LIVERPOOL: WONDROUS PLACE

Music From Cavern to Cream

Paul Du Noyer
Foreword by Sir Paul McCartney

For Una

First published in Great Britain in 2002 by
Virgin Books Ltd
Thames Wharf Studios
Rainville Road
London
W6 9HA

A catalogue record for this book is available from the British
Library.

Plate section designed by Anita Ruddell

ISBN 1 85227 983 4

Typeset by TW Typesetting, Plymouth, Devon
Printed and bound in Great Britain by CPD Wales

CONTENTS

ACKNOWLEDGEMENTS

Thanks are due to all my interviewees down the years. I am indebted for their Liverpool stories to the following: Neil Aspinall, Tony Barrow, James Barton, Pete Best, Alan Bleasdale, Bette Bright, Ian Broudie, Budgie, Pete Burns and Dead Or Alive, Jayne Casey, Frank Clarke, Julian Cope, Elvis Costello, Geoff Davies, Rob Dickins, Bill Drummond, Roger Eagle, Echo and the Bunnymen (Ian McCulloch, Les Pattinson, Will Sergeant, Pete DeFreitas), Ellery Bop, Pete Fulwell, Noel Gallagher, Hambi, Bill Harry, Philip Hayes, Peter Hooton, Mick Houghton, Mick Hucknall, Ian Hunter, Stu James, Phil Jones, Spencer Leigh, Cynthia Lennon, Janice Long, Nick Lowe, Philip Lynott, George Martin, Lee Mavers, Mike McCartney, Paul McCartney, Andy McCluskey, Joey Musker, Alan Peters, John Power, the Room, Willy Russell, Paul Rutherford, Kevin Sampson, Paul Simpson, Alexei Sayle, John Smith and Cook Da Books, Ringo Starr, Derek Taylor and Pete Wylie.

I first met many of these people in the course of assignments for the *NME*, *Q* and *Mojo*; and I am grateful to the various editors who gave me the opportunities.

Several others have helped generously with my research. My special thanks go to Geoff Baker, Jamie Bowman, David Buckley, Ian Cranna, Paul Hemmings at Viper, Ronnie Hughes at Sense of Place, Cathy Long, Doll Makin, Kevin McManus and David Roberts of Guinness Publishing. There is a further list of sources in the Bibliography at the end of the book.

I would also like to thank: Ian Gittins; my agent Ros Edwards at Edwards Fuglewicz; my editor at Virgin Books, Stuart Slater; and lastly but never leastly, all my family and my wife Una.

Paul Du Noyer 2002

FOREWORD

BY SIR PAUL McCARTNEY

The first I thing I knew about music in Liverpool was my Dad playing the piano at home. He was a cotton salesman, who'd learned to play by ear when he was a kid, and then he had a band: Jimmy Mac's Jazz Band. By the time us kids were growing up I'd lie on the carpet and listen to him playing things like 'Stairway to Paradise' by Paul Whiteman, or one I loved called 'Lullaby of the Leaves', and a couple he made up himself. He'd just noodle around and it was lovely to listen to. He had a mate at the Cotton Exchange, another salesman called Freddie Rimmer, who'd come around and play as well, so there was always a musical atmosphere in the house.

Every New Year there was a big family 'do', because it was a big family. My Dad would always say to me, 'Learn to play the piano and you'll get invited to a lot of parties.' That was the rule in his day, when there wasn't much radio or TV. So he'd play old favourites and everyone would join in, getting him drinks, all the old aunties sitting around the room. They knew all the words and melodies. They'd go on for hours, getting progressively more tipsy. But it was fabulous.

And I'd hear the stories from my Dad about Jimmy Mac's Jazz Band and their gigging days. He said, 'We used to have to change our name every time we went back anywhere, because they didn't always want us. If we changed the name they might not remember us.' They went back once as the Masked Players. Things had become so desperate they had to wear masks! So they bought these cheap Woolworths masks and went back to play, somewhere above the Co-op. This was in the 1920s, so it was a hot period for music, with the Charleston and all that. And he said, 'You know, during the evening, the glue started to melt on these masks and ended up dripping down our faces.'

Then you'd go to people's houses and they would often have record collections. I remember my Auntie Jin having 'Tumble along with the Tumbling Tumbleweed.' And then a couple of early Elvis records. So I'd try 'em all, mainly old 78s. I remember putting my cousin Kath's 78s through the clothes mangle, just to see if they'd crack. My brother and I got a big telling-off for that. And yes, they cracked, and she was well pissed-off.

Of course the radio was a big influence, mainly the BBC. My earliest memories would be of *Listen with Mother*, which played a lot of classical stuff. Or you'd go to the theatre and see people like Eddie Calvert. In fact my Dad had been a spotlight operator at a place called the Hippodrome – he used to trim the limelight – so he'd see all the music hall acts come through Liverpool and he'd learn all the songs. And he'd go home between the first and second houses, taking all the programmes that the people left lying around. My Auntie Jin and Auntie Millie would iron them, and he'd take them back and sell 'em to the second house!

But once Lonnie Donegan came along, we got the feeling that we could actually be part of it. We could actually do it. Now, as none of us had any money, it was a great little earner to be a semi-pro band: you could pick up a couple of quid a week, just enough to take your girlfriend to the pictures or something. That was a big incentive.

Then I got into the Quarrymen, through my friend Ivan Vaughan, who was a mate of John's. And we got into the scene. We hadn't realised it, but there were *millions* of groups in Liverpool. Wherever we showed up there'd be another group. There were the skiffle groups, the Roy Orbison sort of groups, the Shadows groups. There were skiffle contests, talent contests – though we always got beaten by the woman who played the spoons – and it gradually developed into the Liverpool scene and became a very rich thing.

But the big factor about Liverpool was it being a port. There were always sailors coming in with records from America, blues records from New Orleans. And you could get so many different ethnic sounds: African music, maybe, or calypsos via the Liverpool Caribbean community, which I think was the oldest in England. There was a massive amount of music to be heard. So, with all these influences, from your home, the radio, the sailors and the immigrants, Liverpool was a huge melting pot of music. And we took what we liked from all that.

And then, when rock'n'roll arrived and we heard Elvis, Gene Vincent, Fats Domino and Little Richard, the game was up. That was it. All hell broke loose. We knew we had to do it for a career. And the rest is history.

It's such a rich history, too. The story of Liverpool music is incredibly rich. As you're about to discover . . .

1. HAPPY HOUR IN THE SAD HOUSE

WHAT HAPPENS WHEN SCOUSERS GET DRUNK. AND THE STORY OF BILLY FURY

In the evening, especially when the sailors are gathered in great numbers, these streets present a most singular spectacle, the entire population of the vicinity being seemingly turned into them. Hand-organs, fiddles and cymbals, plied by strolling musicians, mix with the songs of the seamen, the babble of women and children and the whining of beggars. From the various boarding houses . . . proceeds the noise of revelry and dancing.

Herman Melville visits Liverpool, 1839

Liverpool is more than a place where music happens. Liverpool is a reason *why* music happens. When the author of *Moby Dick* sailed to Liverpool from New York he found a town obsessed by entertainment: there was a physical appetite for life and he was shocked by its ferocity.

Herman Melville's descendant Moby (the singer is his great-great-grand-nephew) came to Liverpool 160 years later: 'We went down to Cream last night,' he said, 'and were refused entry. Which was kind of ironic as they were playing one of my songs at the time! I was amazed at how the women in Liverpool were dressed. The vast majority wore really tight, short dresses. It makes me think people here are more promiscuous. I've never seen anything quite like the girls in Liverpool.'

What is it about Liverpool? Is it something in the water? Why does so much music come from here? Why do they talk like that? Why are Scousers always up to something? And why don't the girls wear more clothes?

Let's take a look. Let's begin where Liverpool did, down by the river. Seagulls wheeling overhead, the phlegm of old men beneath our feet, let's walk the granite lip of Liverpool's waterfront.

Down by the Pier Head, at the foot of the Liver Building, the city sips at a river the colour of tea. At the landing stage the Mersey Ferry boats bob, tenderly crushing fat tractor tyres slung from rusty chains. Evening will arrive any minute now and it will crown the whole scene with a huge tangerine sky. The cares of the day will be carried out to sea on a six-knot ebb-tide. Already you can hear a pub juke-box kick into life. Liverpool lights are coming on. And if the old are going home, the young are just getting started. The music is growing louder, and the first girl's shriek is about to pierce the misty air. This is a party town, and nothing gets in its way.

'Liverpool is an entertainment city,' wrote another visitor (this time Geoff Brown from the *Melody Maker*, in 1976). 'To entertain or be entertained is the one aim of life, once a living has been earned, and there seems damned little difference between the watcher and the watched. The enjoyment of entertainment isn't the desperate and often self-conscious style of the Southerner nor the dour, determined style of the Midlands but an exuberant, robust celebration of the laugh-today-for-tomorrow-we-die sort.'

Inside an hour the streets are rammed. There's smashed glass on a pavement, and the bizzies are on patrol. A bitter wind is whipping in from the Irish Sea, but everyone's dressed for Ipanema Beach. You look at the young women and you remember that the butcher's, baker's and candlestick maker's have all been turned into tanning parlours. Any remaining shops must, presumably, sell the strips of white string that the girls are wearing in the place of clothes. The boys look half-terrified of these perfect orange apparitions, so they turn around and roar obscene abuse at each other instead.

Redundant banks, born again as bars, pump out sounds at club volume. 'Bullet in a Gun', the Paul Oakenfold thing they were all mad for in Cream, is blasting across a back-street: perhaps it will awaken the ghosts of long-gone beat groups, dwelling in the cellars beneath the cobblestones. The entire population of the streets seems gripped by some insane fiesta fever. The boys swill more beer and grow in confidence. In the half light of a side-street, you could imagine you're back in Melville's time, when harlots haunted the sailors' grog-shops, or even in the notorious hell-hole of slaving days, when press-gangs roamed and shanty songs rang out in Paradise Street.

In alleyway shadows a boy and a girl are fumbling. 'Where's yer manners?' she suddenly screams. 'Tits first!'

Liverpool now is the same as it always was: a turbulent, teeming city, alive with vice and excitement. Old Melville knew it as a seaport above all: young Moby might not have been aware of any river, but he was witnessing its legacy all the same. Life at sea is hard. When sailors are ashore their preoccupation is with entertainment. The port of Liverpool was made to supply Jack's every need, whether it be for tarts or tarpaulin. Naturally the town was prepared to offer entertainment too. And that readiness became a civic tradition of the town, an acquired characteristic of its people that shaped their very nature.

That's how Liverpool became the cradle of British pop. It was always a town where entertainment was actively sought. The appetite was sharper and the demand was, well, more demanding. Again and again you hear of people from musical households, and when they go out at night to pay for entertainment, it had better be good. As Andy Carroll will say, 'I've DJ'd all over but Liverpool is easily the best. The atmosphere is like you've just scored a goal, but it goes on all night.' You would hear exactly the same from touring musicians of the old school, from Thin Lizzy to Mott The Hoople.

British people used to sing everywhere: in pubs and public schools, in chip shops and troop ships, in air-raid shelters and charabancs to Blackpool. But people in Liverpool went on singing after the rest of the country lost the habit. There has always been a massive take-up of pianos, guitars and instruments in general: 'Our Treesa takes lessons' as Frank Shaw called the syndrome: 'Playing an instrument in Liverpool you must tackle it as you must tackle life, with a deal of pugnacity, show it who the master is. A pianist need not be a great executant and can neglect niceties. But her audience expects her to approach the piano as a training heavyweight champ will approach his punch-bag. If you have a squeezebox – squeeze it. Set about with bow as if you would saw the fiddle in two.'

In Liverpool, even conversation must work as entertainment: it isn't twinkling or gentle, in the Irish way, but hard, competitive and cruel. But Liverpool art is always trying to turn rage into beauty.

Periodically the place erupts, sometimes with Vesuvian force. Creative individuals don't trickle out from Liverpool's edges: they explode from its very core. The ones the world knows are only the famous ones. In Liverpool there are plenty of stars who don't need guitars. The Crucial Three of our story are not pop stars but night clubs: the Cavern, Eric's and Cream. The Liverpool music story is as much about the audience as the performers; they are but two sides of an equation. From the Beatles to Cream, its successful exports owe their existence to the Liverpool people's love of a good night out and their highly-evolved capacity for telling shit from Shinola.

The street where I first lived was Belmont Road, near Liverpool Football Club. As a child I watched, from an upstairs window, the crowds stream down towards Oakfield Road and the Kop. But I keep discovering things about my street. At one end lived the future comic Alexei Sayle. His Mum was the lollipop lady outside my school. Across the road, the young Elvis Costello would come to visit his relatives. A few doors down from me lived Neil Aspinall, who was the Beatles' roadie and still runs Apple. A few doors the other way is a flat where Echo and the Bunnymen and the Teardrop Explodes first took shape in shambolic rehearsals. Ten doors to the right of mine was a big nightclub, the Wooky Hollow, in the middle of a row of houses. And at the far end of the street was a park, Newsham, in whose public lavatories Holly Johnson had his first homosexual encounter.

And that's no more than an ordinary residential street.

'Deep in the heart of the place,' says a local writer, Ronnie Hughes, 'a constant pop song keeps getting written, which lifts its spirits when sometimes it seems nothing else can. This is not a place that's given up. It's a proud, boastful Celtic city where the lads dream big and talk big and keep writing a big, tuney, hopeful song that could only come from Liverpool.'

The dominant fondness, as we'll see, is for melody and a kind of populist Surrealism. It's a place where everything and everyone has to have another name, as if vanilla reality were just too bland to bear. (The Mersey Tunnel is, of course, the Mousehole.) So you come across pubs whose signs say one thing but which are called something else. One of them was always known as the Sad House. And I used to wonder if it ever had a Happy Hour. Liverpool can be a desperately sad place in some ways, but it's fanatical about its Happy Hour. Liverpool lives for entertainment of every kind. But above all it lives for music.

Music is at the heart of this book, because music is the heart of Liverpool.

As far as Scousers are concerned, Liverpool is not a provincial city, but the Capital of Itself. It's deeply insular, yet essentially outward-looking: it faces the sea and all the lands beyond, but has its back turned on England. There were local men for whom Sierra Leone was a fact but London only a rumour. They knew every dive in Buenos Aires, but had no idea of the Cotswolds. And Liverpudlians speak with merry contempt for their Lancashire neighbours, displaying all the high indifference of a New Yorker for Kansas.

In his innermost heart, the Liverpudlian feels a little sorry for those born anywhere else. In his mental geography it's like that famous cartoon map of Manhattan. To the west there's Birkenhead, then Ireland and America. But look the other way and it's a vague place – here dwell woolybacks – where only the enemy football grounds have tangible existence.

The KLF's Bill Drummond, a Scot who'll figure again in this tale, wrote of his time on Merseyside: 'One of the things I always loved about living in Liverpool is that it never felt like you were living in England. The locals always considered themselves Liverpudlians above and beyond any nationality. Maybe this is because of the massive majority of its population being of Irish extraction and because, as a great seaport, the city had its sights set on the rest of the world and not on London, let alone such cultural backwaters as Manchester.'

Like Ireland – from where it acquired the habit, I think – Liverpool is notorious for the sentimentality of its exiles. Everyone knows of its celebrity sons and daughters, who'll pay the place every compliment short of living there. But the people who stay here all their lives are usually just as passionate. Liverpool's talent for self-mythologising is probably unequalled. A local brochure calls it 'the Big Village at the Centre of the Universe'. Some can't understand why a Scouser would choose to move away.

You won't spend long in Liverpool before encountering the famous quote by Carl Jung, the Swiss psychiatrist, who called it 'the pool of life'. Here's what he wrote: 'I had a dream. I found myself in a dirty, sooty city. It was night and winter; and dark and raining. I was in Liverpool. The various quarters of the city were arranged radially around the square. In the centre was a round pool; in the middle of it, a small island. While everything around it was obscured by rain, fog, smoke and dimly-lit darkness, the little island blazed with sunlight. On it stood a single tree; a magnolia in a shower of reddish blossoms. It was as though the tree stood in the sunlight and were, at the same time, the source of light. Everything was extremely unpleasant; black and opaque – just as I felt then. But I had a vision of unearthly beauty . . . and that's why I was able to live at all. Liverpool is "the pool of life".'

I've never taken Jung's line as a prophecy – just a whimsical play on words, by a German speaker who'd encountered a foreign place name. But his words are seriously revered in Liverpool. That's because, deep down, they are what Liverpudlians really believe. It's the Pool of Life. Just follow the M62.

Two hundred years ago, as Manchester's partner in the Industrial Revolution, Liverpool was a new kind of metropolis. 'The pestilent lanes and alleys,' went a report to the House of Lords, 'are putrid with vice and crime; to which, perhaps, the round globe does not furnish a parallel. The sooty and begrimed bricks of the very houses have a reeking, Sodom-like, and murderous look . . . These are the haunts from which sailors sometimes disappear for ever; or issue in the morning, robbed naked, from the broken door-ways.' It was not yet a large town, but it boasted 2,900 prostitutes. Life expectancy was seventeen.

The streets of Sailortown were a riot of stabbings, drunkenness and carnality. Stepping though them gingerly, the American Consul Nathaniel Hawthorne recorded '. . . the multitudinous and continual motion of all this kind of life. The people are as numerous as maggots in cheese; you behold them, disgusting, and all moving about . . .' Even when the city was prosperous there was awful poverty, and unemployment was endemic because of casual labour. Every Liverpudlian carries a conviction of the city's extremity. Whatever it's good at, it's the best. And whatever is bad here, well, it's the worst you'll find anywhere. The interesting thing is how many locals take a strange pride in notoriety.

This sin-ridden seaport has always been a place apart – a sort of sunless Marseilles that operates on different principles to the rest of Britain. When the Irish arrived in massive numbers it became a Catholic Celtic enclave in a Protestant Anglo-Saxon kingdom. You would scarcely speak of it in the same breath as, say, Chichester or Tunbridge Wells. With its back-alley poverty and idolatrous passion for football, it's been compared to South America. It has a way of backing the wrong side: in the American Civil War it came out for the Confederacy. In 1979, when the British elections brought in Thatcherism, the Liverpool voters opted for Trotskyism.

Liverpool was always trouble. Before the slave trade its first fortunes were made from piracy. There were warships in the Mersey during the strikes of 1909 and 1919, their gun barrels trained on an English city. Tanks and armoured cars have rumbled more than once across its cobblestones. The police were occasionally issued with spears. In a Sherlock Holmes story of 1917, *The Adventure of the Cardboard Box*, Arthur Conan Doyle pits his hero against a gang of Liverpudlians, who perform with unusual savagery; their escapades include sending dismembered limbs to old maids and a brutal slaughter off the shoreline of New Brighton. And the tempestuous, brooding hero of Emily Bronte's *Wuthering Heights*? One very troubled Scouser called Heathcliff.

All ports have an edginess about them. Salt winds whip across the rooftops. The sea air carries a sense of incipient disaster. Like the mining villages inland, coastal towns are marked apart by a communal tradition of grim tidings. Liverpool was the intended destination of the *Lusitania*, sunk by the Germans en route from New York in 1915. The *Titanic*, likewise, sailed with a Liverpool crew. At the climactic moment of the DiCaprio/Winslet movie, when the boat rears up before plunging down, the two words on screen are 'Titanic' and 'Liverpool'. I imagine it struck some people as an apt combination.

As if its insularity and self-obsession were not enough, Liverpool's uniqueness is reinforced every time a local opens his mouth. There is no sound like it. A Liverpool voice is so obviously of Liverpool. It's not English, nor even Northern. It's Scouse, and the Scouser is doomed to stand out, come what may. As Paul McCartney puts it: 'Liverpool has its own identity. It's even got its own accent within about a ten-mile radius. Once you go outside that ten miles it's "deep Lancashire, lad". I think you do feel that apartness, growing up there.'

'People outside hated us,' said Cilla Black, 'because of the way we spoke, especially the fellas, who were very guttural. If you asked for a drink in a pub in Blackpool or North Wales they'd throw you out.'

If it's true, as one theory goes, that human speech began in song, then some accents are always trying to get back there. Liverpudlian is one of them. You could hear that sing-song musicality in the suburban, south Liverpool speaking voices of the Beatles; even their deadpan statements carried a lilt, not to mention timing, of metronomic precision. The north Liverpool dockland voice is harsher, faster, more threatening. It can sound like a rusty sub-machine gun, but it carries the driving beat that powered rock'n'roll. Melody and rhythm were already lurking in the Liverpool accent. It only awaited a few guitars and a drum-kit to liberate them.

The locals spoke with a Lancashire voice until the 1840s; after the Famine the Irish influence grew so strong that a brand new accent came into being. But they were not the only newcomers, of course, and I like to think the verbal stew of Scouse must have a dash of Welsh and a soupçon of Chinese. There is the Liverpool air as well – traditionally a cold, bracing blend of muck and damp – to ensure the accent is not so much nasal as adenoidal. To this day, a bad chest is the birthright of all born on the banks of the Mersey. The raw material of the Beatles' music was the guitar and catarrh.

Because there is no 'th' sound in Gaelic it disappeared from Liverpudlian, replaced by something like (though not quite) a 'd' sound: dee do, dough, don't dee, dough? As in Dublin and Brooklyn, if there is more than one of you then you are 'you's'. Consonants land with explosive force, and the 'ck' of a word like 'cack' is emphasised with passionate saliva, like the Welsh 'bach'. Cool is 'kewl'. Years in exile have diminished my accent gradually: at university down South, however, I quite deliberately stopped myself from rhyming book with 'puke'.

The 'ur' sound is much more difficult to lose, having deep roots both in Irish and in Lancashire. George Harrison's singing voice was noted for it ('You'll never know how much I really curr . . .'). Cilla Black became notorious for it, though she is quite correct to say that it results from an effort to speak normal English: 'When I go, Clur with the fur ur, I'm talking posh.' Among Scousers themselves the sound would be more like, 'Cleer with the feer eer.'

Liverpudlian speech indicates a playful approach to language and logic. Sailors were great importers of foreign words – banana, jamboree, tornado. The port of Liverpool would have heard new words brought ashore on every tide, refreshing the native fondness for verbal novelties. 'Scouse' itself is one example, probably from a Scandinavian seafarers' term for Lapland stew. The wilful twisting of syllables ('antwacky' for antique, 'Parthenion' for Parthenon) is probably Irish, with a dose of instinctive Surrealism. When critics thought John Lennon must have studied James Joyce, they missed the linguistic roots the two men shared. Nor was John's ingenious gibberish entirely drawn from Lewis Carroll and Edward Lear; Ringo's way with word-play ('a hard day's night', 'eight days a week') was nothing special. They merely grew up in a place where people talk like that, all the time.

It was always dangerous to waste time decoding Beatle lyrics. (Why does Desmond change sex during 'Ob-La-Di, Ob-La-Da'? Would semolina pilchards really climb the Eiffel Tower?) Precision is not a characteristic of this city, where the word 'thingy' is indispensable. ('It's a thingy! A fiendish thingy!' cries George in *Help!*) In fact the Liver Bird itself, from the civic coat of arms, was only a medieval draughtsman's vague attempt to draw a cormorant. It looks nothing like one. Thus the Liverpool skyline is commanded by twin monuments to artistic licence.

Surprisingly, it was not until the Beatles that Liverpool was nationally recognised as having its own accent at all. Victorian novelists made no effort to represent it; Liverpool music hall acts favoured a broadly understandable Lancashire voice. The actor Robert Newton, in the 1950 film *Waterfront*, played his Merseyside docker with a Cockney scowl and a touch of Long John Silver.

No sooner had Scouse been discovered, though, than it began to infiltrate the English language: fab, gear, grotty, moggy, y'know, no-mark, made up (as in pleased), fit (as in attractive), give it loads, shag. Nowadays it wraps itself around the tonsils of foreign footballers; the accent of Liverpool's French manager Gerard Houllier became a thing of wonder. And though a force-field still separates Merseyside from Manchester, Scouse has made dramatic inroads in the South Lancashire towns, across into the Cheshire Wirral and even North Wales.

Is the Liverpool accent changing? It probably always is. A university study in 2000 found that cleaner air was having its effect, as well as the influence of national TV. The accent is losing its richness over time. In a very old man, like John Lennon's Uncle Charlie, you hear the warm, thick and loamy blend of Ireland and Lancashire. By John's time this was growing harder, more piercing. At its contemporary worst there is the grating, metallic clang of *Brookside* characters whinging.

Will Scouse survive? There is a bleak outlook for all regional accents. The 'Estuarial' English of the South-East seeps across the land like spilt tea on a tablecloth. Mick Jagger's faux-prole drawl – wiv all its, like, gloh-al stops and all 'at kinda fing, yeah? – is much preferred to anything else. It's the 'Mockney' accent that proper English speakers are now trading down towards. It's the one respect in which the Rolling Stones might eventually prove more influential than the Beatles.

The least appreciated quality of Mersey is its physical beauty. The vast sky overhangs a fine, wide river that curves around the shoreline like a silver scimitar. There is an unsuspected grandeur in Liverpool's setting. From a hilltop or a ferry boat you can watch the weather bearing down on you from Wales. The waterfront buildings are as magnificent as their cousins in Shanghai and Chicago. Inland, outside of Lime Street Station, is an epic Athenian dreamscape: William Brown Street's opulent stretch of Victorian homages to classical Greece, from St George's Hall to the Walker Art Gallery, the Library and Museum, down to the gaping maw of the Mersey Tunnel.

Look in some directions, however, and you'd think Liverpool had a passion for self-mutilation. Some of it is everyday slobbishness – on the pavements, staggering quantities of litter and spit – but the rest of the mess is sanctioned from above. Post-war planning seems like the work of a vindictive chimpanzee. If you believe that beauty and ugliness have a conditioning effect on our souls, then what was done to Liverpool was very wicked indeed. Parts of it appear intended for an earthling colony on Mars. There are nonsensical new roads that go nowhere. Old road patterns with a local logic were destroyed. Condemned streets sprout weeds and stop in dead ends, like those around the old Berlin Wall. Neighbourhoods are gutted to cut tarmac swathes for strangers' cars: they drive through, as disconnected from those neighbourhoods as aeroplanes flying over the North Pole.

In the 1960s the dignified St John's Market, the shopping centre's Victorian heart, was torn out. They replaced it with a box-like retail precinct – nothing so human as a market any more, just a 'precinct'. It's unimproved by an apologetic series of fussy, post-modern facelifts. Listed buildings continue to vanish, usually through the 'dangerous structure' notice that follows decades of neglect, or a mysterious fire. When you demolish familiar places, or obliterate old pathways, you deracinate people, cutting them off from the psychic roots that nourish our sense of belonging. I remember the way commentators condemned the Toxteth rioters for damaging their own environment – yet, whatever they did, it was trivial in comparison with official vandalism. Those rioters had grown up breathing brick dust.

A lot of the decrepitude is not deliberate, of course. It's only what happens when the money runs out. By the docks are mile upon mile of shut-up buildings, surrounded by fences that bristle with barbed wire and signs that bark of guard dogs. There are wastelands, like the scars that heal on a healthy body but linger on a sick one. Some locations maintain a mere Edwardian façade, with no buildings behind, while the side streets fade in urban tundra. It's as if the whole city were just a gigantic plywood film set. And beyond the central stretch are slum-cleared hills, still to find new purposes. While they wait, slowly grassing over, they're like undulating meadows that only want a shepherd and his sheep. Further out, there are handsome boulevards of flaking affluence, reminding us of Liverpool's descent from being one of the richest cities in the world, to one of the poorest in Europe.

There is a legend that Hitler used to live in Liverpool. The story arose from memoirs of his Irish sister-in-law, Bridget Hitler, who says he stayed for a while in Liverpool in 1912; one elaboration is that he worked in the Adelphi Hotel. Historians, unfortunately, say it's unlikely. Yet it's a picturesque idea, in a macabre way, and if he was unhappy here, that would explain the Luftwaffe's special attention to Liverpool in the Blitz. Curiously, Adolf's alleged address was the very last street to be bombed here in the Second World War. But he would not have made a good Scouser: although he had the legs for *Lederhosen*, he lacked all sense of rhythm.

Music, as we've said, is the heart of Liverpool. And from the heart of Liverpool came Britain's first great rock'n'roll star. His name was Billy Fury.

Elvis Presley was not the first rock'n'roll singer, but he was the first rock'n'roll star. Billy Fury was not the first British rocker, but he was the coolest of the first generation. There were Cliff Richard and Tommy Steele and a few others – but only Billy Fury was the real thing. He remains the first charismatic idol to emerge in the story of British rock music.

He got off to a classic, Hollywood biopic sort of start. Born Ron Wycherley, from the Dingle, he'd been a Teddy Boy tugboat worker on the River Mersey. On the night a rock'n'roll package tour came to Birkenhead, he slipped backstage and met the renowned impresario

Larry Parnes: minutes later he was on stage singing his songs. Parnes had already auditioned another young hopeful that night, a compere called Jimmy Tarbuck; but the shy Ron Wycherley was a real find. Sharp, flamboyant, ambitious, Parnes was kingpin of London's Tin Pan Alley – he once claimed he'd invented the term pop music. He would sign up young boys wherever he went and launch them into show business with thrusting new names – Tommy Steele, Vince Eager, Marty Wilde, Duffy Power . . . It's said that Ron Wycherley didn't discover his own reinvention – Billy Fury! – until he read it in the *Daily Mirror* a few days later.

Between 1959 and 1963 the hits came thick and fast for Billy. He was a sex symbol too. Onstage he was beautiful – golden suit, black shirt-collar turned up, his shoulders hunched, pathetically self-protective yet provocative with it. His sullen, hooded eyes were full of hurt, his supplicating voice a troubled, trembling moan. When the drama climbed, his hand reached out and snapped shut. A twist of the wrist and back the hand came, so he could open the palm to see what he's grasped. And find it empty . . .

He's best remembered for the pneumatic melodrama of hits like 'Halfway to Paradise' and 'Like I've Never Been Gone', songs that weren't among the best, or worst, of his work. The best is in a 1960 LP of whispered rockabilly called *The Sound of Fury* – self-written and one of Keith Richards' all-time favourites. He also covered a minor US hit, 'Wondrous Place', and made of it something sexy, epic and shimmering with mystery. (It would re-surface in 1999 for a Toyota ad campaign.) But in the end the formulaic ballads took over, while his own songwriting lapsed.

Though more hits followed, the national arrival of the Beatles, in 1962, was the beginning of the end. Paul McCartney said of him: 'a less furious guy you have yet to meet. A sweet Liverpool guy – the first local man who made it, in our eyes.' Ironically they nearly became his backing group before they were famous, when Larry Parnes came up to Liverpool to audition them.

In the beat group onslaught of the early 60s, solo singers suddenly looked *passé*, especially if they were modelled on Elvis. By 1964, Fury was a Man Out Of Time. Worse, he was running out of time. His health had always been bad. Like Ringo Starr (who'd been at the same school, St Silas's) he'd been a sickly child, forever in hospital. He'd had rheumatic fever, often fatal back then, and grew up believing his days to be numbered. The legacy was a damaged heart, and a series of operations. He retired to a farm in the countryside, and looked after sick animals for the RSPCA. He already owned a racehorse; now he built a bird sanctuary. He told the *NME*: 'One thing about me is that I'm a terrible loner. I think I was born with three brick walls around me. No – *four* brick walls: I knocked the back one out.'

In the early 70s he made a rare appearance. Like a pilgrim I travelled down to London to the Rock'n'Roll Show at Wembley Stadium, where Billy Fury shared an historic bill with Chuck Berry, Bill Haley, Little Richard and Jerry Lee Lewis. In the souvenir *Evening Standard* I read an article about a Teddy Boy revival shop in Chelsea, called Let It Rock. Its owner, a 25-year-old called Malcolm McLaren, gushed that 'Billy Fury is Britain's only rock'n'roll singer of note'. Before going back to Liverpool I visited Malcolm's shop, which would soon be re-named Sex, and developed a fascination for it. When I moved to London I looked it up again, in time to watch punk rock being born there.

I got to meet Billy Fury in 1981. I'd become a writer on the *NME* and he was holding a reception in Soho for a slightly underwhelming comeback record. He looked frail, though still beautiful, and worked the room with tired eyes and a brave display of willing. We chatted pleasantly of this, that and Liverpool, until he was pulled away by a posse of Radio One personalities, who all spoke much louder than he did. Then I was approached by Larry Parnes, brim-full of stories about his dear friend, the recently-murdered John Lennon. Parnes proposed that I visit him for more, perhaps over a weekend in the country. I was politely non-committal, but never considered the offer. Who knows, I might have come home with an utterly unsuitable new name, like Paul Potent or something.

Two years after that came the sad, yet expected news. Billy Fury's cheating heart had stopped beating, once and for all.

Nobody in those pre-Beatle days spoke of Billy Fury as a 'Liverpool pop star'. He never played up the accent. He obeyed the convention, still in force back then, that celebrities should suppress a regional or proletarian voice. He wasn't, in any case, a typical Scouser: 'I never really got into the humour of the Liverpool people,' he once said. 'I was too serious, always worrying about my life and what I was going to do with it. I appreciate the humour now. But at the time I was really waiting to get out.'

In Billy Fury's day Liverpool was less the Gateway of Empire than the Tradesmen's Entrance. In the pomp of its Edwardian prime the port had been a genuine marvel; its splendid waterfront a grand backdrop to the comings and goings of the fashionable and the fabulous. By 1960 it lacked the glamour of those great days. Liverpool was left to get on with its mundane business. Nobody really gave it a thought. Even its football teams languished in obscurity. If the town produced national entertainers, they were simply from 'somewhere up North'.

However a turning point loomed. In the decade to follow, Liverpool would attain stupendous fame. To get a sense of how big the Liverpool myth was set to grow, look at the way Nik Cohn would write about it in his pop history *Awopbopaloobop Alopbamboom*: 'Liverpool is a strange town, it gets obsessed by everything it does . . . In such an atmosphere, hungry and physical, pop could hardly miss. It exploded.'

2. THE SEA OF DREAMS

LIVERPOOL AND THE BEATLES

'Good place to wash your hair, Liverpool. Nice soft water.'

George Harrison

In 1977 there was an almighty row in Liverpool when councillors turned down a Beatle statue. 'They aren't worthy of a place in our history,' said one. 'The Beatles couldn't sing for toffee,' chimed another. 'Their behaviour brought tremendous discredit to the city.' But the group's old agent Allan Williams was very prescient: 'The councillors don't seem to realise just what a world phenomenon the Beatles are. There should be a complete museum and tourist industry in Liverpool.' Paul's brother, Mike McCartney, offered a visionary solution: 'Erect two separate statues. Rotten tomatoes could be thrown at one, and bunches of roses at the other.'

Back in those days, when Merseybeat and Beatlemania were consider-ed dead and buried, the Cavern was only a memory and its home, Mathew Street, had returned to its former obscurity – dingy and sunless, a narrow, crooked thoroughfare with only one pub (the Grapes) and a subterranean punk club (Eric's) to make it worth a detour. A couple of blocks away, the Albert Dock was a rotting hulk, set in a shoreline of dying industries. A mile in the opposite direction, where Cream now throbs and bars vibrate with night-life, there were just more crumbling warehouses, abandoned cars and the oppressive silence of urban neglect.

It took five bullets from the gun of Mark Chapman to change all that – followed, seven months later, by the Toxteth Riots. The shock of the first event, John Lennon's assassination on 8 December 1980, awoke the slumbering Liverpool people to a legacy they'd ignored because they took it for granted. As Stratford-upon-Avon was to Shakespeare, so Liverpool could be to the Beatles. And now, with Lennon dead, the Beatles were not so much old news as an instant heritage industry. The national trauma of the second event – a British city up in flames, apparently gripped by anarchy – encouraged hard thinking about Liverpool's slide from Edwardian prosperity to late century meltdown.

Nowadays you could not walk from the Albert Dock to Mathew Street without encountering Beatle memorials of some sort. Between the piped music of tourist shops, theme pubs and museums, you might hear half their recorded catalogue in the process. If Toxteth had reminded

Margaret Thatcher's regime that you can't expect a city to die quietly, it was Lennon's death that galvanised Liverpool itself. Now that its past was so dramatically sundered from its present, thoughts turned to ways of stopping that past from disappearing altogether.

How would it look to Lennon now? Suppose, to be romantic, he returned from the Other Side by ferry-boat. The Pier Head would surprise him, for the Liver Building is no longer black with velvety soot but hard and bright after sandblasting. The Albert Dock is equally clean: thanks to the steady Covent Gardening of the waterfront, it's more like Disneyland than the clanking, cursing, frowning hell-hole that generations of labouring men knew. Looking uphill he'd see the familiar Cathedral, but its space-age Catholic counterpart and St John's Beacon would still seem odd to his eyes, post-dating the Liverpool he grew up in. He'd wince at the pockets of shabbiness in Lime Street and wonder where Clayton Square had gone. In fact, whole chunks of his familiar streets would be missing, like gaps in old men's teeth.

Had he flown in to Liverpool Airport, of course, he would have found it was now named after him. Wandering up to his old home on Menlove Avenue he'd see a plaque on the front. Across the golf course, Paul's little house is a National Trust museum. Ambling past his old school to Penny Lane – having looked in on rebuilt Strawberry Field – he might have noted the shiny new street sign: 'vandal resistant, UVC protected and fire-retardant' according to the Council. He might chance upon the daily coach-load of Beatle tourists – the barber, shaving another customer, will pause and wave to them. It's been known for such coaches to spot John's Uncle Charlie Lennon, an old man with poor eyesight but pleased to stop and talk. That suburban corner of Lennon's 'Liddypool' is remarkably unchanged since his day.

But if he took a notion, for old times' sake, to go back to Mathew Street, then he'd discover the strangest alterations of all. If by coincidence there happened to be a Beatle convention in town, he'd be startled by the sight of lookalike quartets – they might be Hungarians, Brazilians, whatever – strolling to their next engagement in full Fab attire. Sitting in tourist pubs there would be visitors held spellbound by old associates from Beatle days: faces grown wrinklier with the passing of time, but their anecdotes worn smooth as pebbles in a stream.

The Grapes, where he himself sank many a pint, has happily stopped rebranding itself 'the Famous Grapes', and the cosy White Star around the corner remains true to itself. There are new bars, too: the Rubber Soul, Lennon's, the Cavern Pub. Where the old club stood there is a decent replica, with a 'Cavern Walks' shopping mall above it. Of course, there are plaques everywhere. When they run out of walls, the big plaques will be getting little plaques on them. At least the Plaque Attack is not monopolised by Beatles – one display commemorates all Liverpool's Number 1 records, from Lita Roza, through Cilla and Frankie Goes To Hollywood, to Atomic Kitten and beyond.

There are Beatle statues going up all over. One day they'll outnumber the Victorian war heroes. Around the corner in Stanley Street is a careworn woman representing Eleanor Rigby, made in 1982 by Tommy Steele, one of that first generation of English pop singers abruptly upstaged by the arrival of the Beatles: he sold her to the city for the headline-grabbing sum of Half a Sixpence. Opposite the Cavern, high on a wall, is Arthur Dooley's sculpture of *Four Lads Who Shook the World*, one of the earliest Beatle mementoes, unveiled in 1974. His quartet of cherubs surrounds a Madonna-like figure, suggesting Mother Liverpool and her four most celebrated children. The wings worn by one angel, Dooley explained, were a visual pun on Paul's band of the time. Since 1980, as Mathew Street became the place of Lennonist pilgrimage, the winged angel is often thought to be John.

And if John took a wander to the main road, Whitechapel, he'd look across and find Brian Epstein's shop, NEMS, had become an Ann Summers sex store. But Brian's old lawyer, Rex Makin, remains in his office just beyond: still keeping a close eye on human vice. John would search in vain for the Kardomah Café, or for Frank Hessy's guitar shop. Some of the dereliction might depress him, but the 'civic improvements' that have seen off Liverpool's oldest streets and pubs would dismay him even more. With a last, affectionate glance down Dale Street to the Town Hall, he might float home again, across the universe.

Liverpool has made a big investment in the Beatles, both financial and emotional. The council now estimates that the Fab Four connection is worth £20m a year to the local economy. At the Beatles Shop and the Beatles Story, at Cavern City Tours, are people, sincere in their enthusiasm, who work to make that connection stronger.

The biographical facts of the Beatles' link to Liverpool are well documented. What's more interesting to disentangle is the relationship of their art. The danger is that you're always trying to stuff the butterfly back into the chrysalis: to believe that everything the Beatles became was already there at the start, just waiting to be made manifest. That would be wrong. They became what they did because they were so open to the world around them, and to the experiences that came their way. And, ultimately, we should not try to explain away the magic. John met Paul, a chain of events followed, and unforeseeable splendours resulted.

All the same, you just know that our story would be shorter if the Beatles had happened to come from Grimsby.

If Mathew Street is Mecca, then its holiest shrine must be the Cavern. It was not the only club in town, but nowhere else comes close in terms of Beatle history. Between 1961 and 1963 they played there about 272 times. There have always been people who say the group was at its best there. Those people include the Beatles.

What you have in Mathew Street today is not exactly the Cavern of old, but a respectful modern replica on the same site. The original formed the cellar of a Georgian brick building, part of a complex of fruit warehouses near the docks. Tourists were sometimes told its walls were built thick to muffle the cries of African slaves. This was a fib, but the premises were put to various uses down the years – housing eggs, wine and electrical equipment amongst other things. In wartime the cellar was employed as an air-raid shelter.

It was a man called Alan Sytner who thought of introducing music. He already ran some jazz nights nearby, but he was smitten by the Left Bank romance of Le Caveau club, in Paris, and planned a similar underground lair in Liverpool. The Cavern, named in homage to its French original, opened on 16 January 1957. The attraction that first evening, the Merseysippi Jazz Band, drew a full 600 people, with another 1,500 stuck outside. Sytner's plan was a winner.

What you did not find in the Cavern, in those days, was rock'n'roll. If you were a jazz sort of person, you did not care for the likes of Elvis Presley at all. 'There was much more snobbery than there is now,' says Mick Jagger. 'In the old days, jazz people hated rock'n'roll. I can't even start to tell you much they hated it. I guess they saw it as a threat, and they didn't think that rock people had any technical ability, which a lot of the time was true, but it doesn't really matter; classical musicians used to look down on jazz people, who didn't have as much technical ability. Now musicians and critics alike are more prepared to appreciate lots of different music in one go. But in those days people like Chuck Berry, and blues singers generally, came in for a very patronising time.'

Skiffle, on the other hand, was halfway respectable because it was a sort of folk-blues. This was an era when blues artists such as Muddy Waters and John Lee Hooker were under pressure to play down their electric boogie styles in favour of folk-blues – older, more rural and acoustic – that the educated white market deemed authentically ethnic. So the Cavern welcomed Big Bill Broonzy and, of course, his British disciple Lonnie Donegan. But woe betide a band like Rory Storm and the Hurricanes if they went off-message and broke into a rock number. The Quarrymen played here twice; and Ringo appeared as a member of Eddie Clayton's skiffle act.

An accountant named Ray McFall took over from Sytner in 1959, and from May 1960 he accepted the inevitable and gradually relaxed the anti-rock'n'roll policy. The club was open at lunchtimes as well as evenings, but jazz was soon relegated to the weekends (and disappeared altogether in 1963). Of the Beatles' shows, 150 took place during the day.

One eye witness from 1961 is Geoff Davies, later the owner of Probe Records: 'I saw the Beatles there about 78 times, and it was one of the most exciting things I've seen in my life. The first time I came across them was at an all-night jazz session, and we were horrified to find what we considered a pop band getting in on it. So we got a pass-out at the door to go down the pie stall at the Pier Head. I remember them starting up as we went out and I thought, What a fucking racket.

'But the following week I went to a lunchtime session and there were the Beatles again. And that was it, everything changed for me. They used to do "Money" and extend the intro, really bloody heavy, and then Lennon comes in: "The best things in life are free," in the dirtiest, foulest voice I'd heard in my life, full of hate and sneering and cynicism. I couldn't believe the anarchy. The cheek of them. Everything I'd seen before had been like the Shadows, but the Beatles came on and they didn't give a fuck: backs to the audience, the lot. In between the numbers they'd do TV jingles or any old nonsense, talking like the Goons. And the volume! It was still mostly trad jazz at the time at the Cavern. But the Beatles had amps.

'The concerts they did in Liverpool were completely different to what they did afterwards.'

It was never a luxury joint, more of a disinfected dungeon. The walls ran wet with perspiration. The toilets were squalid, obviously. But no one objected. It's often forgotten how young the crowd could be at those clubs: like the old Marquee in London, the Cavern wasn't licensed (hence the musicians' need to get tanked up at the Grapes beforehand); the raw, pubescent energy of British beat was fuelled on orangeade. In the beginning, before the DJs, pills and lager, dance clubs were a world of live bands and soft drinks. Maybe that atmosphere made for a purer sort of musical communication than later generations became accustomed to. It definitely bred a scene with enough internal dynamism to conquer the rest of the world.

Bob Wooler (who deplored the arrival of liquor in later years) was the Cavern's resident DJ, and a gifted quip-meister in the best tradition of

Merseyside Surrealism. Already pushing 30, he was the scene's hip uncle: his musical influence is incalculable. From 1960, when jazz gave way to rock'n'roll and Liverpool rock began to call itself beat music, Wooler ruled the roost, coining phrases like 'Remember all you cave dwellers, the Cavern is the best of cellars.' He could be a melancholy man sometimes: 'Don't spell my name "Wooller," ' he used to say. 'There's enough "l" in my life already.' He came to call the Cavern's location 'Mythew Street' on account of the misconceptions which grew up around it. (He denies, for example, that he announced Brian Epstein's arrival at the club on the fateful day.) He died in February, 2002 to widespread dismay. His funeral in St Nicholas's church, at the Pier Head, was full to overflowing. Just like the Cavern had been.

When the Beatles became famous the Cavern acquired a magical status. The boys could not play there any more, but great acts came from all over the world. Then, as the Beatle connection grew weaker, things began dying down again.

By 1966, the Cavern was nobody's idea of a goldmine. Poor sanitation had been a constant problem. In a former life the cellar had been a place for imported Irish bacon, packed in ice which drained away. Later owners of the warehouse assumed this drain was a sewer outlet and installed toilets. That was not a problem until the cellar became a music club: suddenly hundreds were using those toilets, not just a couple of workmen. The drain was no more than a hole and sewage started dripping on to railway workers in a tunnel below. The projected cost of installing proper drainage was prohibitive so the Cavern went bust.

Soon, though, new owners came: the old place got a facelift, a drinks licence and, on 23 July 1966, a grand re-opening by the Prime Minister Harold Wilson. The club had a further seven years of life. When I was of an age to 'club it' in town, the Cavern was in its final days, and probably a shadow of its former self. You still experienced a certain thrill descending those hallowed steps (largely mingled with relief at getting past some very unwelcoming doormen); the club's three tubular chambers were still intact and still sweaty; the air was a rancid fug of body odour, cigarette smoke, hamburger smells and a little something from the toilets. An upper room had been added, from the body of the building, and functioned as a disco. But the main stage hosted live music, as before. This being the early 70s, the usual fare was grinding boogie, played by scowling former flower children.

The Cavern closed down in 1973, and the warehouse above it was demolished to make way for a railway ventilation duct (which, ironically, was never built). The cellar itself was simply filled in with rubble.

Eerily, it remained in this undisturbed state, like Tutankhamun's tomb, until 1982. Few of us across the street in Eric's, no more than a couple of yards away, realised the Beatles' home was actually still in existence. The site was now to be re-developed as the Cavern Walks shopping centre. Hopes of restoring the original cellar, however, had to be dropped when it was found that it would be unable to support the new building planned above it. But some of the original bricks were used to create a replica space: it's slightly to the right, rather deeper underground and faces a different direction, but its dimensions are exactly the same and it occupies about three-quarters of the original site. It opened for business in 1984.

For most of us, the Beatles' real career begins in 1962 with their first Parlophone recordings. But there is this argument that, as a live act, their best days were already over. Lennon said it, in 1972: 'We always talk about Hamburg, the Cavern, and the dance-halls in Liverpool, because that was when we were pretty hot musically. We never talk about after that because, to us, that was when live music stopped existing.' Plenty of old fans back him up. But out there, beyond the Mersey, a big world was waiting now.

'Liverpool? I said you must be joking. So what's from Liverpool?' These were the words of the London music publisher Dick James, when his friend George Martin spoke of the new Northern group he'd acquired. But James overcame his professional scepticism when he heard the music – and deciding to be its publisher would prove to be an immensely profitable decision. Historically, that was the last time a figure in his position would express surprise that distant, dreary backwaters might be full of showbiz promise. It wasn't only Liverpool that was about to swim into metropolitan focus, but the provinces generally – and the less posh the better.

On the night of Thursday, 10 January 1963, somebody had stolen 100 tickets for the group's gig at the Grafton Rooms, in West Derby Road, only to find their stub numbers cancelled. The next day, Friday, saw the release of the Beatles' first big hit 'Please Please Me' – and with it, the beginning of the end of their Liverpool lives. Of course, nobody knew this for sure at the time. In the *Sunday Times*, Derek Jewell looked at the group and wondered: 'Although they are probably big (and good) enough to survive the demise of the "beat" vogue . . . they know how cold the wind cuts around Liverpool's Pier Head. And next year, who knows?'

For about the first year of their fame the Beatles were still Liverpool residents, but only insofar as they lived anywhere other than in studios or on the road. They delayed the final move, as Paul McCartney explained to Barry Miles: 'I had this strangely strange entrance into London, coming down from Liverpool where everyone had said, "You'll never make it, coming from Liverpool." Which had angered us a bit, so we stayed up in Liverpool a lot. We didn't just all move down to London, we tried to prove ourselves from Liverpool.' They'd stay at the Royal Court Hotel on Sloane Square (theatrical connections, a very Epstein choice) or the President on Russell Square. By autumn of 1963, all four had moved into a house in Mayfair, though John soon left to set up house with Cynthia and Julian, while Paul moved in with his girlfriend Jane Asher at her parents' home.

Meanwhile they put out their first LP, also called *Please Please Me*. It's probably their least discussed album, and admittedly not their best. But it's interesting because it is their Cavern album – and Hamburg, and the Grafton Rooms and all the rest. Bulked up by cover versions, it sets out everything they had so far taken in (soul, rock'n'roll, old and new pop) alongside their first steps in songwriting. It's a great document, if not a great LP. With a bit of effort you can grasp how startling they must have been for a ballroom audience in New Brighton. But it's equally obvious that the next records – including 'She Loves You' and 'I Want to Hold Your Hand' – display a soaring talent that is purely its own creation. In leaving Liverpool the Beatles were about to become truly themselves.

They also became the Kings of Swinging London. That fabled place was largely a tourist myth, but for the pop elite it was a real and very desirable location. Initially, Epstein introduced his boys into conventional entertainment circles – Alma Cogan, Lionel Bart and Bruce Forsyth all figured. Within eighteen months, however, the Beatles had inspired an entirely new scene into existence, and could move at will through gilded salons of long-haired pop boys, mini-skirted models and Cockney photographers, spiced with high-living hoodlums and slumming aristocrats. One imagines that the Aintree Institute began to seem long ago and far away.

Still, amid the madness, the group had each other. Pretensions were checked; the Beatles moved about in a Liverpudlian bubble. Their gift was for absorbing outside influences while remaining true to themselves. And what the world loved about them, nearly as much as the music, was the wit, the cheek and the exuberance which were suddenly Scousedom's defining characteristics. When their first film, *A Hard Day's Night*, was scripted by Liverpool playwright Alun Owen, it was important that he reinforced the Beatles' image as a travelling circus of loveable wackers

But what did Liverpool itself make of this? The Northern premiere of *A Hard Day's Night*, on 10 July 1964, was to be preceded by a civic reception at Liverpool Town Hall. The Fabs themselves were far from easy about their return. There had been murmurings of local resentment. In the event, their drive into town from Speke Airport was a triumph. Crowds lined the route, and a reported quarter of the city's population thronged around Castle Street for a glimpse of the homecoming heroes on the Town Hall balcony. High on nerves and elation, John offered the multitudes a Hitler salute.

My own recollection is of Liverpool people, adults and children, taking extraordinary pride in the Beatles' success. Their old associates on the beat scene might have experienced more complex emotions, but the city at large, I think, was simply chuffed. There was intense interest in their hair. Small boys raged at barbers' continued imposition of the short-back-and-sides style perfected during National Service. Sweetshops ran a sideline in plastic Beatle wigs, but they were scarcely a substitute. Grown-ups were at first suspicious of long hair. To mothers in Liverpool it carried ancient connotations of poverty and neglect; to fathers it signified an effeminate rejection of man's warrior nature. But the Beatles overcame all that. They were likely lads – no more and no less – and what's more, their hair was cleaner than anybody's.

Criticism became more common later, when it was clear the Beatles had left Liverpool for good. They hadn't simply skipped off down to London for a lark. They were gone, and they weren't coming back. Actually, the widespread notion that the Beatles 'turned their backs' on Liverpool was a tribute to the magnificent insularity of Liverpudlians. They supposed that millionaire entertainers, with the world at their feet and every earthly delight to be sampled, would find the old place perfectly adequate for their needs. What did Belgravia, Manhattan and the Bahamas have that Allerton, Clayton Square and Seacombe didn't?

Whatever the Liverpool view of the boys, the rest of the country was – for the time being – more or less united in delight. Tiny tots and pensioners loved them. Toffs and commoners cheered them, Tory and Socialist beamed approvingly. Dissent seemed limited to the outer reaches of political extremism, from paranoid right-wingers who thought them agents of Moscow, or hard-line communists who saw them as capitalism at its most decadent. In the popular imagination, the Beatles represented youth and irreverence, at the precise point in the 1960s when Britain's establishment was ready to accommodate them. Their official acceptance – culminating in those MBEs at Buckingham

Palace – was all the quicker for the arrival of Harold Wilson at Number 10 Downing Street. A shrewd populist, the first Prime Minister in living memory to speak with a Northern accent, and with a Liverpool constituency to boot, he lost no opportunity to co-opt pop music into his vision of a New Britain: young, classless and modern.

The Beatle-inspired rise in Liverpool's prestige was mirrored, with uncanny synchronicity, by the astonishing ascent of Bill Shankly's Liverpool football team. TV, theatre and the arts fell into line behind the Hit Parade by filling up with Liverpudlian performers and celebrations of the city's supposed qualities: funny, tough, egalitarian. With all of Britain lost in sudden admiration, it was time to tell the rest of the world. And the platform that the Beatles took was a press podium at New York's Airport, on the occasion of their all-conquering American Tour.

According to the US-based Liverpudlian author P. Willis-Pitts: 'When the first tough American journalists lined up to shoot down the mop-headed Beatles, invaders at Kennedy Airport in 1964, within minutes the Beatles had them eating out of their hands, charming the American nation forever. What the Americans didn't realise was that wit and repartee are the substance of Liverpool life and that a group of Liverpool bus drivers would probably have proven just as charismatic.'

The irony was that while so many Americans could trace their personal histories back to Liverpool – whether as emigrants through its dockside, or as slaves transacted through its ledger books – the United States had long forgotten the ties that used to bind its seaboards to the damp, distant port behind Ireland. Apart from a handful of stevedores, retired salts and servicemen, there could have been few with any particular impression of Merseyside – until it acquired a brand-new identity as Birthplace of The Beatles.

It's still impressive to watch old newsreel footage and observe how far the Beatles' mutually-supportive Scouse assurance could take them. Their press conference aplomb was amazing. George thought later that they'd drawn on Liverpool's comic tradition to break down the media, America's first line of defence. In *The Beatles Anthology* Paul accounts for their nonchalance like this: 'Americans all spoke with accents that we like a lot and identified with. We felt we had a lot in common, phonetically. We say "bath" and "grass" with a short "a" (we don't say "bah-th"), and so do they. I think people from Liverpool do have an affinity with Americans, with the GIs and the war and that. There are a lot of guys in Liverpool walking around with cowboy hats. It is almost as if Liverpool and New York are twin towns.'

Soon the group's new champion of the airwaves, Murray The K, was being coached by John to say 'wacker' and 'It's the gear, la". If you were to become a Fifth Beatle you had to learn to talk like one.

Even as very young men, thanks to apprenticeships served in Liverpool and Hamburg after dark, the Beatles were worldly beyond their years. Within a few more years, by 1965, their accumulated experiences were simply astonishing. They emerged from the first flush of Beatlemania both shell-shocked and invigorated. They'd sampled more of life, seen more of the world, been party to more outright strangeness, than most could experience in a lifetime. In a classic artistic progression, their minds now turned to the inner life: of consciousness, memory and the meanings of things. Once they'd conquered the outer world it was time to explore its internal counterpart, a world shaped to a large degree by childhood – and by the city where they'd first drawn breath.

'We came out of Liverpool and we reflected our background,' said Lennon. He claimed his first 'major' piece of work was 'In My Life', and he valued it because it was autobiographical. He always placed much higher store than Paul on songs that grew from authentic personal experience. 'In My Life', in its first draft, was autobiographical in a very literal way. John's initial lyric followed the route taken by a bus from his childhood home in Menlove Avenue to the centre of town: Penny Lane, the Abbey Cinema and Calderstones Park were among the locations listed. Named, too, were a couple of sights he knew to be demolished now: the tramsheds and the overground railway, known locally as the Dockers' Umbrella. It's conventional to think of him as the unsentimental Beatle, but nostalgia was never far from Lennon's mind, and those references underscored the song's essentially melancholy sense of time slipping away. By the final draft (the track appeared on *Rubber Soul*) the Liverpool specifics had been dropped, but the mood remained.

There is a stranger instance of lingering Liverpool influence in a song primarily by Paul. 'As James Joyce reconstructed the Dublin he had fled from,' wrote George Melly, 'so the Beatles rebuilt the Liverpool of their own anonymous childhoods. I can vouch for the imaginative truth of Eleanor Rigby: the big soot-black sandstone Catholic churches with trams rattling past, the redbrick terrace houses with lace curtains and holy-stoned steps . . .' More specifically, the name of Eleanor Rigby herself appears on a gravestone in the churchyard of St Mary's, Woolton (where Paul and John first met, in fact). McCartney believed he had taken the first name from Eleanor Bron, the actress in *Help!*, and the surname from a shop sign in Bristol. When the tombstone theory was put to him he began to suspect a subconscious link: 'I will have been amongst those graves, knocking around with John and wandering through there. It was the sort of place we used to sunbathe, and we probably had a crafty fag in the graveyard.' The Eleanor in question, who died in 1939, had lived directly behind Lennon's house on Menlove Avenue.

Conscious or not, such throwbacks were early symptoms of a trend that would blossom in 1967. The mental retreat to childhood was an emblem of English psychedelia, and would be expressed to perfection by the two Liverpool songs on the Beatles' double A-side of February 1967, 'Penny Lane' and 'Strawberry Fields Forever': a coupling which is possibly their greatest achievement.

There were concerns, in the minds of Brian Epstein and George Martin, that the Beatles might be growing remote from the record-buying public. Meanwhile, at Abbey Road, the group set to work. As the winter nights drew in, they hunkered down to create the Summer of Love. In private they believed the tracks that would become the *Sgt. Pepper* album were destined to amaze the world. And of course they were right. However, Epstein and Martin were less confident. Anxious to put something on the market, they decided on a New Year single to fill the gap until *Sgt. Pepper* would be ready. By Christmas the group had the basis of three new songs: 'When I'm Sixty-Four' was a tune that Paul had kicked around for years, freshly revived in a jokey vaudeville style; 'Strawberry Fields Forever' was a murky tangle of introverted Lennon-isms; and 'Penny Lane' was pure McCartney pop, as bright and breezy as the suburban day it celebrated.

Despite the triumphs of Beatlemania, John had withdrawn into a cocoon of private misery, living in Home Counties isolation amid the slow decay of his marriage to Cynthia. Paul was, if anything, more chipper than ever – Swinging London's most eligible bachelor, fired with a creative energy that placed him for the first time in effective charge of the Beatles' work. February's single would be an overture to psyche-delia's high summer and, in its perfect balance of light and darkness, a brilliant depiction of the partners' stylistic range.

McCartney discounts a report that the two songs were precursors to an abandoned album all about the Beatles' childhoods. Instead, he thinks he may have been moved to write a reminiscence of Liverpool after hearing John's draft of 'Strawberry Fields Forever'. Paul had already fixed on Penny Lane as a potential song title, attracted by its 'poetic' sound in the early version of 'In My Life'. Both sites are within a short walk of Lennon and McCartney's old addresses: Penny Lane was known for the Corporation bus terminus at one end, and still has its barber shop, bank buildings and a nearby fire station. (I'd travel to school on a big green bus marked Penny Lane, though I got off miles before; when the song came out I looked at my bus with new respect and wonder.)

Strawberry Field, in the singular, was a Salvation Army children's home with overgrown grounds where John used to play. 'It was a rather wild garden,' Paul told his biographer, Barry Miles. 'It wasn't manicured at all, so it was easy to hide in. The bit he went into was a secret garden like in *The Lion the Witch and the Wardrobe* . . . a little hideaway where he could live in his dreams a little.' The home has been re-built since then (and gets support from Yoko Ono), but the distinguished front gate remains.

John began writing 'Strawberry Fields Forever' while filming in Spain, on the set of a satirical movie, *How I Won the War*. Returning home he felt a stifling sense of aimlessness, unrelieved by his experiments with LSD. From these conditions he fashioned the psychedelic melancholy of the song. As a lost and lonely adult, he made the garden sanctuary of his Liverpool childhood a symbol of psychic retreat. 'No-one I think is in my tree: I was hip in kindergarten,' he elaborated later. 'I was different from all the others. Nobody seems to be as hip as me, is what I was saying. Therefore I must be crazy or a genius: "I mean it must be high or low." There was something wrong with me, I thought, because I seemed to see things other people don't see.' Acid, for Lennon, was not so much a door to the unknown, as a return ticket to the private trances of his infancy.

The lyric's self-conscious stumbling was mirrored in the music, toiling forward through a sonic fog. Unlike the avalanche of pop-psychedelic imitations which followed, the song drew its power, not from an effort to simulate the alleged insights of hallucinogenics, but from the authentic emotional power of one man's struggle to keep himself together. Along with 'In My Life', Lennon ranked 'Strawberry Fields Forever' among his best songs. In March 1984, just outside the Dakota Building and three years after Lennon's murder on the New York sidewalk, a section of Central Park was ceremonially re-named Strawberry Fields.

For all their differences, 'Penny Lane' and 'Strawberry Fields Forever' broke new ground together, transcending the comic tendency of English place names in song. In its leader column of 1 April 1967, *The Times* showed its approval: 'To see that some apparently ordinary place is unlike any other, and to express for it a nostalgia unmixed with any

ML

chauvinistic notions of its superiority is a pleasant but forgotten art . . . "Penny Lane", indeed, looks back to the days when parochialism was not an attitude to be derided.' In a similar Britpop vein, the Kinks' 'Waterloo Sunset' and the Small Faces' 'Itchycoo Park' would both be in the charts before the year was out. Denied the expanse of space, speed and exoticism that American songwriters took for granted, the English minstrels opted for a sense of place, rooted in the past. But on another level, the physical realities of Strawberry Field and Penny Lane were scarcely relevant: they were secondary to the universal states of being that their respective songs evoked in hearts and minds all over the world.

As sessions continued for *Sgt. Pepper's Lonely Hearts Club Band* through early 1967, the past would cast increasingly potent spells on Beatle imaginations. The Sgt. Pepper name itself was a Surreal collision of stoned West Coast and staid Lancastrian. The legendary album cover had its source in two McCartney memories – one being a 1920s photograph of his father's Liverpool dance band, all posed proudly about the big bass drum, and a more general recollection of Northern municipal parks, with their floral clocks, Edwardian bandstands and stiff presentations to civic dignitaries. Among the characters nominated by Lennon for Peter Blake's famous collage were the wartime Liverpool comedian Tommy Handley (in a cloth cap, next to Marilyn Monroe) and a veteran Liverpool footballer, Albert Stubbins.

Much the same trend towards nostalgia inspired the 'charabanc' theme of the *Magical Mystery Tour* film, based on those proletarian coach excursions that Paul had watched departing from Liverpool for the Blackpool Illuminations or hotspots unknown. Of the songs themselves, 'Your Mother Should Know' was in Paul's tradition of tributes to the tea-dance gentility of his parents' courting days. And John's stream-of-consciousness, 'I am the Walrus', summoned up an ageless refrain from Liverpool playgrounds, 'Yellow belly custard, green snot pie, all mixed up with a dead dog's eye. Put it in a butty, nice and thick, all washed down with a cold cup of sick.' Some say, too, that his 'English garden', waiting for the sun, was Lennon's beloved Calderstones Park, the beautiful tract that lies between Menlove Avenue and Quarry Bank School.

In the long, final chorus of 'Hey Jude', we might just hear the Beatles' own echoes of the Kop – the Merseyside football terraces had adopted Beatle tunes *en masse* in 1963 – and a wistful evocation of the communal solidarity they could no longer experience, even between themselves.

On the *White Album* (alias *The Beatles*), John used the self-referential 'Glass Onion' to name-check the Cast Iron Shore – another childhood retreat, a murky stretch of Mersey riverbank by the docks. In a similar vein, Paul's song 'Mother Nature's Son', he says, took its inspiration from boyhood jaunts in the semi-wilderness of Hale, before a giant car factory was built there, when there was rural isolation by the muddy expanse of the Mersey Estuary.

'Can you take me back where I came from?' sang Paul on the *White Album*; his plaintive call is left to drift across the anarchic squabble of John's 'Revolution 9'. 'Brother, can you take me back?' Reviewing the *White Album* for the *Sunday Times*, in November 1968, Derek Jewell had sensed the lingering imprint of the Beatles' city: 'They are Liverpudlians, and their style is a cocky Liverpudlian two-fingers-to-the-world one moment, with glimmers of moral remorse the next. So the searchers after significance stay tempted . . . They may not be philosophers, but they shouldn't invite equation with the regiment of Liverpool funny men either.'

Naturally the Scouse references could be daft and joyous – whether it's John bawling 'Maggie May' on *Let It Be*, or turning his accent to pantomime effect on *Abbey Road*'s 'Polythene Pam' (its subject 'a mythical Liverpool scrubber' he said, though some other theories exist). More generally, though, the Beatles' final music is rich with awareness of the gulf that separates our early certainties and the world as later experienced. In the mournful 'You Never Give Me Your Money' – written by Paul in the long dark night of the Beatles' break-up – he suddenly grabs ecstatically at an image from adolescence, of himself as a van-driver's assistant for Lewis's Liverpool store – aimless, broke, but wonderfully free from care. As he told Miles: 'I remember thinking, in many ways, I wish I was a lorry driver, a Catholic lorry driver. Very, very simple life, a firm faith and a place to go in my lorry, in my nice lorry.'

Liverpool was, for the Beatles, a beginning rather than a destination. But in their imaginations they never entirely left it. And the city's influence would swirl around the music they made long after the Beatles. As George Melly noted of their *Yellow Submarine* movie: 'The departure for the Sea of Dreams is from the Liverpool Pier Head.'

3. THE FAB FOUR HUNDRED

THE BEATLES' MERSEY MAFIA

There were so many 'fifth Beatles' down the years that the Fab Four could have been the Fab Four Hundred. There is a handful of individuals whose contributions stand out – including Brian Epstein, Neil Aspinall and Derek Taylor. Two contenders, Pete Best and Stuart Sutcliffe, were actually band members for a while. My own nomination would be George Martin. The Beatles really matter because of their records – everything else is peripheral – and as their producer, George Martin was vital in the creation of those records.

Liverpool itself has often been called the fifth Beatle. The character and traditions of the city were so influential upon the Beatles' personalities that the assertion is perfectly valid. And London, which (to reverse Charles Dickens' formula) lies second in my heart to Liverpool, made its own essential contribution. And there is a third town, too, with a credible claim to having made the Beatles . . .

Hamburg and Liverpool were never quite twins, but there was a resemblance: rough and ready Northern seaports where people took their pleasures greedily. Yet Hamburg had suffered even more terribly than Liverpool in the second world war, while its eventual recovery would leave Liverpool standing. The Beatles were first taken there by their agent-cum-manager, a stocky Welsh wheeler-dealer named Allan Williams, and his business partner Lord Woodbine, a calypso singer and Caribbean steel band player.

Williams' city centre joint, the Jacaranda, was frequented by the Beatles. Through his showbiz contacts in Germany, Williams had sent across a local act called the Seniors. Fronted by a dynamic black vocalist, Derry Wilkie, and powered by saxophonist Howie Casey (their line-up would later include Freddie Starr), the Seniors were the first Merseybeat band to make the Hamburg trip, and through the favourable impression they created, Williams gained a useful new market. The young Beatles' lack of day jobs made them ideal candidates to follow. They would need a drummer, and so they recruited Pete Best.

The German city had been almost obliterated by RAF raids, and was occupied by the British until 1951. Life in the ruins had been so harsh that prostitution was common, and vice was made worse by an influx of gangsters escaping communism in the East. The legacy, by 1960, was a thriving red light district in St Pauli, where customers were on the rough side and liked their music loud. 'We were scared by it all at first,' said Lennon, 'being in the middle of the tough clubland. But we felt cocky, being from Liverpool, at least believing the myth about Liverpool producing cocky people.'

Their friend of the time, Astrid Kirchherr, believes that lurid tales of the Beatles' sexual exploits in Hamburg have been exaggerated, but it was clearly a defining experience for these inexperienced suburban boys. The writer Barry Miles suggests: 'Deprived of the familiar friendships of home and family, thrown together in a non-English-speaking culture, they developed a hermetic Liverpool bubble around them: a secret language of wisecracks and references, gestures and behaviour.'

The addition of Pete Best (whose mother, Mona, ran a West Derby hang-out called the Casbah) set the band up for Hamburg, which proved a sort of musical boot camp. Right away they had to match the impact made by Derry Wilkie, especially by his barnstorming take on Ray Charles' 'What'd I Say'. The long hours and raucous atmosphere toughened their style. Playing hundreds of cover versions gave them an eye for song construction. A stint as backing band for the English singer Tony Sheridan was another factor: he was a guitarist of stinging ferocity, while some say Lennon even copied his stage stance.

'That place was the making of so many Liverpool groups,' said the Merseybeat manager Joe Flannery. 'They went out as novices and came back as tight as anything. It was one of the best training grounds. When I first went out there I thought you could have been just across the Mersey in Birkenhead, rather than across the North Sea.'

Bill Harry of *Mersey Beat* strikes a note of scepticism: 'The whole Hamburg thing has been distorted. When the Beatles went to Germany after Derry and the Seniors there was basically only the Kaiserkeller club and the Top Ten. But in Liverpool you had groups playing at well over 300 venues: the social clubs, the ice rinks, the swimming baths, synagogues, church halls, town halls, everywhere. Hundreds of groups playing. Yet people go on about Hamburg, where there were two poxy little clubs and a handful of groups. And what you have to remember also is that there were more Liverpool groups going to the American bases in France than there ever were to Hamburg.'

Spencer Leigh, the Merseybeat historian: 'Lots of groups went to Hamburg and it didn't seem to change them at all, but it certainly changed the Beatles. Pete Best's style of drumming became very forceful; it changed their look, they came back in black leathers, it probably gave them more attack. It meant that people like Cliff Richard and the Shadows became old-fashioned around here.' It's commonly agreed that the Beatles' homecoming gig at Litherland Town Hall – on 27 December 1960 – was so electrifying that it kick-started Beatlemania. From now on, prophesied Bob Wooler, the Beatles would be 'the stuff that screams are made of'.

A few years later, in 1964, Astrid paid a visit to the Cavern. Her companion, the German photographer Max Schler, commented: 'I was struck by the Liverpool kids, they appeared like characters from Dickens, dressed in strange styles, not trying to look rich or smart as kids would still do back in Hamburg. But the city was still devastated from the war, while Hamburg was already rebuilt.'

When the Beatles first sampled Hamburg they were John, Paul, George and Pete – plus Stuart. Their fifth member was somewhat rescued from obscurity by the film *Backbeat*, which was largely about his time in Hamburg. But he played a key role in Liverpool, too. Though his musical input was meagre, Stuart Sutcliffe gave the Beatles some of the intellectual edge that marked them apart in a town crawling with competitors. A teacher's son, he'd grown up in Huyton and went on to the city's College of Art, where he became one of its most gifted students and the best friend of would-be Teddy Boy John Lennon. 'I was always torn,' Lennon said later, 'between looking like Elvis/James Dean and looking like an artist. It's always apparent in my work and in the photographs of me around; there's two kinds of Lennons – there's the one that looks like a rock'n'roller and one that looks like a student or a painter or a poet.'

Sutcliffe felt the same conflict. In 1960 a painting of his was admitted to John Moores' prestigious exhibition at the Walker Art Gallery. He used his prize money to buy the bass guitar that got him into Lennon's group, Johnny and the Moondogs. (It's believed he helped John come up with The Beatles' name, too.) His heroes ranged from Elvis to Modigliani and Rimbaud; he smoked Gauloises and wore dark glasses. In Hamburg he became the lover of Astrid Kirchherr, part of a student circle who influenced the Beatles' look – in particular the 'French cut' hairstyle popular on the Paris Left Bank, which led the band to abandon greasy quiffs for a clean, combed-forward style.

When the boys went home to Liverpool, Stuart stayed behind with Astrid. In 1962, he died of a brain haemorrhage in Hamburg.

Sutcliffe's personal style had been a vital bridge between two contrasting and apparently incompatible aesthetics: the cosmopolitan beatnik and the working class Teddy Boy. He was not alone in this: around Britain there were figures like Peter Blake and Ian Dury who made the same connections. But Stuart Sutcliffe influenced the Beatles, and therefore the world. In Liverpool, the Beatles say, their dash of student artiness would push them ahead of the crowd. A gaunt, moody and beautiful bass-player, with a taste for Gauloises and existentialism, was something you didn't get in Gerry and the Pacemakers.

The next to exit was of course Pete Best, mysteriously sacked by Brian Epstein. 'I missed the bite of the cherry by *that* much,' he told me years later. He was the Beatles' drummer for only two years, from 1960 to 1962, but they were such amazingly busy years that he conceivably spent more time onstage with them than Ringo Starr. What's certain is that Best was a Beatle in their crucial, formative period. His sex appeal was important in building the Liverpool fan base that propelled the band to national attention. And he was instrumental, in Hamburg, in developing the style that would revolutionise popular music.

In rock mythology, Best became the archetype of the pop loser – all the more poignant in downtrodden Liverpool, where the alternatives to stardom seem so much bleaker. While the Beatles climbed to godlike stature, their redundant drummer became a figure in folklore: to be 'the Pete Best' of any band is to be the one who was in the bath when opportunity knocked. I met him in a hotel bar in Westminster. He spoke so quietly it barely registered, and seemed not aggrieved but depressed. He was smart with a neat moustache, like a retired footballer, and lived in the Liverpool suburbs. 'Those are days that are engraved on my mind,' he whispered. 'They were my growing up.'

For reasons that have never been clearly explained, Brian Epstein invited Pete Best to his NEMS record shop office on 16 August 1962, and told him he was no longer a Beatle. Best was devastated: 'I felt like putting a stone around my neck and jumping off the Pier Head,' he said. 'I knew that the Beatles were going places and to be kicked out on the verge of it happening upset me a great deal.' Wasn't he always an outsider in the band? 'No, I disagree. How can you be an outsider when you spend two years of your life with them, living abroad, all in grotty digs, playing on stage for seven hours a night? It was always the Beatles *en bloc*, getting bevvied together, crawling round the record shops for a free listen to the records we wanted to copy.'

There are various theories about his sacking. Spencer Leigh compares the situation to an Agatha Christie murder mystery, where everyone in the Vicarage has a potential motive for the dirty deed. Was it someone's jealousy of Best's good looks and Cavern popularity? Or George Martin's dissatisfaction with his drumming? A symptom of Epstein's thwarted sexual longings? Pete's failure to grow a mop-top haircut? Or his mother Mona's pregnancy, by one of the Beatles' inner circle? All or none could have played a part. Only Epstein ever knew for sure.

For Pete's friend Neil Aspinall, the Beatles' roadie, it was a difficult day: 'I was close to Pete. But it wasn't a conflict of loyalty. Brian wanted to see him, I don't think Pete could drive at the time, so I drove him into town to see Brian. I was in the record store looking at records, and he came down and said he'd been fired. He was in a state of shock, really. We went over to the Grapes in Mathew Street, had a pint. And I just said, "I'm going now." And Pete said, "I'm staying here for a while." I just left. That night I think we had a gig somewhere over the water, Birkenhead side. I had all the gear in the van. So when it was time to go, I just got in the van and drove to the gig. I think that John, Paul and George might have been slightly surprised. But, hey, I'm turning up, this is my job. What happens outside of that is nothing to do with me.'

While the Fab Four went on to glory, Pete Best was left in Liverpool to pick up the pieces. He joined various Merseybeat bands and, after his old group became world-famous, enjoyed some minor celebrity as leader of the Pete Best Band (actually calling one LP *Best of the Beatles*). But the gulf between his predicament and their astonishing ascent was too much to bear. In 1965 he attempted suicide – and was rescued by his mother and brother, who smelled the gas beneath his door. Married with children, Best became a labourer in a Liverpool bakery and then spent 20 years in the Civil Service – aptly, his job was to advise the local unemployed on getting themselves re-started after redundancy.

I asked him if he bore a grudge. 'No. Even now I reflect that I've lost my heritage. You push it into your subconscious but something will trigger it off, like some story about Paul or the news of John's death. But time has mellowed. And over the course of 20 years my lifestyle's changed. I've had to make the best of what's available. There's a lot of fond memories. In four years I saw a lot of life. I can say I did it, it was great to be part of it. And no one can take those memories away from me.'

In 1993 he took early retirement, and makes occasional public appearances. Paul's brother Mike McCartney once designed posters for the Beatles at Mona Best's Casbah Club; years later, he discovered one outside a restaurant toilet in Tijuana, Mexico. 'Of all the toilets in all the places in the world!' Mike laughs. 'I don't know who in the Casbah sold it to them, but you'll have to work it out. I did an interview with Pete when he didn't have his *Anthology* money, because Pete has a lot of fond memories for me. Of all the people who benefited out of that Beatle phenomenon, Bob Wooler and Pete Best are the ones I felt sad for. I agreed, but said the deal is I'll have one of me posters back!'

Pete received his '*Anthology* money' after the release, in 1995, of old Beatle recordings he had played on. 'Pete will earn a decent amount of money,' confirmed the Beatles' spokesman Derek Taylor, 'which is only right. He is a good man, and he deserves it. Being sacked from the band was a great shock for him, but he has remained philosophical about it throughout.'

Elvis Presley had his Memphis Mafia. Roman Emperors had their Praetorian Guard. The Beatles were surrounded by a protective inner sanctum of Liverpudlians. As a group they were immensely open-minded, and struck up acquaintances with anyone – from Eric Clapton to the Maharishi – who might have something to teach them. However, their business life was a different matter. From Brian Epstein downwards, the Beatles' professional world was dominated by trusted lieutenants of impeccable Mersey pedigree: Neil Aspinall, Mal Evans, Tony Barrow, Peter Brown, Geoffrey Ellis, Alistair Taylor, Tony Bramwell and Derek Taylor. Liverpool and full employment are terms we rarely hear in the same sentence, but it wasn't for want of trying on the Beatles' part. They were never equal-opportunity employers.

I'd suggest it was an instinctive defence mechanism, rather than Scouse chauvinism. In one way the Beatles' experience of real life came to a stop when they left Liverpool for London. Removed from their familiar landscape, from the friends and family members who'd known them all along, they entered the artificial existence of celebrity. From that day on, every person's reaction to them was conditioned by the fact of their colossal fame. Who could they trust? Who else carried in their heads a memory of the last fragment of reality they had known? Only the men of their own Praetorian Guard: The Beatles' Mersey Mafia.

'If anyone was the Fifth Beatle, it was Brian.' Such was Paul McCartney's assessment of the Beatles' manager, made 30 years after his death. The fact is that they were going nowhere until their adoption by this starry-eyed young businessman from the record shop down the road. Packed-out Cavern gigs were proof of their popularity on Liverpool's limited beat scene, but it took a man of special talents to translate what the Beatles had, into what the whole world wanted. He steered them to the top at a time when Britain had no pop industry to speak of. And, within three years of his first encounter with the band, they were toppermost of the global poppermost.

A cultured and fastidious character, Epstein stands in elegant contrast to most managerial stereotypes. He wasn't a hard-nosed hustler, in the mould of Elvis Presley's Colonel Parker, nor was he a sharkish Tin Pan Alley operator or a thuggish Mr Big, banging tables and terrorising his witless charges. As with their producer George Martin, the Beatles were blessed in meeting precisely the right individual. In Brian Epstein they found an ally of intuitive sensitivity – who loved them as a teenage fan would love them, could speak to them as an equal, and would oversee their careers with a capable business brain.

He'd been born in 1934 to a prosperous family of Lithuanian Jewish descent, and grew up in a sizeable house on the broad suburban thoroughfare of Queens Drive. (It actually intersects with Lennon's old road Menlove Avenue, close to Penny Lane and Strawberry Field.) In the childhood homes of both Paul McCartney and Cilla Black there stood pianos bought from the north Liverpool furniture store run by Brian's father. The Epsteins' shop grew large enough to incorporate the business next door and became North End Music Stores (or NEMS). There was an assumption that Brian would eventually join his father there. He was an educational misfit, however, who went through a succession of private schools. To the dismay of his ambitious parents, he spoke wistfully of becoming a dress designer.

In the end he was persuaded to enter the family business, and took to it with flair, assisted by the post-war consumer boom that took NEMS into electrical goods and pop records. His entrepreneurial career was interrupted by National Service in 1952 – but the refined Epstein proved unsuited to military life, and was actually arrested for 'impersonating an officer' by virtue of his immaculate clothes and aristocratic manner. Back in Liverpool, where he socialised with the city's theatrical set, he once again upset his family by leaving for a spell of drama training at RADA – The Royal Academy of Dramatic Art – in London. The experiment proved a failure, and 1957 found Brian once more minding the store. At least they had now expanded from the drabness of Walton to the comparative glamour of the city centre.

Behind his failures as a soldier and as an actor there lay the fact of Epstein's homosexuality. In his autobiography *A Cellarful of Noise* (often satirically dubbed 'A Cellarful Of Boys') he reports his Army discharge without revealing details. The book, ghost-written by Derek Taylor, was necessarily reticent about Brian's private life: homosexuality was still illegal at the time. The army, in fact, had readily detected Private Epstein's inclinations, and tactfully retired him on unspecified medical grounds. The RADA stint, meanwhile, was scuppered by his arrest one night in a London toilet; the affair was discreetly resolved by the Epstein family lawyer. On another occasion, Brian was the victim of a brutal beating by a would-be blackmailer.

Whatever the turmoil of his private life, Epstein took his NEMS work seriously and in 1959 assumed control of a new branch, this time in the busy Liverpool street of Whitechapel. Nearby were some other famous merchants: the music stores of Rushworth & Draper and Frank Hessy's, the book-sellers Philip, Son & Nephew and the toy shop Hobbies where Aunt Mimi would take the young Lennon for a treat. Across the road, close to the Kardomah Café, was the warren of eighteenth-century back streets that concealed the Cavern.

Epstein's assistant Alistair Taylor became aware of the excitement building around the Beatles, even if their one known recording, 'My Bonnie', was the rather poor relic of a Hamburg session they'd done as back-up band for Tony Sheridan. It's also likely that Brian too knew something of the Beatles, whether as regular fixtures in the *Mersey Beat* newspaper to which he himself contributed, or as persistent visitors to the shop itself: the group would build its repertoire with feats of memory in NEMS' listening booths.

In fact it was Brian's ambitious stock-ordering policy that helped ensure the Liverpool groups had ready access to US records before their rivals; Taylor recalls stocking the entire Blue Note catalogue. Once signed to Epstein, the Beatles were even allowed access to the shop after closing time, riffling the racks before a gig. Another NEMS man, Peter Brown, remarks that they were kept on their toes by working class Liverpool customers, whose seafaring connections made them so knowledgeable in American music.

Spencer Leigh remembers: 'In 1960–61 I used to go to NEMS to buy my records because NEMS was a very well-ordered shop. There would be about 40 or 50 new records a week and you could be sure that NEMS would have them in. In fact I always remember going in and the person in front of me in the queue said, "Have you got that record of Hitler's speeches, please?" And the person serving – it could well have been Brian Epstein – said, "Yes, here you are." This record must have been total anathema to him. But a customer wanted it, so he would find it.'

Epstein visited the Cavern on 9 November 1961 to catch the Beatles' lunch-time show. His encounter left him smitten: 'I had never seen anything like the Beatles on any stage,' he wrote later. 'There was clearly an excitement in the otherwise unpleasing dungeon, which was quite removed from any of the formal entertainments provided at places like the Liverpool Empire or the London Palladium.' Within a month he was their manager.

Family and friends suspected it was merely the latest of Brian's butterfly enthusiasms, and he was clearly a contrast to his knockabout young signings. (Epstein himself spoke in the clipped tones of pre-war England.) Yet he began to promote their career with earnest dedication. Most local managers of the time were not accomplished men; often their only qualifications were to have a telephone and transport. Brian, however, had contacts, charm and brains. In Liverpool at least, he was a hugely impressive figure.

There were demoralising setbacks at the hands of London record executives, sceptical of the Beatles' appeal, but his fortunes changed thanks to the fateful intervention of George Martin, A&R man at the unfashionable EMI label Parlophone. Epstein then survived the storms of protest that followed his dismissal of Pete Best. At Brian's behest the group abandoned rock'n'roll leathers, and took to wearing suits. The effect was not, as often claimed, to 'tame' their image. Instead it rescued them from a 50s style that was fast becoming *passé*, and cast them in a mode that was utterly new and even strange. (The Beatles were, in fact, rather fond of suits and wore them quite voluntarily, as a glance at the *Abbey Road* sleeve shows.)

Epstein had just contrived the most far-reaching makeover in show business history. If there was a sexual element in his devotion to the Beatles, he was careful not to show it. Rumours spread in Liverpool about a short Spanish holiday he took with John Lennon – in fact John's first national newspaper mention came when he beat up Bob Wooler for suggesting he was Epstein's plaything. The truth may never now be known. What's for sure is that, once in London, he deepened and enriched the young provincials' outlook, stimulating them to greater creativity.

After the Beatles came an entire stable of NEMS acts: many, like Gerry and the Pacemakers, were so successful they made Merseybeat the defining sound of British pop. And, attached as he was to the Beatles, he was equally devoted to his only female signing, Cilla Black. He moved the agency side of NEMS to premises in London, next door to the home of the entertainment elite at the London Palladium. Soon enough, the former Liverpool shop-keeper was negotiating some of the biggest deals in show business history.

In 1965, with America conquered, the Beatles were given their MBEs. Epstein, it's said, was hurt at being omitted – but was consoled by

Princess Margaret's quip that MBE might stand for Mr Brian Epstein. He remained a quietly debonair figure, seen on the edge of Beatle news conferences, delighting in their triumphs and protecting their position as Britain's golden children. However, he formed no significant relationships outside of his work, and evidently suffered from the pressures of colossal success. He'd never been closely involved in the Beatles' music: his input was confined to occasional advice on the best choice of single. And when they stopped touring in 1966, to concentrate on studio work, he was largely without a role in their lives. His last years were marked by depression, unrelieved by new ventures including a West End theatre and the management of a British bullfighter.

He was discovered dead in his Belgravia flat, on 27 August 1967. Nobody can know for sure whether his overdose of sleeping pills was deliberate. It's certain he had been low in spirits, but the best qualified observers, including Alistair Taylor, Derek Taylor, Cilla Black and Paul McCartney, have always shared the coroner's conclusion that the death was accidental. We can easily forget how young the main players in the Beatle drama really were. The group themselves went from mop-tops, to bearded patriarchs, to solo artists before they reached 30. As Cynthia Lennon says: 'I look back at photographs of Brian and, considering he ran the most famous pop group in the world, and he died at 32, it's crazy.'

It's been argued that Epstein was a financial amateur. He made a major blunder in signing away 90 per cent of revenue from Beatle merchandising at the height of Beatlemania. He probably underestimated the market value of Lennon and McCartney's songwriting, too. But the record deals he signed were standard for the time, drawn up before rock artists knew their bargaining power. When the Beatles took off, it happened on a scale, and at a speed, that were entirely unprecedented: Epstein worked in a world without signposts. The Beatles spoke well of him, acknowledging his influence and forgiving his mistakes. All things considered, it's doubtful that anyone could have served them better.

We can imagine him, had he lived to be 64, approaching the twenty-first century as a distinguished theatrical knight. Openly gay and hopefully contented, he would know the place he craved in show business history was utterly secure.

At a Rock & Roll Hall of Fame ceremony George Harrison once said: 'There are supposed to be about 5,000 Fifth Beatles. But really there were only two: Derek Taylor and Neil Aspinall.' You might of course stake a claim for Brian Epstein and George Martin, but Martin himself tends to nominate Neil Aspinall. How does the shadowy henchman feel about it? 'Oh, I keep trying to lay that on George!' he says. 'There is no fifth Beatle. I think if there was such a thing, it would be Pete Best or Stu Sutcliffe, not some outsider who wasn't in the band. A ridiculous suggestion.'

The self-effacing evasion is typical. Yet Aspinall has been in charge of Apple, the Beatles' company, since it began in 1967, except for the brief interlude when their affairs were handled by Allen Klein. Before that he was their road manager and all-round Mr Fixit. Through the madness of Beatlemania, he was by their side. Later, in the unhappy years when the Beatles had ceased to trust anybody, including one another, they still trusted Neil. He is the one constant presence in their story. 'Poor old Neil,' McCartney once remarked to me, coming off another phone call to the Apple office. 'He's been a real solid guy for us. But I don't think we've always been good for him.' Decades of loyal service have been tough on his health.

When the Beatles were a baby-band, Neil Aspinall would ferry them through the Mersey Tunnel to local gigs, humping their primitive gear past squealing fans and scowling Teddy Boys. He drove them down to London for their first auditions with Decca and EMI. He'd been at school with Paul McCartney and knew George Harrison, a boy in the year below. Later on he lived in digs at the house of Pete Best: 'When they came back from Hamburg and needed transport, I had this little beaten-up old van. I was training to be an accountant so I only got £2.50 and some luncheon vouchers a week, which wasn't really enough to live on. So to drive the band around and get £1 a gig, it was found money. At the same time, I'd seen them perform, so I knew I was driving a good band around. I'd normally just take the equipment to the gig and everybody made their own way there. I'd leave the equipment there and go home and do my accountancy correspondence course. Then I'd go back and pick the gear up. If they wanted a lift I'd drop them off wherever. It started that simply.'

When the group moved away from Liverpool he went with them, and in the process acquired a job title: 'We went on the Helen Shapiro tour and the first theatre we got to, the tour manager was a guy called Johnny Clapton. I remember just standing to the side of the stage about three or four in the afternoon when we got there, and Johnny Clapton was saying, "Who's the Beatles' road manager?" I'd never heard the term before, so I didn't answer. So he ended up saying, "Is there anybody *with* The Beatles?" So I said, Yeah, I am! "OK, *you're* their road manager."

Oh, OK! I still don't know what a road manager is, quite frankly. But that's where the term came from for me.'

From Litherland Town Hall to Shea Stadium, his duties multiplied in complexity. But in 1966, quite suddenly, the touring years stopped: 'I was tired. We'd been doing it for a long time. But I don't think it got me down in the same way as it got them down. They were the centre of attention wherever they went and it was always people wanting a piece of them or their autograph, or an interview or whatever. If they'd decided to keep on touring, that would have been OK with me.' Though there was no more road to manage, the Beatles' road manager was still on hand when the group chose to cloister themselves in studios. 'I was there all the time. For them, they were working, they were composing, recording, and on occasions that could get boring for me. But I learned to play chess with Ringo.'

Brian Epstein's death left the band without a business overseer, and once again they looked to Aspinall: 'So I said to them, foolishly I guess, "Look, I'll do it until you find somebody that you want to do it."' Outsiders duly arrived, in the form of Allen Klein and Linda's relatives the Eastmans, but when the dust of the Beatles' split had settled, there was Neil again, looking after the shop. 'I don't really have a job title,' he shrugs. 'I guess I'm just manager of Apple. When the four guys asked me to do this, when they got rid of Allen Klein, they basically asked me to do "it". But "it" was never defined.' Apple vacated its famous Savile Row HQ, but Aspinall carried on, patiently untangling their business problems in a succession of rented premises around London. As the custodian of their archives he became the driving force behind the *Anthology* project, which remains their definitive memorial.

In a world where people jostle for attention on the strength of very slender connections to the Beatles, Aspinall adopted an extremely low profile. He scuttles from the spotlight like a bug whose stone has been upturned. 'Yes. I'm very shy,' he says. 'Or I was in those days. I also thought that all the hoop-la that was going on was not because of me. It was because of them and what they were doing. People didn't want me in the shot, thank you very much. So I stayed out of it.'

His partner through the physical turbulence of Beatlemania was a hefty, bespectacled Scouser called Mal Evans – a Post Office engineer with a part-time job as bouncer at the Cavern. 'We knew Mal because he was on the Cavern door,' says Neil. 'I was ill with a temperature. We were due to come down to London for some radio stuff. In the Cavern, I was, [groans] Oh, I'm not going to be able to make this. So I told them and Brian, I can't drive to London tomorrow. So they say, "Well you'll have to get somebody else, won't you?" No sympathy [*laughs*]. And I didn't have a clue who I could get. I went up the Cavern steps into Mathew Street just to get some fresh air, and Mal was standing there. So I just said to him, "What are you doing for the next couple of days?" Six or seven months later it was really getting too much for one person to handle, and I said to them and Brian that I really need some help. So we asked Mal and he gave up his job as a telephone technician. He drove the van and looked after the equipment after that.'

Mal Evans may have risen from 'humper' to 'personal assistant' but, unlike Aspinall, he found no role for himself in a world without the Beatles. He moved to America where he began his memoirs, provisionally titled *200 Miles to Go* (that being the distance from Liverpool to London). But in 1976, seemingly depressed, stoned and confused, he was shot dead in a scuffle with the Los Angeles police. A down-to-earth character who loved the Beatles, but worshipped Elvis Presley, Evans had been a rock of Liverpudlian strength for the band. But they changed his life and he couldn't find a way to change it back again.

When I interviewed Derek Taylor he was in semi-retirement. Being off the drink he wouldn't meet in a pub, suggesting instead a café near my office and close to Brian Epstein's old London HQ, by the London Palladium. Just across Regent Street was the Savile Row building where Apple used to be. Within the record business he was still revered by PRs and journalists who'd watched him operate in his heyday. 'There's a man I have a lot of admiration for,' one told me. 'He was a man of manners. He had great style. And when you didn't get anything from him, he made you come away feeling you'd been royally entertained.' Another said: 'If I've ever modelled my approach on anyone, it was him. It just struck me that he had this incredibly civilised attitude to the whole thing.'

Raised in the Wirral, Taylor left the Manchester showbiz desk of the *Daily Express* in 1964 to be Brian Epstein's assistant – he'd just helped Brian write his autobiography *A Cellarful of Noise* – and then became the Beatles' public relations man. 'My inclination was always as an enthusiast rather than a relentless hunter down of evil men, which is why I crossed over from writing about the Beatles to writing for the Beatles.' Friendship with Lennon was cemented one drunken night in Paris: 'Are you pretending to be from Liverpool or something?' John demanded. But he could be won over, Taylor recalled, 'once you had proven you weren't from Manchester and therefore useless'.

Derek looked after Epstein's public relations in the media frenzy over Merseybeat, which had no precedent in Britain. 'I remember going to get hold of Cilla Black in a hairdresser's in Liverpool – because if you got to Number 1 you went and had your hair done. It was a more innocent age. The joke of getting your parents a house in the country had been laid out in the 50s: the paradox was that whereas pop stars were seen as very vulgar and crude people, they were in fact very sentimental people who bought their parents homes.'

Within a year he was restless, however, and after a minor tiff with Brian he moved with his wife Joan to Los Angeles. Here his first PR clients were the Byrds, another brilliant group who were transforming the sound of pop. When they toured England, Brian took them to a West Country gig by train, so that they could re-create the scenes in *A Hard Day's Night*. In America, Taylor's gentle whimsy and optimistic world-view made him an ideal mouthpiece for the Love Generation, and in 1967 he helped set up the first great hippy event, Monterey: 'Doing the Monterey Festival was easy. I was never afraid of looking a prat. I sent out a very fancy press release: "Through a gold Californian sky, a festival of great delight and magic . . ." It was part GCE poetry, part journalese and part marijuana, and it was saying this is not an ordinary thing we're doing . . . We were not trained PR men. I wasn't that smooth. I was honest. The Beatles got us pretty well trained to be straight, to be yourself, and that got me by a lot.'

Droll and charming, Taylor acquired a glittering reputation for hip eloquence. He'd need these qualities more than ever when he was recalled to London to become the Beatles' PR again. During their troubled and final years, he was the spokesman for their idealistic but chaotic Apple adventure. 'That was the biggest test,' he told me. 'That was a hard and unhappy time, a lot of the time. The press had turned against the Beatles, and the Beatles turned against Apple. I never lost faith. I still believed in an Apple that was there to fulfil at least some of the promises, to give people a cup of tea if they came in, or a few quid. At the same time we were all having a couple of drinks during the day . . . And what we were trying to do was to save the world. This had gone beyond PR, this had gone to another phase. In my case it was entirely political: we had lots of money and other people had bugger-all, so Apple seemed to me like a wonderful idea.' Was money wasted? 'Well, what is money wasted? It depends on what you think money is for. I've always felt that it was for spreading about.'

Newsreels show Derek, bravely defending John and Yoko in the media circus of their bed-in for peace. Back at Savile Row, his hospitality was legendary. He became an alcoholic in the process. 'So, what with the Beatles falling out, the money running out, my administrative skill being limited, my generosity with their money being unlimited, confusion ensued. Downstairs you had John and Yoko running a peace campaign on a grand scale; Paul was wondering how he'd got into this madness in the first place; George was only interested in spiritual matters; and Ringo was quite indifferent to the whole thing, really. There was a lack of direction, to put it mildly. In Liverpool they were asking, What has happened to our boys? Liverpool has the capacity to absorb all sorts of craziness, from Derek Hatton to Bill Shankly. It's a place which is never short of extremes. But the Beatles even had Liverpool baffled: "They're goin' round in fuckin' dresses now!"' '

When the Beatles split, Derek stayed on for another year: 'I didn't accept the break-up. I'd say: The break-up is temporary. The Beatles will never break up. And they haven't. They can never be ex-Beatles.' Then he took a job at Warner Brothers, eventually becoming its UK boss. His philosophy was unchanged: 'It was always trying to show people a good time, that was the thing. And that meant lunching, parties, receptions, meeting them at the airport with enormous limousines and people with flowers. In Liverpool I'd see that they stayed in the Adelphi and not some modern place.' He'd greet the visiting US acts at Heathrow and drive them into town via Windsor – a big detour, but Taylor always took the qualitative view of life, not the quantitative. When he spoke about the Beatles it was never the statistics of chart success that excited him, but the magical essence he detected at the group's very core: 'I never saw the charts as being the real measurement of value. Real value doesn't necessarily end up in the singles charts.'

He kicked the drink in 1975 and as a Warners executive sponsored several Liverpool acts, especially George Melly, but also Liverpool Express and Deaf School. (When he tried to sign the Sex Pistols from EMI in 1977 he was overruled.) By 1978 he was ready for retirement in East Anglia: 'I began to dread people coming in and saying, "D'you wanna hear the guy's new album?" Because I didn't. I wanted to hear George Formby.' His last project for Warners was overseeing the clever Beatle parody the Rutles. 'After that I realised that was more or less it: I'd done the Beatles at the beginning and the Rutles at the end. Out!' But that was not the end: by 1995 he was back at Apple, hard at work on the *Anthology* CDs, films and book. I'd visit him there, in the company's smart new place in Knightsbridge – no longer dispensing unlimited hospitality, but still the in-house wit and sage, perched above the fray like some benevolent owl.

As a publicist he was a cut above the average spin doctor; he had the sense to know that the spinner is not the ball. 'Anyone can do it,' he said of PR. 'There's no mystery to any of this. On the other hand, what I love about soccer, or tap-dancing, is that there's no deception there. I'd watch John Barnes on TV, taking those corners, and say to my wife as a joke, "He's bullshitting, it's trickery." Because it so obviously *isn't*. It's all so wonderfully honest . . . Artists are reachable, and so deeply human and insecure, that if you can slot into that – the fact that we're all little children, weak, we're all in this struggle to get by as best we can – then you can become a publicist and you can become their friend.'

Derek Taylor died in 1997, leaving the magnificent *Anthology* book as a memorial. 'If you want to think I'm a bit of a Charlie,' he once told me, 'I still believe that we come back, and that your body is just like a coat and hat that you take off, and you're still here even if you're dead.' On the dangers of fame, he wrote: 'I would guess that there is no combination of weapons more dynamic than a strong childhood within the closeness of Liverpool, a sense of humour and a belief in a power higher than ourselves.'

4. 'SAND FOR BREAKFAST IN THE MORNING, BOYS!'

THE SEA AND THE SOUNDS IT BROUGHT INTO PORT

Of all the sea-ports in the world, Liverpool, perhaps, most abounds in all the variety of land-sharks, land-rats, and other vermin, which makes the hapless mariner their prey . . . And yet, sailors love this Liverpool; and upon long voyages to distant parts of the globe, will be continually dilating upon its charms and attractions, and extolling it above all other sea-ports in the world.

Herman Melville, *Redburn*, 1849

Once it was a city filled with people from elsewhere – from Ireland, from China, from Timbuctu. Its trade was in the transportation of commodities, but also of human beings, who journeyed for profit or pleasure, or out of poverty and persecution, or at the insistence of the slaver's whip. Above all Liverpool was the original Atlantic City, grown in might and notoriety by serving as England's gateway to the New World. In Sefton Park stands a statue of Christopher Columbus, inscribed with the words 'The discoverer of America was the maker of Liverpool.' If that's true, then it would make Columbus the forefather of Merseybeat, too, because the Liverpool rhythm is more than anything the pulse of America.

For years the symbolic Scouse character, practically the civic mascot, was the docker. Before that it was the seaman. More recently, I suppose, it's been the bloke on the dole. But those old maritime traditions survived, permeating generations who have never spliced a mainbrace or slung a hook. Liverpudlians of all backgrounds have unconsciously modelled themselves on these men. From the dockers they took a stubborn solidarity, from the sailors a whole raft of un-respectable attitudes. The uncertainty of casual labour and the binge mentality of shore leave still condition the Scouse way of spending. The drunken sailor's approach to financial planning is very evident. (Armies of Liverpool clerks, in the marine insurance trades, must have been of the opposite type, but their legacy has been mysteriously obliterated.) Generations of labour struggles seemed to instil a dogged ethos of equality. Hardship bred stoicism, and windfalls encouraged generosity. The appetite for entertainment remains ferocious.

London's port was bigger, but it contributed a much smaller proportion of the capital's culture. In Liverpool the sea and the docks determined every facet of life. In terraced homes and high-rise hutches you would always spot a mantelpiece or cabinet full of global paraphernalia: keepsakes from the Orient, souvenirs of Panama, knick-knacks from Newfoundland. Ringo Starr: 'I always wanted to be a merchant seaman. It was like an automatic thing for me, going away to sea . . . Everyone in Liverpool had a camel saddle in the corner, because in every other house someone went to sea and would bring all this crap back.'

For most of English history Liverpool was just a fishing village. It has no Roman remains, little that's medieval or quaint. In that respect it's like an American city; it really got going around the same time as New York. By European standards, Liverpool was born yesterday. And that made Melville's heart sink: 'And this is England?' he groaned with disbelief, sitting in his first Liverpool tavern. 'But where are the old Abbeys, and the York Minsters, and the Lord Mayors, and coronations, and the May-poles, and fox-hunters, and Derby races, and the dukes and duchesses, and the Count d'Orsays, which, from all my reading, I had been in the habit of associating with England. Not the most distant glimpse of them was to be seen . . .'

On the Liverpool dockside, Melville prayed that if Adam and Eve are immortal, they would not be punished with such a sight as this. Yet, those squalid, wicked old docks were romantic in a certain light. At the passenger embarkation piers, Europeans ceased to be so, and began to become Americans. The congressmen and mobsters of tomorrow, their ancestors mustered here. Australia too was largely populated from this port. Between 1830 and 1930, nine million emigrants set sail from Liverpool. From these quays were dispatched the latest instalments of Charles Dickens's novels, to be tossed to clamouring crowds, down at the foot of Wall Street. From here, Dickens himself sailed to write his *American Notes*, having enjoyed his last meal at the Adelphi Hotel, remarking that Liverpool lay second in his heart to London.

Seven miles of docks spread along the Mersey shores. By 1912 they claimed fifteen per cent of all the cargo in the world. There were cranes from here to the misty distance. In the paintings of Atkinson Grimshaw, jewellers' shops rub shoulders with pawnbrokers', and gaslight dances on rainy cobblestones. Giant silos arose, and the world's biggest bonded warehouses. From Birkenhead the one o'clock gun boomed daily, across the tugboats and dredgers, the pilots and the ferries, the luxury liners and the cargo ships.

Along the land there sprang up teeming streets to house the mass of unskilled workers who kept this vast anthill in motion. Mean tenements, stinking courtyards and unwholesome hovels were the first develop-ments, then the regimented terraces that have sometimes survived to the present day. Slums grew up in the shadows of massive, fortified dockyard walls – built extra thick, the better to separate property from poverty – like peasant huts beneath a castle's ramparts.

Plenty still gets shipped through the port – more than ever before, in fact – but since containerisation began in 1955, the need for human hands has fallen drastically. Dockers belong in black-and-white photos now. Goods in big tin boxes don't need processing on the spot, either, while the boats that bring them are self-sufficient beasts. For those and other reasons, employment in all sorts of industries around the Liverpool waterfront has been vanishing for decades. Everything from sugar refining to banking has been hit, gone the way of sail-makers, bakers of ships' biscuits and carvers of ships' figureheads – all those stout timber Highlanders and busty wooden mermaids.

Passenger ships disappeared, as well. The transatlantic liner trade moved gradually to Southampton, being more convenient for London. (That is why the *Titanic* sailed from there, though still with a Liverpool captain and crew. One survivor recalled the Scouse ship's purser calling to his doomed shipmates, 'Sand for breakfast in the morning, boys!') The dockside lost the glamour of its elite visitors. No more the movie stars and millionaires, the playboys, the writers and the royals. Nowadays they fly instead, and the Adelphi Hotel is no longer the haughty old dame that defied the locals to enter its revolving doors.

The port lost its traffic in celebrities, and commodities now pass through in sealed containers. But Liverpool's past has been preserved in the genes of its people. Some of those ancestors were seamen who stayed behind, others were emigrants too poor to travel further. Every colour and creed was represented in a city which, like New York, had so little indigenous heritage that it became the creation of its immigrants.

There might be a poetic irony, as some like to point out, in a former slaving port becoming the principal conduit for black music imported from America. Despite some grimly picturesque legends to the contrary, though, slaves were not physically shipped through Liverpool; they appeared here only in the shipping clerks' ledger books. It's true the trade was once important to the city's wealth. The painter Fuseli visited, and thought he could 'everywhere smell the blood of slaves'. There was also the retort of an eighteenth-century actor, tormented by a tough Liverpool audience: 'I have not come here to be insulted by a set of wretches, every brick in whose infernal town is cemented with an African's blood.' The city's own black population, however, is largely descended from free-born African seamen who married into the population.

In 1839, our visitor Melville was struck by the confidence of black American sailors on the pavements of Liverpool. The paradox was that this town, with its bloody history, seemed to him more tolerant than his homeland: 'In Liverpool indeed the Negro steps with a prouder pace, and lifts his head like a man . . . Three or four times I encountered our black steward, dressed very handsomely, and walking arm-in-arm with a good-looking English woman. In New York, such a couple would have been mobbed in three minutes; and the steward would have been lucky to escape with whole limbs. Owing to the friendly reception extended to them, the black cooks and stewards of American ships are very much attached to the place and like to make voyages to it.'

So there were Chinese cooks, Somali poets, Scottish engineers, Lithuanian Jews, Nigerian crewmen. But, by an overwhelming majority, the dominant mass of newcomers came from Ireland. And that changed everything in Liverpool, forever. If Irish people had green skins, then the typical Liverpool complexion would be a delicate shade of mint.

There was a documentary filmed of the Beatles' conquest of America, in 1964, with wonderful footage of their arrival into New York's airport. Amid the screaming, sobbing teenagers are a row of jokers holding placards that say stuff like 'Beatles Are Starving Our Barbers' and 'Beatles Unfair To Bald Men'. Perhaps they were put there by newsreel people, who'd failed to foresee the event would be sufficiently sensational on its own terms. If so, they were not the only ones to misjudge the occasion. If you replay the scene with a freeze-frame DVD, you'll notice another knot of deafened protesters, waving a banner that tells the Fab Four: 'England Get Out Of Ireland'.

To that sort of slogan, the comedians of the day used to reply, 'Only if you give us back Liverpool.'

The mop-topped quartet were an odd target. Genetically and culturally, the Beatles' city is inextricably tangled up in Ireland – or 'west Liverpool' as Ken Dodd calls it – and the Beatles' bloodlines are no exception. An actual Irish accent is far less common than it was, but the playgrounds still abound in ginger mops and freckled Celtic faces. For any Liverpudlian, Dublin is still a familiar-feeling place, and the stag-night boys pour off the boats with vomit on their shoes and a family address in their pockets.

Kings of Olde Englande liked the idea of Liverpool because it was a useful troop depot for quelling the Irish. The traffic went both ways, however, especially in the 1840s, when the Famine years sent a full quarter of Ireland's people to Liverpool. Many of them then went on to

America, others stopped at the Mersey. But for a simple twist of fate, John F. Kennedy might have been a gas-fitter in Fazakerley, and Grace Kelly a Saturday girl at Littlewoods.

More and more would follow, for there were tunnels to be dug, docks to be excavated and railways to be laid. Casual, unskilled work was the order of the day, and big Catholic churches rose up around the docklands, looking down on scenes of phenomenal overcrowding and unparalleled squalor. The Irish presence was, of course, so large that it transformed the city's accent. Ringo Starr remembered the fighting on Orange Lodge Day and St Patrick's Night: 'That's how it was, Liverpool being the capital of Ireland, as everybody always says.'

The Irish dimension had a warping effect on local politics. For decades, certain Liverpool constituencies returned Irish Nationalist MPs. The Labour Party had to go Catholic to get elected, while Conservatives played the Orange card. Liverpool often showed the potential to become England's own little Ulster. It had the poverty, the bigotry and (even without Ringo) the great big noisy drums. Happily, though, it never had the guns or the ultimate determination to take that route. If you look around you will still discover the odd wall shouting 'No Popery'. A vandalised bus shelter might bear the inscription '1690' (being the year of King Billy's Protestant victory) or 'IRA', but sectarianism has declined steadily, and nowadays it rarely gets past the graffiti stage.

The Irish shaped many facets of the Scouse character – a taste for defiance and a subversive way with verbal ingenuity among them – but their greatest contribution was the view of music as one of life's necessities.

Generations of Irish settlers and their descendants kept the old traditions alive. Like exiles everywhere, they were often more zealous than the people back home. The purist tendency encouraged ceili bands and Gaelic refrains, but the more common influence was simply a love of singing out loud, for the family or the pub. The favoured tunes might come from Dublin or Hollywood, Sligo or London. More often than not they were country and western. The impulse to perform was the most important thing – and participation was encouraged. Hundreds of Liverpool rock musicians grew up with that culture in their backgrounds.

There is a big Irish strain in English pop, generally, though it's mostly accounted for by the combined dominance of Liverpool and Manchester. At the Q Awards ceremony in London a few years ago, Bono of U2 gave a speech wherein he surveyed the assembled superstars, triumphantly claiming them for his homeland. He'd nod towards Morrissey: 'One of ours!' Towards Paul McCartney: 'The Beatles. One of ours!' The Gallagher brothers: 'Oasis. One of ours!' A couple of years before that, I watched him leading U2's Zoo TV tour in the North-western USA: 'Rock'n'roll loves the places where it rains,' he called to the crowd at the Tacoma Dome. 'Seattle! Dublin! Liverpool!'

Though it's always overshadowed by the Irish connection, Liverpool's Welsh legacy also runs deep. In 1813 a tenth of the town's population came from Wales. The Scouse-Welsh (some call it 'Squelch') presence has been steady for centuries – not surprising in view of its closeness. The musicality of the Welsh nation must to some degree have infiltrated the city's sensibility, via parlour room performance and chapel choirs. It struck me as funny that a Liverpool record shop would rack its Welsh CDs in the 'World Music' section, when you could see Snowdonia from the roof.

Liverpool's own folk music was shaped by the nearness of the Celts and the dominance of the sea. And what's remarkable is the extent to which it's always been sung by actual folks, as opposed to white-collar hearties in weekend woollies. It's true there is a strong tradition, too, of academic enthusiasts and middle-class keepers of the proletarian flame. They are not to be sneered at. But Liverpool was a town where rough-and-tumble Dock Road pubs, town centre hen parties and family get-togethers might resound to 'Maggie May', 'The Orange and the Green' or 'In My Liverpool Home'. One of the earliest Liverpool-related hits was the 'Theme from Z-Cars', adapted from a local sailor song, 'Johnny Todd', that every school kid used to know.

Nationally, Liverpool folk music has meant the Spinners. They were an oddity, being skiffle players who moved on to folk instead of rock, and they were only one-quarter Liverpudlian. But it was their home through a 30-year career. As Spencer Leigh says, 'Folk music was very big in Liverpool. The Spinners' folk club was very influential, and they stayed in this community. Even at the height of their popularity they were still performing here every Monday night. I always felt with the Spinners and Jackie and Bridie and Bob Buckle and the others, you could tell that a lot of these people had been school teachers. There was a tendency to lecture the audience.' Nevertheless, their annual Philharmonic shows were a civic institution, and they preserved or popularised such renowned Merseyside songs as 'The Leaving of Liverpool', 'Fried Bread and Brandy-O', 'Liverpool Barrer Boy', 'Maggie May' and Cilla's favourite ('Oh, you are a mucky kid . . .'), 'Liverpool Lullaby'.

Elvis Costello served his apprenticeship on Liverpool's folk circuit; the young folk artist Kathryn Williams is another graduate. John Lennon was scornful of the scene, apart from a few Fenian rebel songs and 'Maggie May', of course, but Paul McCartney was such a fan of Dominic Behan's 'Liverpool Lou' that he recorded it with the Scaffold. Pete McGovern's song 'In My Liverpool Home' was started in 1961 and is still being written. He continues adding verses, bard-like, to commemorate new events. But the chorus at its heart, with the 'accent exceedingly rare' and the 'statue exceedingly bare' strikes a chord all over Liverpool. The song rolls up and down like a boat on the waves; and, like the ocean, it can seem to stretch forever: there exists a 70-minute version that features the Spinners, Mike McCartney, Adrian Henri and 'Sinbad', the window-cleaner from *Brookside*.

Not so much rooted in the land as tossed by the sea, the folk music of Liverpool is naturally more surf than turf in flavour; the shanty resonates in odd places, from Shack's *H.M.S. Fable* to Lennon's 'Give Peace a Chance'. But it never entered the bloodstream of British rock in the same way as the rustic folk styles of England, which were adapted by Bert Jansch, Fairport Convention and Nick Drake, and taken up by Traffic and Led Zeppelin. As usual, Liverpool and England seem eerily disconnected, while Uncle Sam lives just the other side of Ireland.

Liverpool's links with America might have been even stronger if only the South had won the Civil War. Commercial self-interest led the city's merchants to support the Confederacy. This port had done well out of slavery, after all, and now it prospered by shipping slave-state cotton. Nobler souls, the mill-workers of Lancashire supported Abe Lincoln, despite his naval blockade of their factories' raw material. But Liverpool had no such scruples, and in its yards built warships for Dixie. The Confederacy kept an embassy here (it's still standing) and even as Atlanta burned, Rhett Butler's money was snug in a Liverpool bank. Strangely, the last official act of the Civil War occurred at the Town Hall, when a Confederate captain formally surrendered his ship, the *Shenandoah*, to the Lord Mayor.

It's always been said that Liverpool led British pop because of its transatlantic trade with America. The explanation was trotted out so regularly that it began to seem rather pat and simplistic. Did Scouse urchins really loiter about the gangplanks of US merchant ships, hoping to score some unheard rock'n'roll? Did Cunard Yanks, those flash local lads who worked the New York liners, come home laden with R&B rarities? Were Liverpool ballrooms really alive with jive-talking GIs, set to hip you to the secret sounds of Motown and Mississippi?

When a theory gets long in the tooth there is a temptation to rubbish it from sheer boredom. And the Cunard Yanks idea has enjoyed decades of acceptance. Where does the truth lie?

We'll meet the now-deceased Roger Eagle later in our tale. But let's note for the moment that he was a DJ of legendary knowledge who helped begin the ultra-hip underground of Northern Soul, and then set up the most influential club in Liverpool, Eric's. He once said, 'Liverpool is the most American of English cities. It's got the most intensely aware soul music black community in the country. They're getting American records in so fast they're probably getting them before they're properly released in the States. It's like a sinew that goes across the Atlantic.'

Did that sinew stretch to Liverpool's whole population? It's known the town joined the jazz age at the first opportunity. Local writer Frank Shaw: 'I have heard that the first jazz was heard in this country from the Dixielanders in Liverpool. It is sure that no place in the UK welcomed it as Liverpool did.' We're told that in Bootle in the 1920s every neighbourhood had its jazz band, and the music arrived on brown-coloured discs brought home from the States by sailors. There is to this day a Liverpool combo called – brace yourself – the Merseysippi Jazz Band; they've played together for 52 years, were the first act to appear at the Cavern, and the young John Lennon referred to them as 'those old buggers'.

But the strongest sign of Liverpool's affinity with the American South is its passion for country and western. In the 1950s the town was said to have more country groups than Nashville itself. As Billy Fury said: 'Before rock'n'roll, I'd been into country and western music. Actually, in Liverpool, everybody used to play country and western, Hank Williams or whatever. Anything with some real lyrics about a bit of trouble or a bit of heartbreak.' In a study called *Nashville of the North*, Kevin McManus found that country music gained its first foothold in Britain in Liverpool, and the usual source of records was the sea. 'Elsewhere in the UK,' he says, 'country music was all but invisible.'

An ex-docker named Hank Walters has been a musical fixture on Merseyside almost as long as the Merseysippi Jazz Band. He formed the Dusty Road Ramblers in 1953 and started the Black Cat Club four years later: 'You won't find any country music in Britain as long ago as that,' he claims. They'd advertise on factory notice boards – country is working man's music, through and through – and watched the scene explode. (The actor Ricky Tomlinson was one of hundreds performing in that period, assisted by a large Stetson and the stage name Hobo

Rick.) In the 1970s I worked on a Kirkby factory floor where one wall carried a giant portrait of Che Guevara – specifically to irritate the management – while at the other end a hot-wired hi-fi played George Jones and Merle Haggard, morning till night.

When skiffle hit Britain around the mid-1950s it proved wonderfully compatible with Liverpool's country leanings. If there is such a style as Merseybeat then country music is one of its foundations. Future beat musicians would also be absorbing country via the rockabilly licks of Elvis Presley's guitarist Scotty Moore, but local crossover was even more pronounced. Country and rock acts shared the same bills: Hank Walters played the Cavern and the Beatles went to the Black Cat Club. There was considerable overlap of repertoire and personnel. It's something that would mark the Mersey bands apart. The Stones and Eric Clapton would take up country later on, while coming down off psychedelia, but it wasn't what they grew up with; only in Ireland, in Van Morrison, do you find deep country roots entangled with R&B.

Country music might still be unfashionable in Britain, yet it's a cornerstone of the nation's best-loved band. It's an overlooked facet of the Beatles' style, but it was there from the beginning. On the Quarrymen's business card John Lennon had printed 'Country – Western – Rock'n'Roll – Skiffle'. Ringo Starr's first musical memory was of the cowboy Gene Autry, singing 'South of the Border'. He recalled of country: 'A lot of it was around from guys in the navy. I'd go to parties and they'd be putting on Hank Williams, Hank Snow and all those country acts. I still love country music.'

'There is the biggest country and western following in England in Liverpool, besides London,' John told an American interviewer in 1970. 'I heard country and western before I heard rock'n'roll. The people there – the Irish in Ireland are the same – they take their music very seriously. There were established folk, blues and country and western clubs in Liverpool before rock'n'roll.' He claimed the first guitar he'd ever seen was being played by a Liverpool man in a cowboy hat, and that he began imitating Hank Williams when he was fifteen.

George Harrison was influenced by everything he heard as a child, not omitting Max Bygraves' 'You're a Pink Toothbrush'. But he reserved particular praise for Jimmie Rodgers, the white bluesman who pre-dates Hank Williams and effectively founded country music. Rodgers' 'Waiting for a Train' was among the records that George's seaman Dad brought back from New York – along with the machine to play them on – and it led the boy to take up guitar. He developed his craft by copying the chords from a Chet Atkins LP. In emulation of Atkins he graduated to an American electric Gretsch guitar in 1962, bought off a sailor who'd advertised it in the *Liverpool Echo*.

It's true the Beatles' take on Nashville style was often jokey, for even if they loved it, British acts have rarely felt able to play country with a straight face. In the Beatles' repertoire the overtly country-flavoured numbers such as 'Octopus's Garden' or 'Don't Pass Me By' were whimsical filler tracks. But they also deployed country with subtlety, in ways that owed nothing to pastiche. Listen to 'Baby's in Black', to George's solo in 'All My Loving', or his playing throughout the mid-period albums *Help!* and *Rubber Soul*. John cites 'I Feel Fine' as one of many songs written with that style in mind.

There are probably various reasons for country's appeal to Liverpud-lians: it's gritty but sentimental, it has deep Celtic roots, it's within the reach of amateurs with an urge to perform. But it's also clear that it found its first home in England by virtue of the River Mersey, and the ships that sailed from there to the United States. The boyhood experience of George Harrison is but one of countless examples that fit the Cunard Yank theory, or some variant thereof.

When we come to rock'n'roll, though, the picture is less certain. Bob Wooler was the DJ at the Cavern in its prime, and a man who introduced the Mersey groups to much of the material they would build their sound around. But he was scornful of Cunard Yank talk: he just didn't think the bands, Beatles included, played anything that wasn't readily available in the shops. The most scientific analysis was done by the Merseybeat historian Spencer Leigh: 'I took every cover version that had been recorded by a Merseybeat group and asked, Who did the original, did it come out here? And in every instance, there were about 130 of them, the answer was Yes, the record had been released here. So people like Charlie Feathers [the early rockabilly star], whose records weren't released in this country, nobody thought of covering. I think this explodes the myth of the Cunard Yanks, because they would surely have brought in some records that never came out here.'

Paul McCartney's abiding memory of learning new material was the entire days spent in record shop listening booths – Brian Epstein's NEMS store in particular – learning a new number off by heart. Spencer Leigh again: 'Brian Epstein would get those records in the shop quickly and people would learn them quickly. Though the Cunard Yanks theory did apply to jazz records in the early 50s, and to country and western music, it didn't really apply to beat music. I can't find a single song in the Beatles' repertoire that has come from a Cunard Yank.'

Or, as Stu James of the Mojos puts it: 'I know I never bought a record off a sailor.'

The local promoter Sam Leach, an important figure in the scene's development back then, believes that merchant seamen were useful only for bringing in US records that friends already knew and wanted, but couldn't yet buy. Leach also credits the Liverpool musician Kingsize Taylor: like his southern counterpart Mick Jagger he was on US mailing lists, 'and it was he who introduced much of the new music to Liverpool. For that reason, many aspiring musicians – including Lennon and McCartney – flocked to his shows, eager to learn and copy his latest imports.' Other colossal influences were the rock films of the time, such as Presley's *Jailhouse Rock* and Eddie Cochran's 'Twenty-Flight Rock' cameo in *The Girl Can't Help It*. Finally, faint as it was on 50s wireless, there was Radio Luxembourg as well, to compensate for the near-total absence of rock on the BBC.

And yet . . . The notion of naval intervention is firmly supported by The Beatles and their associates. Ringo Starr: 'We were very lucky coming from Liverpool because it was a port and it seemed that half of Liverpool was in the Merchant Navy. All these records were coming from America, so you could find out about Arthur Alexander and people like that.' Ditto John Lennon: 'Liverpool is cosmopolitan. It's where the sailors would come home on the ships with the blues records from America . . . We were hearing old funky blues records in Liverpool that people across Britain or Europe had never heard about.'

In *The Beatles Anthology* their producer George Martin says: 'I think that the so-called Beatles sound had something to do with Liverpool being a port . . . They certainly knew more about Motown and black music than anyone else did, and that was a tremendous influence on them.' While their road manager Neil Aspinall adds: 'Through the merchant seamen you could get a lot of American records that weren't being played in England. And whichever of the bands heard a record first got to do it.' Meanwhile Ringo's Dingle homeboy Gerry, of the Pacemakers, recalled: 'When I was a kid every street had a pub filled with music and it was the seamen home from the States and all over the world playing music.'

It didn't require a mass importation of vinyl to shape the city's tastes. Communal listening was the norm back then, not the exception. Whole streets gathered around a single family's gramophone. Young enthusiasts like Lennon and McCartney would take three bus rides across the city to hear somebody's copy of a Little Richard B-side. An influential character, a Bob Wooler or Hank Walters, could expose a multitude to musical obscurities. Greater than the odd vinyl rarity, though, was the influence of transatlantic seamen on the cultural climate of Liverpool: in the Dingle, in 1957, you could believe yourself nearer to Baltimore than to Buckinghamshire.

One more ingredient must be added to the mix. In both world wars American servicemen were garrisoned in Liverpool in large numbers. For many years after the second world war there was a massive US military base at Burtonwood, just outside the city. You can still see a few disused hangars across the fields from an M62 service station. The Yanks left many other traces of their presence. The men were reputedly well-disciplined, but nobody mistook them for Cistercian monks. More than one Liverpudlian girl has gazed out to sea, like Madam Butterfly transposed to Everton Brow, cradling a 'Burtonwood babe' and thinking wistfully of its long-gone Daddy in the USA. The base recurs in numerous memoirs of Liverpool music: black GIs were fond of the clubs in Liverpool 8, and brought their records with them, while local country and western acts consoled homesick rednecks at the base itself. When Ringo's stepfather Harry got work as a painter and decorator at Burtonwood, the lad was guaranteed a supply of DC comics and hot jazz. In countless small ways, Burtonwood helped prime Liverpool for rock'n'roll.

The Cunard Yank school of thought has taken a battering lately, and it was never an adequate explanation for Liverpool's unique susceptibility to American music. Nearly all the imported music in Liverpool was available to anyone in Britain, though Liverpool might have had a few weeks' lead time. The real difference was that Liverpool wanted this music more badly; its craving was stronger; and once it had learned the words it took those songs to its heart and howled them back at the world. Liverpool made more music than most cities, and made it more passionately, because it was in the personality of Liverpool to do so. And Liverpool has the personality it has because it is a seaport. Liverpool only exists because it is a seaport. Its virtues and vices, its accent and attitude, its insularity and its open-mindedness, are all derived from that primary fact.

The first Liverpool artist to reach Number 1 was Lita Roza, in 1953; she was also the first British girl to reach Number 1. It's perhaps unfortunate that she achieved this with a rotten song: 'How Much Is That Doggy in the Window?' ('the one,' it specified, 'with the waggly tail'). But that's show business. Lita despised the song herself: she was made to record it by her A&R manager at the record company, a man called Dick Rowe, later famous for turning down the Beatles. She made a virtue of never singing it again. The song was much admired, however, by the young Margaret Thatcher. No doubt it was the title's way of putting a financial consideration above the emotional aspect that spoke so deeply to her soul.

The second Liverpudlian chart topper was almost the singer Russ Hamilton with his 1957 song 'We Will Make Love'. A strike at the record pressing plant, apparently, stalled him at Number 2. 'It was so popular,' he's said, 'that even the dogs in the street were singing it.'

Luckier, at least for a while, was the sleepy-toned crooner Michael Holliday, the first Liverpudlian to have two Number 1 hits. In 1958 came a cover of Burt Bacharach's 'The Story of My Life' and then a song called 'Starry Eyed'. A former seaman from Kirkdale, he developed a Bing Crosby style and sang each week at the Burtonwood Base, which might account for his leaning to American songs like 'Sixteen Tons', 'The Yellow Rose of Texas' and 'The Gal with the Yaller Shoes'. His Western drawl was heard to pleasant effect in his theme song for Gerry Anderson's cowboy puppet series *Four Feather Falls*. The mellow assurance was deceptive, however, as in private Holliday was a troubled man. It seems he was tipped over the edge by a tax demand in 1963. He shot himself dead and left a note for his wife that read, 'By the time you receive this, I trust I shall be in the land of Nod.'

By far the biggest figure of that pre-rock era, though, was Frankie Vaughan. Cilla Black queued for his autograph; in Paul McCartney's memory, he was the major Liverpool star. He was born Frank Abelson, to a family of European Jewish stock: the story is that when he tried to think of a stage name, his grandmother said 'Whatever he picks, he'll still be my Number Vorn.' The hits were a strange mixture of big-voiced melodrama ('Garden of Eden', 'Tower of Strength') and outright cheese ('Green Door', 'Hello Dolly') though the career-defining routine was his top-hat and cane number 'Give Me the Moonlight'. His dazzling, ready smile and dark good looks made him a movie contender. It's sometimes thought (though incorrectly) that his move into films inspired a *Liverpool Echo* headline 'Frankie Goes To Hollywood'. He was happily married and, while in the States, famously spurned the advances of Marilyn Monroe. Unusually for a Scouse pop singer, he spent the final years of his life as Deputy Lord Lieutenant of Buckinghamshire.

And then there was Billy Fury, followed by the Beatles. The Liverpool contribution to popular music was only just beginning. And when it did, the contribution was so enormous that, for a year or more, there was only one force in the Hit Parade, from top to bottom. They called it Merseybeat.

5. BEAT CITY

MERSEYBEAT; BRIAN EPSTEIN'S BOYS; BRIAN EPSTEIN'S GIRL.
AND HOW AMERICA LEARNED TO SAY 'RANDY SCOUSE GIT'.

*By night they flood out into the raw mistral that rips in from Liverpool Bay; over
two hundred semi-professional trios and quartets on Merseyside, trailing their
electric guitars, drums, voices and amplifiers into cars and vans. From New
Brighton Tower to Garston Baths the 'beat' (beat for rhythm, not beatnik) groups
thump, shout, kick and tremble in pubs, clubs and church halls . . .*
Derek Jewell in the Sunday Times, September 1963

Liverpool was, for a couple of years, the world capital of pop and to
come from anywhere else was a terrible curse. The local promoter Sam
Leach points out that, for 51 of the 60 weeks between April 1963 and
May 1964, there was a Merseybeat record at Number 1. For two of the
remaining weeks, the top slot was occupied by Paul McCartney's
discoveries Peter and Gordon, with his song 'World Without Love'.

The Beatles have never lacked for recognition, but Merseybeat in
general has been pushed out of memory. Yet it took British pop music to
another level. Before Merseybeat the native rock'n'roll trade was a junior
branch of show business – a sequence of hiccuping, twitching novelty
acts. Now it became a defining force in British culture. For the first time
there was mass hysteria and media obsession, and pop achieved the
previously unthinkable status of cherished British export. To this day
the Merseybeat formula serves as blueprint for rock bands everywhere:
four or five young men on drums and guitars, keyboard optional. U2,
Radiohead and R.E.M. are all in the tradition, nowadays so natural as to
be taken for granted. We tend to credit the Beatles with everything, but
they did not create Merseybeat. They certainly led the scene to national
recognition, but they were products of that scene, not its inventors.

The skiffle star Lonnie Donegan, though not from Liverpool, was
more adored on Merseyside than anywhere else. Before he cashed in
with comedy hits like 'My Old Man's a Dustman', he fired off a volley of
cool, rocking songs such as 'Rock Island Line' and 'Lost John'. His skiffle
was a sort of goosed-up folk blues – part Woody Guthrie, part Leadbelly
– that chimed right away with Liverpool's traditions of US country and
Celtic styles. It was fast, easy to learn and sounded good on cheap
acoustic gear – even the washboards you'd find in a Liverpool backyard.
All in all, it was ideal for people gripped by a psychotic need to get up
and entertain one another. Ideal, in other words, for Liverpudlians.

When the skiffle craze died down around the end of the 1950s, washboards got returned to Mum's scullery. But Liverpool's kids – John Lennon was only one of hundreds – were bitten by the bug, and now traded up to full rock'n'roll. The line-up of Cliff Richard's group the Shadows was one pointer. Beat groups learned those numbers, since that was what their audience knew and called out for. But the Cliff-style, stand-alone frontman lost ground to harmony vocals by the players themselves, while the Shadows' meticulous instrumentals got sidelined by something more raucous, powered by rhythm guitars, bass and drums. It was not unique to Liverpool, this new formation, but the city came to dominate by sheer force of numbers.

There was always the love of a good song, too. American musicals were the backbone of any local record collection – occasional Broadway songs found their way into the beat group repertoire, such as the Beatles' 'Till There was You' – and young Liverpudlians fell eagerly on their modern successors. Chiefly that meant the sophisticated pop being written in New York's Brill Building by the likes of Leiber and Stoller, Goffin and King and Bacharach and David, recorded by harmony groups such as the Coasters, the Drifters and the Shirelles. Combining this with smart black pop arriving from Tamla Motown – early heroes being Smokey Robinson and Marvin Gaye – the Liverpool musicians found a new source of inspiration. Just as well: the supply of 1950s rock'n'roll hits had begun to dry up. Brill and Motown music was clever but not so obscure that scholars pored over it. In Liverpool the call was always for music that entertained.

Nobody really knows how many beat groups there were in Liverpool, but the total would run into several hundred. No other town came close, including London. It's a sign of the standards reached that Gene Vincent's return gig in Liverpool, in 1960, could feature Allan Williams' mostly local support bill. Merseyside had a well-developed live circuit to nurture these acts: apart from city centre clubs there were numerous suburban 'jive hives', factory social clubs and parish halls. The consequence of playing such everyday venues was that Mersey groups acquired the common touch of people's entertainers, not the cult intensity of in-crowd favourites. It was an education that would give them a head start over the rest of the country, but eventually tell against them.

In the pre-disco age, bands were hired so people could dance – all speeds and styles – and they had to learn quickly. Liverpool was a tough school for live musicians, full of folks who reckoned they could do better, and patrolled by territorial gangs of tanked-up knuckleheads.

Litherland Town Hall, Garston 'Blood' Baths and the Grosvenor 'Brawlroom' in Wallasey were just a few of those suburban killing floors, where the Beatles and their peers learned it would never be enough to stand about looking pale and interesting.

For the upper echelon there were prestige central venues, primarily the Cavern, the Mardi Gras and, in nearby Temple Street, the Iron Door. The latter, like the Cavern, had first emerged as a jazz hang-out but eventually surrendered to rock'n'roll. One legend says it acquired its iron door after the wooden one got smashed in by axe-wielders chasing Derry Wilkie. Meanwhile the elite of the scene, Beatles included, could assemble after hours at Allan Williams' upmarket Blue Angel club in Seel Street – attractions ran to topless waitresses and live fights with baby bulls, and distinguished guests included Bob Dylan and Judy Garland. A beatnik favourite was Williams' Jacaranda, in Slater Street; it was visited, in 1984, by the nostalgic ghost of John Lennon, reportedly seen arguing with the 1959 barmaid, a woman called Audrey. Tourists, living or dead, will find that both the Blue Angel and Jacaranda are still standing and once more trading under their old names.

Impressively, the Liverpool scene was big enough to support its own weekly music paper, Bill Harry's *Mersey Beat*, which he'd begun at art college after switching allegiance from jazz to rock'n'roll: 'I was writing to the *Daily Mail* saying what is happening in Liverpool is amazing, it's like New Orleans at the turn of the century, but with rock'n'roll bands instead of jazz. No answer, of course. And the *Liverpool Echo* didn't do anything on the scene. The advertising column on their front page said 'Jazz', and no matter how much the clubs asked them, the *Echo* would not change it to feature rock'n'roll. And all the Northern media was based in Manchester: though Liverpool had a larger population, all the news was Manchester-biased. Bob Wooler and I made a list of 300 local bands, yet no one knew about anything outside their own immediate neighbourhood.'

Mersey Beat became the grapevine that allowed a coherent scene to develop. 'I didn't know what to call it. But I pictured our coverage as like a policeman's beat. So I thought Mersey Beat. It was purely that: the word beat wasn't used for the music at the time. The venues were called jive hives and the groups were called rock'n'roll groups. The Beatles' name was not taken from the beat of the music but from John and Stuart saying they should be an insect name like Buddy Holly's Crickets. So it became Beetles and John thought of putting the "a" in it.

'Groups then started calling themselves beat groups. The whole city became aware of the music, with *Mersey Beat* coming out. Suddenly in the tailors' shops you had the dummies with guitars. You saw all these groups' vans in the streets now: they started travelling all over the region.'

Harry took his brainchild to the local venues and shops, including NEMS: 'In July 1961 Brian Epstein ordered twelve dozen copies of issue number two, an incredible amount for a provincial record shop. The entire front cover was about the Beatles recording in Hamburg. And I got John to write a piece for me which I called "On the Dubious Origins of The Beatles. Translated from the John Lennon." He was so delighted he gave me everything he'd ever written, about 250 poems, stories, drawings, and I used them as a column called Beatcomber.

'Epstein got so excited by the paper he asked if he could be my record reviewer, and his reviews appear in issue three. He took advertising, and the only other thing on the NEMS page was a piece by Bob Wooler on the Beatles, saying they were musical revolutionaries. Every time I dropped copies around to NEMS, Brian would call me into his office, offer me a sherry and want to know all about it. He saw something in this scene on his own doorstep. He asked me to arrange for him to go to the Cavern. In his book he comes up with this thing about a guy coming into the shop and asking for "My Bonnie" but he'd been discussing the Beatles with me for months already.

'I was in the office all the time: I did the writing, design, advertising, circulation, the lot. At times I was working 100 hours a week, collapsing with the blood coming out of my nose. Did an interview with the Swinging Blue Jeans once, they had to get an ambulance and take me to hospital.

'There was an amazing folk scene, too, and the biggest country music scene in Europe. Add the poetry and the black music scenes, and it was incredible what was happening in that city. I don't think it ever happened anywhere else. You get books saying, "Oh, as soon as the Beatles happened, everyone was suddenly on the streets with guitars." But the whole thing happened prior to that.'

By 1963 the Beatles were attracting the attention of serious commentators, who looked too at the city they were beginning to symbolise, and the music scene they grew from. Here's Derek Jewell, writing in the Sunday Times in September: 'Although there is no pat explanation for Liverpool's gift of early impetus to this music in Britain, there are many clues. It is a big, in-drawn city, sustaining its own self-centred life. It has a tradition of home-brewed entertainment, based on a rash of clubs which thrive, too, in its hinterland. The opportunities for semi-pros are immense, and its outflow of entertainers (Handley, Askey, Ray, Vaughan) has always been unparalleled.'

But any goldrush will leave some casualties by the wayside. One such was the Liverpool rock scene's first local legend, Rory Storm. It's rather a sad tale.

His real name was Alan, the son of Ernie and Violet Caldwell. His sister Iris was George Harrison's first girlfriend. But his hunger for stardom was exceptional; he took his stage name to the point of telling people to call his mother 'Mrs Storm'. She was in fact her son's most fervent fan, a motherly figure to many beat musicians, and supported Rory in all his endeavours. He began with a skiffle act, the Raving Texans, but was among the first in town to upgrade to rock'n'roll. By the end of the 1950s Rory Storm and The Hurricanes were Liverpool's top band.

The great peculiarity of Storm's character was that he spoke with a severe stammer, which always disappeared when he was performing. A flamboyant Teddy Boy, he had a vast blond quiff that he would ostentatiously comb on stage: in old black-and-white photographs he seems to be built entirely of silver. He was an athletic man, a natural extrovert, given to daredevil stage leaps (he once broke a leg jumping from a balcony for a photograph). He'd wave the mike stand around and, strangely, pour lemonade over himself. I'm told he was once apprehended by a railway porter on Bootle station for writing 'I Love Rory' on a wall. The other groups worshipped him; George Harrison longed to join the Hurricanes but was told he was too young.

Rory found a local drummer, another refugee from skiffle, called Richard Starkey. He lured the boy with promises of a summer season at Butlins holiday camp in Pwllheli, where each week brought a fresh coach-load of excitable girls. In line with the Hurricanes' big-thinking policies the drummer was allocated a new name, Ringo Starr. (This era would be lovingly re-created in a 1973 film featuring Ringo with Billy Fury and David Essex, *That'll Be the Day*.) Starr's reputation grew so fast in his time with Rory, that he was eventually poached by the Beatles to replace Pete Best.

For a while Rory Storm stayed in contention, despite the loss of his drummer. Iris Caldwell went on to marry the beat singer Shane Fenton, later known as Alvin Stardust, who has compared the Hurricanes' live sound to the early Rolling Stones. Others suggest that Rory had all the potential of his nearest London counterpart, Rod Stewart. Like Rod, he was a keen footballer, too, and captained a Merseybeat XI with Freddie Starr: Storm, of course, loved to be photographed in net-busting action and would insist on taking every penalty. However the music world was moving on and Rory Storm was not. It's a telling point, made by Mark

Lewisohn, that on the night the Beatles played Shea Stadium, the Hurricanes' engagement was the Orrell Park Ballroom. Possibly motivated by some lingering guilt, Brian Epstein paid for Rory to record the *West Side Story* number 'America', producing it himself with Ringo in the background. It brought no real improvement in the group's fortunes.

By 1971 it was obvious that Rory Storm would never achieve the rock'n'roll stardom that his whole existence once seemed geared towards. Despondent, he became a barber, then a salesman. He was depressed by a split from his fiancée; his mother Violet, by some accounts, seemed to share his disappointments to the extent of deepening them. A year later they were both devastated by the death of quiet, reliable Ernie Caldwell. Storm grew ill and took to his bed with Scotch and sleeping pills: his intentions are unknown, but his body was discovered there by Violet, who took her own life on the spot. At Rory's funeral he was carried by pall-bearers from the Merseybeat scene, to the accompaniment of Gerry Marsden's 'You'll Never Walk Alone'.

Gerry Marsden, like Ringo, came from the docklands of Dingle. He got a job on the railways, he played skiffle and then got himself a beat group, the Pacemakers, who served their time in Hamburg. They were game entertainers, these boys, who could play anything in that week's Hit Parade if it's what the crowd wanted. Having a piano-player made them a bit different, too, and offered them some range. Gerry had a funny way of holding his guitar high on his chest: it was so he could see his fingers.

Brian Epstein watched them in action at the Cavern, and saw in Gerry something of the same star potential he perceived in the Beatles and Cilla Black. He brought George Martin to see them play in Birkenhead, and they were duly signed to an EMI label, Columbia. Once in the studio they were more compliant than Lennon and McCartney, and readily agreed to cover the song, 'How Do You Do It?', that the Beatles had rejected. Good thing, too. It got them to Number 1 straight out of the traps, and a month before the Beatles at that. Paul McCartney would recall much later: 'The first really serious threat to us that we felt was Gerry and the Pacemakers. When it came time for *Mersey Beat* to have a poll as to who was the most popular group we certainly bought and filled in a lot of forms, with very funny names . . . I'm not saying it was a fix, but it was a high-selling issue, that.'

In fact Gerry and the Pacemakers made pop history by taking their first three singles to the top. The second was 'I Like It' – not a complex song, for sure, but for my money the happiest pop music ever made. It caught the surge of youthful optimism in the air in 1963. In its perfect match of energy and innocence, it's a type of pop song that could never be duplicated in more knowing times. Gerry was on TV and all around the country, pop-eyed, bandy-legged, singing with a wide, froggy grin that shaped his Liverpool twang.

The third Number 1 was destined for glory. 'You'll Never Walk Alone' was a well-known number from Rodgers and Hammerstein's musical *Carousel* – which made it rather old-school for young beat fans, but Liverpool still loved those American show tunes. The Pacemakers' version was strong and sincere, and when it got noticed by the crowd at Liverpool's football ground, the song became an anthem. The team, as it happened, was powering ahead after years in obscurity, and the parallel rise of Liverpool's pop and soccer was lost on nobody. 'You'll Never Walk Alone' was not by the Beatles and it wasn't even Merseybeat, but it became synonymous with the Liverpool Sound. It's still sung to this day, of course. But, to watch the Kop at that time, in all its scarf-waving celebration of civic solidarity, was to witness something extraordinary. It used to move me to tears.

More hits followed – the fourth single, 'I'm the One', was only kept off the top by the next Liverpool sensation, the Searchers – and, amazingly, there would be another timeless anthem among them, 'Ferry Cross the Mersey'. It was more evidence of Marsden's songwriting talent – confirmed soon after by a superb ballad called 'Don't Let the Sun Catch You Crying' (its title was not original but the song certainly was). But such a dazzling run could not last forever. And when, around the mid-decade, pop began to change in deep, strange ways, Gerry was one of the many Mersey boys who opted out: 'I never liked the Beatles' psychedelic situation at all,' he said later. 'It just wasn't the Beatles to me.'

He never developed any further as a rock star, though he survived in show business. He had success in the West End (*Charlie Girl*, with Anna Neagle), in children's TV (*Sooty and Sweep*), panto and cabaret. He still tours the country, and latterly resembles Ernest Borgnine. His two return visits to the charts have been slightly macabre. In 1985, as the Crowd, there was a Band Aid-style version of 'You'll Never Walk Alone' for the 55 victims of a Bradford City fire disaster. Thus he became the first act to have two Number 1 hits with the same song. Four years later came another charity chart-topper when he teamed with Paul McCartney, Holly Johnson and the Christians to sing 'Ferry Cross the Mersey' for families of the Hillsborough victims. He still lives by the Mersey, still married to the girl who inspired 'Don't Let the Sun Catch You Crying'. He was never in any sense cool. But he's always been hugely underrated.

For a kitsch souvenir, you might try a cheerfully feeble feature film made in his heyday, called of course *Ferry Cross the Mersey*. The story was slight, starring Gerry as a semi-fictional beat boy from 'over the water' (as the Wirral side of the river is locally known) who leads his band through various scrapes and larks. It was all a cut-price *Hard Day's Night*, likewise in black-and-white, but the River Mersey looks gorgeous and there is good live footage of Cilla, the Fourmost and others, including a young Jimmy Saville, in action as one of the earliest club DJs. When the ballroom sequences were shot at the Locarno, a real traditional gang-fight erupted and was duly filmed in best cinema-verité style. The plot (written by *Coronation Street*'s creator Tony Warren) called for Gerry and the boys to commute on scooters, on a ferry boat that's still operating today, and if you take that ride you will hear the movie's theme song played over the speaker system. Do the ferry employees hear it at night in their dreams?

The writer Johnny Rogan has suggested: 'If Cilla Black had died in 1967, she'd have been regarded as one of the greatest British singers of all time.' Elvis Costello, you will find, is fiercely protective of her reputation. And another Elvis, resident of Graceland, used to keep her records on his personal jukebox. She was Britain's best-selling female singer of the 1960s and, of all Brian Epstein's acts, probably the dearest to his heart. Being signed to Brian was not always a guarantee of the best management, but it did secure access to Lennon and McCartney originals, a recording deal with EMI and the production services of George Martin. And 'Our Cilla' was not a girl to waste those advantages.

To later generations she became entirely known as a TV institution; for a long spell she was, like Gerry Marsden and Jimmy Tarbuck, one of those bubbly Scouse celebrities who seemed to have squatters' rights on light entertainment programmes. In time she left music behind to present the country's favourite game shows, and she began the twenty-first century in television rivalry with her Liverpudlian contemporary, Anne Robinson of *The Weakest Link*.

But Cilla's first job in show business was to make the tea in the Cavern office. She was in fact the quintessential Scouser: a docker's daughter from the Catholic enclave Scotland Road. In the family parlour stood a piano from the Epsteins' North End Music Stores, just up the road. When the 60s started she was a typist in town who spent her lunch hours watching the beat groups at the Cavern, where she picked up some spare-time work. Soon she was to be found on stage as well, performing guest spots with Kingsize Taylor and the Dominoes, the Big

Three and Rory Storm and the Hurricanes. (Sometimes she would duet with Ringo on his big number 'Boys', but turned down a chance to go with the band to Hamburg.) One night at the Iron Door her girlfriends urged the Beatles to give Cilla a go. 'OK Cyril,' John Lennon said. 'Just to shut your mates up.' She sang Sam Cooke's version of 'Summertime', and her career was on its way.

It was Lennon who recommended 'Cyril' to Epstein. 'I fancied Brian like mad,' she recalled. 'He was gorgeous. He had the Cary Grant kind of charisma, incredibly charming and shy. He always wore a navy-blue cashmere overcoat and a navy spotted cravat. I know now it was a Hermés but then I still knew it was expensive.' She failed an early audition for him, backed by the Beatles, but he saw her again at the Blue Angel and changed his mind. For her Parlophone debut she was given John's song 'Love of the Loved', but the smash hits really began in February 1964 with a Bacharach and David number, 'Anyone Who Had a Heart' and a tremulous Italian ballad translated as 'You're My World'.

For the rest of the 60s Cilla Black was pretty well unbeatable. She would never be admired as much as Dusty Springfield, her nearest rival, and could not match the decadent dolly girl aura of Marianne Faithful. Nevertheless she entered the hearts of the nation. It was so often said she was the next Gracie Fields that it became a self-fulfilling prophecy. But there was still a run of superlative songs: between her own taste, her husband/manager Bobby Willis and George Martin, material was obtained from the most impeccable sources (John and Paul, Randy Newman, her great admirer Burt Bacharach) and her chart run was sustained brilliantly. In 1967 she even went psychedelic for a moment, borrowing George Martin from the Sgt. Pepper sessions next door to record a weird thing called 'Abyssinian Secret'. But Our Cilla was never destined to do weird.

Epstein is said to have remained devoted to her, but she was also very demanding of him: of all his clients she alone had the power to wrest his attention away from the Beatles occasionally. Like all the more conventional pop stars, Cilla aimed to become an all-round entertainer, and in 1967 was offered her own BBC television series. Brian Epstein took the contract to study it: in fact, it was still in his hands when he was discovered dead, two days later. Cilla was away at the time, and found he had left a message asking her to contact him urgently. Perhaps for that reason she has always repudiated the suicide theory.

But the series went ahead, in 1968, complete with a slinky theme song donated by Paul McCartney, 'Step Inside Love'. Though her recording career was patchy after that, the glory years began again in

1983 with a TV show, *Surprise Surprise!*, that specialised in family reunions. A few years after that came *Blind Date*, initiated by another old Cavern-goer, John Birt: 'I suppose her chief qualities,' he said, 'are the classic Northern virtues of warmth, good humour and the enjoyment of others; they allow her to oversee the show in a non-threatening, non-sexual way.'

She'd become a sort of electronic emissary from old, matriarchal Scotland Road: a simulated neighbour from your virtual community. Liverpool remained the centre of her social life until her own mother's death in 1996. 'We may not live in Liverpool,' she said of herself and Bobby, 'but our whole life is there. You've got to understand that we are still very clannish. All our cousins, nieces, nephews are still in Liverpool, and it's still like a village there. Most of my friends are still in Liverpool and nothing goes on there without me knowing about it.' Bobby Willis's death in 1999, and Linda McCartney's a year earlier, spelled the end of two exceptionally stable celebrity marriages.

She has often said she would rather be remembered as a singer than as a TV presenter, and in 2001 planned a return to music with a 'clubland re-recording' of 'Step Inside Love'. If the strategy is not a success she would not be destitute. She always had good legs for panto, for example, as demonstrated by a raunchy routine for the Queen on that year's *Royal Variety Show*. The voice is not universally enjoyed, it's true. Years ago in pantomime, she appealed to the audience for advice on killing the baddie. 'Sing to him!' piped up a child in the stalls.

Billy J. Kramer came from Bootle, at the other end of the docks from Gerry Marsden's Dingle. Like Gerry, though, he had a job on the railways, played at the Cavern and came under the gaze of Brian Epstein. He was really called Billy Ashton but found Kramer in a phone book. (The 'J' was a casual flourish.) Brian then went to Billy's manager, one Ted Knibbs, and paid him £25 to secure the boy's freedom. Brian teamed him with a Manchester backing band, the Dakotas, swopped his old school glitter jackets for the black Dougie Millings suits worn by the Beatles, and duly placed him at Parlophone with George Martin.

Handsome, clean, well-groomed in a slightly old-fashioned way (his hair was still combed back, not forward), Billy was not a rocker in the Lennon mould. Nevertheless it was John who recommended him to Brian and supplied his first hit, 'Do You Want to Know a Secret?' Soon Billy was at Number 1 with another Lennon and McCartney original, 'Bad to Me'. As the third of Epstein's Liverpool stable to reach the top – after Gerry and the Pacemakers and the Beatles – Billy J. Kramer's success confirmed Merseybeat as a full-on phenomenon. Brian organised elocution lessons for the Bootle boy, hoping for opportunities in acting, though nothing transpired.

He was lucky in having John and Paul around to supply their surplus songs, and scored again with 'From a Window' and 'I'll Keep You Satisfied': nowadays among the least-known Lennon and McCartney numbers, but OK in their day and still fine for the sweet of tooth. He found his biggest song, however, in a spurt of independence, when he insisted on recording 'Little Children', by the gifted US writer Mort Shuman. He displayed taste, too, by covering Burt Bacharach's 'Trains and Boats and Planes'. His great mistake, however, was to turn down McCartney's offer of 'Yesterday': 'I said, I don't like it, it's boring, Paul. I want a rock'n'roll song.'

Billy's blunder was understandable. He'd become known as a slightly damp balladeer, whereas he yearned to prove himself with tougher stuff. In fact you can hear recordings of him on a US tour in 1965, rocking up a storm. But he became one more casualty of the shift in rock's sensibility, and could not compete in a post-Merseybeat era. A worrier by nature, he had always struggled with fans' attention and drank more than he should. A career in tailspin made his habit worse, and the pretty-boy looks would take a hammering. He recalled being with Ian St John after a Liverpool game: the footballer introduced him to a girl who said, 'Billy, you used to be a nice-looking guy. What the hell have you been doing with yourself?' He walked away, he says, and didn't drink again for five years. He moved to America, even worked as an alcohol counsellor, and played the nostalgia circuit.

Then there were the Fourmost. They suffered from a lack of Brian's time and attention. On the other hand their NEMS connection brought the all-important link to Lennon and McCartney. When they asked John for a song, he gave them 'Hello Little Girl', saying he'd written it on the toilet: no writer's block for the Beatles in 1963, clearly. It got them a Top 10 hit and gave them a career. The next, 'I'm in Love', was written by the Beatles especially for them. They found another winner elsewhere, called 'A Little Loving' ', but then began to flounder. They could rock convincingly, as proved by a B-side version of the Isley Brothers' 'Respectable', and chose well with a cover of the Four Tops' 'Baby I Need Your Lovin' '. But they lost one member, Mike Milward, to leukaemia in 1966 and retreated from battle with the psychedelic era by taking refuge in comedy. Next thing you knew they were doing George Formby routines and, so far as the charts were concerned, that was that. Cabaret was always there for them, at least.

Epstein's touch, though spectacular, was not infallible. The evidence was a boy called Tommy Quickly (born Thomas Quigley). He went to the lesser-known Piccadilly label, and was therefore without the services of George Martin. His statutory Lennon and McCartney song, 'Tip of My Tongue', was among their least distinguished. 'He was an exciting stage performer,' recalls Spencer Leigh, 'and there is a live version of "I Go Crazy", the James Brown song, which is very good. He was going to record a version of the Beatles' "No Reply" but he messed it up and the session was aborted.'

More legendary than most, however, were a band briefly signed to Brian, the Big Three. Other musicians on the scene seemed to regard this band with awe. They were the original power trio, real sonic bruisers who'd built themselves the biggest amplifiers – nicknamed coffins – that anyone had ever seen. Drummer Johnny Hutchinson, bassist Johnny Gustafson and guitarist Brian Griffiths were respected by Lennon for their rawness and their ability to spot a good song, being the first to cover 'Money' and 'Some Other Guy', the latter a Merseybeat classic. They recorded it for Decca after coming home from Hamburg, but struggled to find equally good material. The group believe they were pressurised to play in softer styles than suited them. There are some surviving tracks cut live at the Cavern, though, which testify to their savagery – and you get to hear Bob Wooler introducing them as 'the boys with the benzedrine beat.' Those were more innocent times.

The Searchers are in many ways the connoisseur's Merseybeat band, and in their prime made music that sparkles like champagne. They would experience mixed fortunes in later life: of the four founders, one went to prison, one joined the civil service, and the other two carried on, but in rival versions of the group. While they were at their peak, however, the Searchers laid down some tracks that are as durable and influential as any in rock history.

Hitting Number 1 with their first single, a Drifters cover called 'Sweets for My Sweet', they became the fourth band in that tidal Mersey wave of 1963. They were also the first non-Epstein act – they'd made their name at Les Ackerley's Iron Door club, rather than the Cavern, and signed to Les before joining a London big-shot named Tito Burns. They lacked access to Lennon and McCartney songs, but it was really the Searchers' *sound* that was so special – the radiant, chiming twin guitars above all – and Epstein would openly regret his failure to acquire them. Signed to Pye they were looked after by an ambitious executive called Tony Hatch, who wrote their second single 'Sugar and Spice'.

The lack of a great songwriter in their ranks was obviously a drawback, though the same was true for everyone in 1963 except the Beatles. Even Jagger and Richards took a while to get going. For their first LP the Searchers relied mainly on American songs from their Hamburg and Bootle repertoires. Its wonderfully period sleevenotes offered a glimpse of the guys' private selves: Michael Pender liked leather jackets and pale blue shirts, lime milkshakes, rum-and-Coke, blondes and Everton; John McNally disliked 'conceited people'; Tony Jackson favoured football, girls and 'genuine friends'; Chris Curtis was troubled by rain and British winters.

Curtis in particular, the nervy, intense-looking drummer, was skilled at picking US cover versions, and the group recorded some beauties: 'Needles and Pins', 'When You Walk in the Room', 'Goodbye My Love ' and 'Don't Throw Your Love Away'. (They were only stopped from scoring four consecutive Number 1 hits by Gerry and the Pacemakers' 'You'll Never Walk Alone', but then they did the same thing to him.) The sheen of their vocal harmonies survived the replacement of bassman Tony Jackson with Frank Allan, while the founders McNally and Pender continued to blend their two guitars to shimmering effect.

Those twin six-strings – they didn't use a Rickenbacker twelve-string until later – were vital to the Searchers' magic. George Harrison was moving toward something similar at the time – heard to best effect on 'A Hard Day's Night' – and both bands were to be a profound influence on the Byrds' Roger McGuinn. One can see why: the Searchers had the same skiffle background as every other Merseybeat band, but they were rare in keeping a folk-ish element in their music (that debut LP, for instance, has a version of 'Where Have All the Flowers Gone'). McGuinn was an American folkie himself, an experienced twelve-string player, who shared Bob Dylan's interest in the fusion of folk with electric rock. Like every US musician, McGuinn and his fellow-Byrd David Crosby were galvanised by the arrival of the Beatles, but they both admired the Searchers too.

In the musical evolution of rock, the Searchers' effect on the Byrds was key. 'McGuinn's been in there all along,' Elvis Costello said to me. 'There wouldn't be any R.E.M., any Tom Petty without him. It's a part of the musical language that he and the Searchers and George Harrison put in there.' Within a few months the Byrds' influence was looping back on the Beatles: the legacy is best described as a jangling, spacious style of guitar pop that recurs down the decades. It's a shame the Searchers' gradual disappearance from the charts meant they were seldom remembered when the credit was being handed around.

They carried on performing, however, and even made a well-received album comeback in 1979. Chris Curtis had left long before, but the drummer had one more footnote to contribute to rock history: in London he tried to launch a group called Roundabout, with keyboard-player Jon Lord and guitarist Ritchie Blackmore, but his involvement was short-lived. They in turn became Deep Purple, the country's greatest hard rock act after Led Zeppelin. And Chris Curtis went to work for the Inland Revenue in Bootle. *C'est la vie.*

McNally and Pender, meanwhile, dissolved their long partnership in 1985 – not without bitterness – to continue as two separate groups, the Searchers and Mike Pender's Searchers. The original bassist Tony Jackson suffered various problems with his health and his business, and he had a spell in prison in the late 1990s on a charge of threatening behaviour. He was luckier, though, than the Searchers' first frontman Johnny Sandon; he hanged himself on Christmas Day 1996.

Behind the front rank was a whole army of beat volunteers. The luckiest were those whom Brian Epstein chose for his own: he might have neglected them in favour of the Beatles, but the prestige he brought with him was, according to Spencer Leigh, 'definitely a good thing, because very few of the other managers did very much. There's a famous saying about Joe Flannery that "Flannery will get you nowhere." Poor old Joe, he managed his brother Lee Curtis and kept him in Hamburg too long. Lee Curtis was an anachronism, he was too late for the Elvis era and too early for the Tom Jones era, and he looked wrong. There was no way he was going to make it in 1963. When Brian Epstein was getting rid of Pete Best he offered Pete to Joe Flannery, who put him with Lee Curtis and the All-Stars. But he wasn't able to do the deals that Brian Epstein did.'

The Beatles' name will live forever more. Gerry and the Pacemakers and Billy J. Kramer will at least live wherever pub teams do pop quizzes. Most Merseybeat acts, however, will have to make do with whatever fragments of their repertoire they managed to record. For a whole bunch of them the chief souvenir is a double album, *This Is Merseybeat*, originally released in two volumes by the Oriole label. Their man John Schroeder simply turned up in Liverpool, invited acts to the Rialto Ballroom and taped whatever they played at him. For all the knock-kneed, breathless desperation of their trebly and sore-throated assaults on sundry R&B standards of the day, the groups' efforts possessed enough nervous energy and innocent excitement to make the results largely likeable.

Among the best is Faron's Flamingoes, possibly the first British band to cover a Motown song, in this case 'Do You Love Me'. Faron, whom Bob Wooler dubbed 'the Panda-footed Prince of Prance', sings his heart out. They were desperately unlucky to see their version beaten to the charts by Brian Poole and the Tremeloes (especially if, as Faron claims, Poole got the lyrics off him in return for a Scotch).

The Swinging Blue Jeans were a rare example of a non-Epstein success story. With unlikely origins in trad jazz, they rocked up their act in Hamburg and were Cavern regulars even before the Beatles. It was the Beatles' version of an American hit, 'Hippy Hippy Shake', that inspired them to record it, securing them a Number 2 hit in Merseybeat's golden year. (It also won them an appearance on the first ever edition of *Top of the Pops*, along with the Rolling Stones.) The follow-up, Little Richard's 'Good Golly Miss Molly', was slightly too similar, but they came back with a smouldering take on the Betty Everett song 'You're No Good', which remains one of the greatest Liverpool records.

The Merseybeats were altogether sultrier, favouring a romantic Latin-lover look – ruffles included – that set them apart from the mob, as well as a penchant for ballads. The group's nucleus of Tony Crane and Billy Kinsley began in their mid-teens as the Mavericks; becoming the opportunistically-named Merseybeats, they scored with dreamy hits such as 'I Think of You' and 'Wishin' and Hopin''. And when Merseybeat fell out of fashion they extended their shelf-life with a swift truncation of name to the Merseys. From this period came the marvellous 'Sorrow', imitated by George on *Yellow Submarine*'s soundtrack ('With your long blonde hurr').

By the time Merseybeat had acquired nostalgia value the Merseys traded back up to their full title. Tony Crane took the revived Merseybeats into cabaret, while Billy Kinsley formed Rockin' Horse (who would for a while be Chuck Berry's backing group). The mid-70s found him in a soft rock outfit, Liverpool Express, who were signed to Warners by Derek Taylor and enjoyed hits with 'Hold Tight', 'You Are My Love' and 'Every Man Must Have a Dream'. Unfortunately they were caught in that awkward time, post-hippy, pre-punk, without the credibility of either, and only the middle of the road for a home. Today, Crane and Kinsley are back together in the partnership that began more than 40 years before.

The Undertakers were all-out rockers with a gusting saxophone for added honk. As the name would imply there was a certain degree of top hat and funeral car nonsense involved, but they are often mentioned in the same breath as the Big Three: rock'n'roll heavyweights, Cavern naturals. The 'nearly man' of the story was their singer Jackie Lomax. He'd been signed by Epstein to NEMS and, after the manager's death, was adopted by George Harrison for the Apple label. Here he issued the Harrison-penned single 'Sour Milk Sea', delivered an LP called *Is This What You Want*, and even sang back-up on the Beatles' 'Dear Prudence'. And, with that, he more or less walked into the mist of Merseybeat history.

Liverpool groups were like little gangs – a mentality that's helpful when your audience is full of big gangs – and solo singers rarely prospered. The scene was even less congenial for girl acts, yet there were several with the spirit to give it a try. Some, like Cilla, got their chance through guest-spots for the boy bands: a couple of girl songs in the set could bring a welcome dash of variety. Even before the Beatles, Liverpool produced a nationally-known act in the Vernons Girls, named after the football pools firm where they worked. They had a few minor hits, such as 'Lover Please' and 'You Know What I Mean', but were chiefly famous for their residency on the *Oh Boy!* TV show. There was an all-girl band called the Liver Birds, long before the TV sit-com, who even played a residency in Hamburg.

Bill Harry: 'There were so many girl groups. People say there were no female acts on Merseyside, but I listed over 50 of them in Liverpool, a tremendous amount. And of course the Liver Birds became very big in Germany, where they stayed and had hits. And all the Liverpool groups going to the US bases in France had to take a girl singer. So all these office girls, typists, you name it, were suddenly going over to France to sing with the local groups: Faron's Flamingoes and everybody.'

The overlooked heroine of this era was Beryl Marsden. Though no relation to Gerry she was Merseybeat aristocracy: a gutsy R&B singer who signed at sixteen to Decca Records. Still under age, but with a special work permit, she braved the lion's den of Hamburg, too. By one of fate's occasional quirks, John Lennon had planned to give her his song 'Love of the Loved' but was prevailed upon to keep it in the NEMS family; so it launched Cilla Black's career instead. She made some feisty recordings all the same, including 'Breakaway' and 'I Know (You Don't Love Me No More)', and would later work in London with Rod Stewart in Shotgun Express.

It's striking that for all the vibrancy of Liverpool's black district in Liverpool 8, Merseybeat remained a largely white phenomenon. Its musical origins were mixed: Merseybeat players had learned a lot from black America, but their performing roots were in skiffle, country and folk. The Liverpool 8 writer P. Willis-Pitts, a beat musician of the time, reports a lack of black interest in the guitar, Merseybeat's basic vehicle. There were some older jazz players, like Odie Taylor, whom John and Paul watched at the White House in Duke Street. But the great favourite was vocal harmony music – itself, some say, a survival of African oral traditions – and the coolly aspirational style of shiny-suited doo-wop acts. In Liverpool 8's night life, in fact, there may have been as much emphasis on dancing to records as performing on stage.

There was also the racial separatism of the town itself. If black beat groups had arisen they would have found it one thing to play in Liverpool 8, but quite another in Walton. That degree of informal segregation would have extended to audiences too. In Merseyside clubs and dancehalls, considerable thought-power went into finding something to fight over. A gang from another neighbourhood was always sufficient provocation. Another colour was just ideal. Sometimes it's just not worth the trouble of stepping outside your own patch. One way or another, black musicians were isolated from the Merseybeat mainstream.

Yet there was a richness of musical heritage in there. Liverpool 8 was commonly settled by black seafarers, who brought not only the music of their African or Caribbean backgrounds, but also the songs they picked up on their travels. Harmonic collisions of all sorts were known. There had been, for example, a long tradition of immigrant Irish women marrying black sailors, with all the musical potential for merriment and lament that this implies. Derry Wilkie, of the Seniors, who first led Merseybeat to Hamburg, was the son of a seaman and grew up on a diet of calypso, country and Irish ballads.

Wilkie was unusual in fronting a white rock group, rather than joining in a vocal harmony act, but his upbringing was fairly typical. Sugar Deen of the Valentinos had a Glaswegian mother and a Nigerian sailor for a father. His American role models were Frankie Lymon and the Teenagers, the Ink Spots and Shirley and Lee, whose records came through Burtonwood Base. Eddie Amoo of the Chants (and later of the Real Thing) had a Ghanaian father and an Irish grandmother.

Joey Ankrah, the leader of the Chants, first sang in his Ghanaian father's choir at the African Churches Mission. Influenced by US acts such as the Ravens and Flamingoes, again discovered via Burtonwood contacts, the Chants had a vocal sophistication that was the envy of their Merseybeat peers. They were backed on occasion by the Beatles, and Brian Epstein undertook to manage them before he got distracted. They were in time signed to Pye, and had support from Liverpool's formidable political leader Bessie Braddock, but were finally sent to undeserved obscurity.

Through into 1964, Liverpool remained the Apple of England's eye, the pride of Great Britain and – increasingly – a source of wonder to the world. There was only a tiny fraction of the media we have today, but what little existed was infatuated. Everyone was talking about this damp, grubby town that nobody had thought twice about for 50 years.

The Associated Rediffusion company came up to have a look, for a documentary called *Beat City*. The writer and narrator, Daniel Farson, spoke in clipped tones and wore a tweed jacket. 'To my mind,' he marvelled, 'Liverpool is the strangest of all the cities of the North . . . hard-living, hard-drinking, hard-fighting, violent, friendly and fiercely alive.' With his brave crew, and sounding like a plucky Victorian captain in some savage, distant land, he ventured into the depths of the Cavern. But of course it was already too late. The club was rammed, admittedly, and the music rocked, but it was no longer creating anything. The scene was a done deal and everyone knew the dress code because they'd seen it on TV shows like this one.

'Invasion of the Liverpoplians' was a typical music paper headline of the day. *Thank Your Lucky Stars*, the big pop show of 1964, had a Mersey special with Cilla, the Beatles, the Searchers and Billy J. Kramer – so successful was the show that it was the British entry in that year's international TV competition. A beat group was invented called the Wackers, who were in fact from Manchester. That may not sound like a scandal of Watergate proportions, but to those on the scene it was a sign of the desperation other towns were feeling. Polite young Merseyside men, up at the Oxbridge colleges, were suddenly talking Scouse for the first time in their lives.

Liverpool, so often out of step with the national mood, was now its very model: cheeky and young, un-posh, un-stuffy, democratic to the boot-heels. Screaming Lord Sutch proposed a National Museum of Pop, to be built in Harold Wilson's constituency of Huyton. The idea of a pop museum was, back then, the greatest absurdity imaginable, but nobody could fault the location. The Prime Minister revelled in it: his predecessors, Harold Macmillan and Alec Douglas-Home, were Edwardian aristocrats, whose hearts were in the grouse moors, but Harold was a very modern politician, and a shrewd populist. He seized the opportunity to present awards to the Beatles at the Variety Club of Great Britain: 'I'd just like to say thanks for the purple hearts,' quipped Lennon on the stage. 'Silver!' shouted Ringo. 'Oh yes, sorry about that,

Harold.' The PM laughed gamely with the audience, though it's by no means clear that he grasped what had been said.

Big new factories arrived on Merseyside (often thanks to Wilson's influence) and a young generation of shop stewards, supremely self-confident, arose with them. At the weekends they would dress up for the match – white shirts, narrow black ties, sharp grey suits – and sway in full-throated triumph on the Kop or at Goodison Road. As school-children we were taken to exhibitions of city regeneration. I remember how I gasped at the planners' balsa-wood models: audacious schemes for a space age metropolis of towers and walkways in the sky. I was amazed by the architects' impressions of futurist piazzas, full of sleek, laughing people in car-coats.

I honestly couldn't wait.

The strangest sight of all was Merseybeat's impact on the world beyond Britain's shores. Thanks to the impression it made, big doors were opened to British music. Before the Beatles there was no sense, internationally, that Britain was a natural home of pop, but suddenly you had Chuck Berry coming up with a title, 'Liverpool Drive', for an LP called *St Louis to Liverpool*. Chuck had, of course, been quite the demi-god to Liverpool groups, but it's unclear whether he had even heard of the place twelve months earlier.

Motown's boss Berry Gordy was even quicker off the mark. The man whose label had been to Merseybeat what gasoline is to a flame, now arranged for Diana Ross and the Supremes to rush-record an album of Beatle covers called *A Bit of Liverpool*.

American recognition of the Liverpool upsurge was occasionally bizarre. In 1967 The Monkees followed up their hits 'I'm a Believer' and 'Last Train to Clarkesville' with something called 'Alternate Title (Randy Scouse Git)'. As Mickey Dolenz explained to *Mojo*: 'We were over in England and the Beatles threw a party for us. There were limos outside and always screaming girls. I was just sitting in a hotel suite trying to document what was going on in a kind of poetic way. The title I got watching *Till Death Us Do Part* – I just heard it and said, "That's a cool term, but what the hell does it mean?" And it was something like "sex-crazed Liverpudlian jerk". RCA in England told me they'd pull it from the album unless I came up with an alternate title. So I said, "OK, 'Alternate Title' it is." ' Stranger still, the 'randy Scouse git' was actor Tony Booth, playing Alf Garnett's idle son-in-law and target of his Cockney rage. Booth was the father of Cherie Booth, future wife of Tony Blair.

The legendary 'British Invasion' of American pop began with Merseybeat but soon fused with music from across the country – from London, Belfast, Newcastle – and lost its Liverpudlian connotations. In all, though, it remains a truly odd phenomenon in rock's history. From Hollywood to Microsoft, baseball caps to Batman, American products have colonised the modern world. Only in rock'n'roll has another country significantly reversed the flow. Britain took the ultimate American invention, re-arranged its ass and shipped it back.

The British were not, on the face of it, the race that anyone would have tipped for this job. The English in particular were not a funky people. Their menfolk danced like Douglas Bader. It was a land where reserve was valued over exhibitionism, where enthusiasm was suspect and quiet irony the favoured means of subversion. English music was sometimes beautiful, often witty, but never sensual. Yet it seems all it needed was a push. And that push, when it came, came from England's least English city. Frigidity has never been a characteristic of seaports. When the levee broke, it was the Scousers wot broke it.

The only obvious reason why the British were so successful at adopting rock is the language factor. Speaking English made them all the more receptive to American culture, and better placed than other countries to imitate or infiltrate it (like the English actors in early Hollywood). With the heroic exception of Billy Fury, the first English rockers, such as Tommy Steele, Cliff Richard and Marty Wilde, grew up too soon to have assimilated Elvis Presley, Chuck Berry and the gang. Rock'n'roll was a thing they had to learn, like car maintenance or Arabic. But the wave that followed – Lennon, McCartney, Jagger, Townshend – were young enough to have absorbed it from the start. Because of Elvis, they had a sense of rock as something vast and mythic. And to the Liverpudlians, American music was not so much something new, as something in the bloodstream.

In the immediate wake of the Beatles, American taste in Limey imports was not impeccable. The second biggest act was the cloddish Dave Clark Five, from Tottenham N15 ('the Mersey Sound with the Liverpool beat' went their US publicity). There were the useful Hollies, Cavern regulars from Manchester. Also from Manchester were the quaintly hopeless Freddie and the Dreamers and the limply winsome Herman's Hermits (whose singer Peter Noone was actually from Liverpool). By 1965 there were better and harder R&B bands: the Animals, the Who, the Rolling Stones. A year later came Van Morrison's Them.

The combined forces of Merseybeat and British R&B made massive changes to American music. Their influence took root among young garage bands across the nation, whose members would become the superstars of tomorrow: Bruce Springsteen, Tom Petty, Kiss. The Liverpool effect upon the Byrds was epoch-making. Bob Dylan himself was fascinated. The Beach Boys knew it was time for a re-think. All across the States, youths threw off their mental Bermuda shorts and fantasised about red buses and Royal Guardsmen. They formed groups with names like Sherlock Fogge, affecting deerstalkers with their newly grown hair.

Coals were being returned to Newcastle by the boat-load. A rising generation of country musicians, such as Roseanne Cash, Dwight Yoakam and Steve Earle, worshipped John Lennon as much as the memory of Hank Williams. Even the supremely authentic black bluesman Robert Cray was inspired to pick up a guitar by the Beatles. Over the longer term, it would be silly to claim that US musicians drew deeper nourishment from Billy J. Kramer than from John Lee Hooker, or from Gerry Marsden than Woody Guthrie. But it was often these flimsy British acts who first demonstrated the glamour and fun of pop and, what's more, made it look achievable. After all, if Herman's Hermits could make hit records and get themselves chased by screaming chicks, who the hell couldn't?

Back home, practically the last act to scramble aboard the Merseybeat bandwagon were the Mojos. They were not the biggest, but they were one of the best, and their story is in some ways emblematic of the whole era.

Stu James, their singer, was a pupil at the Liverpool Institute, though a few years younger than Paul McCartney and George Harrison. He was therefore of the first Liverpool generation whose musical inspiration began with the Beatles themselves: to him, they weren't Cavern rivals, or even pals. They were divinities.

'Suddenly there came a day when you heard about what was going on at the Cavern,' he remembers. 'That's where it all began. The word at school, at the Institute, was the Beatles. This thing was actually happening with some guys who'd been in our Fifth Form. Geographically, it was an easy walk at lunchtimes down to the Cavern, and Sunday nights I'd go to Mrs Best's place in West Derby, where they played as well. From there it escalated to charabanc outings to Manchester or Crewe or Preston to see them. And you were very partisan: if you liked the Beatles you couldn't like Rory Storm or anyone else. But I was absolutely *obsessive* about the Beatles, and I could recite their set list to you.

'The Beatles' Hamburg record with Tony Sheridan, "My Bonnie", was the first one that came into Liverpool. If you were fanatical about the Beatles, that was a moment of great excitement: that was the first piece of plastic, and we all charged round to NEMS to pick it up. This was the first opportunity to take them home with you. Where we heard everything first was in the Cavern from Bob Wooler. It was a big deal if you could get in the DJ box and actually talk to him, and I remember one day how I'd proudly acquired this Chuck Berry greatest hits album by sending away to America, so I took it in to him saying "Hey, look at this Bob!" And John Lennon came over: "What have you got there?" I think he actually bought it from me for four quid. I was really proud.

'Everything that happened to a band was new, back then. Just hearing them on the radio was a high. Today they probably would have been on John Peel or Steve Lamacq, but the whole process was new in 1962. And the night that the TV cameras came into the Cavern to film the Beatles was an incredibly big deal. They sang "Some Other Guy".

'A large proportion of the people at the Cavern didn't go to local places like Litherland Town Hall. Whereas the Tower in New Brighton would have a real mix of Teddy Boys and whatever, those of us at the Cavern felt we were a bit arty. It was quite a cool place. It wasn't just everybody that went to the Cavern: there was a feeling of clique-ishness. Take away the smell of disinfectant and you felt good about being in there. I didn't like the older-looking groups like the Searchers. I associated them with the Iron Door club and somehow that was uncool. I have to say, though, that their records have stood the test of time, and are very much in the line of pop you can hear in the La's. But you either went to the Cavern or you went to the Iron Door: I don't think I even went there once.

'One of the keys to it was that Cavern bands always sounded very loud. The way that place worked, with the three tunnels, if you sat in the middle it seemed incredible. Compared to the London acts like Joe Brown, who were almost cabaret entertainers, our bands were scruffy. But the biggest thing for me was just how loud these bass coffin amps could be, and that was so obviously different to what you saw on the TV. And I did think the Big Three and the Undertakers were very credible, not that we would have used that word. They sounded very tough and were probably the best musicians.

'The first band I had myself was a local group in Penny Lane, with guitars from mail order catalogues, and it was all Tommy Roe and Buddy Holly. Then I was in a band called the Nomads: they weren't school mates, and I had to go miles on the bus to Anfield. I'd be playing Jerry

Lee Lewis stuff on a piano with a mike stuck in the top. The first recording we made was when John Schroeder of Oriole came to the Rialto to record the local bands, and I'm singing "My Whole Life Through" which I wrote, a bit of a "Hippy Hippy Shake" rip-off. We didn't get paid, though I still get publishing royalties. I just wait for the day when somebody like Eminem decides to sample it.

'We started to get gigs, and I remember being thrilled to play about 24th on the list of a Cavern all-nighter. It all took off when we did an American song, "The Mashed Potato", which we'd ripped off from Jackie Lomax in the Undertakers. It all went mad: they started screaming and going bonkers. We'd obviously moved up a couple of notches overnight.

'The breakthrough was a songwriting competition at the Philharmonic Hall, organised by this publisher. I won that: I think I got a tape recorder, and we got a publishing deal. But we had to change our name since there was another Nomads somewhere; since we always did the Muddy Waters' song "Got My Mojo Working" we then became the Mojos. If we had any individuality around town, it's that we weren't so much a harmony group as blues-based. I was a Chuck Berry fanatic but the bass player, Keith Karlson, was more anorak-y and into more obscure tracks. We got this manager, Spencer Lloyd-Mason, who was bit of a playboy from Ainsdale or Southport.

'And then we went to Hamburg for a five-week stint at the Star Club: it was January and freezing cold, but it was the first time I stayed in a nice hotel. A very happy month. You'd always do three or four hours a night with big drinking gaps in between. There was a caff next door where you'd go for soup, bread and beer. The audiences were all male, and there were nights when barnies broke out, but that was nothing new, because all the gigs in Liverpool were like that too. It was like you'd suddenly see half the audience had disappeared, because there was a massive fight going on. I remember the police having to get us out of one gig in Aigburth. They were very violent. In Penny Lane Hall, you'd see the crowd swirling like a kaleidoscope with the fight rushing round and chairs in the air.

'Through the publishing deal we also got signed to Decca, and once we could add the magic words "Decca Recording Artists" to our posters we were away. The Mojos were very much the second generation, at least two or three years younger than the Beatles and the Searchers, but people in London were still saying "We must have a Liverpool band on the roster." It was so hot. Everywhere we went, people had fake Liverpool accents: "A'right la?" I wasn't even like that myself. You could get a shag just by speaking in a Liverpool accent.

'In Hamburg we made "Everything's Alright": I think there was a rush because the Liverpool thing had been around for two or three years. I remember walking home from the Star Club, thinking of a jazz song called "Moanin'" and trying to work out a bluesy way of singing in the gaps between the riff. Terry, our keyboard player, worked out a way to do that. There were bits in the song that were clearly influenced by "Twist and Shout" but what was original was the riff at the start, and singing in between it. We might also have been influenced by Tony Sheridan, who was brilliant, like Ray Charles incarnate.

'So then we did a theatre tour with the Dave Clarke Five, the Hollies, the Kinks and Charlie and Inez Foxx. We started at the bottom of the bill, in Coventry, but when we had a big hit with "Everything's Alright" we overtook the Kinks. We still got on well with Ray, but less well with the Hollies: we'd never played theatres before, you see, only clubs, and I think we quickly grabbed lots of the Hollies' act, in terms of being more outgoing and running around the stage. I think Graham Nash was somewhat peeved about the whole thing.

'The second was an eight-week tour with the Stones. But I spent absolutely zilch time with them, because they'd arrive in Black Marias with police escorts.

'"Everything's Alright" was raved about, but it was diminishing returns after that. We didn't know what it was about the song that everyone loved. It had been so spontaneous, but now we sat around analysing our own song. We sort of tried playing it sideways, found a riff that was just a bit different, and ended up with a pastiche of our own track. Which was a disappointment to people who thought we were a highly imaginative organisation. With the benefit of hindsight, we should have stuck to our guns and done the blues stuff, like Mose Allison's. We did record "Spoonful" but they wouldn't let us put that out: they wanted the poppy harmonies, and in those days bands had no control at all.'

When the Mojos' next single failed to chart, Stu James recalls, 'we saw the writing on the wall'. But he persevered with a new line-up that included the well-respected drummer Aynsley Dunbar and their tour manager's son Lewis Collins (who'd once been a ladies' hairdresser with Mike McCartney, and would become a TV star as one of *The Professionals*). Strangely, they tried storming the charts with 'Goodbye Dolly Gray', an old soldiers' favourite from the trenches. 'The producer's idea,' sighs Stu. 'A horrible record. He told us anti-war songs were big that year.'

The band's last days were spent in Africa, where they were booked to play a residency. 'It was a wonderful gig, with lots of shagging, good money, the sun was shining and we only had to play two or three hours a night. And that was probably the last place on earth where people still thought it was really cool to come from Liverpool. The women thought they'd died and gone to heaven, and so did we. Everything was provided, we had lovely bedrooms. But I was lying by the pool one afternoon and thought, "I'm 23 now, this really isn't going in the right direction." We gave up after that.'

6. TONIGHT AT NOON

THE DEATH OF MERSEYBEAT. SOME LIVERPOOL POETS AND BEAUTIFUL LOSERS

The most romantic way to enter Liverpool is from the sea, but the next best is by train. The experience starts with the sweeping view from Runcorn Bridge, which carries you across a wide, sleepy expanse of Mersey water and marks, to my mind, the unambiguous beginning of Northern England. The final loss of prettiness, announced by a brutalised industrial landscape, might be felt with a pang by some incomers, but my own pulse quickens. Soon the track is lined with overspill estates, which are in turn succeeded by the south Liverpool suburbia of Lennon and McCartney's childhoods. On the brink of the city is the station called Edge Hill: hence the wonderfully apt expression 'getting off at Edge Hill': Liverpool was always lustful, but it used to be Catholic too, and the only birth control was *coitus interruptus* . . .

Suddenly the sky goes out. You're in deep canyons and rumbling tunnels, hacked from primeval sandstone by thousands of nineteenth-century Irish labourers; the walls are now black with soot or green with slime, enlivened by the occasional greeting such as 'Cockneys Die'. There is a drama about it all. You won't see daylight again until you're in Lime Street Station, the end of the line, with a sense of having gone underground and now emerged in some other world. Which, to be fair, you have. It's not everyone's cup of tea: 'Previous to entering Liverpool,' wrote one of the first passengers, in 1835, 'you go through a dark, black, ugly, vile abominable tunnel 300 yards long, which has all the horrors of banishment from life – such a hole as I never wish to go through again.'

The walk along that platform from the London train to Lime Street's concourse is invariably thrilling to me. But sometimes a homecoming can mean a kind of defeat.

I'm thinking of the unsuccessful beat boys, back in the middle 1960s. Here's where so many thwarted pop musicians returned back North, careers gone south, their dreams all cracked and battered. The run from Lime Street to Euston was in theory the location of that railway sequence in *A Hard Day's Night*. In Alun Owen's screenplay the train scenes separate the pandemonium at one end from the madness at the other; sealed in a couple of carriages the four boys are at leisure to flirt with girls, taunt the authorities and bat the banter up and down. Those compartment trains have gone now. But how many musicians must have sat in them and fantasised about the kind of Beatlehood awaiting them in the smoke, just the other side of signing some papers in Manchester Square and Denmark Street. How many must have sat in those same compartments, gloomily chugging home, wondering why the plans had gone awry.

Nowadays the 1960s are remembered more for Swinging London than for Merseybeat. Just as plays are staged in the provinces before they're presented to the London West End, so the Liverpool tumult was, with hindsight, no more than a dress rehearsal for the century's most hyped decade. By 1966, fashionable attention was firmly back on England's capital, and it's stayed there ever since. When London's finest pop songwriter, Ray Davies of the Kinks, came to compose 'Waterloo Sunset', he was originally thinking of twilight on the Mersey not the Thames. (Davies was a melancholic writer, always drawn to autumn not spring, who would have been struck by Liverpool's fall from grace, and who treated Swinging London as a source ripe for satire rather than celebration.)

Of the Merseybeat groups, only the Beatles really made it on an epic scale. Their contemporaries had drifted back to the city in threes and fours. You would spot them, has-beens at 24, standing at bus-stops or telling their war stories in pubs. The most determined of them refused to disband; so they played at cabaret clubs, ageing gamely in the glam-rock 1970s, grown men with leathery faces and feathery haircuts. By the 1980s, some of them found their most regular bookings came from playing redundancy parties on the Dock Road. The better-known groups had sufficient fame to make good dough on the nostalgia circuit. Their careers might be condensed to two or three hit singles to be replayed forever – sometimes in medleys to alleviate the band's boredom. But so what? Working life was meant to be boring, from the Ford plant at Halewood to the Birds Eye frozen food factory in Kirkby.

The Beatles took themselves, their music and everyone else to a new place when they moved on. As George Melly put it, they didn't go down with the Liverpool ship, but neither did they take the showbiz lifeboat. Other Liverpool stars were left with a sense of life as a long anti-climax, stretching out ahead of them. 'It's like being 20 and scoring the winning goal in a Cup Final,' one of them said to me. 'How are you ever going to match that feeling again?'

Most of them eventually settled for a normal existence: poor, tormented Rory Storm was the exception rather than the rule. A few of them became celebrities all over again. There were soap stars: Geoffrey Hughes, who was *Coronation Street*'s Eddie Yates, had been in the Travellers (he'd also be Paul's voice in *Yellow Submarine* and join *The Royle Family*); *Brookside*'s Ron Dixon was once the leader of Vince Earle and the Talismen and also played with Rory; Clive Hornby who plays *Emmerdale*'s Jack Sugden was in the Dennisons. Of the comedians, Freddie Starr went on to national fame (or even infamy), Russ Abbott of the Black Abbotts likewise. Jud Lander of the Hideaways joined the music business and plays harmonica on Culture Club's 'Karma Chameleon'. An ex-Merseybeat, Billy Butler, became the star DJ of Liverpool's local radio and is probably more well-known in the city than anyone else in this book, apart from the Beatles and Cilla.

The Cavern's DJ Bob Wooler had watched the ascent of Merseybeat at close quarters, funnelling wondrous puns into his microphone as he went. So it's appropriate to quote his comments on the decline. In 1971, just after the Beatles' painful separation, he wrote of the golden age: 'That was many hit parades ago, when our budding Mersey Beat scene was a comparatively innocent Garden of Eden with no sign of the Apple let alone the serpent! I guess the beginning of the end came when the cream of the scene sort of EMIgrated . . . The nation was afflicted with an acute attack of mal-de-Mersey! Scouse was as "out" as Strauss . . . There followed more hang-ups than an orgy of Roman crucifixions . . . All the same it was swell while it lasted.'

Indeed it was. To a great extent, it was the innovations of the Beatles which hastened Merseybeat's demise. Having ascended to some higher realm of pop existence, they pulled the ladder up behind them. Posterity has passed a harsh verdict on Merseybeat because its other acts were so completely overshadowed by the Beatles. However many of them were extremely good within their period, even if they knew no way out of it. Most were dynamic on stage, and were unfortunate in never being recorded in a way that did them justice. As Nik Cohn wrote, looking back from a more sophisticated but somehow less joyful time, 'Right here, I wouldn't mind swapping.'

What went wrong for the Liverpool Sound? Nothing in pop is designed to last forever, but Merseybeat had once appeared omnipotent. Within a year it vanished so completely that it was hard to believe it really happened at all. Even now, when we're surrounded by the re-cycled past on back catalogue CDs and in long, retrospective magazine articles, Merseybeat has left eerily little trace.

The roots of the problem can be detected around 1964–65. By now the British teens could experience American music for themselves.

Chuck Berry was touring in the flesh. Little Richard and Jerry Lee Lewis were finally on TV. More importantly, so were the stars of Tamla Motown, who visited Britain on package tours, while their records gained ever more efficient British distribution. Once, Liverpool had brought American music to Britain. Now it was here, Britain had no more need for Liverpool. There had been that fine Liverpool version of 'Baby I Need Your Lovin'', for instance – but who needed the Fourmost when you could have the Four Tops?

Liverpool was the Cinderella City of the 1960s. When the clock struck midnight its finery, just like Cinderella's, turned back into rags.

If its nemesis could be summed up in one word, that word would be psychedelia. It wasn't just Swinging London that usurped the Liverpudlians' supremacy. Liverpool had, for a while, been the English Memphis. By 1967, the *Rolling Stone* writer Ralph J. Gleason was calling San Francisco 'the American Liverpool'. The comparison was a little flattering: in reality Liverpool pop was finished, while San Francisco symbolised Flower Power and a rising concept of music – what it was for, how it might sound, and where it might take the enlightened spirit.

Personally, I well recall that legendary Summer Of Love in Liverpool. In 1967 I remember flowers and incense. I myself wore a robe that swept down to the ground. There was strange, unearthly music playing and people chanted syllables from an esoteric language. But that's because I was an altar boy. The climax of my year was to serve at the opening ceremonies of the space-age Catholic Cathedral. Of the legendary hippy Summer Of Love, I saw no sign. Even Ringo admits it: 'A lot of Flower Power didn't translate in, say, Oldham or Bradford, and not really in Liverpool.'

The Beatles' greatest songs of that year, 'Penny Lane' and 'Strawberry Fields Forever', celebrated their childhood memories of Fifties Liverpool and not the Liverpool of 1967, where my own childhood was taking place. It was now a good place to have come from, but not a groovy place to be. It was not a Love Town. The golden moment had passed, and the circus moved to a land where the beautiful people sat in wildflower meadows partaking of LSD – not in Northern pubs, supping mild and bitter.

This brings us to what might be called the Surrey Conundrum. Why did the art school R&B bands of South-east England become the new rock aristocracy, while the Liverpool boys (the Beatles, as usual, excepted) got consigned to cabaret or civvy street? From London and the Home Counties came the Rolling Stones, the Yardbirds, Fleetwood Mac, the

...verpool, the wondrous
... itself, by the silver
...tar of the River Mersey.

(MERSEY PARTNERSHIP)

...Vith your looks and my brains, son...'
...in's first real rock star Billy Fury, with his
...tor and manager Larry Parnes. (PICTORIAL
...S)

...ocal idols on the brink of their recording
...ract, but the Beatles still play second fid-
...o an Irish showband flown into Liverpool
...ne date only. (PICTORIAL PRESS)

PAVILION LODGE LANE
PHONE ROYal 5931

ON STAGE FOR
ONE NIGHT ONLY
MONDAY, 2nd APRIL
COMMENCING 7-30 ——— DOORS OPEN 7 P.M.
FLYING VISIT OF "IRELAND'S PRIDE"!!
THE ROYAL SHOW BAND
(WATERFORD)
Winners of the Carl-Alan Award for the outstanding
Showband of the year
ALSO—"MERSEYSIDE'S JOY"
THE BEATLES!!
LIVERPOOL'S OWN BEAT GROUP
All Seats bookable.   Prices from 3/6 to 7/6
Box Office open 10 a.m. to 5 p.m. Daily
A NIGHT YOU MUST NOT MISS

◀ Returning in triumph,
America conquered, the
Beatles survey their spiritual
home from the balcony of
Liverpool Town Hall, 10
July 1964. (LIVERPOOL POST
& ECHO)

▼ Celebrating the launch of
*Sgt Pepper's Lonely Hearts
Club Band* at Brian Epstein's
home in Belgravia, 19 May
1967. The manager would
be found dead at the same
address just three months
later. (PICTORIAL PRESS)

▲ Surprise, surprise! 'Our Cilla' at the Cavern Club in 1963, awaiting her blind date with destiny.
(LIVERPOOL POST & ECHO)

▶ 'The Best of Cellars': Cavern Club rocks to th Clayton Squares, 1964. Clayton Square itself, th days were numbered.
(LIVERPOOL POST & ECHO

▶ McGough, McGear a Gorman, collectively th Scaffold. (PICTORIAL PRE

▲ Gerry and his
Pacemakers take that
immortal Ferry across the
Mersey, 1964. (LIVERPOOL
POST & ECHO)

Liverpool's cleverest ... n, Ken Dodd, enter- ... s the Mayor. (LIVERPOOL ... & ECHO)

Hi Jo Hi!': the band that ... ght Liverpool music ... from the point of ... ction, Deaf School, in ... 5. (© SEAN HALLIGAN)

▲ Elvis Costello: love lies down with treachery, hope is a delusion (DAVID CORIO/S.I.N.)

Who and more. The Yardbirds alone would give us Jeff Beck, Eric Clapton and Jimmy Page – and therefore the core of both Cream and Led Zeppelin. All these artists shared a grounding in the purist blues scene, which Liverpool largely shunned.

Take Muddy Waters. After he played in Britain in 1958, some young people were never quite right in the head again. Minds were blown by this man: the clanking, metal music that reared up from an electrified Mississippi swamp, his mighty stance of imperial dignity, the mad, voodoo poetry of mojo charms and 'John the Conqueror root' and seventh sons, and how his huge cheeks wobbled when he growled about being a nat'ral born lovin' man. You never got *that* off Tommy Steele. By the time he was back in Chicago, those traumatised young people were plotting the birth of British R&B. But not, for some reason, in Liverpool.

Spencer Leigh: 'The interesting thing about Liverpool is that the blues passed it by. The jazz musicians were very impressed when Muddy Waters came to play at the Mardi Gras Club, but it didn't seem to influence the beat musicians at all. A lot of them say they saw Buddy Holly in 1959 and it was like St Paul on the road to Damascus, that was a big event. But Muddy Waters, they don't mention. Pete Best did say that in Hamburg, when they had to keep going for hours at a time, they would sometimes do 12-bar blues that would go on forever. But the Beatles didn't record any blues until "Yer Blues" on the *White Album*.'

The Liverpool guitarists favoured rhythm and picking (learned from Eddie Cochran and Chet Atkins respectively) over the blues styles studied down South. For his own part, George Harrison found a way forward by incorporating the sitar, but the players who became guitar heroes were from the blues camp. White boy blues enthusiasts triumphed because their style could develop – into acid rock, psychedelic boogie, virtuoso solos or even heavy metal. Clapton and co were at least equipped to compete in the age of Jimi Hendrix.

What's more, as serious-minded student types, those Southern boys could talk the talk. According to Mick Jagger, groups like the Stones and the Pretty Things, 'had a good overall history of the thing, blues, country, rock, black music, jazz, whatever . . . It's that middle class knowledge, the sense of history, and the desire to know everything, how Slim Harpo's harmonica licks work.'

Another problem, obviously, was the Mersey musicians' failure to follow Lennon and McCartney as songwriters. Was it for lack of talent? Or was it their detachment from the cultural upheavals of the day? We know they seldom shared the emerging psychedelic mind-set. Spencer Leigh offers another suggestion: 'As well as the blues, you don't have a

Dylan element on the Liverpool scene. They seemed to shun folk rock, you had hardly anyone trying to do Dylan-type songs.' There were some honourable exceptions, like Jimmy Campbell of the Kirkbys, but most Merseybeat efforts at composition were chronically unambitious.

The Merseybeat acts were mostly working class lads, whose values were those of traditional entertainers. They never had the scholarly obsession with obscure blues that Jagger, Richards and the others had; they liked the bright, accessible pop of Tamla Motown and the Brill Building. They had no interest in the emerging 'counter-culture'; their roots were in semi-pro show business. When pop became rock and rock went weird, around 1966, the Liverpool groups were left behind. And with the rise of DJ-dominated discos, the beat groups weren't even needed for dancing to. They faced oblivion or exile on the chicken-in-a-basket circuit. Cream and the rest became rock gods; the Swinging Blue Jeans became a good night out in Widnes.

Liverpool lost its supremacy in pop music, but suddenly became famous for pop art. The impetus this time came not from ordinary Scousers, but from a bohemian district up the hill from the town centre. Beginning at Hardman Street, the quarter encompassed two Philharmonics (the pub and the concert hall), the Art College and University, fanning out through wide, handsome streets of Georgian houses around the Anglican Cathedral. While locals always referred to the area by its postal name of Liverpool 8, one day it would be globally known by its Domesday Book title: Toxteth.

Liverpool 8 claimed a unique place in the civic psyche. For most of white Liverpool this enclave up the hill, especially the central drag of Upper Parliament Street, was the dubious abode of coloured people. Liverpool is territorial at the best of times; add the extra complication of race and you had a virtual no-go zone. The tall, well-proportioned townhouses had originally been built for Liverpool's affluent classes. The location gave them a commanding view of the maritime highway and freedom from the pestilent airs of the dockland slums. Now carved up into rented tenements, the buildings were often slums themselves.

Sloping down to the South Docks, Toxteth was the most exotic vestige of Liverpool's history. It contained the oldest Chinatown in Europe. There were shops and drinking clubs to cater for every race on earth. There was a sexy, disreputable atmosphere you did not encounter in ordinary Liverpool. And the college element brought yet another flavour. As in London's Notting Hill Gate, the cheap flats of Liverpool 8, and the sense of its separation from English respectability, attracted young and rootless intellectuals. The ready availability of drugs did no harm, either. In the imaginations of suburbia's most adventurous escapees, like Lennon, McCartney and Stuart Sutcliffe, Liverpool 8 represented glamorous non-conformity. They once played a club here as backing band for Janice the Stripper. In essence, this place was the anti-suburbia of your rebellious dreams.

George Melly wrote of that era: 'There is no doubt in my mind that the crater of the volcano was not London, but Liverpool . . . Liverpool 8 had a seedy but decided style; its own pubs and meeting places; it was small enough to provide an enclosed stage for the cultivation of its own legend.' In 1967 the *Daily Telegraph*, no less, produced a special on 'the New Culture of Beat City.' The prince of it all, perhaps, was a roly-poly poet and painter named Adrian Henri. With his fellow poets Roger McGough and Brian Patten he was responsible for a Penguin paperback, *The Mersey Sound*, which became the best-selling poetry collection of all time. And, this being Liverpool, Roger McGough found time to be in a chart-topping pop group, the Scaffold, as well.

Once again Liverpool was not a provincial outpost but a creative hub which attracted progressive thinkers from far and wide. Henri would play host to the American beat poet Allen Ginsberg – who was, in his heart, something of a Beatle groupie and was moved to declare, 'Liverpool is at the present moment the centre of the consciousness of the human universe.'

One day, the obscure performance artist Yoko Ono materialised, as Spencer Leigh recalls: 'I am very proud of the fact that I touched Yoko Ono before John Lennon did. She came here in 1966 to the Bluecoat Chambers and had a "happening". I had never been to a happening before, but it sounded very exciting and mysterious and avant garde so I went along. She invited members of the audience to wrap her up in bandages, so that is why I touched her before John Lennon did. I was doing her feet very delicately while Adrian Henri was doing the top half. She was covered in all these bandages and I remember John Gorman of the Scaffold shouting out, "You're wanted on the phone!"

'You could really see the influence she would have on John Lennon's work. She had the black bags on stage and she invited people to come up on stage and take their clothes off inside the bag. About eight people did. It was an entertaining evening which went on for about two hours. Part of it was just watching her eat a tuna fish sandwich. At the end of the happening she put a vase on the table and her husband Tony Cox smashed it and invited people to come up and take a piece. So I did and

Yoko Ono said, "I want us all to meet in ten years' time and piece this together." I've never met her since.'

Adrian Henri was from Birkenhead, the grandson of a Mauritian seaman. During the Blitz he'd watched Liverpool in flames across the Mersey, and would say the sight of fire reflected in the river water haunted him forever. He moved to Liverpool 8 in 1957: 'Liverpool in the 1950s,' he recalled, 'seemed to me like Paris in the 1920s.' He drank in Ye Cracke, the art school local frequented by John Lennon, and eventually taught painting. His own style was pop art, though he favoured homely images from working class Liverpool over the flashier icons of Americana. 'The pop artist,' he said, 'stands with one foot in the art gallery and the other in the supermarket.'

In his poetry, too, he was closer to Scouse populism than to high culture. He recalled a disastrous early reading when the audience grew bored: 'Every poem from then on had to have a surface meaning,' he decided. 'Maybe you could get to another meaning by reading it, but it had to mean something immediately.' In his poem *I Want to Paint*, he expressed an ambition to paint 'pictures that tramps can live in . . . pictures that teenage lovers can send each other'. He became such a symbol of 60s art that his name cropped up on a Jam album, *This Is the Modern World*, getting a credit off Paul Weller 'for foresight and inspiration'; one track, 'Tonight at Noon', borrowed its name from a Henri poem, itself derived from a Charlie Mingus jazz record. 'Tonight at noon,' wrote Henri, 'a tunnel full of water will be built under Liverpool.'

Surreally-enhanced Scouse settings were a feature of his work: he'd see 'Marcel Proust in the Kardomah eating Madeleine butties dipped in tea', or a beautiful Polish gunman, dripping in blood, collapsing in a Liverpool 8 alleyway. He'd paint the Liverpool landmarks towering over a luscious tropical rainforest, or Hope Street taken over by festive skeletons from the Mexican Day of the Dead. In one of his greatest canvases, *The Entry of Christ into Liverpool*, we see a magnificent procession of Henri's friends and heroes (figures include the Beatles and Roger McGough), through a Lime Street streaming with banners.

Henri had staged joint performances with Liverpool groups and in 1967 formed one of his own, the Liverpool Scene. In the aftermath of Merseybeat there was a more educated class of bands emerging, with greater leanings to blues. From the Clayton Squares he took saxophonist Mike Evans; from the Roadrunners came Mike Hart. A gifted guitarist called Andy Roberts also joined. They were championed by John Peel, who produced their first album, *The Amazing Adventures of . . .* Its cover showed the band and friends outside the Hardman Street pub O'Connor's, gathered about its landlord Jimmy Moore: O'Connor's had the look of a Wild West saloon, but its dour interior became a spiritual home for Liverpool bohemians, while its dingy entrance became a place for student white boys hoping to trade with the black merchants of Liverpool 8.

Rock star was perhaps the least successful of Adrian Henri's incarnations, and though the band had its moments – including a support tour for Led Zeppelin and an appearance on the same Isle of Wight bill as Bob Dylan – they barely made it to the 1970s before splitting. Adrian stayed in Liverpool 8 for rest of his life, and died on 20 December 2000, just hours after the Council had voted to make him a Freeman of the City.

The honour was shared with his fellow Mersey poets Roger McGough and Brian Patten, who said at the ceremony: 'The Freedom of Liverpool has been given to me by my best teacher: the city itself.' A few months later I ran into Patten at the Chelsea Arts Club, where it fell to me to inform him that O'Connor's was nowadays a fun-pub called Bonkers. He flinched.

Roger McGough was a docker's son who went to university, and in his poems caught the wayward nature of Liverpool speech. Of the musicians, only John Lennon really matched him for that. It's not surprising that McGough was drafted in by the makers of *Yellow Submarine* to give its script a tang of that Scouse whimsy which could easily pass as psychedelia.

His parallel pop career began when he met Paul McCartney's younger brother Mike. Though employed by day in Andre Bernard's hairdressing salon (an establishment for upmarket ladies, opposite the Adelphi; it's now a burger joint), McCartney had artistic ambitions: he designed posters for his brother's band and was infatuated by photography and Surrealism. He found his way up Mount Pleasant to the basement of the Hope Hall (later re-styled as the Everyman Bistro) where a curious group of young experimentalists were gathering. 'There they were, these strange people,' Mike recalls, 'Adrian Henri, Roger McGough, John Gorman – he was a telephone engineer, who knew how to make free phone calls all over the world – the painter Sam Walsh. It didn't have a name, it was just a collection of people. In fact it was originally called the Merseyside Arts Festival.

'We attracted this underground movement: Ginsberg and the beat poetry was getting to Liverpool then. Merseybeat was going on at the same time. We're doing this up in Hope Street, our kid and the beat groups were down in the centre of town, in the Cavern. We're near the art school and the university. That's your marketplace. So our thing was different: it was poetry, art, comedy, rhythm and blues. We'd go into town to see the Beatles and sometimes they'd come up to see us.'

One day the TV people came to Liverpool to investigate these mixed-media happenings. McCartney, by now trading as Mike McGear, was performing comic sketches with a loose grouping called the Liverpool One Fat Lady All-Electric Show. It was the TV people who picked a trio from the chaos: in Gorman, McGough and McGear they'd found a talented clown, a bespectacled intellectual and a good-looking boy whose brother was in the Beatles. The new group took its name, the Scaffold, from a Miles Davis record.

'We were satirists,' says McCartney. 'Our main thing was to comment on life. A ladies' barber, a Post Office engineer and an English teacher, jobs for life, and they dangled this carrot, said "Would you like to go on the telly?" So all these serious jobs, we just jacked them in. We realised that when comedy got to a wider audience it would be good to include music. We couldn't do rock'n'roll because we couldn't sing or play instruments. But we had this Cockney dirge, "2day's Monday", and George Martin was interested in producing it. We liked that idea, not because of the Beatles but because he did the Goons. We went on *Juke Box Jury* with it and Spike Milligan said, If there was a comedy chart this would go to Number 1.

'Now that we were involved with George Martin and EMI we went to Brian Epstein and said, You've got all the pop groups, but can you do a theatre comedy group? He goes "My dear boy!" – 'cos he was a failed actor – "Of *course*. We'd *love* to have you aboard." So we thought, with his enormous NEMS agency we had nothing to lose.'

But the Scaffold were frustrated by Epstein's stalling over their next single, 'Goodbat Nightman,' built around McGough's wry commentary on the Batman craze then raging. 'It was released too late. Died a death. We got disillusioned with Brian after that. I went out with him in Wheeler's in London and said "Brian, it's like a racetrack and we're on the outside. All your heavyweights, the Beatles and Cilla and Gerry are on the inside. It's just not working for us." He says, "Oh I quite agree, Michael." I felt like hitting him, to tell you the truth. So we left.

'There was this other song I'd written where we'd thank the audience for coming along: "Thank you very much for keepin' the seats warm" and so on, just to close our show. So we recorded "Thank U Very Much", a good strong track. We had a hit there – it was Harold Wilson's favourite record – and it got us on the telly in a major way. *Top of the Pops!*'

By November 1968, Paul was no longer the only McCartney brother to top the charts: the Scaffold scored a Christmas Number 1 with 'Lily the Pink'. The song was just as insanely memorable as 'Thank U Very Much'. And thanks to Lily, the Scaffold were propelled from a world of fringe theatre groups and college satire fans, on to the lucrative cabaret circuit. 'We'd created this monster of success,' says Mike, 'but it was the wrong success and we got disenchanted. You stuck to your songs and played the same bloody thing every night. We were bored and the audience was bored. That's the tragedy of Scaffold, that we were known more for the silly songs because they reached more people, than the stuff we really enjoyed doing, the satirical comedy and the poetry.'

So the Scaffold resigned from pop and submerged their act inside a new ensemble, Grimms: the name came from their initials plus those of Andy Roberts from the Liverpool Scene and Neil Innes and Vivian Stanshall of the Bonzo Dog Band. (It was Mike who'd secured the Bonzos' appearance in the Beatles' *Magical Mystery Tour*.) There were contributions too from Adrian Henri, Brian Patten and others. Grimms' shows were an often inspired collage of rock, comedy and poetry, and a chance for the ex-Scaffolders to rediscover the edgier aspects of their act. But the troupe was unwieldy, bedevilled by drink and personality clashes. One night, as their tour bus reached Huyton, McGear declared, 'Stop the coach, I want to get off. And I did.'

The Scaffold re-appeared a few years later, signed to Warners by Derek Taylor, where Paul McCartney produced a stirring version of the Dominic Behan folk song 'Liverpool Lou'. Mike McCartney would subsequently concentrate on photography; Gorman became a regular on children's TV. McGough remains that rare thing, a genuinely popular poet; in 1996 he collected an OBE from Buckingham Palace on the same day as Cilla Black, while Paul McCartney became a knight of the realm.

If Lime Street was for some the Boulevard of Broken Dreams, then its minstrel-in-residence was Jimmy Campbell. As a songwriter he often took for his setting the train back to Liverpool, following another disastrous encounter with London. Of all the unrecognised talents who fell as anonymous foot soldiers in the 60s beat campaign, Campbell was the best. He was, if you can imagine such a thing, a sort of Scouse Nick Drake; happily he did not die, but his reputation lingers only in the heads of dedicated collectors in far-flung territories. In Liverpool, where he lives to this day, almost nobody knows his music.

Campbell played in one of those innumerable Cavern bands; his was called the Kirkbys, at Bob Wooler's suggestion, after the district they came from. What made them interesting was that they attempted what so few of their peers did, and went psychedelic. They changed their name to the much spacier-sounding 23rd Turnoff – though its cosmic mystery is simply a reference to Junction 23 of the M6, the exit for Liverpool. As 23rd Turnoff they recorded a delicate Campbell song, 'Michelangelo', which should have been among the greatest hits of 1967, but was instead ignored. There is some posthumous justice in the fact it's now regarded as a psychedelic classic by fans of the genre.

The end of the 60s saw a new vogue for sensitive singer–songwriting types, in the manner of James Taylor and the re-vamped Cat Stevens, and with this niche in mind the solo Jimmy Campbell made a series of albums. He was helped by Tony Crane and Billy Kinsley of the Merseybeats and, in between his own records, also played in Kinsley's early 70s band Rockin' Horse. In the space of four or five LPs Campbell wrote perhaps a dozen classics, maybe more. The best of these was an epic production 'Don't Leave Me Now', full of Campbell's specialisms: hurt, rejection, insecurity. It's to be found, if it's to be found at all, on the LP *Half-Baked*, which Campbell deplored for the lavish string arrangements added by the record company – though I find his frail, bony voice benefits from all the sonic upholstery.

Billy Fury covered a few of his songs including 'Green Eyed American Actress' and 'That's Right That's Me', but Campbell's talent was largely unrecognised. The kazoo-blowing George Formby side of his stuff – there is one track called 'Adrian Henri's Party Night (at O'Connor's)' – could be hard to take, but the prevailing tone was of the romantic optimist, forever nursing love's new bruises. A typical title, 'Another Springtime's Passed Me By', finds him pulling out of Euston Station with fresh failures to ponder. If art could be its own reward, though, Jimmy Campbell's story would be one of immense success.

With the glorious exception of *Sgt. Pepper*, the psychedelic years were arid for Liverpool acts. There were minor hits in 1966 – 'Lady Jane' and 'Dear Mrs Applebee' – for a singer called David Garrick, whose publicists claimed he had once sung the opera *Pagliacci* at the Cavern, for a bet, and that his interests included Buddhism, stamp collecting and Arabic. His LP, *A Boy Called David*, is hopeless.

What's significant is that Garrick was backed on stage by a Liverpool/Welsh band called the Iveys. With a few line-up changes, they became Badfinger, and their story is the saddest and most terrible of all. They're remembered best for a hit record they did not write, 'Come and Get It', which was a gift from Paul McCartney. Yet they're seldom linked with a classic song they did write – 'Without You' – because the hit version went to someone else. If Badfinger have earned themselves any kind of place in rock mythology, then it's for something else entirely.

The bleak and best-known fact about Badfinger is that the band's two principal songwriters, Pete Ham and Tom Evans, both hanged themselves. Pushed to the brink of despair, they shared a soul-destroying sense of personal failure that tormented them beyond endurance. Ham and Evans' suicides have always cast a macabre, backwards shadow across the music they made.

In 1966 the Iveys were a Swansea club band. But destiny arrived one fateful night, in the unlikely shape of a silver-haired Liverpudlian called Bill Collins. He road-managed the Mojos, whose line-up at this stage included his son, Lewis. One evening in Wales the Iveys supported the Mojos, and Bill liked what he heard, especially the sweet, imploring voice of their sandy-haired lead singer, Pete Ham.

Visiting the Welsh boys at their parents' homes, Bill Collins persuaded the Iveys to give up their day jobs and move to London, where they and the Mojos would share a communal house in Golders Green. Here they got the gig with David Garrick. Newly togged up in Swinging London finery, the four young Iveys were Carnaby Street dolly boys, with high Regency collars and back-combed bird's nest hair. When Dai Jenkins, the guitarist, grew homesick for Swansea, Bill Collins replaced him with a contact from Liverpool, the 20-year-old Tom Evans. Possessed of dark, gypsy good looks, Evans was more boisterous than the gentle Pete Ham. But the two men hit it off. A friend from those Golders Green days, Viv Jones, recalls: 'Tom coming into the group really changed things. He was a very strong personality, who didn't always go along with Bill, whereas the Swansea boys were very much "Yes Bill, whatever you say." Tom was more streetwise.' On a small tape recorder the two men wrote songs together by the dozen.

The big break came through Collins' connections at the Beatles' new Apple label. Through his friendship with the Beatles' assistant Mal Evans, he got a tape to the band themselves. Paul McCartney was encouraging, though he doubted there was a hit single there. George Harrison was more positive, and declared that Apple should sign them. John Lennon agreed.

There was soon a feeling that the Beatles might be grooming the Iveys as a band in their own image. The resonance of Pete and Tom's harmonies, and the quartet's interplay of plaintive melodies with sweaty rock'n'roll, could not have been lost on the masters of Apple. The bass player, Ron Griffiths, recalls: 'The ultimate goal was to get a recording contract. But to get one from Apple was *really* exciting. You'd walk in the door and trip over James Taylor's legs. I was in the studio the day they were recording "Get Back" upstairs. Yet we were still living in Golders Green, getting £8 a week each.'

At Apple's prompting they found a new name, Badfinger. However Apple was collapsing around them. With the Beatles hardly speaking to each other any more, the label sank into inertia, and Badfinger were left in limbo. Ron Griffiths: 'We'd been submitting songs of varying quality to Apple and they metaphorically binned it. So I bleated to one of the music magazines that the Beatles weren't giving us any assistance. Paul McCartney read this article. He'd been approached to do songs for *The Magic Christian* [a movie starring Ringo with Peter Sellers] and he'd already written "Come and Get It" for the film. So he came to meet us all at Golders Green. We were awestruck.'

Produced by Paul, who also played piano, "Come and Get It" was a Top 10 hit on both sides of the Atlantic in the first months of 1970, propelling Badfinger to overnight celebrity. By the time they appeared on *Top of the Pops* to promote it, however, their line-up had already changed. Poor Ron Griffiths had effectively become the Pete Best of Badfinger, his crime being to marry his pregnant girlfriend.

Ron returned to Wales and a job on the factory floor, while the radio was still playing the hit record he had appeared on. To replace him, Bill Collins once more looked to Liverpool, and a guitarist called Joey Molland. To accommodate the newcomer, Tom Evans switched to Ron's old role on bass, occasionally using the Hofner Violin model made iconic by Paul McCartney. Now that the Beatles were officially disbanding, Badfinger came to look like the anointed successors. An *NME* piece from the time has the band posing for shots in the Cavern; the writer marvels at Joey Molland's 'incredible facial similarity to the pensive side of Paul McCartney'. It's left to the cautious Pete Ham to plead, 'We're a first Badfinger, not a second anybody!' But in 1970 the question of a 'new Beatles' was a global obsession, and for Badfinger there was no escape.

A little-noticed track on their first album was Tom and Pete's 'Without You'. Pete composed the verses ('I can't forget this evening, and your face as you were leaving . . .') after a tiff with his girlfriend. For his part, Tom had a chorus in search of a song: 'I can't live, if living is without you.' The partners combined their respective scraps and duly made a song from them. A year later when they were recording again, the American singer Harry Nilsson – himself a longstanding Beatle pal – came into the room to introduce himself. He invited the band next door to hear something he had just finished. Badfinger were understandably amazed by what they heard. Lushly orchestrated and passionately sung, Nilsson's version of 'Without You' elevates the song to new and majestic levels. Among the most enduring pop singles of all time, it's been covered by dozens more artists, and in 1994 it was a global hit all over again, this time for Mariah Carey.

For the moment, all looked sunny in Badfinger land. Band members played on Lennon's *Imagine* sessions, Ringo's hit 'It Don't Come Easy' and George's solo album *All Things Must Pass*. From sharing a suburban house in Golders Green, they went on to rent an actual stately home. After the years of struggle and frustration, they were famous, respected, working in harmony with each other, and looking forward to a fabulous future.

But there were warning signs. Though it's much admired by US fans of British powerpop, Badfinger's melodic and versatile approach was going out of style in their homeland, where the post-Beatles audience was falling for glam rock, prog rock or teenybop. The band turned to America, and Bill Collins found them a US manager called Stan Polley, who promised they would soon be millionaires.

At Polley's behest, Badfinger toured America constantly. However Apple disliked the next album and rejected it. The day was saved only when George Harrison stepped forward, and volunteered to produce the second attempt. The gem of these new sessions was a Pete Ham song, 'Day After Day', featuring a slide guitar part by George, and it gave Badfinger their third worldwide hit single. In February, 1972, 'Day After Day' was in the US Top 5, rubbing shoulders with Nilsson's version of 'Without You'. It seemed that nothing could now go wrong for Badfinger.

Yet their days at Apple were numbered. With its founders scattered and absent, the label became moribund. Polley took his band to Warners, and reassured the boys that fortune was just around the corner. But it was a corner that Badfinger never seemed to turn. Joey Molland and Tom Evans grew increasingly suspicious of Polley. Evans once recalled: 'I started demanding things. I figured I wouldn't see the money so I might as well get something. I wanted a house and a Porsche: I crashed it but I kept the house. We were treated like kids when it came to money.'

Suddenly, Warners pulled the next album off the market, claiming financial irregularities. To the bewilderment of the band, they were now being sued by their record company for the return of money they had never received. It was a mortal blow. Pete Ham was devastated by

Badfinger's predicament. By now he lived in Weybridge, in Surrey, where his near neighbour was Tom Evans. On the night of 23 April 1975 the two men went out drinking, and discussed their problems. When Tom gave him a lift home, in the early hours of the morning, Pete left him with the words, 'Don't worry, I know a way out.'

On the following morning, 24 April, his partner Anne awoke to find that Pete had not come to bed. She went downstairs to the garage, where he would sometimes work on his music through the night. It was here that she discovered his lifeless body, hanging from a rope tied to a beam. Nearby was an upturned stool, and a half-empty bottle of wine. First on the scene was Tom Evans, contacted by the distraught Anne; he then informed the police. Later, Anne noticed something else in the garage. It was a hand-written note, which said:

Anne
I love you . . . I will not be allowed to love and trust everybody. This is better.
Pete.
PS Stan Polley is a soulless bastard. I will take him with me.

Badfinger disbanded. Their London rehearsal rooms went to a new group called the Sex Pistols. In a grim twist, Molland was recording in LA with Mal Evans, Badfinger's old benefactor, when Mal was shot dead. Disputes about Badfinger's money, especially the songwriters' royalties for 'Without You', grew tortuously complex, with all parties claiming a share. Though the group re-formed, and Tom was getting some money, he was shockingly careless with it. His musical hopes were blighted. He began to talk repeatedly of suicide. Most of all he had never recovered from the death of his soul-mate Pete Ham.

In Surrey, on the night of 18 November 1983, Tom phoned Joey Molland in the States and had one more argument. His wife went to bed. In the morning she found her husband had not joined her. Tom Evans' body was discovered hanging from a tree in his back garden.

7. A CUT ABOVE THE REST

HOW ERIC LED HIS PEOPLE OUT OF THE DARK AGES

Nothing is sadder than the recently fashionable. When the 60s died there was a pervading sense that Liverpool's time had died with them. Pop is always a barometer of Liverpool's self-esteem, second of course to football, and musically the early 70s were a bleak time. The closest Liverpool came to a legendary record was the Kop choir segment on Pink Floyd's *Meddle* album. The fact that Little Jimmy Osmond should score a hit called 'Long Haired Lover from Liverpool' somehow confirmed the worst. Only the tragically unhip Osmonds could still think of Liverpool as a happening reference point.

Giving birth to the Beatles seemed to leave Liverpool exhausted. In the early 1970s a sort of post-natal depression still afflicted the city's music scene. There was a comic rock band called Supercharge, who were good musicians, very likeable and specialised in witty pastiche; they put some life back into the local live circuit with pub residencies; but they were the tail-end of a previous generation and not the start of a new one. And there was certainly nothing of sex, danger or mystery about them. Another success story was a troupe of children called Our Kid, who had a big hit in 1976 called 'You Might Just See Me Cry'. The music was awful, naturally, and nobody I knew could mention them without feeling pain. But they were undeniably authentic. All that corny stuff is very Liverpool.

The true extent of Liverpool's fall from grace, however, could be summed up by saying that in 1972 it wasn't as hip as Wigan. Wigan? That music hall joke of a town down the road? That was a bad state of affairs. And the reason was that all over Lancashire, outside Liverpool's invisible city walls, there was Northern Soul. Like the blues before it, this particular strand of black American music passed Liverpool by. Though the movement grew from Britain's love of Tamla Motown – itself popularised by the Beatles – the passion for rare soul imports really took off in Manchester, especially at the Twisted Wheel, and spread throughout the North-West.

In time the major shrine became the Wigan Casino, and it drew soul pilgrims from across the land. The clubs in Liverpool's city centre were pedestrian affairs, but a few miles out in the sticks you were in a different world – and, frankly, a more exciting one. A final irony was that Liverpool was still playing its old role of music import specialist: some Northern Soul records were arriving via Burtonwood, while the scene's leading DJ, Rob Bellars, was collecting his supplies at the docks.

In the desolation of the 1970s, two very different bands emerged to salvage the pride of the Liverpool music scene. Without them it had threatened to become the same as Anytown, UK. And if Liverpool cannot be its own thing, then it really ceases to be anything.

This first of these bands were Liverpool's first black pop stars, the Real Thing. Their style was a million miles from the urgent sweatiness of Northern Soul, being instead a radiantly uptown affair in the tradition of the Temptations and Philadelphia funk. They were Britain's best selling black group of the 1970s.

When Eddie Amoo, aged eleven, went to the Empire to watch Frankie Lymon and the Teenagers – a US rock'n'roll vocal act – he got the same charge that his white contemporaries received from the Liverpool visits of guitar-slingers Eddie Cochran and Buddy Holly's Crickets. From neighbourhood *a capella* sessions he moved on to form the Chants with Joey Ankrah. For all their expertise, however, the appeal of close-harmony acts was on the wane in the early 60s, and would not revive until the surge in Motown's popularity later in the decade. By 1976 Eddie joined his brother Chris in the Real Thing, who came to national notice via the TV talent show *Opportunity Knocks*.

They struck up a collaboration with David Essex, touring with him and covering his songs, but broke through on their account with a Number 1 hit 'You to Me are Everything', followed by 'Can't Get by Without You' (Number 2) and followed this up in 1979 with 'Can You Feel the Force'. The Amoo brothers developed as songwriters, and the Real Thing's albums showed a more serious side than those splashy, disco-pleasing singles would indicate: 'Children of the Ghetto', from their Liverpool 8 song-cycle on *4 From 8*, was in the socially-committed vein of latter-day Marvin Gaye and Stevie Wonder; it's since been covered by Courtney Pine and Philip Bailey. A decade later their hits were remixed and became big hits all over again, and they continue to perform to this day.

The second band that stood between Liverpool and extinction was Deaf School.

They were formed at Liverpool Art College, John Lennon's *alma mater*, and, like Supercharge, thrived on the developing pub circuit. They were in the Bowie and Roxy traditions, which had been very big in Liverpool, but there seemed to be dozens of them on stage, like a low-budget cabaret revue. The focal points were a suave young crooner with a moustache, one Enrico Cadillac, and a sexy, upbeat girl in 60s styles called Bette Bright. A guitarist, Clive Langer, looked serious and bespectacled, so you assumed he was the musical genius. There was a comedy vicar called the Reverend Max Ripple, and another lounge lizard named Eric Shark. In fact there was a pile-up of competing looks to accommodate, and a corresponding jumble of musical elements, from Tin Pan Alley to Brecht/Weill cabaret to rock'n'roll satire.

Bette Bright (who was actually Ann Martin, from Whitstable in Kent) remembers: 'We started a band that was supposed to be interesting, just kind of different. Originally there were a lot more people in the band – early on it was a bit ridiculous – but it gradually got more serious. Eventually the numbers kind of whittled down to about eight.'

They won the *Melody Maker*'s Folk/Rock contest in 1975, which led to a record deal with Warners and their 1976 debut LP *2nd Honeymoon*. They were massively backed by the company at first, and launched in America with high hopes all round. However, this was also the year of punk rock, and Deaf School suddenly seemed wrong. I know I divided my time that year between Sex Pistols gigs at the 100 Club in London and trips to Liverpool, and despite my affection for Deaf School I recognised the problem. Theirs was a sort of provincial take on Kings Road camp, whereas the mood of punk was something harsher. Fey pastiche was making way for dirty realism. In the end they made a few more, largely unfocussed albums in the 70s, before dissolving.

Yet Deaf School had been a great thing for Liverpool in two ways. Firstly they were a compelling if chaotic live event, a hundred times more interesting than anything else available in the mid-70s. And secondly, they were the first young group to provide the scene with a post-Beatle focus. A new generation of music fans and would-be musicians found their earliest role models in Deaf School. Its personnel would be the germ of Mathew Street's revival.

Bette Bright: 'I think we were a really good band who happened at a really bad time. Punk came along and because we were so different to all of that – although all the time we were changing – we got lumped with this "art college" image, which is really unpopular. I mean, we were a really great live band. But with all that punk thing, the fact that you were Deaf School, you couldn't do anything right. You couldn't cross the road. It was terrible. And that used to really piss me off.

'The way we went about things I don't think we'd ever commercially have been successful. When we started out it was the pub bands like

[Ian Dury's group] the Kilburns that we really liked, and we only set our sights at about that level. And a lot of the time the record company wanted us to compromise, for example to change the name because the BBC wouldn't play us. It got to the stage where there was a lot of talent in that band that couldn't be used. It was better to split up and let people continue along their own paths.'

They were in fact an impressive nursery for talent. Steve Lindsey, who liked to call himself Mr Average on account of his semi-detached Bebington upbringing, went on to form the Planets. The drummer Tim Whittaker was a gifted artist and, as a drummer, hugely admired by local players like the Bunnymen's Pete DeFreitas. Sadly, he died in 1996. Steve Allen, the former Enrico Cadillac, would later found Original Mirrors with Ian Broudie, and is nowadays a music industry big-shot, having become Senior A&R Director at WEA/London's Eternal label, where his successes have included Eiffel 65. Clive Langer would become one of the best-known producers of the next decade, working with Madness, Teardrop Explodes and Elvis Costello (with whom he wrote the immortal 'Shipbuilding').

Bette Bright went on to make some fine pop tracks, in her inimitably excitable vocal style, including 'Hello I Am Your Heart', 'When You Were Mine' and 'My Boyfriend's Back'.

Derek Taylor, who signed the band to Warners, told me: 'I had one or two failures. I had Deaf School. I worked very enthusiastically for Deaf School, because I thought they were fabulous, and I used to bore the pants off people about them. But I haven't the sort of voice that lingers in people's minds. It's got a certain pitch and I can see people thinking, Why doesn't he stop? But I won't forget Deaf School. They were a great group, we knew that, you knew that, Liverpool knew that. So I'd be going "Deaf School! Deaf School! Listen to Deaf School! Like The Byrds, these are not people who will ever be forgotten. They may not become rich and they may not become famous. But remember, you heard it here first!"

'You have to have faith in your own judgement. Long after it was all over, one of them told me, "We were always too big, there was always too many of us, we were all over the place." I said, "Well, there was always that risk, you were too expensive to transport, every fare counted, and Warners spent a lot of money." But that didn't mean that they weren't worth pushing, because they had real merit.'

When Liverpool roused itself once more, salvation came from another cellar in Mathew Street, directly opposite the rubble-filled remains of the Cavern.

Roger Eagle had already earned himself a niche in musical legend through his time as a DJ at the Twisted Wheel Club in Manchester. He'd worked there as long ago as 1963, using his boundless knowledge and enthusiasm to bring rhythm and blues to a new audience. In the process, he effectively laid the foundations for Northern Soul. Like any self-consciously underground scene, the Twisted Wheel crowd defined themselves in opposition to the pop charts – which is how Eagle came to mark 1963 with a ritual onstage burning of the Beatles' second LP. Equally symbolic was Roger's gesture the night the Rolling Stones stopped by: they heard him play the original US versions (in precisely the same order) of each track on their debut LP.

Eagle was really a missionary at heart, fired by violent passions for the music he believed in. Tall enough 'to wind the Liver Clock' as Liverpudlians say, he'd actually been born in Oxford, was a distant relative of George Bernard Shaw, and drifted North to the Twisted Wheel, where he found his real vocation in life. He took to managing bands and moved across to Merseyside, where he began promoting shows at the old Liverpool Stadium. This backstreet venue had formerly been a boxing arena, where dockers roared nightly ('Hit 'im Joe, 'e's not a holy picture!'), and seediness still hovered over it. I used to queue for Eagle's gigs, and I'd watch Allan Williams, still on the scene, gamely working the line with a fistful of flyers and a mouthful of hyperbole.

With Deaf School's road manager, Ken Testi, he schemed to create a club of his own. Roger told the *Melody Maker* he was dreaming of a club like New York's Bottom Line – discerning yet adventurous, offering bands a stage between pub gigs and major theatres. He was eerily clairvoyant as to what the new place might achieve and what its problems would be. To run a club in Liverpool, he said, needs someone 'who is very heavy or very lucky or can strike up a relationship with the people who are heavy. There's almost nobody capable of doing that. I don't know if I am but I'm gonna have a pretty good shot at it. You've got your law on one side, the drug squad over there, your gangsters over there and you've gotta go down the middle. That's basically the reason there's no breeding ground for groups.'

Then he brought in a graduate of Liverpool University called Pete Fulwell. Pete had come into the music business through designing posters – an early Led Zeppelin effort had brought him to the attention of their manager Peter Grant, who became something of a mentor. They'd acquired premises in Mathew Street, a venue which had, in fact, recently been trading as the New Cavern . . . Pete Fulwell: 'We'd bought the Cavern, a world brand! We could have called it the Cavern, but with typical arrogance went, "No, this is us. This is now. We'll carry the spirit on but it's got to be ours." So it was Eric's. Ken Testi came up with the name, partly as a spoof on 60s discos like Samantha's, and partly because it was a name he'd use pulling women at parties, pretending he was someone called Eric.'

Eric's opened in October 1976 with appearances by the Stranglers, the Runaways, the Count Bishops and the Sex Pistols. The club décor was left over from a previous incarnation, the Revolution, featuring gigantic papier-mache busts of Fidel Castro and Che Guevara. Those icons of Marxist-Leninism would presumably have looked with approval on the new proprietors, who were not the world's greatest capitalists. 'Very early on,' says Fulwell, 'we decided it wasn't a business. To make it a commercial business would have stopped it being what we wanted it to be. So we decided, "Fuck it, the job is to keep it flying as long as possible," knowing it was going to crash.'

For Roger and Pete, in fact, Eric's became a grand experiment, or a sort of human laboratory. And their prize specimen was a girl called Jayne Casey.

Casey was a refugee from children's homes across the water, in the Wirral. She arrived in mid-70s Liverpool with a mission to re-invent herself. Like many free spirits in that post-hippy, pre-punk lull, she turned to hairdressing: 'A Cut Above The Rest, it was called. They employed me because I looked like Marilyn Monroe. I had gorgeous blonde curls and big tits. So I shaved me head! Oh dear. All our posse met at that shop. Because I was bald I was on reception in the window. It was a real macho culture at the time, and because of the way I looked you attracted people to you who were looking for something else.'

Within weeks she'd collected Pete Burns, who would later form Dead Or Alive: 'He was about fourteen, he used to hang around until we gave him a Saturday job. We sacked him after a few weeks because he was just so rude. But after we sacked him I'd see him around, and he was so ironic, and so scarily rude, that you kind of got on to his humour. I got him back to work at the shop and there was another girl there, called Lyn, who became Pete's wife.'

Her next acquisition was another teenage misfit, Holly Johnson, an effeminate, Bowie-worshipping boy from Wavertree. Jayne then left the hairdressers to set up a second-hand clothes stall, Aunt Twacky's, in that obscure backwater with the strange allure, Mathew Street. Yet another young boy, this one called Paul Rutherford, would come along to gaze at her. Eventually his mother arrived and persuaded Jayne to let him work there. Holly and Paul would one day form the core of Frankie Goes To Hollywood. Others in the gang included the future actress Margi Clarke, from Kirkby, and her brother the budding playwright Frank Clarke. With Pete and Lyn Burns, these acquaintances became spectacular apparitions on Liverpool's intolerant streets. Their preference for gay hang-outs – the Lisbon, Sadie's, the Masquerade – was a sexual choice for some of them, and a bid for safe haven by all of them. Their very existence testifies that Liverpool's punk scene had significant gay beginnings.

Jayne attracted the attention of a very different figure, too: the ageing veteran of Mathew Street's original golden age, Cavern DJ Bob Wooler. 'He used to follow me round when I first hit town,' she says. 'I had a bald head and the street would stop when I walked down it. I noticed this guy who kept following me – I thought he was a pervert! – but eventually he came up and introduced himself. He was really interesting because I was so young and he was full of the stories of that period. He said, "There's been a girl like you in town before," and it was Thelma McGough. He said she opened the first boutique in the city and she was the first girl to wear a mini dress. He used to tell us stories of the kids who'd been out in town before us, because we thought we'd invented it.'

It was only a matter of time before Jayne and her menagerie were noticed by the would-be impresarios who'd bought the club up the street. As Jayne recalls: 'Roger comes in to my stall and says, "Got a club openin' on Saturday night! I want you and all your mates to come!" What a man. Normally we couldn't get into gigs because we looked so weird. We had to go to these scummy little gay clubs down in basements, though they didn't really like letting a girl in. We were put off by his arrogance, but at the same time mesmerised that somebody wanted us to go to his club. "Oh my God, he wants us!" '

Eric's drew a diverse crowd. There were even matinee shows, without a drinks license, for younger teens. Its toilets were legendarily squalid, but the club became a daytime drop-in centre as well as niterie, under the benign supervision of Doreen Allen on the door. The night the Clash played, the audience included eighteen-year-old Philip Hayes: 'My Mum had got me the biker jacket for me birthday, the black leather jacket like the Clash wore, so I go to the gig really excited in me brand new jacket. Me mate, who had long hair down to his waist, Jayne Casey cut a bit of his hair off to put on the front of her head, 'cos it was lovely bright carrot-coloured. He was mortified!

'After the gig I'm at the bar and there's Joe Strummer, he buys me a pint. I'm like, Oh that was so excitin'! And he says, "C'mon, we're goin' to the Swinging Apple for a bevy." I was all for it, knockin' about with the Clash. But me mate wouldn't go with me, with his long hair, he goes, "It's a skinhead club, we'll get battered." So that sparked following the Clash, bought their album in Probe Records, all in that same area. Probe was where you got all your indicators from, learned what was cool.'

But punk was not the only flavour available. Reggae was strongly favoured by the club's DJs, while Roger took every opportunity to extend the booking policy. The writer Kevin Sampson remembers, 'It was very influenced by New York. There were more musical rows in Liverpool over the Velvet Underground versus the Doors than over the Clash versus the Pistols. My memory of sitting in Eric's, trying to make a pint last forever, was of the most played record on the jukebox being "Suzanne" by Leonard Cohen. Everyone goes on about seeing the White Riot tour or the Stranglers, but I remember seeing Matumbi there, Prince Far-I or Rockin' Dopsie and His Cajun Twisters, apart from the Adverts and 999 and the Clash. And I wouldn't value one above the other.'

The Lightning Seeds' Ian Broudie: 'Growing up at that time, when Eric's was going, definitely affected me. More than the Beatles, in a funny way. I'm very influenced by Patti Smith and Television and the New York groups, even if no one hears it in my records. Jonathan Richman as well. Even the Lovin' Spoonful. They all connect up.'

Pete Fulwell: 'There was a strong affinity with New York; we were always being compared by the Americans to CBGB. Punk was part of the mix, but our perception was that punk was wider than the leather jackets and spiky Mohicans. It ranged from Jonathan Richman to the Damned. It was an attitude rather than a dress code. It was a brief period when people were open to things.'

The musician Paul Simpson: 'It was kind of an art school scene, not that any of us went to art school, but Eric's was quite unique. It didn't look like other punk clubs. We didn't dress in bondage gear. Everyone was more creative. Everyone looked very individual. We weren't following a London blueprint.'

Fulwell: 'In one of the last conversations I had with Roger, he was saying he'd only just come to terms, finally, with the fact that it was a punk club. Because that wasn't what we'd set out to do. The intention was to create a music club, period, that presented the best popular music and the cutting edge as well. So there would be jazz and folk and blues and R&B as well as rock. But at the time we started it, there was this huge wave starting to break, and that over-rode everything. We ended up just surfing along on the top of it.'

* * *

Eric's spawned a succession of beautiful monsters, who would outlive the club and perpetuate its memory. Yet the classic Eric's creation would rise and fall within the club's own lifespan. This was the band that Jayne Casey fronted, Big In Japan, whose story involves another extraordinary visitor to the city . . .

Bill Drummond was a tall, handsome Scot from a small town in Galloway. His travels brought him to Liverpool, where he worked at the Everyman Theatre building stage sets. From here he moved down to Mathew Street to work in Ken Campbell's Science Fiction Theatre Of Liverpool – part of the arts, market and café complex known as the Liverpool School of Language, Music, Dream And Pun. Outside was its celebrated bust of Carl Jung – destined, alas, for decapitation. It was the beginning of Bill's mystic attachment to Liverpool in general and Mathew Street in particular: he decided Jung's 'Pool of Life' could be precisely traced to an ancient spring, located below a manhole cover not far from the Grapes pub. And while Bill made scenery, a young guitarist called Ian Broudie provided music.

Drummond made another key acquaintance when he went to watch Dr Feelgood play the Stadium, and encountered Roger Eagle quelling the crowd. He agreed to lend Roger his handyman skills in setting up Eric's, and thus became part of the clique now assembling there. It was Deaf School's Clive Langer who suggested he form Big In Japan. (Their name came from a favoured joke in music circles, used to describe struggling acts who saved face by claiming to be really successful somewhere else.) They'd last for only a year, but their importance is astonishing.

'One day,' remembers Jayne, 'this weird guy came into Aunt Twacky's when I had the bald head and this pyramid eye make-up and he started freaking out, saying "Oh my God, this is amazing!" It turned out it was Ken Campbell, and he'd come to Liverpool to put on this play the *Illuminati*. He decided there and then to put his play on in the café that we had in the building. He brought Keith Allen in. Bill Drummond was the set designer, and Ken wanted me to be the singer. I said, "Get lost, I can't sing," but we'd get drunk and they'd egg me on. So I took a part in the play and got to know Bill. Now he was putting a band together and asked me to be the singer. He said, "It's not about singing, it's about the way you look." We had two songs, Big In Japan, and one where I read out the charts! I said I'd only keep on doing it if my friend Holly could join.'

The band rehearsed using Deaf School's gear at Eric's. Pete Fulwell: 'Roger and I worked together with Big In Japan, in as much as it could be managed, because they were all strong characters. We helped, but "managed" is too formal a word.' These characters now included Bill Drummond, Ian Broudie, Jayne Casey and Holly Johnson. Though the group lasted for little more than a year, 1977 to 1978, others who would pass through the ranks included Budgie and Dave Balfe. In fact, considering the destinies of these individuals, Big In Japan was a kind of academy to rival Eton and Oxbridge.

Wealth and fame awaited them all in different degrees, which was not the fate you would expect of such a shambolic outfit – they were much more playful than their counterparts in London punk, and quite the opposite of careerist. Budgie would eventually join the Banshees, becoming Siouxsie's drummer and partner. After the Teardrop Explodes, Dave Balfe became a record mogul who made his fortune from Blur's label Food Records. The fates of Broudie, Drummond, Johnson and Casey we'll explore shortly. Collectively, though, they were a sort of billion dollar quintet.

Jayne: 'Bill didn't play that much but he was very conceptual, had loads of great ideas, and I think Holly and I together wrote the best songs, but our songs would often get thrown out because Bill and Ian would try and dominate. Years later Bill said, "We should have just stuck with yours and Holly's songs, because we'd created this character for Big In Japan but kept trying to make it a proper band, whereas the value of Big In Japan was really at the other end of the scale." '

Did she think they were an influence on the bands that formed at Eric's after them? 'We had an influence because we were definitely *not* what they wanted to be! I was so arrogant and really horrible. We were the most damaged children society had turned out that year! And we all just happened to be on stage together. And that was most probably a bit of a driving point for the other bands. The competition drove other people forward. What they loved about us was that loads of kids were fed up with that narrow way of looking at things, and we turned up looking as we did, doing what we did. To them it was like a gateway. They just clung to us; it wasn't that they loved us, but they loved what we stood for, the way we weren't going to go for that working class macho shit.'

Eric's escaped involvement in Liverpool's thuggish club wars: the city's night-life had been the scene of backdoor intimidation and murderous rivalry since time immemorial. 'Partly,' explains Fulwell, 'we weren't in the club business; we weren't competing with the other clubs. We were seen as music biz rather than club biz.' Eric's was also under the benevolent eye of a powerful local figure, a 'Mr Big with a Rolls Royce and various bits of armoury in the glove compartment. We were under his protection. And I think we were his pets, really, a place to take his mates down to the zoo to see these curious creatures.

'What we weren't protected from, though, was the politics of the police and clubland, and I think we were a soft target when they wanted to appear to be taking action. I don't think they had the intention of closing us down, they just didn't realise how fragile we were.'

The big bad city could not be pacified forever. I was in the club one night when the police raided. It was an intimidating sight. The music was turned off and sergeants strolled about in the gloom, brandishing the 'staffs', or nightsticks, that were a peculiarity of the Liverpool force. Constables, meanwhile, moved from table to table, demanding details of the food we had eaten and, strangely, taking little test-tube samples of the beer in our glasses. Any drinker without food was cautioned that an offence may have been committed under the licensing laws. Eric's was just one of 235 known late-drinking clubs, and probably the most peaceful. But clubland was causing more concern than ever in Liverpool, after the case of four assailants who had visited a suburban house and tried to remove the victim's feet. The trial had failed to secure any convictions.

'I tried to have a relationship with them,' Fulwell says of the police. 'They came one night and I was asking them if there were any problems, was there anything we should be doing. I remember one of them saying, "I really fancy a drink." I said, "Well, let me take you down to the bar. What do you fancy?" He says, "Oh no, I can't drink alcohol when I'm on duty." I said, "Do you fancy a Coke, then?" It wasn't until afterwards that I learned that was code – a "drink" wasn't a drink. But we weren't part of that world. Two weeks later came the big raid.'

The 'big raid' occurred in March 1980, when the Psychedelic Furs were playing, supported by Pete Wylie's Wah! This time the police brought dogs to the party as well as sticks. According to a report of the time: 'Three van-loads of people were taken away and eleven arrested. Two members of the band were arrested, then they ripped the seating in the food bar with razors, punched people in the stomach, and emptied the contents of their handbags on to the floor.'

Pete: 'The reality was that for several years we'd been trading at a significant deficit and juggling with our creditors. The police did one big raid – why they did it was anybody's guess, certainly the way they acted was less than respectful. But the impact of that raid was on our creditors, who thought the police were going to close us down, so they all wanted their money at once. Wylie did his "I Fought the Law and the Law Won" sub-set – one of the great moments in the club's history.

'I think nobody was more surprised than the police that the house of cards collapsed But economically, it just didn't stand. Most of the time there was just a handful of people there. Plus there was the old joke about how many people does it take to change a light bulb at Eric's? Thirty. One to change the bulb and 29 on the guest list . . .'

A protest demo in town by Eric's regulars got some publicity but the club was already dead. My last part in the saga, some months later, was to meet the Psychedelic Furs' singer off the London train at Lime Street and show him the way to court to answer the drug charges. He'd made a brave attempt at smartness, but could not hide his nerves. He'd been advised there would be no point in pleading Not Guilty.

Roger Eagle's dreams survived the demise of Eric's. I came across him at the bar of another club a while later. The trouble with Eric's, he decided, was that local economics were against them – even at the lowest prices, it was still too expensive for most kids, especially without a name band to tempt them. His next ambition was to open a joint where young punks would hear Ornette Coleman, the jazz player, or even see similar music legends play live. It would be healthy for the next generation of artists, he argued, like his current discovery Mick Hucknall of the Frantic Elevators. He was initiating Mick in classic soul, just like the stuff he'd played back in the Twisted Wheel, but Roger couldn't move the group from Manchester to Liverpool without them losing their dole.

Sure enough I would sometimes run into Hucknall at Roger's next club, Adam's, where the live attractions included soul legend Junior Walker. 'Roger was on a mission to promote soul,' says Fulwell. 'He pumped music into people.' And the future star of Simply Red was probably his most successful student: Doctor Eaglestein's Monster. 'Roger was always teaching you,' adds Jayne Casey, 'but in a way that was not oppressive to a young person. He had a way of inspiring you. It was an amazing experience to be educated by Roger Eagle. He adopted me as his daughter.' According to Bill Drummond, Eagle summarised his philosophy as 'Brutality, Religion and a Dance Beat . . . Without these three ingredients pop music is nothing. All great pop music, from John Lee Hooker to the Bay City Rollers, from Captain Beefheart to Augustus Pablo, from the Buzzcocks to Johnny Kidd and the Pirates has it.' Sadly, in 1999 he died of cancer, aged 56. Bill Drummond constructed a memorial in the form of a cabinet housing what remained of Roger's record collection.

'Eric's belonged to a lot of people,' is Pete Fulwell's verdict, 20 years on. 'You're seeing that expressed now, with all the different memories. A lot of people felt ownership of it, and that's what it needed to make it work. A lot of people have a strong sense that they made it work, they led it. I was interested in scenes. And here was a great opportunity to watch, like in a laboratory. That opportunity hadn't existed since Merseybeat when Bill Harry covered the Cavern.

'It's a fascinating thing, the way scenes develop. In different cities, at different times, to different degrees, you have locations where a curious interaction takes place between opinion leaders, fashion, music enthusiasts, subversives and conformists, a melting pot. In the early stages there is a management role, providing a stage for it, exposing it to itself through the media – and you played a part in that, as did Tony Wilson at Granada TV – that location sees itself reflected through the media and begins to be driven by that reflection. But after a while it becomes self-managing, it tells you what it wants. Seeing it as a venue where bands play to an audience, and the effect of those bands on that audience, misses the point. The people in a scene are at least as important as the people on the stage. The scene that springs up – that's the wondrous place.'

It was more than pride that led Eric's owners to reject the New Cavern name. It would have repelled the people they hoped to attract. There was no particular hostility to the Beatles in the 1970s, but among the young there was a strong sense that they belonged to the previous decade; it was time for the next generation to assert itself. The solitary example of Fab nostalgia then in evidence, Dooley's statue of *Four Lads Who Shook the World*, was just above Eric's entrance, by the old Cavern sign, and it was considered a bit of a joke. A cycle of years must be completed before the past can be assimilated. In 1977, The Beatles were just too recent.

Holly Johnson expressed the ambivalence felt in his age-group towards the Adrian Henri generation in Liverpool: 'In our opinion they were the Boring Old Farts or Hippies . . . They had all known the Beatles; "yawn, yawn" was our attitude. Although there was a hidden respect for and curiosity about what that generation had achieved, we were too cool to applaud those who we thought applauded themselves.'

Punk was not the only music on Eric's menu, but it was punk that offered the quickest route to forming your own band – just as skiffle had done for the Merseybeat boys a generation earlier. This time around, the legendary visitation was not by Lonnie Donegan, but by the Clash.

The night they played Eric's, 5 May 1977, was to be the turning point in Liverpool's musical fortunes.

In the crowd that night were two boys who had known each other from school, Pete Wylie and Ian McCulloch, and a student from the Midlands called Julian Cope. By evening's end they were all acquainted and resolved to found their own group, the Crucial Three. It was a characteristic of the Eric's scene that grand plans might be hatched, reputations inflated and feuds pursued – all without an actual note of music being played. Sure enough the Crucial Three would not play a single gig or make a record. In fact, never were three egos less destined to co-exist on a permanent basis. However, of all the imaginary bands in Mathew Street that year, the Crucial Three would at least live up to their name. McCulloch formed Echo and the Bunnymen, Cope the Teardrop Explodes and Wylie a series of groups that were more or less called Wah!

8. THE SKY ALL HUNG WITH JEWELS
ECHO AND THE BUNNYMEN

The first time I saw Echo and the Bunnymen play they were like a little clockwork band. Three withdrawn individuals, just about kept together by a drum machine perched on a plastic-backed chair. That night in the Everyman Bistro, the new group played their frail, tick-tock tunes, and looked as if they might split up on the spot if someone asked them to. Will Sergeant says of those early gigs: 'Whenever we broke a string, that was it. We had to go off.' Yet there was a definite magic being born. They got better by the day, and nearly became the biggest group in the world. Sometimes I think they were the second-best band to come out of Liverpool.

At first I'd been attracted by the absurd name: as with their friends the Teardrop Explodes, these soft and voluptuous titles were against the grain of punk harshness and brittle new wave. Liverpool was turning into a world of its own again. Though they were not to discover drugs until much later, both groups seemed to be taking psychedelia as their musical starting point – picking up the baton where their Merseybeat predecessors had let it drop. Down in London, though, it was Echo and the Bunnymen's name that made my employers, the *NME*, reluctant to cover them at all.

Given the go-ahead, I went to meet them on Orange Lodge Day, 1979. The town was a mass of cheering crowds and flag-waving children, all pipes and drums and police-leave cancelled, the muggy summer air thick with beer breath and jubilation. Arriving at the Everyman I met Bill Drummond for the first time when he crashed through a door, attempting to carry a speaker cabinet and shake my hand at the same time. We then went to a house nearby where Mac – as McCulloch became known – was getting ready to meet his public. While Les Pattinson (bass) and Will Sergeant (guitar) fretted, Mac displayed his Olympic-standard talent for late running, taking an age to prepare his hair.

After Big In Japan, Drummond and Dave Balfe concentrated on their own label, Zoo, based in Chicago Buildings, just across Whitechapel from the site of Brian Epstein's NEMS. They offered management as well as production, opening their accounts with debut singles by the

Teardrop Explodes and the Bunnymen. Bill had worried about me seeing the group so early in their development. As it happened, I found the Everyman show just as beguiling as the records I'd heard. But his first words to me when they slouched off stage were, 'Sorry, that was a bloody shambles.' I made a stumbling effort to interview them, not getting much except that Mac's ambition was to become rich and buy France. Nevertheless I went home happy that night. I walked down Hardman Street and watched a chip shop in flames, while a fat Orange Lodge boy played the accordion outside.

The Crucial Three had never quite happened, but its members would all play in the overlapping bands that formed spontaneously around Eric's. McCulloch started the Bunnymen when Julian invited him to support the Teardrop Explodes. Mac – a short-sighted Bowie fanatic, already a pop star in his own mind – recruited Will Sergeant, the brooding guitar boffin, and Les Pattinson, the amiable bass-player who built boats for a living (Les had once had a band called the Jeffs, whose members had to change their names accordingly). Their insularity was instinctive. 'There's a thing between us,' they told me, 'that we do think we are Bunnymen. And another member, a drummer, he might not be a Bunnyman.'

Drummond stepped in after watching their support slot. He fell in love with the name, donated by a friend of the group, and began to conceive of Echo as a Nordic rabbit god and the Bunnymen as his followers. Disturbingly, the cover photo of their debut LP would accidentally feature an evil rabbit head – if you viewed it from the right angle – formed by some gnarled trees and the bass-player's right hand.

They overcame their early mistrust of drummers, acquiring Pete DeFreitas to boost the power of their sound. Even so, DeFreitas sometimes seemed an outsider in the Bunnymen. 'He was in a way,' Les concedes. 'But that was only because he was a public schoolboy. He thought we were the three Stooges. He was from a totally different background, totally different part of the country. But I don't think he knew how much we liked him for that. Me and Will would take the piss out of him. He came from Oxfordshire, so we'd go, "Where's that? Is it by Wales, or something? We should call you Taff." So we did!'

One of their early producers was Ian Broudie, later of the Lightning Seeds. He says, 'Separately, what they're playing didn't seem that great. But somehow, when the four of them touched together, it ignited the blue paper. You could say to them, "Play A to D." They'd all join in and play A to D, and it would just sound great. The four of them created some kind of chemical reaction.'

It was Rob Dickins, later the MD of WEA, who signed them to that company's new imprint Korova, having watched them play the London YMCA with the Teardrop Explodes and Joy Division: 'The singer looked so charismatic,' he remembers. 'He was beautiful. His voice had that Jim Morrison ring to it. The songs weren't well formulated, but you saw "Star" in neon above his head.' Mac was also perfecting his rivalry with Julian Cope. What I remember most about the YMCA night was meeting him in the Gents', and being challenged to deny that the Bunnymen were easily better than the Teardrops.

For a while, nothing stopped the Bunnymen. The first album, *Crocodiles*, was full of atmospheric strangeness; it's worn well, especially the re-worked version of their Zoo single 'Pictures on My Wall', the booming 'Rescue' and the dark psychodrama of 'Villiers Terrace' ('You said people rolled on carpets but I never thought they'd do those things . . .') The next, *Heaven Up Here*, had a fine track in 'All My Colours' – 'the first song where we proved we could connect emotionally,' says McCulloch – that suggested the Bunnymen's strengths lay in dreamy abstractions, not in stadium-pleasing posturing. Another haunting song, 'The Disease', he called 'a kind of anthem for the Liverpool suppressed, for those who saw their potential in human terms and not in terms of having or not having a job.' The best Bunnymen music always was dream-like, with disembodied phrases drifting across the brain. The meaning was fragmented but the emotional tone consistent.

Never knowingly undersold on their own legend, the group were now aspiring to magnificence. Taking his cue from the band's own genius for self-esteem, WEA's Rob Dickins chose to promote *Ocean Rain* with the slogan 'the greatest album ever made'. History might judge otherwise, but the record remains as close as the Bunnymen ever came. Acoustic guitars and gorgeous string arrangements define its sound, key tracks including 'Silver', 'Seven Seas' and their finest composition, 'The Killing Moon'. 'Kissing music, songs to fall in love to,' proclaimed McCulloch of the record's lush romanticism. It was recorded in Paris, after Mac decided he would sing better in the City of Light. But, with typical indolence, he ran out of time and had to add his vocal tracks back home in Liverpool.

On record sleeves they posed amid the splendours of the natural world: mountains, skies, glaciers and lakes. Nothing was cramped, or dingy or mean. Would-be challengers, from U2 to Big Country, were tongue-lashed in McCulloch's interviews. He was Mac The Mouth, and very good at it. He was amazingly vain of his appearance, too, but became a genuine pop pin-up. And there were some fine hits, such as 'The Back of Love' and 'The Cutter'. McCulloch contributed his looks, his low, plaintive moan and mistily poetic lyrics. 'I was everything from existentialist to metaphysical,' he told me years later. 'I never knew what either of them meant. It just meant that I was bluffing: "I've got an English A-level so I'm gonna use it . . ." Since then I've grown to know that everyday language and emotions are better than imagined ones. I've had enough experience of emotional ups and downs to know what I'm writing about.'

Like McCulloch's beloved Liverpool FC, the Bunnymen's legend owed much to a visionary Scottish manager called Bill – in this case Drummond, not Shankly. The city was already high on its own mythology, but it took Bill Drummond to put the place on a ley-line (even if, on closer inspection, it ran only through his head). 'It comes careering in from outer space,' he explained, 'hits the world in Iceland, bounces back up, writhing about like a conger eel, then down Mathew Street in Liverpool where the Cavern Club – and latterly Eric's – is.' The line apparently went on to New Guinea and then back into space. He once dreamed of having the Bunnymen play a gig in Iceland while the Teardrops played in New Guinea – while he stood on the manhole cover in Mathew Street where the cosmic energy line met the Pool of Life.

Just as Drummond saw Liverpool as a cosmic crossroads, not a provincial outpost, so he encouraged the Bunnymen to revel in majestic follies that would become folklore. There was for example the 'Crystal Day' in May 1984, when fans joined the band in a 24-hour 'happening' in Liverpool: apart from a choir recital in the Cathedral, and a gig in St George's Hall, participants had to eat at the group's favourite café, Brian's Diner, take the Mersey Ferry, and attempt a mass bicycle ride in the streets, along a route that Bill had mapped in the shape of Echo the Rabbit God. Another time, bored with tour routine, he planned an itinerary for the boys that took them from New York to the Outer Hebrides to the Albert Hall.

I caught up with them on the Hebrides leg, at a gig on the Isle of Skye. Bad weather had forced me and my photographer, Pennie Smith, to get a taxi right across Scotland from the nearest open airport, Inverness. Our £70 fare would be the talk of Skye for days after; it seemed to induce more reverence in the locals than the band did. Most of the fans, in fact, were outsiders – like the Bunnymen themselves they saw the jaunt as a holiday. Bill swept his hand across the wonderful landscape. Northern grandeur, he told me, was what the Bunnymen represented. 'I always think of the Jam as a housing estate group. That's what they aspire to, they're not reflecting anything that's glorious.' We travelled on by ferry to the Isle of Lewis. After a Stornoway show, Bill drove me up to the ancient stone circle at Callanish, where – in pitch darkness – he lay prostrate in what could have been a burial site at the centre. I know not what primal forces he'd disturbed, but the car's battery seemed to go flat. When we finally moved off, a mysterious rabbit appeared in the headlights, running ahead of us like a spirit guide.

A year or two later, the surprise resignation of Bill Drummond looked like the first wheel dropping off the Bunnymen's bandwagon. 'It was weird,' agrees Will. 'He'd always been the one forcing us to make it more extreme. He took us on to a certain level, then he said, "I don't want to be a manager any more".' Of his decision, Drummond told me, 'I've never been happy with the straightforward thing. One of the reasons for Echo and the Bunnymen not being U2 or Simple Minds is my attitude to things. If I'd been managing the Beatles, instead of playing Shea Stadium I'd have had them playing a week of dates wherever Buddy Holly's plane crashed, to a few cows in celebration of Buddy Holly.'

In 1987 I stopped by the Bunnymen's HQ off Mount Pleasant. There was a new American management team, now, whose brisk manner contrasted with the lethargy I detected in the band themselves. 'They were really good managers,' Mac told me after the inevitable parting of the ways, 'but I don't think they really got the band, or understood how fragile it was at that point. We were breaking apart. The entourage was splintering.' That day, Pete DeFreitas was absent at first: 'Phoned him last night,' someone mumbled. 'Said he'd be comin' but he sounded weirded out.' Pete eventually did arrive, wearing full motorcycle gear and the face of a mildly bewildered flowerpot man. There were still tensions, I learned, about him absconding a while back, throwing himself into a doomed group called the Sex Gods and going on a lurid American 'lost weekend' of rock'n'roll debauchery and regular car crashes. He was accepted back into the fold but not with full-member status.

There were tensions with McCulloch, too, as Will told me later: 'It became horrible, a real us-and-him situation, fuelled by him being out of his head all the time. He's two completely different people. Sometimes he's totally brilliant, another day you just know he's going to be a turd.' Mac was feeling his own brand of pressure: 'It was verging on madness, I was losing me sodding mind. I flew a lot in the last few years, just to get away from the tour bus, get a bit of space for meself. But I was feeling more isolated.'

'It would always start with these little divisions,' remembers Les. 'He was always getting drunk and talking about how we were going to make the greatest thing ever – and the next day he just had a hangover.'

All the same, observes Will, 'that's when we took off in America. We were hot on the heels of U2, we really were.'

The hard fact was that U2, the Dublin joke band of Bunny banter, were becoming hideously successful. The question was, Did the Bunnymen have the drive to even compete? The pressure to get global success manifested itself in the studio, where the band were caught in a crossfire of well-meaning advice. Rob Dickins of WEA recalls several rows about the choice of producers, but remains philosophical: 'They could be contrary, but I'm a fool for that Liverpool charm. As difficult as they can be, it was always funny . . . I was always trying to make them bigger than they perhaps wanted to be. Bill and I thought they would be the biggest thing ever, but I'm not sure they bought that. You can never be accused of selling out if you don't hit the big time. U2 have got a million critics. But if you're Mark E. Smith, you're cool. I've never really gone for that ticket.'

For their part, I think, U2 saw the Bunnymen as a parable of talent wasted through lack of ambition. They would always ask me how the Bunnymen were doing, and express regret that things were not going better. McCulloch recalls the 1980s as 'a difficult decade to keep your integrity in. We never lost ours, but we lost our grip on what was cool. From 1979 to 85 we were the hippest band on the planet, and the best. Then the Howard Jones/Nik Kershaw decade battered us into sub-mission.'

The next few years were messy indeed. McCulloch called a band meeting: 'I said, "Let's all get together and get totally bevvied-up one afternoon. I wanna talk about things." And I basically said we should knock it on the head. Maybe with Bill Drummond around I'd have been talked out of it. But I just didn't have the energy any more.' Will Sergeant took the news without enthusiasm. 'Mac leaving really cheesed us off. We'd done a lot of work to get to that point.' To Mac's surprise, the pub summit did not spell the end of the Bunnymen. The obstinate Sergeant would not let it lie, and recruited a new singer called Noel Burke.

Then came tragedy. A rehearsal was arranged for the new line-up, their first session together. But the drummer never made it. Riding his motorbike up to Liverpool from the South, on 14 June 1989, Pete DeFreitas was killed in a crash at Rugeley, Staffordshire.

As Pete's partner in the rhythm section, Les the bassist felt a special desolation: 'It was like we were into another language together . . . We named my little lad Louis, after Pete's middle name.' (Despite the inter-group rivalry, Julian Cope was always close to Pete, whom he describes as 'peaceful in his head'. For Julian, 'Pete DeFreitas dying was an enormous thing. He was a fantastic inspiration because he was just so out there. He was much more out there than me, I was just fucked up on drugs.')

Les: 'I still think of him. I still think of him almost every day. The longer you live, the more people die around you, and you can't describe it to anyone. Heaven is a place in people's heads. I'm always thinking of Pete, so that's my heaven for him. When Pete died I had this image of him, at the funeral, that he was bouncing from every star, like a satellite, from Australia and back.'

Still, the Bunnymen trundled on, while Mac had a solo career. Neither party was doing well. And the singer had let himself go. 'I could always drink a lot. I was a great drinker. But the greater you get, the more you drink. And the more you drink, the more your head gets done in. My being pissed was coming out as belligerence. I think I started trying to be macho. Not in a rock'n'roll way, just . . . Probably because I grew up feeling like . . . I wasn't the cock of the school, put it that way. Being able to drink a lot makes you feel you've qualified as a proper bloke. The sensitive side to me was getting lost. Instead of being proud of myself, which was how I'd always felt, there was self-pity. You can sell nothing and still be proud of yourself, and that will sustain you. But I knew there were certain songs where I just didn't pay attention. So there was a lot of bev going down, amongst other things. It just became a spiral of sadness. I got scared and used drink to enable me to say, "I'm still right, I'm still great."'

Will and Mac sank their differences and reunited under the name Electrafixion. 'I didn't like the name from day one,' says Mac. 'We'd gone through hundreds of names in rehearsal: but none of them were Echo and the Bunnymen and that was the problem.' Les Pattinson, meanwhile, had set himself up with a sandblasting business in Lancashire.

By 1997 the three were back together as Echo and the Bunnymen, and made a successful come-back album, *Evergreen*. A year later McCulloch recorded the official England World Cup song, '(How Does It Feel to Be) On Top of the World', with fellow Liverpudlians John Power of Cast and Tommy Scott of Space, plus the Spice Girls. Ironically his chart competition came from the Bunnymen's old producer Ian Broudie and his own soccer anthem 'Three Lions'. Though Les would bale out soon, and Will would still despair of Mac, the Bunnymen march on.

At their peak, Echo and the Bunnymen were a great Liverpool band. Their cockiness was not the urchin exuberance of Scouse tradition, but they glowed with a defiant pride, just the same. The band's attitude, which their overseers have found both enchanting and infuriating, is that failure and success are not what matters. It's your dignity that counts. Your panache. Such self-respect is not universal in Liverpool, but it's a characteristic of the city's better self. Despite their success they remained residents. 'Liverpool's great,' Mac told me, 'though we've never written a "Penny Lane" or a "Strawberry Fields". I wouldn't miss the recognition, if I left. I'd like to be able to walk down to the shops and not hear someone goin' "Band's fuckin' shit," just loud enough for you to hear it.'

Les listened in, and frowned thoughtfully. 'I'd miss me big chair that I get carried around in.'

This reminded me why it was never a good idea to interview the band together. But I pressed on. Were they more confident these days?

'I still get tense,' decided Mac.

'Yeah, sometimes I'm tents,' said Les. 'I felt like a marquee yesterday.'

Will Sergeant said he thought of himself as more of a teepee.

In a sleevenote to one of their compilations, Bill Drummond said that, for him, the Bunnymen's music summoned up 'memories of lies, deceit, hatred . . . loss of innocence, missed opportunities . . . petty rivalry and Pete DeFreitas dying.' But also: 'a glory beyond all glories . . . this golden light shining down on you, bathing you, cleaning all the grime and shit from the dark corners of your soul.'

9. 'I'VE REALLY FAR-OUT THINGS TO TELL YOU'

JULIAN, BILL, COURTNEY, PETE AND ANDY: WEIRD STUFF GOING DOWN

'Liverpool . . . a great school to become a rock star.'

Courtney Love

Julian Cope and Pete Wylie once had an Eric's band called the Nova Mob, whose chief aim was to raise a petition demanding that Big In Japan split up. In the event they secured a mere nine signatures, several of which were from members of Big In Japan itself. 'I was pissed off,' wrote Cope. 'I mean, where was people's pettiness?' Rubbing salt into the wound, the Nova Mob's own drummer, Budgie, defected to the enemy.

Julian now joined McCulloch in something called Uh? They evolved into A Shallow Madness, but soon separated. Mac pursued his own destiny, while Cope and Paul Simpson became the Teardrop Explodes, their name taken from a DC comic. Big In Japan's Drummond and Balfe, now of Zoo, became the Teardrops' managers, producers and label owners. Balfe even joined the line-up on keyboards. Simpson left when he found the group's pop leanings 'too cheesy' for someone of his Fall/Pere Ubu leanings, and formed the Wild Swans. Another temporary member was Alan Gill of the Wirral-based Dalek I Love You; they were almost the only electronic group around, inspiring another Wirral outfit called Orchestral Manoeuvres In The Dark.

Julian Cope was an outsider, up from Tamworth in the Midlands to attend a teacher training college. He was polite and middle class, too, but his uncool friendliness won people over. 'It took no time,' he writes in his book about that period, *Head-On*, 'getting used to the Liverpool attitude – it was so hard-faced, I fell deeply in love with it.' In early performances he looked nothing like the pop star he later became; while McCulloch dripped mystique, Julian merely dripped. He looked gauche and plain. However he underwent a transformation after the Teardrops were signed to a major label and began having hits such as 'Reward' and 'Treason'. Growing into his self-adoring frontman role, he acquired grace, glamour and an abiding rivalry with Ian McCulloch.

Deaf School's Clive Langer, who'd made a name for himself producing Madness, oversaw some of their first album, *Kilimanjaro*, and all of their second, *Wilder*. The former carried a cryptic sleevenote for the benefit of the Bunnymen, 'Hop Skip and Jump; Wait for the Bump' while a song on the second, 'Culture Bunker', expressed Julian's jealousy towards their singer: 'I feel cold when it turns to gold for you.' But the early 80s were a golden time for both the Teardrop Explodes and Echo and the Bunnymen. 'Bless my cotton socks I'm in the news,' sang Cope on *Top of the Pops*, and indeed he was.

So I jumped at the chance, in November 1981, to observe the Teardrops' return to the clique they'd sprung from. Though Eric's had gone, the regulars were reunited by Roger Eagle: he staged a season of Teardrop nights, called Club Zoo, in premises on Temple Street. The shows were almost secretive, supposed to build by word-of-mouth, and I watched the band play on the opening night to about 30 onlookers, all of whom they knew personally. How much of a gulf would Julian's new fame have opened up between him and the old gang?

'Is it all right like this?' he appealed from the tiny stage. 'Oo are yer?' came a sarcastic shout. 'There's no Marlboros in the ciggie machine,' someone grunted in the darkness. Liverpool's ego-debunking process was in full effect.

He invited requests. A chant went up for 'Geno' by Dexy's Midnight Runners. Another voice asked the drummer to expose himself. The event, I felt, was on the brink of collapse.

'Are you all OK?'

'Nah, we're just peasants.'

The band unveiled a new song 'Like Leila Khaled Said'.

'Wow, that was emotional, man,' sneered a gap-toothed rockabilly named Boxhead. Cope snapped, and leaped into the crowd to wrestle him. 'Scrap!' panted the excited crowd. 'I'm warnin' yer, Julian,' said his tormentor, head now wedged between Cope's hip and elbow, 'I'll tell me mam!'

Sitting at the bar, Roger Eagle smiled wearily at me: 'I'm just sitting here, looking smooth. Trying to look as if I'm in control of things.'

A year after that the Teardrop Explodes were no more. 'For Julian,' his friend and press officer Mick Houghton told me, 'success does not breed success. It breeds confusion.' They were commemorated in a posthumous album, *Everyone Wants to Shag The Teardrop Explodes*. Mick Houghton reflected: 'Looking back on it, I think the Teardrops did too much press. With Julian I helped to create this affable monster. Over certain periods he was everywhere, and it contributed to his mental downfall, I'm convinced of it. There was a point when Julian's press was out of all proportion to the amount of records he sold. It was so easy with him, everyone wanted to talk to him. You knew you would come away with enough copy for half a dozen features. Most artists have very little to say.'

He retired for a while to Tamworth. In the second volume of his memoirs, *Repossessed*, he writes: 'I lay morbidly fearful of *Top of the Pops*. Was this to be my life from now on? Peering fearfully at the uncoolness of my more successful friends in a mute discontent of quivering, impotent envy?' Over the years he took an erratic path; there was an album called *Fried*, on which he appeared with a large shell on his back, apparently under the impression he was a turtle. 'I think I took too much acid, actually,' he told me. 'It got annoying, being so paranoid. I'd be sitting at the window, waiting for people to come round so I could freak out. I'd get fans calling on me. When you've got a small, concentrated amount of fans they're really weird people. They'd come from miles away, knock on the door and say "We have LSD for you." '

He decided it was time to shape up: 'I really resented being seen as off my tree. I was a bit skew-whiff, but never off my head . . . So I got into being really healthy. I got into speed-walking.' He was dropped by two record companies. We saw little of him until 1990 when he turned up at anti-poll tax demonstrations dressed as a seven-foot space alien called 'Sqwubbsy', wondering whether to assassinate Margaret Thatcher.

The last time I met Julian was at his home in Wiltshire, where he lived with his beautiful American wife Dorian and their daughters Albion and Albany. The Cope household was a pleasant domestic jumble of Frank Zappa tapes and Thomas the Tank Engine toys, but Julian had become a New Age mystic. 'I've really far-out things to tell you,' he said. In appearance he was a lean, fire-eyed ragamuffin of a man, with half his head shaved. As always, though, he was engagingly enthusiastic. Part of his musical charm is that, no matter how implausible his lyrics, his delivery seems incapable of insincerity. 'Since 22 December 1989, I have been in a different spiritual state. I now term everything before that date, "pre-vision".'

Nursing a mug of tea he talked about his visions. Once he was 'astrally projected' from a hotel room in Liverpool. He described the experience as looking like the cover of Deep Purple's 1971 LP *Fireball*; a spinning diamond entered his skull, filling him with light, 'like a cosmic petrol pump attendant'. Sometimes there were voices, too, with messages such as 'to penetrate the diamond, the pituitary gland gets torn on its axis and frees'.

I asked him, for no particular reason, whether he still took drugs. 'They were important to me,' he confirmed. 'But in 1985 I stopped taking psychedelic drugs. I was off them until December 1993, and then I took three mushroom trips. But that was more because of *The Modern Antiquarian*.' This was a book he wrote on archaeology. 'I thought, What can I bring to the party that no-one else has? A-ha! LSD and mushrooms. But all I do now is walk every day.

'It took me a long time to realise I had anything going in the psychic areas. I just thought, Oh, I'd be perfectly normal if it wasn't for the fact that I was on drugs. I realised that the voices were saying, "You've got to work like a bastard." So I've worked constantly and the vision state has never left me. I have to speak out: the voices have told me I have to stop fucking around. I'm here to build up a trust in the far-out, the unknown. Basically I'm a pagan. I'm a New Age Pol Pot: it's the Land! The Land! The Land!'

The mercenary world of Tin Pan Alley seemed a million miles from this gently intense dreamer in his Wiltshire hamlet. Could he, I wondered, ever get back in the swim?

'No. I can't do that. I can't bear the city. I've become so mystical now. I'm like an artist in the hills. The day that I go down to Sodom will be the day that it all goes off.'

Julian has kept on working like the 'bastard' he aspires to be: more records, more books, including the two autobiographies and a history of Kraut-rock. 'I have a lot to do before I'm 60,' he says. The key is persistence. He remembers the second Teardrops single 'Bouncing Babies'. 'Even after that they were still talking about getting another singer in. That was persistence on my part. And Will Sergeant [the Bunnymen's guitarist] became good-looking! He was actually known as Baked Beans On Toast Face. You can do it. I will persist!'

In the end, I was rather sorry to leave. Going downstairs, he cocked a leg over the Mothercare safety gate. 'I've just got to pursue it until I'm so insane that they put me away. I have back-up. My wife and mother-in-law are not saying, "You're a fucking kook, Julian." They're saying, "You're a vibe, Julian. Keep it together." '

What became of that shadowy figure behind the stories of Big In Japan, Echo and the Bunnymen and the Teardrop Explodes? After managing the Bunnymen, Bill Drummond took a post at their record company, WEA, but his heart seemed not to be in it. Though he had the capacity to be Mister Sensible when required, the daily grind of meetings, strategic lunching, schedules and negotiations left him unfulfilled. I met him in 1986 when he told me he had 'retired from telling other people what to do'. Instead he was releasing his own album, *The Man*. 'I haven't gone out to make a successful record,' he reassured me, 'I've gone out to do the opposite. I can safely say no thought has gone into the making of this record whatsoever.'

He made the album in his native village of Newton Stewart in Galloway, in the hall where he'd seen his first live act, a skiffle group of convicts from the local gaol, where his father was a Church of Scotland chaplain. There was a track on *The Man*, 'Ballad of a Sex God', written for Pete DeFreitas, and another called 'Julian Cope Is Dead'. This particular song, partly a riposte to Julian's own 'Bill Drummond Said', was a whimsical Scottish jig whose lyric urged the singer to accept a career-boosting bullet in the head. Mostly, Bill explained, it was about the way the music business gradually saps your will.

A year later, Drummond's revenge upon the record industry was under way. He formed the KLF with Jimmy Cauty, and the pair released a fusillade of hit records, some under the name the Justified Ancients Of Mu-Mu, or JAMS; as the Timelords they had a Number 1 hit with 'Doctorin' the Tardis' and on the strength of their experience wrote a book *The Manual (How to Have a Number One the Easy Way)*. As the KLF they topped the chart with '3am Eternal' and then persuaded Tammy Wynette to join them on 1991's 'Justified and Ancient'. Though a Scot, Bill's affinity with the Northern hemisphere extended to the North of England, and the Justifieds' magnificent single 'It's Grim Up North' featured name-checks for some of Merseyside's rarely-celebrated outposts such as Kirkby, Maghull, Runcorn and Skelmersdale.

From the merely strange, Bill's activities went to full-on weird. The KLF left a dead sheep at the door of the 1992 Brit Awards Party. In 94 they presented the Turner Prize winner Rachel Whiteread with a £40,000 'worst artist' prize. They also unveiled an art-work of their own: the one million pounds they had earned from music, nailed to a board. In August they took the money to the Isle of Jura and claim to have ceremonially burned it all. If the 'Pool of Life' under Mathew Street has true powers of magical possession, Drummond is Exhibit A.

Bill's adventures in the Hit Parade would coincide with the Bunny-men's doldrum period, and his former charges looked on in awe. 'There was some envy,' Mac allows. 'But I was dead proud of the KLF thing. I just thought, "You sodding maverick genius bastard." He's spent seven years managing a band and then he becomes a sodding pop star. Great pop songs. But the burning of the million quid, I don't know where I stand on that. I thought it was funny at first, then I thought, He could have given me half of it. I taught him all he knew . . .'

*　　*　　*

'Before Liverpool,' Courtney Love has said, 'my life doesn't count. Ian McCulloch and Julian Cope taught me a great deal. I owe them a lot. Listen to the way I write and sing: I stole a lot from them, including this way of playing with stupid stereotypes. I learned that arrogance is not necessarily a bad thing. Liverpool had been a great school to become a rock star . . .'

The future rock star and widow of Kurt Cobain arrived in Liverpool in the early 80s when she was about fifteen, on the latest stop in a life of travels, traumas and perpetual incident. In her own way Courtney was in the great tradition of American imports that galvanised the Liverpool music scene. 'From nowhere,' wrote Bill Drummond in his book 45, 'this loud-mouthed American punkette with bleached hair turned up in Liverpool. She seemed to love everybody and she'd got LSD . . . She turned a Liverpool generation on. Our generation. A generation that had never been into drugs; we were quite happy with our pints of mild and our rum-and-blacks.'

She'd hit town with her girlfriend Robyn, having made Julian Cope's acquaintance in Dublin. As Paul Simpson of the Wild Swans now recalls: 'I was sharing the top floor flat in a large Victorian house with Echo and the Bunnymen drummer, the late great Pete DeFreitas. The flat's previous occupants had been Julian Cope and his first wife Kath, who had recently separated and needed someone to keep an eye on their belongings. Courtney had been shadowing Julian around London, pestering him with talk of putting a band together. Anxious to get rid of her, he passed the parcel by suggesting she look us up and do her band recruiting in the petri-dish of talent that was Liverpool.'

Courtney: 'This trip was one of the most important things of my existence.'

Simpson: 'Courtney and Robyn arrived from Lime Street Station by taxi, looking like a pair of dishevelled gargoyles. After the initial shock had worn off we begrudgingly gave them what had been Julian's bedroom at the back of the house, on the understanding that it was just for a week or so until they sorted themselves out with a flat of their own. In 1982 Echo and the Bunnymen and the Wild Swans were the coolest things happening on Merseyside, and we didn't take kindly to having our style cramped by these loudmouthed Robert Smith lookalikes.'

Cope has recollected her as 'amazingly horrible . . . The first person I'd met who was almost intolerably crazy.' She cultivated a bitter feud with Pete Burns. Her initial infatuation with the Bunnymen cooled considerably, possibly with Julian's encouragement. When I met her again in New York, many years later, she was hopeful of some reconciliation with Julian ('I think our kids are destined to hang out together'), but still dismissive of McCulloch. 'He hadn't done anything,' she sniffed, comparing Mac's sheltered life at that point with her own. 'He used to wear a big thick coat and glasses and hang out with Pete Wylie and mumble. A working-class boy who hadn't done anything.'

Paul Simpson remembers Courtney and Robyn trying to form a group with two other residents of the house, a drummer called Paul Green and a guitarist, Mike Mooney, whose mother lived across the road. She later claimed that Mooney took her virginity, which he's denied. 'Months went by,' says Simpson, 'with no signs of our American friends leaving, and after some alarming discoveries and a little unpleasantness we had recourse to throwing their suitcases down the stairwell.'

On the night I met her in New York, Courtney was in nostalgic mood, surrounded by the other members of her band, Hole. She made a point of relating her Liverpool stories in a Scouse accent. Unfortunately she speaks Scouse about as skilfully as Dick Van Dyke spoke Cockney in *Mary Poppins* (her speech was also very slurred, for some reason) and I think it irritated her, in front of her group, that I couldn't always follow.

'And the guy who claims I didn't lose my virginity to him, but I did,' she said, of Mike Mooney, 'I got along with his Mum. She brought me "butties" from over the road. "Would you like tomatoes on yer butties?" This was in Toxteth. Have you ever been to Toxteth? It was on Devonshire Road, right by Sefton Park.'

Thanks to Dave Balfe, Courtney and Robyn almost became Liverpool's next pop creation: 'He said he wanted a female duo like Soft Cell. He gave us a Fairlight and a four-track and we couldn't do shit. So we came back and we did this rap thing: "Julian, Julian, where have you been? Out in the alley with the tom cats again. Julian, Julian, where are you now? Off to answer the cat's miaow." Really stupid fifteen-year-old rap. I went on about porridge, because all we had was porridge, and Earl Grey without milk and sugar. We had no money, we had cider to drink, we had Woodbine cigarettes. So we weren't the ones. But then Dave Balfe went out and found Strawberry Switchblade instead.'

It's terrible to speculate on how Pete Wylie might have reacted if he had been denied success. Had he been forced to watch the Crucial Three's other two thirds – Julian Cope and Ian McCulloch – patrol the privileged realm of pop stardom without him, I doubt whether he could have stomached it. (Twenty-five years later he has not forgotten that Ian McCulloch has an Eric's membership card one number above his. Nor has Mac allowed him to forget.) His career was, in fact, destined to be a fairly rough ride. But he lived up to his self-proclaimed legend, scored some real chart hits and, in his big millennial number 'Heart as Big as Liverpool' has gifted the city with an impassioned anthem for the new century.

He cut a swathe through Eric's tangled band history, surfacing in the Nova Mob (with Cope and Budgie), the English Opium Eaters (with Ian Broudie and Paul Rutherford) as well as the Crucial Three – who never actually played, of course – and several more besides. He worked for a while in Probe, as well as in Eric's, and looks back on the whole scene with unabashed nostalgia: 'In my mind Eric's was like the Left Bank of Paris: it was a bunch of like-minded beret-wearers going, "My God, you too feel existential about your life!" But the thing that people forget was that, just as important as all the future pop stars, were the guys who never became famous, the Boxheads, the Jamies, the Kevins. We were all part of one big thing. My thing about all these Liverpool guys, Bob Wooler, Geoff Davies at Probe, the Eric's guys, is that I am a sentimental twat, and I love all of them. I know it now.

'The Beatles were problematic for me starting out: the first song I ever wrote was about being in the shadow of John Lennon. We felt like the shallow ripples from their era. So, in the punk era, we determined to become the big stone thrown into the pool. Everything in Liverpool was "From the home of the Beatles!" so we made a deliberate effort to ignore it. But without them, we could have been Herman's Hermits. And now of course I love them. But the best thing punk did was to say "Be an individual". That's why we never formed "punk bands". We didn't want to re-create anything that had gone before, whether it was the Beatles or the Sex Pistols.

'In 1980 I wanted to be in the Clash but I wasn't doing *Wah's in Their Eyes*, I was still doing Pete Wylie. One day me guitar went missing, me pride and joy, and I told Mick Jones [of the Clash], 'cos me and Paul Rutherford had started hanging round with the band, they actually adopted us. I asked Mick if he'd come with me round the guitar shops in Liverpool and help me find a new one. He was my hero: imagine a kid going up to anyone these days and asking that. I'd never recorded a note at that stage. But the punk thing was, you hung round with the bands. And he went round all the shops in Liverpool with me, trying the guitars out and says, "I've got a better guitar for you in London." And he gives me this 1959 Les Paul Special that Steve Jones of the Pistols had used. I say to him, "Mick, there's no way I can afford this!" And he says, "Pay me when you're famous".

'He always said that me and Paul Rutherford were going to be famous. And he got us to form a band called the English Opium Eaters, with

Budgie and Ian Broudie and Jamie Farrell. There was a night a few years later when were on *Top of the Pops* doing "Come Back" and the Frankies were on with "Two Tribes" and I rang Mick to say, "We've done it."

'I never paid him for the guitar, though.'

Eric's owner Pete Fulwell watched Wylie in another of his incarnations, the Mystery Girls, with Pete Burns. He observed that normally when a band comes on the audience all move forward, but in this case they all moved back. So impressed was Fulwell, though, that he gave Wylie some money to record a demo, with the warning that if he didn't, he'd be barred from the club. Roger Eagle was disinclined to issue the result – a thrilling guitar thrash called 'Better Scream' – on Eric's own label, so Fulwell put it on his own imprint, Inevitable. Wylie also found himself a bass player, Carl Washington: 'He was the coolest man in Liverpool, just the most stylish motherfucker you ever met. I said to the guys in Probe: "If he played bass I'd have him in me group." Then one day I see him and he's got this bag. It turns out he's just bought a bass, so I say, D'you wanna be in a group?'

The band was christened Wah! Heat and their second release, 'Seven Minutes to Midnight', made Single of the Week in every music paper. I duly shot up to Lime Street to interview Pete and got the group its first *NME* front cover. I found a motor-mouthed individual, sitting in the Grapes, who talked up a storm and took a Death or Glory view on everything, from his career to the next pint of Higson's. 'The important thing about the Liverpool scene,' he says, 'is none of us took drugs at the time. People always presumed I was a high energy speed freak, but I wasn't. I did an interview saying there were no drugs in Liverpool, then I found out the lads downstairs were speed dealers! But I never had any. But it was also a funny scene, a Spike Milligan version of punk.'

They signed to a big record company (the first of several he would pass through) and made a slightly unfocussed first LP, 1981's *Nah Poo The Art of Bluff*. But then, in 1983, Pete became a pop star: "Story of the Blues" was a hit and that changed everything. My dream had come true. But you know the cliché: Be careful what you dream of in case it does come true. Suddenly everyone is clamouring for the follow-up, and I say, But there is no follow-up. We're not a pop group, trying to churn out hit after hit. We never felt that duty, which bands are trained to have now, to do hit after hit. But then we did "Hope" and to this day it's more requested than "Story of the Blues". There are two parallel universes: one is pop success and the other is me, and sometimes they accidentally converge.'

I do believe he loved the attention, however. I remember how pleased he was when a reviewer described him as 'a swaggering poet ruffian':

'That's the best thing I've ever been called,' he told me at the time. "Cos it's got a bit of romanticism and nobility to it, and the intellectual thing. But at the same time it's got the ruffian element to counterbalance it. So it's not simply some wet, but something with bottle.'

His chart form was erratic, and Wah! evolved though various changes of name (the Mighty Wah! and Shambeko Say Wah! among them). Though he bought a house in Liverpool, Disgraceland, he acquired a reputation as one of London's premiere liggers. It was predicted his gravestone would read, 'Here lies Pete Wylie. Plus one.' He also fell in love with the late 80s dance scene: 'I had the first acid house party in Liverpool,' he claims, 'and that's a fact. I went to Probe and asked them if they had any acid house, they said, There's a rack of it there, you can have it for nothing. 'Cos no one was buying it yet. Mick Jones came down with Big Audio Dynamite. And Patsy Kensit. And this lad no one knew, James Barton [the future boss of Cream]: it was the first time he saw a proper acid house party.'

Disaster struck one night in 1991: 'I leaned back on a fence in Upper Parliament Street and fell into this basement, no stairs, and I hit a wall on the way down: broke me back, was almost crippled, and my chest bone, missed my heart by a quarter of an inch.' The fire brigade had to be called just to reach him. 'They have to ask you, if you know your name and I go, "You should *know* my fucking name." Just laughing. I didn't want them to take me to the hospital. I'm going, "But I've been invited to a party across the road." But there was no party, it was an hallucination. For the first four days in hospital they thought I was going to die.'

A long convalescence gave him much to meditate upon, including unemployment and the heartache of his daughter, Mersey, being taken to live in Australia by her mother. 'But confidence is a groupie,' says Pete. 'You think you're doing nothing special and suddenly people love you, they want to hang out with you, girls want to have sex with you. And then, when your records ain't doing so good, you can't work out why that same equation isn't working. And the key to being in a band is confidence. I had motor-boat confidence: just put me foot down. I used rock'n'roll as therapy, replacing the love I didn't have from me Mam.'

The old Eric's comrade Dave Balfe, now at the Columbia record company, signed Wylie to a new deal. An album was recorded, but then the label dropped him without warning. The shock almost sent him over the edge. Then there came a court conviction for threatening behaviour in the course of a phone call: 'I've never had a fight in me life,' he says. 'The only violence I've used has been against certain guitar chords. But after 40 years of living as a half-decent human being I gained a criminal record for doing my Joe Pesci thing. But it was Joe Pesci played by Michael Crawford.' A spell of community service followed.

Meanwhile the aborted Columbia album was picked up by another company and appeared in 2000 as *Songs of Strength and Heartbreak*, a characteristically passionate work with the outstanding 'Heart as Big as Liverpool'. Another release was his career overview *The Handy Wah! Whole*, whose tortuous title indicates the love for punning he picked up from Cavern original Bob Wooler: 'He was the link between Merseybeat and our scene: he gave us legitimacy. He'd sit there with his hand on your leather jeans, going "I love to see you young people promoting rock'n'roll." I saw him all the time, and he never forgot a thing about you. Like all of us, he loved the fact it was a scene. He loved Eric's. And he was the King of Puns, which of course I'm stupid for meself . . . And he was the first club DJ. He was a God to me, and I quoted him in a song: "Turn the hi-fi high and the lights down low." Which he use to say at the Cavern.' Wylie is currently considering an album to be called *Pete Sounds*.

'I found a new kind of confidence after the accident,' Wylie says today. 'I have a knack of doing things that people will respond to. After the accident I thought, there is life beyond being a teenage rock star with the cheekbones and swinging guitar. That was all I wanted before. But now I'm fighting that idea that no one over twenty has got any value or creativity.'

Orchestral Manoeuvres In The Dark were not the coolest graduates of the Eric's scene. I always found the other musicians apt to snigger at them. Julian called Andy Leo Sayer. It's true they were outsiders to an extent, signed to Manchester's Factory label rather than Zoo, and came from across the water in the Wirral. Nor were they ever blessed with that panache – the certain swagger of dress or personality – that you found in all the others. But what they did have was talent and solid chart success. Who's to say the sniggering wasn't tinged with a bit of jealousy?

Of the core duo, Andy McCluskey and Paul Humphreys, it was McCluskey who did the talking and has stayed the course. He'd been in school bands around his home town of Meols: 'teenage sub-prog nonsense, with angst-ridden lyrics,' he calls them. His Road to Damascus gig was not the Clash, but Kraftwerk: 'That was the most significant moment. Hearing "Autobahn" on the radio gave me an inkling, and seeing them at the Liverpool Empire in 1975 was the first day of the rest of my life.'

Schooled in electronic keyboard sounds, therefore, OMD were in a different tradition to the guitar-based pop that had driven everything from Merseybeat to punk: 'I'd found my alternative before punk,' he says. 'But the punk inability to play was something we clasped to our bosoms: they played with three chords and we played with one finger.' The catalyst, just the same, was Eric's club: 'There's no way in Hell that Paul Humphreys and I, with our tape recorder, could have played pubs like the Moonstone: we'd have got bottled off. We started purely because Eric's was there.'

They knew of Zoo's Dave Balfe through his membership of synth band Dalek I Love You – McCluskey even sang with them briefly – and were encouraged by that group's use of drum machines and tapes. Through the Eric's connection to Tony Wilson in Manchester, they sent him a tape and hoped he'd put them on his local TV show. Instead he signed them to his brand new label, Factory.

'Dave Balfe still says the biggest mistake Zoo made was not signing OMD,' says McCluskey. 'But we were just amazed to be on any label. We weren't made to feel unwelcome at Eric's, but we were always the outsiders: because we came from the other side of the river, and didn't live in bed-sit land; and also because the music we were making was different, more electronic and German-influenced than the guys in town.'

By 1979 they'd signed to the Virgin subsidiary Dindisc. Post-punk music was dominated by the provinces, especially the North: 'Just for a brief moment,' says Andy, 'the music industry got de-centralised. A&R men were going to clubs like Eric's, discovered weird bands and were prepared to sign them. Nowadays they wouldn't dare sign anything different.

'Tony Wilson had been mad enough to say we were a pop group and should be on *Top of the Pops*. We were offended to be called a pop group! And yet, though we were influenced by such unusual music and never imagined we could sell lots of records, we were naturally distilling from Kraftwerk the most melodic elements.

'The high points of OMD was that first *Top of the Pops* – how utterly gob-smacking to participate in this iconic part of British social history – and also our first record, holding "Electricity" in my hand and thinking, "This is my record, that me and Paul wrote in his mother's house, in Meols." And then to stand on stage in front of tens of thousands of people who are going bonkers because of a song you wrote. That's a drug, and I miss it.'

Pop stars or not, OMD were never 'poet ruffians' or charismatic loons. 'Electricity' had all the innocent wonder of 50s Wirral schoolboys: there was a touch of the Airfix kit and school pullover about them. Even at their chart peak I found them a neat, conscientious pair, very thoughtful. They wore soberly meticulous clothes. 'We're not a publicity band,' Andy told me in 1981. 'We're not faces on posters. And we choose to be like that. We're anti-personality cults. If Spandau Ballet didn't dress the way they do, would they still sell a quarter as many records? We're pretty plain to look at. We do dress in a certain manner, but it's just, like, clean and tidy, "modern" in the loosest sense of the word.'

After 'Messages' came 'Enola Gay', 'Joan of Arc' and more. But Andy was already absorbed by the business side of pop life: he would fret and tut about the poor organisation of a tour, about the record company contract or potential group conflicts, and the inconstancy of the media. He would brood on the role of pop music in the world. But he was learning lessons that would prove invaluable later. He and Paul continued to live on Merseyside, even if OMD's schedule ensured they saw little of their homes.

'We finally cracked America,' he says now. 'But in the process it cracked us. The band disintegrated, Paul had enough of touring. We were exhausted and skint: we were selling records, but the more we toured the more it cost us. By 1988 we owed the record company a million pounds, having sold millions of records. So we did a "Best of" to cover our debts. A second-hand car and a little cottage were all I had to show for ten years of success, and not because I'd blown it on mansions or on yachts that I sank around the world.'

He slogged on for a while without Humphreys and had a few more hits, including 'Sailing on the Seven Seas'. But by 1996, he says, 'OMD were considered 80s has-beens, Radio 1 wouldn't play it, Woolworths wouldn't stock it. We'd had eighteen years so I couldn't complain. I was determined not to become a sad pastiche of myself, playing to ever-smaller audiences until I was on the chicken-in-a-basket circuit: "Here's one you might remember: Ee-nowlaah Gaay . . . Oh, and keep your cards because I'll be calling the bingo later!" I didn't want to spend the rest of my life in a Groundhog Day, repeating things I'd done when I was 24. I wanted to do something new.'

That 'something' would turn out to be the hugely successful girl group Atomic Kitten, to whom we shall return.

OMD are a reminder that, even in the 70s, there were more strands to Liverpool music than the standard pop guitar jangle. In common with a lot of the pre-La's, Eric's generation, he was not obsessed by the Beatles: 'They seemed like ancient history; we were teenagers and they belonged to the time when we were children. We wanted something new, and that's why I got interested in synthesisers. It was a rejection of the immediate predecessors, which all good young musicians do.

'When I got older and really listened to the Beatles' albums, I recognised their genius. Now that I've mellowed and realise I'm not going to change the world with my music, I think about them as songwriters. And next to Lennon and McCartney everyone else pales into insignificance. The fact they came from Liverpool is intimidating: not only will you never be the best in the world, you'll never even be the best in your home town. Mind you, we're now apparently ahead of Ken Dodd in the Guinness book. So we're catching up with them!

'What remains is this. Pop music is what I've done. It's not like I've invented a cure for cancer or solved world hunger. But just for three minutes of somebody's day, and maybe for millions of people, something I did lodged in their life, and that's an incredible feeling. The money was great, the travelling was amazing, the ego massage was wonderful. But feeling that I did something that millions of people still listen to – that is the ultimate prize.'

10. EXQUISITE FOOLERY

EVERYONE'S A COMEDIAN IN LIVERPOOL. EXCEPT TOMMY SMITH

Liverpool has sometimes seemed to possess comedians more numerous than humorous. For better or worse, all those TV comics have been the voice of Scousedom for decades. A few were genuinely great while others scraped along by trading complacently on the native reputation for wit. That reputation was generally deserved, but wit is a mercurial quality, apt to abandon those who try to serve it up professionally. I've found myself reduced to tears of mirth by everyday encounters with Liverpool civilians, especially on factory floors, but I've watched with cold indifference the fellows in frilled shirts at the microphones. Ordinary Liverpudlians 'do' funny, all the time and very well; the TV Scouse comedian, however, is an unreliable replica of his street-level original.

The Liverpool reputation for humour appears to have taken root in the reminiscences of seamen, and from the experience of conscripts in the two world wars, when thousands of men from all regions of Britain were suddenly thrown together for the first time. The Scouser was, according to legend, the one with all the back-chat, the inclination for a sing-song, and probably wanted to be the shop steward too.

Just as in the music of Liverpool, performing standards were driven up by competition from the audience. To go on stage in a city of natural comics, or passionate singers, parlour pianists and blister-fingered guitarists, you had to be better than good yourself. The inescapable cliché became that living conditions in Liverpool had bred a resilient spirit: 'Everyone's a comedian round here,' the line would go. 'If you didn't laugh you'd cry.' Even a cliché can tell a sort of truth, of course, and this one does. Humour is psychic self-defence in a world where precious little is yours to control. Around the old docklands of Liverpool, where the Scouse mentality was defined, laughter was the only luxury that anybody could afford. Few men enjoyed the usual source of status, namely wealth, so they valued other qualities. An ability to fight, to entertain, or make people laugh: these were skills an ambitious chap might cultivate.

For speed of wit and tongue, of course, that man might find his wife at least as capable. There was a verbal equality of the sexes in slum life that persists in our own time. No macho swaggerer through Saturday night clubland can be guaranteed safety from the spitfire lips of those Liverpool girls, least of all when they're in gangs and the old squealing feeling has descended upon them.

In the earliest days of radio, and through to the 1950s, Britain was kept amused by the great Liverpudlian comedian Robb Wilton. Paul McCartney recalls getting his autograph. John Lennon went through a phase of watching Wilton and others at the Empire after a day at art college. He was particularly taken, apparently, by Wilton's classic discourse on The Day That War Broke Out ('My missus says to me, Well, what are you going to do about it?') It's been claimed, though impossible to prove, that Wilton was the first to say you had to be a comedian to live in Liverpool. Yet he rather played down his accent – the time had not yet arrived to parade your Scouseness as a virtue in itself.

Wilton's contemporary was Aigburth's Tommy Handley, another radio legend, chiefly remembered for his wartime show *ITMA* ('It's That Man Again') and the rash of catch-phrases he launched from it: 'Can I do you now, sir?' and 'I don't mind if I do' and TTFN or 'Ta-ta for now'. It was largely thanks to Handley's show that non-Liverpudlians came to know the term Scouser: over the years it would replace 'wacker', which had in turn displaced 'Dicky Sam'. His comedy had a deep streak of nonsense to it – he stands in ancestry to the Goons and Monty Python – which might be why John Lennon put him on the *Sgt. Pepper* sleeve. Upon his death he was given a national send-off at St Paul's Cathedral, where the Bishop of London pronounced: 'The flame of his genius transmuted the copper of our common experience into the gold of exquisite foolery.'

Handley's accomplice in that 'exquisite foolery' was Deryck Guyler, whose character Frisby Dyke was taken from the name of a Liverpool draper's shop. Handley and Guyler eschewed the stage Lancastrian voice of Wilton and the others, preferring the greater levels of absurdity they could achieve with their Mersey accents: another of the catch-phrases, 'Don't forget the diver, sir' was comprehensible only to those who'd watched a certain one-legged swimmer, at New Brighton, passing the hat around. Guyler himself became a mainstay of TV comedies, playing the genial copper PC Corky for Eric Sykes and the cantankerous caretaker, Potter, in *Please Sir*.

From deepest Toxteth, Arthur Askey was an early possessor of the Liverpool Institute desk inherited by Paul McCartney. The old comic had supposedly carved his name on it. 'Big-hearted Arthur' insinuated himself into the public mind via some catch-phrases of his own, notably the Liverpool tram-conductors' 'Aythangyew!'

But greater than Askey, or his fellow funnyman Ted Ray, was Robb Wilton's most devoted student Ken Dodd. The last graduate of the live varieties circuit that thrived before television, as recently as 2001 this buck-toothed institution was still captivating provincial theatres with five-hour marathons. He'd declare at the point of unconditional triumph: 'Right! Lock the doors! Nobody's going home tonight!' He seems to have been around Liverpool for ever. As Roger McGough said, locals spoke of him as they might talk of the Pier Head. The Beatles supported him in 1961: a traditionalist in his musical tastes, he tried to get them thrown off the bill. Decades after the demise of music hall his act still parodied its staples: the sand dancers, the operatic tenors, the drum and trumpet turns.

Liverpool has long supplied him with subject matter: 'In Paris all the chairs and tables are out on the street. In Liverpool we call it eviction . . . We've always been environmentally conscious in Liverpool. We've had unleaded churches for years.' The larky allusions to Diddymen, jam-butty mines and tickling sticks could be wearying, but one distinguished drama critic has suggested Dodd's Surrealism – that word again – is in the same Lewis Carroll-to-Edward Lear lineage that delighted John Lennon. (Despite the 1961 unpleasantness, Dodd and Lennon did appear on TV together a few years later, and the atmosphere crackled with mutual hilarity.) Non-Liverpudlians were always surprised to find that Knotty Ash was not another invention, but the actual village-turned-suburb that Dodd has lived in since childhood.

He is not in the proletarian Scouse tradition of dockland funnymen. Dodd represents a Liverpool character less often celebrated: the droll suburban sceptic, the Dale Street cotton clerk or low Tory stockbroker in the lunchtime pubs of Hackins Hey. Most of those men have gone now, just as surely as their cloth-capped adversaries in the labour unions. And when Ken Dodd goes, there will be nothing left to remind us of their whimsical side.

At the same time he's one of Liverpool's most successful recording acts, up there in the hit statistics list with Cilla, Billy Fury, Frankie Vaughan and the Beatles. The tunes have typically been those cheery numbers designed to send a comedy crowd out with a spring in their step ('Happiness', 'Love Is Like a Violin') or else the heart-tuggers, like 'Tears', that showcased his surprisingly impressive voice. His attachment to the science of comedy is well-known. He's made a systematic study of jokes all his career. Once, on Parkinson's show, he advanced his theory of regional comic tastes. 'You can tell a joke in Glasgow and they won't laugh in Manchester,' he stated. 'Yes, why *is* that?' asked Parkinson, intrigued. 'Because they can't hear you,' Ken Dodd explained.

For a long time Dodd was kept in chuckle bullets by the unsung genius of Liverpudlian comedy, the writer Eddie Braben. Born in the Dingle, he'd begun writing jokes while selling fruit and veg in St John's Market; his Ken Dodd connection flourished for thirteen years. However, it was Braben's work for Morecambe and Wise that brought his craft to a peak of perfection. From 1969 onwards, working alone and under huge pressures, he'd post his scripts down from Liverpool to the country's most famous and most demanding double-act. It was a hellish process for him: 'like putting your brain through a mincing machine', he called it. But it was Braben's scripts, developed from his own shrewd reading of the two men's personalities and relationship, that created the Morecambe and Wise of entertainment legend. And, once more, the tone was of deep Liverpudlian unreality: a sketch about Eric's fast-growing moustache seeds, the typewriter made out of a bicycle or the self-multiplying absurdities in the 'play what Ernie wrote'.

And then there was Jimmy Tarbuck. It's difficult now to imagine a time when Jimmy Tarbuck was considered cutting edge. But in the euphoria of Merseybeat, in 1963, he possessed the cheeky image, the urchin hairstyle and the wacker accent that allied him in the public mind to the Beatles. Just like them he'd slogged around for a while, but his sudden ascent to the pinnacle of show business looked every bit as giddy. Appointing him as the host of *Sunday Night at the London Palladium* seemed no more than natural. In 1963, British TV's weekly climax must without doubt be handed to a young Liverpudlian. The connection was quite genuine. Tarbuck had gone to the same school as John and George, he'd played the Cavern and now he was knocking around London in the Beatles' gang.

Barely a year later, though, their respective outlooks would begin to diverge dramatically. Tarbuck's achievement was to evade the same oblivion that met the lesser Merseybeat boys, and to accompany 'Our Cilla' behind the velvet rope of Light Entertainment Royalty. There followed the long decades of unchallenging TV and pro-celebrity golf that so enraged the next generation of comics. His sharpness relaxed into self-satisfaction. He'd once promised better than that.

But if edginess were all you needed, Freddie Starr would have been the daddy of them all. Here was the 'Hannibal Lecter of Comedy', he who allegedly ate the hamster, and was somehow more threatening than all the radical young alternative comedians put together. Real name

Freddy Fowell, he'd appeared in a 1957 Liverpool film, *Violent Playground*, but his performing roots were in Merseybeat. He joined the Seniors to sing alongside Derry Wilkie: signed to Fontana they were the first of that Liverpool generation to record. Drunken hell-raisers by all accounts, they soon imploded, leaving Freddie to join the Midnighters and change his name to the suitably nocturnal Starr. The musical career stumbled on, through Hamburg, Decca studios and yet more bands. The trouble was that nobody remembered Freddie the singer so much as Freddie the clown. Even he disliked the records.

The comedy career that followed was seldom jovial. He met with fantastic success, but there was always something disturbing in Starr's barbed-wire persona. The Elvis and Hitler impressions that he stuck with, for just a little too long, looked more like symptoms of mania than mirth. He never did eat the hamster – the newspaper headline was a PR coup – but he did tip maggots on to an audience. The son of a bare-knuckle fighter, he was born poor and grew up hurt. There was drinking, divorce, debt and long-term addiction to contend with, as well as eventual rejection by entertainment's ruling powers. He was, in his own dark way, a brilliant symbol of the emotional violence that can lurk inside successful comedy. 'He gave the people what they wanted,' wrote the *Sunday Times*' Georgina Howell. 'In other words he undermined their collective identity, he selected prominent individuals and held them up for humiliation, he divided and he ruled, he turned the audience into victims of an anarchic and exuberant manipulation. He mined a vein of latent hysteria that connects embarrassment with humour and results in an electric sense of release.'

You had to laugh, or else you'd cry.

'My contribution to the history of comedy,' Alexei Sayle once said, 'is that I was the first comic that genuinely didn't care whether the audience liked me or not.' It's true. Alternative comedy was invented by a Liverpudlian from Anfield, Manx on his father's side and Lithuanian Jewish on his mother's. If Liverpool had dominated comedy of the old school, through Sayle it set the craft in a new direction.

Of the comic wave that rose to prominence in the 1980s, via the Comedy Store, *Not the Nine O'Clock News* and *The Young Ones*, Alexei Sayle was almost the sole working-class voice. That's not to say that he remained a working-class comedian: 'I'm not performing to miners' clubs in Northumberland,' he admitted. 'I'm not performing to hard core proletariat.' And his training ground was London, not Liverpool itself. But he represented millions in the post-war world, upwardly mobile, cut adrift from their roots by mass education, yet still unsure of their incorporation into the middle class. Eventually, by sheer weight of numbers, that generation (of teachers, social workers, media types and sundry professionals) would transform the British middle class into something like its own liberal, dressed-down image.

Sayle's comedy was in the middle of these changes, and he understood them. What's more he was a student of the comic art, just like Ken Dodd. I once went with him on a pub crawl around South-west London, but had the presence of mind to make some notes: 'His favourite Hammersmith pub. A powerfully stout rather than flabby man, a head that's nearly all face, a tough stubble which merges, somewhere, with the brutal crop he calls a haircut.' If there really was a thin man inside of him trying to get out, I thought, then it was not surprising: the fat one was wearing *his* suit. Over it all, he wore a rather handsome camel-hair coat. He could have passed for a right-wing agitator, but was actually a former member of the Liverpool chapter of the Communist Party of Britain (Marxist Leninist), an organisation with a name longer than its membership list.

He'd been to the same school as Ian McCulloch and Pete Wylie, though a few years ahead of them, then left Liverpool to go to art college in Chelsea. 'I always thought I was going to London,' he told me. 'It was taken for granted I wasn't staying in Liverpool. It was just automatic.' So he found himself in the Kings Road at the start of the 1970s, having missed the abolition of the Swinging 60s by a matter of months. It was a bit of a disappointment. 'I'd never met anyone from a public school until I came to Chelsea, and I couldn't work me way into the gang. It took me about two years. I did genuinely think I'd be walking down the Kings Road for a week, then people would be going, "Hey! A'right Lex?" Y'know?'

The degree that he picked up was useless, but the experience was invaluable. 'You got very good at spotting trends. Being a "good" fine artist is not about having any talent or skill, but about spotting the minute variations of trends – a dab of paint here, or putting black borders around your photographs of piles of dirt in the Pennines. At art school they sort of tell you that you've got a vision. Most of the time they're lying, 'cos you're just there to make up the numbers. But most people get convinced while they're there that they've got some unique vision to share with the world. I carried on believing, I suppose.'

He washed dishes, worked on tube trains and taught general studies to day-release pupils. He also did nine months in the civil service, in the DHSS (Architects Division): 'There were four of us in my office. One of them was learning to play the balalaika and writing a novel; one of them was having an affair with one of the architects; there was me, I was writing film scripts; and there was one woman doing all the work. It was a kind of lifeline, the civil service. We could afford to be optimistic because we came from an optimistic generation. We had the civil service and it'd keep you going until you found out what you wanted to do . . . I was lucky that no one ever took me seriously, in a way. If anyone had ever given me a half decent job it I probably would have stuck with it.'

He got his start in stand-up at the Comedy Store: 'I thought there was both an audience and a performing style out there that wasn't being exploited. But you had to mentally visualise it for yourself because there was nothing. I mean, there were vague hints like Jasper Carrott and you'd think, Well, it might be interesting to do something a bit like that. What you thought was, I could do a lot better than that. Then there was all the new wave stuff, Elvis Costello and that, and you thought, Well, there's an audience there that's vaguely like what I might like to perform to. But it was genuinely, basically, a case of inventing it all for myself, really.

'What I like about it is that it's a craft. It's a very finely-honed craft. And I'm good at it. It gets very technical, so comedians even like me and Rik Mayall tend to talk in code a bit. It's partly a familiarity with your material, having actually honed it in performance. You take a piece of material and you work it for five years and it gets a gloss on it, so every single word is exact, has an exact purpose, every single word is leading up to a laugh. It's actually beautifully polished. I love that.

'It's also being able to improvise, having a quick mind and lots of energy. Those traditional values. There's always been a misconception, starting with old Lenny Bruce, that if you feel ill you can go on and babble about it. But you don't. If you feel ill, you go on and still do the best show you can. Old-fashioned professionalism.

'I'm very bad-tempered. I'm constantly fairly pissed off with the way things are, one way or another. It's just finding a way that's funny. I think my delivery does spring out of, I suppose, deep down being very angry with things . . . It's partly showing off, and part of showing off is taking the piss. Walking down Lime Street and taking the piss out of people there. Sort of dive in and poke at them. The thing that makes humour interesting is that it's completely inexplicable. It's a kind of code, you either twig it or you don't. You can talk about technique, but there's always something indefinable at the end of it. Something that remains elusive.'

Much has happened since the night of our pub crawl. Alexei Sayle has written books, made films, and invented characters who include the curly-permed, oddly tragic Liverpool comic Bobby Chariot. And his favourite Hammersmith pub has been demolished. I like the books the best of all his work. The final story in his collection *Barcelona Plates* is called 'The Last Woman Killed in the War': it's one of his most serious, and Douglas Adams called it a masterpiece. I love it in part for its descriptions of the Anfield streets where Sayle and I grew up. Once they were alive with little shops but, by 1999, the Liverpool football ground 'seemed to have grown like some giant cane toad, squat and carbuncular and fed itself off the vitality of the whole area. All the shops had been burnt down or been bricked up or had big bites taken out of them. Apart from a couple of Chinese chip shops. The only putting up seemed to have been road signs and little aluminium fences at every road junction and street corners, as if the inhabitants if not fenced in would fling themselves under the wheels of any passing car.'

There could be great things still to come from Sayle. As he used to say on stage when things were going badly: 'I'm an experimental comic. And parts of me aren't finished yet.'

For each of Merseyside's great comic institutions, from Deryck Guyler's washboard to Paul O'Grady's Tranmere trollop Lily Savage, there is unfortunately a Stan 'the Jeermans' Boardman, or a dozen others too terrible to mention. Music and football have brought glory to Liverpool, but comedy's contribution has been a somewhat mixed affair. So, for that matter, has television's.

The first identifiably Scouse TV programme I can think of was the police series *Z-Cars*, which began in 1962 and took for its setting the fictional Newtown, very like the overspill developments then being built around Liverpool. There were still not enough local actors to guarantee the authenticity of its accents, which occasionally got no further from RADA than Birmingham. But it was a tough, intelligent and ground-breaking show in its time, chiming with the contemporary taste for gritty Northern realism. With a couple of rare exceptions in old school TV drama, and Alan Bleasdale's *Boys from the Black Stuff*, very little has equalled it.

Situation comedies have occasionally been even more regrettable than the worst of the real-life Bobby Chariots. There was a 70s sit-com, *The Wackers*, too wretched to recall. The twin creations of animal rights enthusiast Carla Lane, *The Liver Birds* and *Bread*, were too cosy for many locals' taste. But even worse was watching documentary indictments of the city, whether about the Adelphi Hotel's apparent eccentricity, or *Mersey Blues*' police detectives in cahoots with drug dealers.

The Liverpool soap opera *Brookside* has, in its favour, a proud record of sponsoring local writers and acting talent. I've watched it from the start, on the opening night of Channel 4 in November, 1982; and, like any long-term follower of such shows, I nurture the conviction it's not as good as it used to be. But that is probably wrong. Thinking back, Brookside Close had plenty of eminently forgettable residents among its fondly-remembered giants. (In a reversal of television tradition, *Brookside* seemed to generate convincing working-class types, while its middle-class inhabitants were cardboard cut-outs.) *Brookside* used to have a plodding, social-issue-by-numbers way of parading its political conscience. Now it's attached to fast, flashy grabs at every fashionable anxiety. Like a junkie in need of a fix, it's always seemed to crave the short-term ratings boost of a murder, a fire, a rape.

Alan Bleasdale once said of *Brookside*: 'It's hard enough being a playwright and I wouldn't want to knock it for that. But Liverpool people don't like it, and it's not Liverpool. It makes the people appear to look ugly and unpleasant and humourless. It misses out all the emotional generosity.'

No sooner have *Brookside* actors had the chance to evolve their characters into interestingly rounded, dramatic creations than a script-writing U-turn sees them change their personalities like werewolves. Cast upheavals have ruled out even the theoretical possibility of stable family units. Sex themes are covered with a tabloid prurience, the tackiness undiminished by pious 'help-line' announcements over the end credits. But I carry on watching, all the same. Somehow I cannot imagine life without Jimmy Corkhill.

A lot of the best early *Brookside* episodes were written by Jimmy McGovern: his by-line was usually a guarantee of something more than run-of-the-mill. There has been no stopping him since then. *Cracker* is the most famous of his creations; there have been docu-dramas on Hillsborough and the 1990s dock dispute, *The Lakes*, *Priest* and more. It was an argument about *Brookside*'s refusal of a Hillsborough story line that made him leave. However he would re-visit the subject in *Cracker* as well as in *Hillsborough* itself.

Bleasdale's greatest achievement, *The Boys from the Black Stuff*, will be discussed in the next chapter; his stature as a dramatist is secure. In the words of another Liverpool playwright (and an early author of *Z-Cars*), John McGrath, 'Alan Bleasdale's writing comes out of that torrent of words that has been flowing out of Liverpool in so many ways since Tommy Handley and Arthur Askey joined forces with James Joyce to produce John Lennon, the Scaffold, Adrian Henri, Roger McGough and

Brian Patten, way back in the 60s . . . He never lost the sharp comedy of the Liverpool street, second only to its close neighbour Dublin for Surreal wit and Byzantine inventiveness in sarcasm, pun and patter. And for its ability to express strong emotion.'

The most successful of them all, however, is Bleasdale's friend Willy Russell. They all look alike, these bearded Scouse left-wing ex-teacher playwrights (McGovern is another one). Bleasdale told me that Russell used to get drinks bought for him in pubs for writing *Black Stuff*, while he himself was thanked in the streets for *Educating Rita*. I once went to visit Willy Russell in his office next to the Everyman Theatre, and asked him why Liverpool was so prolific in drama. 'There are probably more practising artists concentrated in Liverpool than in any other area of the country,' he said. 'You only have to put a sign up saying Scripts Wanted and everyone in the city is bloody writing one.

'I've pondered why it is, and I don't really know why it should be Liverpool and not Blackburn. I suppose the Irish influence must be important, and the fact that Liverpool has got its own identifiable language, which has got no root with the rest of Lancashire. The Lancashire accents overlap and are related, but you've suddenly got this cut-off line, round to the Bay, and it's a language all of its own.

'The Liverpool dialect is a terrific medium to work in, very fast and exclusive. I suppose it's like painters who painted in certain areas because of the sunlight or sculptors who worked where the clay was good. It would be stupid to ignore this language. The only time I object to a Liverpool tag being put on me is when it suggests a parochial quality, which I refute completely. I always quote Isaac Bashevik Singer who says, If you write about any place well, you write about everywhere.

'The danger in Liverpool is that chauvinistic Liverpool sort of thing, which is well akin to nationalism. I've seen a few things on stage here which are the equivalent to that awful Scottish New Year's Eve TV. And if I see that I run a mile.'

Russell is yet another product of the Liverpool music scene: 'My first-ever group was an attempt to be like the Shadows, before we got to know about the Cavern and the Beatles.' Seeing the Beatles, he once said, changed his life. 'When I was fourteen I walked into the Cavern and saw the bloody Beatles. It gave me something, it gave me identity. I'd be on the school bus the next day and all those pricks who were having a go at me, well, they didn't know about the Beatles. It was so intoxicating.'

He played in a band with Tommy Evans, later of Badfinger. 'He was a really good guitarist so I picked up things from him. Then about 1963 the Dylan thing happened, so I started to play contemporary folk music as it was called. Later I got into traditional music, a lot of fiddle and tenor banjo, then I was doing folk clubs as a singer–songwriter. You had that great platform in those days, it was a great place to learn how to hold a house. I always knew my limitations, and after I'd been at it for fifteen years I'd really seriously started to write plays, so I let it lapse.'

He drew on his stock of self-written songs for *Blood Brothers*, a long-running West End hit about a Liverpool housewife and her twin sons, raised apart. There was a comic play, *John, Paul, George, Ringo . . . and Bert*, that spliced the Beatle saga with fantasy. *Shirley Valentine* and *Educating Rita* became hugely popular films. The list is a long one, to which he recently added a much-praised debut novel, *The Wrong Boy*, about a teenager's letters to Morrissey. One project that never came off, however, was the screenplay that he wrote for Paul McCartney, *Band on the Run*. 'Good script as well. When I first heard that song I thought there was a great idea for a film in there. And when he asked me to write a movie for him, I threw this back at him. He was quite surprised because he'd never seen it in film terms.

'The plot was just about a guy who'd become a very jaded but highly successful cabaret act, filling concert halls, who's well pissed off with it. And there is a band who just cannot get their act together, playing in a pub four streets down from this concert. They end up in a huge fight and have to get out of town, cross-cutting with him, who actually walks off stage in the middle of a number and never comes back. He just pisses off. The two of them meet up and he disguises himself and joins that band. I suppose the film very much picks up on what McCartney did when he first took Wings out on the road, just turning up and playing. And by the end of it he realises that he'll have to leave this band anyway, because he'd destroy them if he stayed, and he has to go back and face things. You can't walk away, you have to go through whatever's happening to you in life.

'There was always a dispute about the end of the film because it didn't end happily. Paul wanted it to end happily and I didn't!' The idea finally ran out of steam when Paul left for a tour and found himself locked up in a Japanese prison on drug charges.

Russell attributes his faith in drama – the spoken word over the written – to the time he spent teaching in a dockland comprehensive. 'I used to have a class called 4WD, that were like the classic impossible class. They'd given up on this 4WD mob. Everyone had them for just half an hour a week, and I had them for something called English/Drama so I could do what the fuck I pleased with them. Went in the first week, tried to hand out some pens and paper and say, Let's establish exactly who's at what level, and I didn't even get a name written down on a piece of paper.

'So the next week I thought, Fuck this, so I went in and said, We'll try some drama. "We will fuck," said this voice from the back. "I'm not poncin' round doin' no fuckin' drama." So I said let's get the desks back, that took 30 minutes then the bell goes and I'm left with all the bloody desks to put back. And this went on for weeks. It sounds like a laugh now, but it was agony. I could have taken the easy option, because no one cared about them. I could have said let's take a ball and play football on the field. In the end, in complete desperation, I went in one week, there was complete pandemonium in this class, and instead of shouting I just started telling a story about two kids.

'The noise stopped, they all started listening. Didn't know where the hell I was up to, 'cos I hadn't invented anything. Got to the end of it, they all went out in silence, came back the week after, this voice goes, "You gonna tell that story again?" I hadn't planned anything, but I started to make up a bit more. This went on for six months. You'd look up and these huge lads were rapt, like infants.

'I made an absolute connection with the way to treat working class culture, because it's still carried by the spoken word. It does not trust the written word. It never has. There's no basic working-class trust in the written word, because they've often been abused by it.'

As a writer Russell is firmly in the Liverpool populist tradition he shared with another friend of his, Adrian Henri. Poets and playwrights can be entertainers too: 'You've got to engage the audience. If you don't engage them at a primal magic level, you won't be able to sell them anything. I use entertainment as a very noble word. It's dead easy to be un-entertaining. Anyone can write tragedy. It's comedy that's the real difficult stuff.'

But the city can do horror, too. In the past few decades it has produced both Ramsey Campbell and Clive Barker. The latter has said that his taste for imagined other worlds was sparked in Penny Lane, in his 1950s childhood, by a display in the Co-op window advertising Sugar Puffs.

The pretty nurse in Paul McCartney's 'Penny Lane', selling poppies from a tray, 'feels as if she's in a play'. It's a common sensation in Liverpool. You can be in a pub, or on a bus, or behind the shelter in the middle of the roundabout, and somehow get the impression that everybody is reacting to everybody else and speaking from a very well-written script.

The Bakerloo Line is not like that. Life on Merseyside has a peculiar vividness. It's lived as though on a stage. There are no spectators because everyone is obliged to take a part.

The favourite variety of dockers' humour was giving names to other people: making them more than real by casting them as characters. So there would be the Weightlifter (he'll wait while you lift), the Lazy Solicitor (who falls asleep on a case), the Mangy Kitten (gets on a bus and says 'I've got no fur').

And what of the city's thespian talents? In days gone by the acting profession was rather reserved for the upper classes. Liverpool produced the likes of Rex Harrison and Derek Nimmo, whom nobody would have figured as Scousers. After them came Glenda Jackson and the wonderful Rita Tushingham. And we must never forget Leonard Rossiter: for his immortal portrayal of the hangdog office fantasist, Reginald Perrin, I'm sure he drew on his former life as a Dale Street insurance clerk. Norman Rossington was similarly gifted. There is a McGann brother everywhere you look. There are now so many TV roles for Liverpudlians that the drama schools must struggle to meet demand. The parts will probably be in *Brookside* rather than *Twelfth Night*, and in commercials for oven chips rather than luxury cars. But what the hell – at least you're in show business.

The most successful actor of them all is the city itself. It even has an agent, in the form of the Council's Film Office. It's always been a favoured location for movie makers, whether playing itself or impersonating somewhere else. Thanks to Liverpool's monumental civic buildings it is good at playing Russian cities, and has done so in many films, from *Red October* to *Yentl*. It has been Hitler's Berlin for *Indiana Jones and the Last Crusade*. It has been 1920s Paris in *Chariots of Fire*. The list of specifically Liverpool films is long and goes back right back to the Lumière Brothers in 1897. It appears in fantasy form in the Beatles' *Yellow Submarine*, and through a nostalgic gauze in Terence Davies's elegiac reminiscences of 50s childhood, *Distant Voices, Still Lives* and *The Long Day Closes*. Teddy Boy toughs maraud in *Violent Playground* (1957) and *Dangerous Youth* (1958). Occasionally film-makers have preferred to use a stand-in for Liverpool: this was the case in *A Hard Day's Night*, while *Educating Rita* and *Hear My Song* exploit the family resemblance of Liverpool's sister city Dublin.

The romance of Liverpool's maritime skyline, and the feral hedonism of its night-life, are wonderfully captured in Frank Clarke's *Letter to Brezhnev* (1985), which I would nominate as the definitive Liverpool film. (As, in fact, did George Harrison.) Frank's sister Margi Clarke plays one of two Liverpool girls (the other is Sandra Pigg) who look for love in the Saturday night fever of the State Ballroom, and find their prize in a couple of Russian sailors on shore leave.

During its making I went out to Kirkby to watch Frank Clarke and his crew in action, filming a sequence set in a suburban pub. The real-life landlord stood behind his bar in the next room, looking harassed. The locals apparently knew him as the Sheep ('because he baa's people out'). Today, though, there were glamorous actresses, lights, cameras and action, and he couldn't get anyone to drink up and go home.

The film, Frank Clarke assured me, was going to be 'just so fuckin' brilliant you wouldn't believe it.' He'd written the script after his Dad was made redundant: 'Thatcher came into power in 79 and she finished up the B&I ferries. Me mum and dad ran the bones off their arse and me, their only lad, I had no work and couldn't help them financially. So I thought, Fuck this, I'm gonna go out and write a play and make a few bob. So I wrote *Letter to Brezhnev*.'

Channel 4 was about to launch. They saw Frank's script and put him to work on *Brookside*, and although he didn't like the show, it taught him some technique. He also wrote for *Coronation Street*, where Margi has appeared as an actress. Willie Russell was an early admirer of Clarke's raw style and even appears in the film. Meanwhile in the pub, Margi's character is fresh from the chicken factory, dressed in a greasy white coat that is authentically smeared with poultry innards. 'I feel like Quasimodette,' she says.

'When I say *Letter to Brezhnev* is about Liverpool,' Frank explains, 'it's not about all that alright la', wack, la' depression stuff. It's about two girls who know, at the beginning of the night, that something is just around the corner for them, something really exciting – and all they have to do is reach out and grab it. And that something is love. For one of them it's a deep, spiritual love. For the other one, played by me sister Margi, it's love of the minge: she wants fillin'. She's talking through her fanny most of the film.

'I'm havin' a ball,' he cackles. 'And if I never make another film again I don't give two fucks. I made this. I'm not arsed.'

The director calls for hush. The extras adopt their positions. An assistant puffs artificial cigarette smoke out of a box. Filming resumes.

'You know the casting couch?' Frank whispers to me, casting an eye across the crowded room. 'If I'd had a casting couch doing these auditions, I wouldn't have a dick left by now.'

*   *   *

At the old Pavilion on Lodge Lane, the Memory Man would challenge his audience by asking, 'Who holds an English soccer cap, an England cricket cap, a Lonsdale belt and a Rugby League cup final medal?' The answer was, of course, the pawn-broker in Smithdown Road. I only mention it to remind us that football is not the only sport on Merseyside. Here is the home, after all, of the Grand National. There is apparently an abundance of quality golf-courses. The city is renowned for the boxers its slums have raised, such as John Conteh; there are cyclists and snooker stars as well. But rugby is little-liked, despite the proximity of its great League bastions in south Lancashire. And there is less interest shown in cricket than you find anywhere else in England. When it comes to daily life and mass-attendance, football is the ruler of Liverpool's heart.

In the second half of the twentieth century, as the city's other claims to fame began to dwindle, music and football grew in stature, to the point where they're now the first things any foreigner would think of when Liverpool is mentioned. Each has had its good times and bad, but together they've saved the city from slipping out of international memory. Whatever the British might think of their wayward seaport, music and football give Liverpool prestige in the eyes of the world. No wonder the city authorities are coming to see them as economic assets as well as cultural jewels.

When Bill Shankly led Liverpool Football Club from years of obscurity to the start of unparalleled success – surpassing their previously superior neighbours Everton – the Kop became a national symbol. By an extraordinary coincidence, the team's resurgence occurred precisely at the time of the Beatles' rise and Merseybeat's supremacy. And it was the Kop, that swaying mass of humanity at one end of the Anfield ground, which synthesised the two phenomena. In everyday media discourse in the 1960s, 'the Liverpool sound' was freely used to embrace the music of the terraces as well as of the groups.

While there was nothing new about supporters singing at football matches, the Kop was in a league of its own. It was not just the sheer size and acoustic resonance of that particular stand. Nor was it the natural civic pride they could bring to their renditions of Beatle numbers. What would amaze outsiders was the Kop's instinctive unanimity. It seemed to think as one: a gigantic, single organism that symbolised the wit, musicality and solidarity of the whole city. The fans' adoption of Gerry and the Pacemakers' current hit, 'You'll Never Walk Alone', was both instantaneous and permanent. If Rodgers and Hammerstein had sat down, all those years previously, and deliberately tried to write an anthem for Liverpool and its people, they could not have come up with anything better.

The puzzling detail to note – and still the subject of pub-table conspiracy talk in Liverpool – is that the Beatles, of all people, never showed any interest. The passion for soccer was left to the lesser lights of Merseybeat. It's remarkable the four most famous Liverpudlian males in the world were almost the only four indifferent to football. The popularity of Billy Liddell, the Reds' great star of the 1950s, led reporters to call the town 'Liddellpool', which sounds very Lennon-ish. But apart from John's casual addition of Albert Stubbins to the *Sgt. Pepper* sleeve, and the occasional request from their office for Cup Final tickets, football did not impinge upon the Beatles' world. Had they been forbidden by Brian Epstein to speak openly of their Red or Blue sympathies, for fear of alienating half their local fan-base? No. The Beatles, says Paul, just 'weren't very sporty'.

With odd exceptions, notably Rod Stewart, indifference to the beautiful game was characteristic of rock culture for many years. Musicians and music fans were often devoted to football, but it somehow inhabited a different compartment of existence. In Liverpool this separation of the passions was evident on the relatively foppish Eric's scene. As Pete Wylie says: 'No one at Eric's talked about football . . . I was into music completely and that was an important thing. You would have been seen as a part-timer if you could also like football. The idea of being able to like two things at once was bizarre! Football was working class, and although we were working class we also had this thing of being classless and we weren't going to be categorised. To some extent we rebelled against that football culture – but then we rebelled against everything. I rebelled against being from Norris Green, from being from that kind of background. At Eric's and in that whole scene, I had mates like Paul, Holly, Pete Burns who were openly, outrageously gay. They could be totally out of the gay closet, yet you hid in the shadows as a football fan. I lived in the football closet!'

It's a view shared by Michael Head of the Pale Fountains and Shack: 'Being brought up in the north end and on the streets of Kenny, for me to get into music – it just wasn't what people there did . . . To get into music, to start going to places like the Everyman, I was leaving something behind, going into a totally different territory.'

A few years later, though, Ian McCulloch was fond of comparing the Bunnymen to his beloved Bill Shankly's Liverpool FC. What had changed? 'If you're cynical about it,' suggests Kevin Sampson, 'the sea-change is in the perception of football as something that's fashionable, instead of something that was always seen as lumpen and yobbish. Certainly there was nothing that squared less with the Bunnymen's view of themselves. They saw themselves as the coolest band on the planet. They were Johnny-come-latelies on the football scene. If they had that passion they were hiding it under a bushel, because it was seen as the antithesis of what indie music was all about.

'And you could understand it, because if you think about the successful football teams of the time, you were talking about men with ludicrous amounts of upper body strength, moustaches and very short shorts. It's difficult to justify having an emotional allegiance to that sort of thing!'

It was the scally tribes of the 1980s who re-made the link between Liverpool music and football. (As we'll see later, the figureheads of the new alliance would be a band called the Farm, managed by Kevin Sampson.) Ian McCulloch was simply recognising the altered situation. And the scally generation of Liverpool youths were as likely to find their musical joy on a dancefloor as on a stage: 'There was an instant connection between the football crowd and the acid house crowd,' remembers Sampson. 'It was suddenly just what everyone did. Instead of drinking ten pints of lager you would pop five pills and apparently girls came up and wanted to lick your face.'

On the national stage as well, eventually, football came in from the cultural cold. Sampson: 'There was the 1990 World Cup, Paul Gascoigne bursting into tears, the Taylor Report insisting that stadiums had to be all-seated; these things conspired to make football accessible and trendy to people who previously poured scorn over it.' One could also mention the parallel effects of Nick Hornby's book *Fever Pitch*, easing the game into chattering-class acceptance, and the media's adoption of 'lad' culture. There was the elevation of Manchester United into a quasi-national team, lionised far beyond their natural catchment area. (This was an especially galling development for Liverpool supporters, who'd long contrasted United's supposed glamour with its lack of actual trophies. As the Mancunian team prospered, they came to supplant Everton as Liverpool's classic grudge fixture.) Lastly there was the advertising agencies' recognition that football, newly absolved of its male, prole and hooligan past, was a potent device for selling anything to anyone.

Suddenly the passion that Liverpudlians had always felt for football had become the 'passion' that Coca-Cola were sponsoring. The idolatry that used to inspire those little shrines in terraced houses – red or blue-coloured candles, around a holy picture of the team – could be mimicked in smartly ironic ads for yuppie cars. The football club 'supporter' – in the dour old sense of supporting, meaning to carry a burden – with his community-rooted loyalties was replaced by the giggling football 'fan', who could be enchanted by the brightest bauble in the shop. The dark, atavistic, tribal underworld of football allegiance, of 'Munich 58' on Liverpool walls and 'Hillsborough 89' on their Manchester counterparts', was resolutely ignored.

We walked on, through the wind. Walked on, through the rain. Our dreams, quite frankly, were tossed and blown. But we walked on, walked on, with hope in our hearts.

Then we said, 'This is cack. Let's go home.'

For a year or more we'd been collecting footballers' autographs, and tramped the dreariest avenues of suburban Merseyside to obtain them. Enough was enough. It's not that our boyish adulation of these sporting gods had waned. But you get bored. And the autographs just weren't selling like they used to. And then there's your nerves. Things like the Tommy Smith Incident. It all gets to you in the end . . .

While it lasted, though, the scheme had been a money-spinner. It all began with Liverpool's stylish left-winger Peter Thompson, in this way.

Official histories say little of my part in building Bill Shankly's classic 1960s Liverpool team. But now I shall break my silence. In 1963 my family stayed in a village of 'holiday chalets', nestling on some rain-lashed promontory of the North-west coast. The chalets lacked gaiety, and most other amenities, but in their favour they were co-owned by Peter Thompson, then a young player with Preston North End. It so happened that Shankly wanted him badly. Peter Thompson visited our chalet one evening, and I urged him to join Liverpool. This he duly did and, with the team now complete, the Reds embarked on three decades of unparalleled footballing triumph.

I look for no reward. One simply does one's bit.

It was great to get Peter Thompson's autograph that night, but even better was to take that autograph into school and be offered money for it. Clearly this was the racket to be in. In those days Liverpool and Everton installed their young married players in club houses around the suburbs. The schoolboy grapevine had most of the addresses, a little detective work revealed the rest. We'd simply pay them a visit.

You'd knock on the door and there would appear the player's wife, who was about 20, or 45, or something. You would say 'Is so-and-so in, please? Please can we have his autograph, please?' The amazing thing, looking back, is that so-and-so would always emerge at the door and sign our books without complaint. Nor did it seem to annoy them that the same small boys were returning for their autographs on a regular basis.

The Liverpool and Everton men were equally decent. Anfield skipper 'Big' Ron Yeats was a vast Scotsman of fearsome aspect but friendly disposition; the Blues' Roy Vernon, a Welsh international, would always stand us tea and biscuits. (I read of his death, in late 1993, not having thought of him for 25 years, and I was struck by just how sad I felt.) There was Alan Ball, not much taller than we were. Gordon West, Gerry Byrne, Alex Young ('the Golden Vision') and Brian Labone were others whose semi-detached privacy we repeatedly violated.

Ian St John was idolised by Liverpool boys; getting his autograph six times was sound business. His house seemed wonderfully modern: a sort of split-level, Scandinavian ranch-o-luxe style, with little dark green coniferous things planted outside. It offered one of those glimpses, which 60s children so relished, of an amazing future – a future which, for some reason or other, never actually happened.

But the turning point was the Tommy Smith Incident. Here our tale takes on a darker aspect. Why did his wife let us in the house? She must have *known* he was asleep on the sofa! We'd have gone away peacefully. Given Smith's terrifying reputation in those days, who wouldn't? Did she *want* to see carnage on the shag-pile?

'Tommy,' she said. 'Wake up, Tommy. These fellas want your autograph.'

This was madness. Obviously the woman had completely forgotten who she was married to. Tommy Smith was feared by everyone. Opposing centre-forwards sustained career-abbreviating injuries just by thinking about him. There was a fashion on the Kop for calling Liverpool's three midfield men 'the Good, the Bad and the Ugly'; but it never caught on, probably because the last two adjectives seemed to be Tommy Smith's alone. When he wrote his autobiography it was called *I Did It the Hard Way*, and nobody ever stood up to say, 'Oh no you didn't!'

How to describe Tommy Smith's expression this fine day? Like a bear with a sore head? No, that would be too amiable. Like a bulldog chewing a wasp? Too hail-fellow-well-met.

In fact he looked the way Tommy Smith *would* look if he'd just been abruptly woken up from his afternoon nap to find a couple of spindly kids in his living room, holding out their scabby little autograph books and saying 'Please can we please have please . . .'

We knew fear at that moment, and we understood mortality. Tommy Smith regarded us through those tiny, and very far from Bambi-like, eyes. His breathing was heavy. His sleep-creased features, the famed complexion that made Mount Rushmore look like a Camay advert . . . Given the choice, you'd rather be gazing at something else. You'd rather be a million miles away. You'd really rather not exist at all.

'Please can we please . . .'

Then something very strange and rather magical happened. Tommy Smith smiled.

'A'right, lads?' He reached out for the first pen and autograph book. 'How's it goin'?'

We'd survived. But one's bottle goes. It was time to get out of the autograph game. Make way for new kids, younger and hungrier. Our market was saturated, anyway. (As indeed were our trousers, if memory serves.) When you come through a near-death experience like that, you feel you have been spared to serve some higher purpose with what remains of your time on earth. The last autograph I ever got is the only one I still have. It's Jimmy Tarbuck's, signed at Anfield on a match programme in 1965. I could never sell it. I don't mean for sentimental reasons. I just mean I could never sell it.

11. BEATEN CITY

ALL THE GRIM STUFF. AND HOW ENGLAND FELL OUT OF LOVE WITH LIVERPOOL

'Her majesty's poor decayed town of Liverpool.'
From a 1571 petition to Queen Elizabeth I

In your Liverpool slums
You look in the dustbin for something to eat
You find a dead rat and think it's a treat
In your Liverpool slums.

Football terrace song, 1986

Slavery and famine are the mother and father of Liverpool. No wonder the child grew up so troubled. All the same, it's a melancholy thing to see your home town in ruins. It happens after wars; it happened to Liverpool and other British towns after the Blitz. But here it happened again in peacetime, in the 1980s. You'd walk along streets of empty shells of homes, bordered by wasteland. Over there were busted relics of commerce and manufacture. In the mind's eye you'd recollect them in the bustle of their prime, maybe not pretty and not necessarily prosperous, but alive and inhabited and purposeful. Everywhere you looked was not what you remembered. Most Liverpudlians will share this internalised experience, and to understand them you need to be aware of it.

Liverpool came to occupy a new and special place in the British imagination. If the 1970s had been a time of anti-climax, accompanied by a gentle subsidence into semi-obscurity, then the 1980s saw Liverpool's old fame replaced with infamy. Suddenly, this was Bad News Town. Somebody dubbed it the Museum of Horrifying Example. Urban riots, radical politics and economic meltdown made it emblematic of the era's downside, just as Stock Exchange roaring boys were symbols of the opposite. Violence, strikes and the two football disasters of Heysel and Hillsborough heightened the city's notoriety.

Back in the 60s, Liverpool had seemed the focus of a revolution. But the revolution was more apparent than real: just a minor shuffling of elites, as the exhausted old order made room for some energetic newcomers. It turned out that Liverpudlians were not in the vanguard of this movement, after all, they were just its mascots. When grey day dawned and normality returned, Liverpool was back at the bottom of the heap. And national affection had curdled into contempt. The Gods seemed of a mind to punish the place in jealousy of its brief dance in the sunlight. What happened was that the Beat City became the Beaten City. The free marketeers who gathered around Margaret Thatcher were the first to make public their dislike of everything the place represented. Eventually, in slyer ways, the liberals would follow suit.

If this was Ginsberg's 'centre of human consciousness' then it looked as if the world had just had a lobotomy. Was this the town that taught the world to sing? Hard to believe in all that stuff any more.

The curse of unemployment struck very hard. The city was slowly drained of people, creating a Scouse Diaspora. The bourgeoisie was long gone; the town which once had more millionaires than any outside London was now called 'the Bermuda Triangle of British Capitalism'. Thousands of slummies were replanted in the Lancashire overspill estates; and the better-off kids who'd gone away to college were not coming back. Scatterlings of Liverpool were to be observed everywhere. Workers might travel across to Europe; you'd see them on the Continental boats, with spirit levels sticking out from duffel bags, or on cold morning squares in Amsterdam and Dusseldorf, awaiting the man in a van. They stood along side the Turks and Algerians, the new *Gästarbeiten* – guest-workers – of the European Union.

Others, unskilled, would drift across Britain to mooch around holiday resorts, where they helped to spread the image of shiftless, shifty Scousers. In 1987 there were 5,000 Liverpudlians in Bournemouth, of whom the police alleged 2,000 were engaged in crime. Some had casual work in hotels and catering, but still signed on for the dole. Feared and loathed by locals, they colonised their own pubs and clubs.

As a boy I walked past the colossal, grand and grimy buildings of Liverpool and wondered what went on there. Now, as buddleia bushes grew from rooftops, the question could only be, What *used* to go on there? Once, the men would meet and grunt a standard greeting, 'Where yer werkin'?' By 1980 I noticed it had been trimmed to 'Yer werkin'?'

Pop groups came from London to play benefit concerts for the unemployed. Even the Bangles had noticed our fallen state – their hit version of the dole-lament 'Going Down to Liverpool' ('to do nothing'), conjured a surreal vision of sun-kissed Californian girls in the cigarette fug of Bootle DHSS. Meanwhile the leftists organised grand marches. Liverpool had become a Jarrow for the Giro age. It seemed to have lost its purpose to exist.

Decline was not always accompanied by dereliction – sometimes by the opposite. City business streets used to be blackened canyons, whose sides were thickened by honest dirt. Now they were blasted clean, as pretty as the day they were made. But nothing went on there. The shopping streets had shouted with traffic. By Whitechapel there used to be a policeman in a black and white box, among the fumes and din, with upraised hands in giant gauntlets. Now the junction was 'pedestrianised', prodigiously littered, swept only by wind from the river. You'd see outdoor traders, who stood along the pavement with their merchandise in cardboard boxes. Unshaven men sold razor blades. Grim-faced men sold party balloons. Ragged, unhappy women held out bunches of lucky heather.

The economic rhetoric of the time spoke of belt-tightening, of sacrifice for the greater good. But this language of sacrifice had an echo of clubroom generals in the first world war. Pain was not to be distributed equally; from those with least to give, the most appeared to be taken. The Liverpool workforce of the 1980s found itself the cannon-fodder of an economic coup. Capital was becoming more global by the day. Footloose and fancy-free, it skipped capriciously from one continent to another. The view from the Mersey shore was that the money-tide was going out, and it was never coming in again.

Mrs Thatcher's new government did not create these conditions – they'd been in the making for decades – but her Party embraced them, and worked along the grain of the new reality, while the Labour Party still pretended to oppose it. As with her next adversaries, the mining towns, she could more easily countenance Liverpool's ruin because there were so few Tory votes to be lost there. Again like the mining towns, there was an ancestral dislike of the place, ideologically rooted in disputes of the past. Perhaps that antipathy was compounded, in Liverpool's case, by its iconic place in the myth of the 1960s, a decade that she and her associates repudiated, and which Liverpool represented. Psychologically, there was a poignant contrast between Mrs Thatcher's supposed 'corner shop' mentality – thrifty, snobbish, respectable, narrow – and the personality of Liverpool – sloppy, generous, improvident, grand of gesture and sentiment.

Into all this arrived Derek Hatton, sleek and cheeky, deputy leader of the Labour-controlled Council and a hero of the party's far-left Militant Tendency. Their supremacy served to further isolate Liverpool from the mainstream of British politics. Militant was troubling the Labour Party everywhere, but Liverpool was its fortress. It was born here, not because socialism was strong, but because Labour was weak. Nationally, the British Labour Party inherited Liberal intellectuals and Methodist working men; but Liverpool's organisation was shaped by conspiratorial Irish nationalists and anarchic casual labourers. Religious divisions scrambled party loyalties. Strikes were often wildcat, beyond the unions' control. The corruption of Liverpool politics was, like the waterfront architecture, normally compared to Chicago's. And when the Catholic Mafia passed into history, the moribund rump of Liverpool Labour was Militant's for the taking.

Culturally, Hatton's battalions were unlike the Labour generation then arising in London. Perhaps because they did not share the hippy past of so many Southern leftists, they were indifferent to the newly-favoured 'issue' politics of race, gender and ecology. They could be openly contemptuous of conservation; Adrian Henri called them 'savagely Philistine'. Their agenda was socialism, nothing more and nothing less. But the Labour Party was quietly dropping socialism. Thus, for the next ten years, Liverpool played an interesting role in the psychodrama of the British Left. Neil Kinnock, by confronting Hatton, began Labour's long climb back from electoral decrepitude. The process was completed by Tony Blair. For New Labour to triumph, Liverpool had to be humbled. Blair's father-in-law was, of course, the actor Tony Booth, 'randy Scouse git' of *Till Death Us Do Part*; in real life Booth was now a wild-eyed, grey-headed figure, and a loose Old Labour cannon. He stalked the Blair family battlements like the ghost of vanquished Liverpool socialism.

Thatcher's time in office saw another surprising development. Liverpool's showbiz contingent gave their allegiance to the Tories. London media types were nonplussed, but it was not so strange. After all, Cilla Black and Jimmy Tarbuck were Scouse celebrity exiles in the stockbroker belt. They'd always hated Labour's taxation policies, which were so galling to self-made people, free of guilt about silver spoon backgrounds. A few rungs lower down, comedian Stan Boardman was even more outspoken. And the DJ Kenny Everett appeared on stage at a Thatcher election rally, heaping derision on Labour's leader Michael Foot. These people were not Tories at all, in the traditional sense, but robustly Thatcherite populists who, like her, despised the liberal culture-mongers. The stars' opinions were disliked back in Liverpool, too – but their audience now was Middle England, not the Liverpool dockers or Alexei Sayle's social workers.

Then the city had some riots. Their suddenness and scale amazed the nation. But there was a residual habit of rioting in Liverpool, anyway. Whether it was over religion, a strike or the price of fish, the streets of Liverpool had always seen astonishing conflicts. In 1775 a row about sailors' pay led to a cannon attack on the Town Hall. The spring riots of 1909 did not fizzle out until the autumn. One of the bloodiest clashes occurred in William Brown Street in 1919, when the Liverpool police themselves went on strike. On 5 July 1981, it was the turn of Toxteth, or more specifically the Granby ward of Liverpool 8.

For two sensational TV nights, this inner city slum enacted England's oldest nightmare: the rabble of masterless men, roaming in fire and ruin. Liverpool's sky glowed red across the Mersey, and among the casualties was the old Rialto Ballroom, scene of pre-war foxtrots and the recording of those 1963 *This Is Mersey Beat* LPs. Across the main streets, police lined up in medieval battle rank, with helmets, sticks and shields. There was charge and counter-charge, petrol bombing, looting and the first CS gas used outside of Ulster. Welsh coppers, swiftly drafted in, sang 'Men of Harlech' like the soldiers in *Zulu*. National reporting of the trouble adopted the area's official designation, Toxteth, and the name won such renown that even the locals took to using it.

Being in a partly black neighbourhood there was an ethnic dimension to the fighting, but not on the part of the rioters themselves – unlike the police, they were a model of racial integration. In the avalanche of explanations that followed, unemployment was the favourite culprit, followed by police harassment. I don't doubt the honest rage that Granby youths felt. I got the impression, however, that they also rioted because it was exciting. If you're going to have a revolution, as D.H. Lawrence said, have it for fun. And for the attention. And for all the free gifts you liberate from local shops. It looked so attractive, in fact, that rioting quickly spread to every part of Britain, including the Liverpool suburbs. Eventually, calm would descend again on Toxteth and rain dampened the embers. But after the police withdrew, only drug dealers could feel optimistic about the business climate going forward.

There was no doubt that unemployment was crippling some people's spirit. In November, 1982, there was a five-week TV drama called *The Boys from the Black Stuff*, which stirred the whole country. Its impact was comparable in scale to *Pop Idol*, but from a tradition of serious TV drama that has now been dismantled. Written by the Liverpool playwright Alan Bleasdale, *The Black Stuff* was unforgettably bleak; it followed the misadventures of a Merseyside building gang against the backdrop of a collapsing local economy. The characters – most memorably the sociopathic Yozzer Hughes – struggled and floundered as unemployment stripped away their self-respect, their families' stability and their own grip on reality. In all, it was a masterpiece of nerve-scraping pathos.

During *The Black Stuff*'s run I arranged to meet Bleasdale at the Albert Dock, which was derelict at the time; to get us inside, he had to find the cocky watchman. The muddy, redundant docks were a sorry sight. He suggested what was going wrong with Liverpool: 'It's the multinationals, it's the fact we're at the arse-end of the Industrial Revolution and every other bugger's whipping past us, and the fact that Liverpool faces west, which was great because of America but is now buggered up because of the Common Market. And Margaret Thatcher doesn't help because she's a cow of the first order and she puts a cold, unemotional face on politics – as if nobody up there really cares.' The building trade, as Bleasdale noted, was emblematic of contrasting strands in Liverpool's workforce. On the one hand were the casual labourers, picked or dismissed on a boss's whim. On the other were the skilled men, inheritors of the craftsmanship that had fitted out the luxury ocean liners, not to mention the city's splendid pub interiors.

What's your next project, I asked. 'I very much want to write a love story,' he said, and laughed. 'Set in Cheltenham!'

Back in London I watched the Carnaby Street shops stock up on Yozzer Hughes T-shirts. His famous lines, 'Gizza job!' and 'I can do that!' became the waggish catch-phrases of the year. I remember two novelty singles being released, one by the Black Stuff Boys and one by Yozzer's Gang: the latter combo dressed identically in donkey jackets, with comedy black moustaches.

Actually, there was nothing but admiration around Britain for Bleasdale's achievement. However the obsession with Yozzer betrayed a worrying trend. He represented a sea-change in national perceptions of the Liverpool character. Britain had fallen out of love with Scousers. The refrain had gone from 'Yeah yeah yeah' to 'Gizza job' in just 20 years.

Worse was to come, though. Football had been the city's last success story. Now it became the source of utter anguish. On 29 May 1985, Liverpool travelled to Heysel Stadium in Belgium for the European Cup Final with Juventus of Italy. Trouble was seen to start in sections of the crowd about half an hour before kick off. No effective measures had been taken to separate the rival factions. When a contingent of Liverpool fans gave chase to a group of Juventus supporters, a crumbling partition wall gave way and 39 people, mainly Italians, were either crushed or trampled to death. After a five-month trial, fourteen Liverpool fans were given varying sentences for involuntary manslaughter. English clubs were banned from European competition for five years, Liverpool for ten. Heysel Stadium itself was demolished.

Though Liverpool and its fans could hardly claim to be the injured party in all of this, it was unfortunate that Heysel did so much harm to the reputation of the city and the club's generally peaceable supporters. There were numerous untruths and small injustices in the official reactions and in the media coverage, but given the greater misfortune of so many deaths, there was little that could decently be said out loud in Liverpool's defence. Silence and condolence were the only appropriate responses.

Four years later came an even more terrible event. On 15 April 1989, Liverpool supporters travelled to Hillsborough, Sheffield Wednesday's ground, for an FA Cup semi-final against Nottingham Forest. I had a brother among the crowd at Liverpool's end, and watched with mounting horror the TV scenes of slowly unfolding catastrophe. My brother survived but 96 did not. Spectators still entering into the stadium tunnels were, unknowingly, pushing against a mass of bodies trapped against the cages at the pitch perimeter. Among the suffocating press of congested Liverpool supporters there followed a sequence of unspeakable suffering and ultimate tragedy.

The shock felt by the whole country was naturally experienced most deeply in Liverpool. The silence in the city that Saturday evening, and all through Sunday, was an eerie phenomenon. The football club's Anfield ground became the focus of mourning. The workings of grief were quiet, steady, massive.

Down in London, however, at the offices of the *Sun* newspaper, there was a different mood in the air. Sunday had been a day of numb incomprehension on Merseyside. Survivors were in shock. Families of the bereaved had much to do and more to absorb. But if Liverpool was preoccupied, the phone lines between Sheffield and London were busy indeed. By Monday night the *Sun*'s editor felt confident of his headline for the following morning: 'The Truth'. Beneath it ran three subsidiary headlines: 'Some fans picked pockets of victims'; 'Some fans urinated on the brave cops'; and 'Some fans beat up PC giving kiss of life'. As it happened, not one of these things was true. Nor, as further alleged, was a dead girl abused. Fans did not urinate on dead bodies, and they did not attack rescue workers.

By the next Sunday, a left-leaning pundit on the *Sunday Times* weighed in with his own reflections: 'For the second time in a decade a large body of Liverpool supporters has killed people.' (Heysel seemed to have entered conventional wisdom as a pre-meditated act of homicide.) 'The futile erection of football into a cult is the city's only modern acquaintance with excellence, matches elsewhere being the one chance to swagger and intimidate ...' If the Sheffield police bore any responsibility, he decided, it was 'for not realising what brutes they had to handle'. He then turned his gaze to the scenes of mourning in Liverpool: 'The shrine in the Anfield goalmouth, the cursing of the police, all the theatricals, come sweetly to a city which is already the world capital of self-pity.'

This was a period of Southern ascendancy in British politics. We saw the renewed dominance of London after the temporary vogue for provincialism. Like the supporters of the London football clubs, who waved five-pound notes at the Merseyside fans – shouting 'D'you know what this is?' or singing 'You'll never work again' – the *Sun* had succumbed to the less attractive side of Cockney swagger. The *Sunday Times'* eccentricity is harder to explain. But neither paper was, in the end, dramatically out of step with shifts in national sentiment. Official reports and independent investigations would exonerate the Liverpool fans at Hillsborough, but the city's stock was once again diminished.

Hillsborough encouraged Liverpudlians in their insularity. The *Sun* saw its Merseyside sales decimated by a boycott. Mistrust of the media grew. It's true the disaster had won some sympathy for Liverpool and occasional admiration of its communal spirit, at a time when such spirit was felt to be disappearing from national life. However, deeper down it reinforced a feeling that Liverpool was trouble and, worse, maudlin with it. 'Self-Pity City' became a recurring headline. The evident rift between sentimental Celtic Liverpool and stoical Saxon England was never wider – until a decade later, of course, when the death of Diana revealed some unsuspected similarities.

Adrian Henri painted the Anfield pitch, buried beneath the sea of flowers and football scarves, with all the passionate engagement he had brought to his portrait of the Kop in full voice, painted twelve years before. He wrote a poem, too, on the day after the disaster: the heart-rending *The Bell*; from his Liverpool 8 house he had heard the Cathedral's bell toll once for each person dead. It was inevitable that one song, 'You'll Never Walk Alone', became the Hillsborough mourners' anthem and the victims' epitaph. In the Liverpudlian heart, music and football fuse at such moments. Punished by tragedy and vilified by the ignorant, the city sought consolation in its old song of fellowship-in-adversity.

12. GIVE IT LOADS

FRANKIE AND A FLOCK OF POP GROUPS; ALSO ELVIS COSTELLO

When Eric's went the way of all fleshpots, the Liverpool music scene lost its spiritual HQ. Manchester, however, still had the Hacienda and Factory. Even the suicide of Joy Division's Ian Curtis brought a kind of renewal there. When his band-mates re-grouped as New Order, they built on Manchester's heritage of Northern Soul to make an alliance of white indie style and black American dance. With A Certain Ratio (whose stirring single, 'Shack Up', was a Northern Soul standard) they shunted music forwards by marrying ghetto funk to European elec- tronica, filtered through a peculiar Northern bleakness.

Liverpool audiences were receptive to New Order, but the city's musicians still displayed a preference for melody over rhythm, and – apart from OMD and Dalek I Love You – for guitars over synthesisers. As the 1980s dawned, the Teardrops and the Bunnymen were the keepers of the flame. Stereotypes held that Manchester music was dour, for all its dance ambitions, and much attached to the grey raincoat, whereas Liverpool was arty and psychedelic. As Ian McCulloch told the NME: 'Probably the main difference is that Liverpool bands have always written songs, whereas Manchester has always been the place that's gone for grooves.'

Other locations embraced electronica: in Yorkshire were Soft Cell, Human League and Cabaret Voltaire; down in Basildon, Depeche Mode. These people moved from 'industrial' avant garde to chart-bound synth-pop. Meanwhile from the Midlands came the punk-ska music hybrid known as 2-Tone, led by the Specials and taken up by Madness of Camden Town. In Bristol musicians drew on the jazz and dub reggae strands that were strong there, which you can trace through the Pop Group to Portishead, Tricky and Massive Attack. 'Dahn sarf' in London's East End, punk became a boot-boy mutant known as Oi. Everywhere else, they just banged dandruffed heads to heavy metal.

Yet, amid the fragmentation, the 1980s would still be an heroic decade for Liverpool music, whatever the city's fortunes in other respects. Bill Harry points out that on 28 January 1984, there were more Scouse acts in the Top 20 than since 1964. They were: Frankie Goes To Hollywood ('Relax'), Paul McCartney ('Pipes of Peace'), Joe Fagin ('That's

Livin' Alright'; from the Blackstuff-lite TV series *Auf Wiedersehen Pet*), John Lennon ('Nobody Told Me'), China Crisis ('Wishful Thinking'), Echo and the Bunnymen ('Killing Moon') and Icicle Works ('Love Is a Wonderful Colour').

Though Eric's was dead, the club had a couple of posthumous gifts for the world. The first of these arrived in the ever-astonishing form of Dead Or Alive's Pete Burns: the sharp-tongued boy from Cut Above The Rest, who knocked around with Jayne Casey and Holly Johnson. The *Rock Family Trees* compiler Pete Frame, who chronicled the Cavern and Eric's generations, penned a vivid description of Burns in 1980: 'a strange character – probably the most bizarre fucker on Merseyside: a psychedelic Sitting Bull with gold rings on his nose, a cosmetic blitzkrieg of eye shadow and rouge, cascades of elaborate ear-rings, several pounds of beads and bones hanging round his neck, and a tonsorial superstructure like a Rasta Tony Curtis modified by 5,000 volts of live wire up his anus.'

Burns was one of those figures who seemed born to hold court in Eric's; it was inevitable he would have a band before long. There was the Mystery Girls with Cope and Wylie, then the group he formed with Martin Healy, Nightmares In Wax. The latter group had a streak of Gay Gothic about them, like the sound of subterranean pleasure dungeons. In a rather terrifying club I was taken to, the all-male clientele were writhing in the half-light to Pete's version of KC and the Sunshine Band's 'That's the Way (I Like It)': 'Now that I'm old enough to know what I like,' howled Burns' lyric, 'I like big heavy muscle boys on motor bikes.' His appearance put some in mind of London's foppish New Romantic scene. But the lonely heroism of Pete Burns, I thought, was that he walked mean streets where you were more likely to meet scallies with Stanley knives than photographers from the Sunday colour supplements.

He and Healy struggled to assemble Dead Or Alive: 'We could never get musicians,' Pete explained, ''cos they thought we were fruitcakes. The thing about that band was that it attracted real loonies. We started a group because we'd stolen a keyboard and thought we'd better do something with it. We're still on the run from some people.' An early drummer and stabilising influence was the excellent Joey Musker, who'd also played – surreally – with the latterday Fourmost. When I interviewed the band in 1981, Burns gave a virtuoso display of acidic Eric's bitching:

'Liverpool bands always pick arty names and I just hate being associated with that arty movement. The other day I picked up this fanzine and someone had said to Ian McCulloch, "Isn't Pete Burns the ace face in Liverpool?" and he goes "Oh no" – through his short-sighted eyes – "I don't think so. He's just a moron in a black suit." And that really upset me, 'cos I'd hate to see Echo and the Bunnymen go on stage with a dead lead singer. There's a thing about certain Liverpool bands that they have to bitch about each other in the press. *This* isn't bitching – this just serves as a warning to him, 'cos I won't go around bullshitting about it. I'll stick a mike-stand up his arse if he starts slagging me through the press. And it would be awful to see McCulloch in a shroud, 'cos I fucking will kill him if he does that again.'

The rest of the band looked uneasy during this speech. But Pete was undeterred: 'There's been so many successful Liverpool bands, and everyone's in awe. But they're just no one to me. And if that happens again, it'll be no teeth.' Doleful old Joey Musker leaned over and offered Pete a large plastic bag. 'Here y'are, Pete. Put that over yer head.'

'I've looked the way I am for years,' Burns went on. 'I'm not part of a movement. And that Blitz thing [the London New Romantic club] makes me wanna die. I mean, I go to work like this!' (Admittedly, his workplace was Probe Records, rather than, say, the Seaforth Docks.) 'I go to the doctor's like this, the toilet like this. I look like whatever I wanna look like. I can't be different or I'll be unhappy . . . It isn't for want of attention because, as hard as this might come to you, I *hate* people staring at me. I hate walking in somewhere and everyone'll go quiet.'

Life could not be simple for a boy who was so uncompromising, yet sensitive with it. He sighed that he had lost count of the genitals flashed at him. It upset him, he said, and put him off his food. When the group were shown on local TV, Martin's Grandad said that Pete should be shot. Violence seemed to wait for him on each Liverpool street: 'At one point I was barred out of every club, gay, straight or music venue, just for looking odd. In the end I retired from going out. I've had a taxi drive up the kerb at me, I've had someone try to push me out of a bus. I've been smashed across the head with a wine bottle and a brick. I could never hope to understand it.'

His childhood was disturbed. He said he had 'a loonie background. I grew up really fast. At fourteen I was bringing up my parents. I was taken out of school at fifteen 'cos the pressure was just too much. I had to get a psychiatrist to take me out of school. The schoolkids were just twats. So now I think I'm having the childhood that I missed. I'm in a circle of people that accept me. I am clever. The only thing I can't do is fix a plug. But when it comes to survival instincts I can do it. I'm quite tough. I'm living out all my fantasies. I'm being everything I wanted to be. If you want to be the Empire State Building, some way you can do it . . . That's my philosophy of life.' By four o'clock the next morning I was in Pete's flat, with his wife Lyn, watching his video of *Deep Throat* and stroking a dead stoat that he'd stuffed with a rolled-up copy of the *Liverpool Echo*. There was also a squirrel with a bullet hole its head. And Pete showed me his collection of nuns' bones. It was lovely.

Within a few years only Pete Burns remained of that line-up; he signed to Epic in London, who teamed him with the hot-shot production team of Stock, Aitken and Waterman. Dead Or Alive adopted the gay disco sound called Boystown, or Hi-NRG – a fast, electro-funk hybrid – and Pete became a global star with 'You Spin Me Round (Like a Record)'. By the 1990s his career was kept afloat by a loyal following in the Far East. Eric's most wayward child was, finally, Big In Japan. 'A lot of bands disappear completely and end up down the Portobello Road selling bruised fruit,' he said. 'But that wasn't going to be me.'

Apart from Dead Or Alive and the off-shoots of the Crucial Three, there was a tough guitar act around that post-Eric's time called Ellery Bop, fronted by a macho rocker named Jamie and his quieter sidekick Kev. They were referred to (out of earshot) as 'the Thug and the Drunk'. Jamie used to work as 'security' in Eric's, where he was given to wading into any fracas. 'I got paid for hitting people, basically. When Eric's closed me whole world finished.' Kev did not actually play, but supplied moral support and the financial proceeds of certain business dealings. Jamie once threatened to beat up Pete Wylie, who talked him into taking up the guitar instead. But his own career in live performance was frustratingly brief: 'There was always trouble,' he told me. 'I hate playing live 'cos I'd get so worked up and nervous that if anyone was being funny I'd end up getting off and fighting them. And I thought, If we carry on like this, we're gonna get people comin' along just 'cos they wanna fight me.'

Jamie struck up a close, if incongruous, friendship with Julian Cope, eventually signed to a London record company and recorded with Ian Broudie. But he made no headway in the capital and his passionate idealism could not carry Ellery Bop to the next stage. Sitting in the Grapes in Mathew Street, his intensity and optimism had sounded invincible. But over the next few years, when I'd meet him in London, he would seem like a fly trapped in a web. He could be truculent: once, in Trident Studios, the hapless Marc Almond wandered into our room, whereupon a brusque dismissal from Jamie (who had a low tolerance for fops) sent the Soft Cell man scampering like a startled faun. It was a loss to rock'n'roll that Ellery Bop did not become successful. They could have been contenders.

By 1984 the whole of Britain was using the Liverpool expression 'give it loads.' And they'd learned it from the lips of experts: Frankie Goes To Hollywood.

In the years since Big In Japan, Holly Johnson had made more music, and drifted into a new band called Sons Of Egypt. Another Eric's face, Paul Rutherford, had been singing and dancing with Hambi and the Dance, where his presence brought a touch of gay disco to the rock world. By the time he and Holly were united in Frankie Goes To Hollywood – the name derived from a Frank Sinatra headline – the line-up was a sexual summit meeting of gay subculture and three decidedly straight Scousers. The latter, who would be dubbed the Lads, were an electrician called Nasher, a joiner called Mark O'Toole and a recently redundant wood-machinist called Ped. Paul, in particular, made their stage act a spectacle of perverse glamour, while the Lads developed a tough variant on the white funk being popularised by Spandau Ballet and the Thompson Twins. There were dancing girls, black leather costumes, chains and whips.

I organised a feature on them for the *NME*, and blanched when local photographer John Stoddart sent me shots of Holly performing mock-fellatio with a knife at Paul's crotch. Between the Frankies and occasional visits by Pete Burns, *NME* colleagues were asking me what had happened to macho Liverpool. The TV show *The Tube* filmed a Frankie set at the State Ballroom, and by late 1983 they were on Trevor Horn's ZTT label, releasing a track called 'Relax' that most of the band did not play on. Despite a belated BBC ban, it became a monumental hit. In the long hot summer of 1984, 'Frankie Say' T-shirts were everywhere. So was their next Number 1, 'Two Tribes'. When they reached the top with third single 'The Power of Love', they'd matched the achievement of their predecessors Gerry and the Pacemakers (whose coffers they'd already replenished by covering 'Ferry Cross the Mersey' on the B-side of 'Relax').

Near the end of 1984 I went with the group on their first American tour. In New York, to Holly's delight, he met Andy Warhol – a dizzying moment for the Wavertree misfit who'd named himself after a Warhol character in Lou Reed's 'Walk on the Wild Side'. And Frankie really did go to Hollywood, where they filmed a cameo in a Brian De Palma movie. From Paul Rutherford I learned the meaning of the group's new song title 'Krisco Kisses', this being a US brand of cooking oil. (But it was no concern of mine, I thought, what consenting adults did in the privacy of their own frying pans.)

ZTT had been reluctant to let the Frankies go on tour, fearing their live skills could not match the dazzling studio concoctions of Trevor Horn. These shows, therefore, were seen by the band as a declaration of independence. And while they could never live up to the phenomenal hype surrounding them, the Frankies were indeed a funky rock'n'roll band. The New York audience was sceptical, but Atlanta loved them. Leaving the gig, fans were battering at the tour-bus windows and the band's adrenaline was racing. At those times the Lads looked as wired as you'd expect of any three scals, plucked from nowhere and set to bask in a sudden mad access of sex, cash and attention. 'How are you feelin', Mark?' I'd asked, when he came off stage, red-faced and gasping. 'Fuckin' *smaart*! What, girls grabbin' yer nuts an' everything? Fuckin' *grate!*'

And yet, though I didn't know it at the time, this was the precise moment Frankie began to break up. Bad blood between the band, their managers and ZTT was mingling with resentments in the band itself. Cue the arrival of Holly's new boyfriend, Wolfgang Kuhle – often cited as the Yoko Ono of the story. He'd met Johnson in a London gay bar a few months earlier and now they lived together. He had just flown out to New York to join Holly, who invited him to stay on the tour. ('For some reason, however, this was not a popular decision with the rest of the band,' he reflected later.) The atmosphere around the group was distinctly subdued.

One evening I sat in the hotel bar with Paul Rutherford. His Eric's pedigree was one of the longest, having formed Liverpool's first punk group, the Spitfire Boys, around the time that Jayne Casey was joining Big In Japan. As well as being the handsomest, best-dressed member of the Frankies, he was invariably easy-going. Suddenly and silently Holly materialised, with Wolfgang at his side, and sat at our table. It transpired, to my dismay, that Holly was cancelling the interview I had been flown over, at the band's expense, to conduct for the *NME*. His decision was based, he said, on a previous article by a different writer. Gesture accomplished, he and Wolfgang then retired into their private world.

While recriminations flew among the band, its management, PR and record company, I withdrew for something to eat with Paul, who seemed to watch the whole charade with humorous resignation. In a revolving restaurant upstairs, as the darkening Georgia sky scrolled past, he shrugged and smiled. 'I just like getting to see the world, I suppose. Sound like a beauty queen, don't I? I wanna travel and meet people.' His mind was still trying to process all he'd seen on that American trip, and coping with the mixed sensations that people often have when they first achieve success. 'I think you're always slightly disillusioned when you get to places. It's like, the Empire State Building isn't as high as you think it is. The Eiffel Tower isn't as high as you think it is. But it doesn't matter.'

He thought back to Liverpool. 'It made us as strong as we are,' he decided. 'It took these five scallies to do it, to stand up and not be pretentious about it. And to laugh at ourselves. Everyone mentions the Beatles to us, especially in America. But we don't bear much relation at all, or to most bands from Liverpool. We all hung round on the same scene, but we've got nothing in common with Echo and the Bunnymen when we're on stage, or on record. In the dressing room later, *that's* where the similarities might start.' Spookily, far across the room, a cocktail pianist had started playing 'You'll Never Walk Alone'.

'Where you're from does make you what you are,' he reflected. 'But do you *owe* it to that place? It's like this whole thing of turning your back on it: "Oh, you've moved to London now." I dunno, they lay on this really weird guilt trip. I personally had a really hard time there. I used to get kicked in the face at least twice a night for being a puff, and dressing weird, being a punk or whatever. I had a horrible time at school. I don't particularly have fond memories of the place, although it's great when I go back now. I always had a better time when I got out. It's necessary to move out. It's a small place. You have to move out if you're going to be as successful as you want to be.'

Like all the Frankies, he was touchy about the notion they were puppets of their record company: 'No-one buys *my* trousers for me, you know? If anything, ZTT just marketed this crazy little entity.' Had he enjoyed the controversy that surrounded them? '*Yiiisss!* Loved it! None of us *felt* controversial. It was just us being ourselves . . . There's this thing, isn't there, that an artist has to have this mystique about them. And they don't. Most people in bands are quite thick, all they wanna do is play music. But they mask it with "I like this painter, and that painter." It's bullcrap . . . But we are definitely leftists. That's socially inbred by being from Liverpool. You just don't dream of voting any other way.'

When the Frankies went home they set, pessimistically, to recording a second album. The group dynamic between homo and hetero had become a fault-line, with the Lads inclined to rock, Holly and Paul to dance. The result was a tougher sound – including the next single 'Rage Hard' – but lacking the sparkle of its predecessor. They called the album *Liverpool*, and packaged it with a grainy black-and-white photo of the Mersey waterfront, as if staking their claim to artistic authenticity and roots credibility. But there were now disputes about anything and everything, and the band could not survive them. Perhaps it was true, as Pete Burns suggests, that the Frankies' rise had been so sudden, their move to London so quick, that they missed out the Liverpool nurturing period that might have bolstered their internal solidarity.

Holly alone was able to build a reasonable solo career, though not before a bitter court battle with ZTT. In 1991 he was found to be HIV positive; in 1994 he published his autobiography, *A Bone in My Flute*. In recent years he has concentrated on painting: works at the Royal Academy's 2001 Summer Exhibition were heavy on male bodies and naked penises. His health, he reported, had improved through the 90s thanks to combination therapy. He declared himself 'very happy to still be alive'.

The curious quality of other Liverpool pop in the 1980s was its wilfully lightweight nature. It used to puzzle some observers, who thought a beaten-up old pug of a town like Liverpool should be inciting music full of rage. Instead it was fey, dreamy and pretty. It's striking that Liverpool has never produced a heavy metal band of any consequence. Nor was there much of a market for the hard-core punk, whether Cockney boot boy or anarcho-vegetarian, that flourished elsewhere. The local taste was for a playful escapism. That, and far-fetched names . . .

Period examples include the Lotus Eaters, who enjoyed a gossamer summer hit in 1983, 'The First Picture of You'. An innocent-looking duo, they were the former Wild Swan Jeremy Kelly and a future don of Liverpool dance music, Peter Coyle. They could not have been less rock'n'roll. Touring in support of Big Country, they let it be known they liked to play a game of golf wherever they went. An equally restrained, tuneful affair were China Crisis, who had a run of ethereal, murmuring hits including 'King in a Catholic Style', 'Black Man Ray' and 'Wishful Thinking'. Then there were the Pale Fountains, whose fanciful name became most people's idea of stereotypical Mersey drippiness. That was not entirely fair to the band, but their true worth was not apparent until years later, when the leader Michael Head launched a new career in Shack. And likewise the Icicle Works, led by Ian McNabb. They had one hit, 'Love Is a Wonderful Colour', and deserved a few more, but the best work came in the singer's solo music.

The craze for cryptically winsome names would reach its zenith in A Flock Of Seagulls, fronted by the sculpted hair of Mike Score. Their biggest British hit 'Wishing (If I Had a Photograph of You)' was blippy synth-pop, typical of the time, but with a superior tune and plenty of swing. Their greatest achievement, however, was to ride the tide of Limey music that the newly-launched MTV was breaking in America. Though they were not an act built to last, you can measure their impact on US trash culture by a stray reference in Quentin Tarantino's *Pulp Fiction*. It occurs when gun-toting Samuel L. Jackson is menacing some cringing student drug-customers, and signals his contempt by calling one of them 'Flock of Seagulls'. (By a further irony, Jackson would turn up in 2001 as a real-life devotee of Liverpool. Spending time in the city on a local movie, *The 51st State*, he remarked to *Esquire*: 'The people that live here have great spirit. They're really hard-working but seem downtrodden by everyone around them. Even right next door in Manchester they always seem to be looking down on Liverpool, but they go there to party. It's a hard-partying city.')

The new importance of video had worked in A Flock Of Seagulls' favour. However, others bands suffered. Signed to major labels in a spray of champagne, the following months would see them lumbered with appalling videos, filmed at colossal expense, promoting records that negated all the promise of their demo tapes. The latter effect was normally thanks to another expensive item on the band's debit account, namely a hot-shot producer, employed by the record company to make their new boys sound like a composite of everything that was already in the charts. It was disappointing to watch some eager young acts arrive from Liverpool, and climb mere inches up the slippery pole of stardom before sliding to the floor. But that's show business.

Among the more fortunate was Colin Vearncombe. The name of his group, Black, signified a break with Liverpool's florid trend, and was at all events an improvement on one of his youthful efforts, the Epileptic Tits. Long years of service were rewarded by a late 80s classic, 'Wonderful Life', and his other hits 'Sweetest Smile' and 'The Big One'. Vearncombe's style was wispy to the point of weightlessness, but – rather like Ian Broudie – his way with a tune concealed more complex intentions. 'What really annoyed me,' he once said, 'was when people asked, "If it's such a 'Wonderful Life', why don't you smile when you sing the song?" That, however, wasn't the idea at all. If they'd listened to the words they would have realised how ironic a song it really is.' He also wrote a song that he dedicated to the people of Liverpool: it was called 'All We Need Is the Money'.

Another significant name to surface around now was Henry Priestman. He'd led a new wave group, the Yachts, who'd been signed to Elvis Costello's label after supporting him at Eric's. But their records were ordinary. He made greater headway, creatively at least, with a later band, It's Immaterial. A *Sunday Times* profile of the group, in 1983, offers a typical glimpse of that scene: the musicians share flats around Sefton Park, sign on the dole every second Tuesday, hang around in cafes where they read the music weeklies and despair at the success of their rivals: 'There's a group called A Flock Of Seagulls live round here. They used to be the blokes in the pub you wouldn't even talk to. Basically we thought they'd never make it. Now they're bleedin' millionaires.'

Henry's day would come, however. At 1983's Larks In The Park show, which also featured the budding Frankie Goes To Hollywood, he'd been impressed by an *a capella* act called the Christians. At first he arranged for them to add their vocals to It's Immaterial's music, but then became a full-time Christian himself. With the addition of his songwriting and instrumental abilities to the group's exquisite harmonies, the Christians were made.

They were a family act, initially, specialists in black harmony who had grown up on the Temptations and Persuasions. There were eleven Christian children, born to an immigrant Jamaican engineer and his Liverpudlian wife. (Their eldest child, Pamela, became a go-go dancer at the Blue Angel Club and enjoyed a brief romance with John Lennon; she also dated Rory Storm.) Two of the brothers, Roger and Garry, sang in a 70s soul group, Natural High, and were no strangers to the loon-pant or Afro. They appeared on the TV talent show *Opportunity Knocks*, singing the Persuasions number 'People Get Ready'. They were, alas, defeated by a 76-year-old man playing a one-stringed violin.

Their only Number 1 record would be the collaborative version of 'Ferry Cross the Mersey', performed with Paul McCartney and Holly Johnson for Gerry Marsden's Hillsborough appeal. But there were plenty of hits, of which the earliest, 'Forgotten Town', caught the urgent claustrophobia of urban Liverpool in a bleak time. Other numbers struck the same note of protest, soulfully expressed. Maybe the greatest of their songs, however, was the one that exposed a streak of romanticism beneath the grit. 'Greenbank Drive' is a dreamy celebration of a Liverpool road that bears comparison to its geographical and spiritual neighbour, the Beatles' 'Penny Lane'. Gary and Russell Christian have recently reunited with Priestman for tours.

*   *   *

Would Elvis Costello count himself as a Liverpudlian? 'The situation is confusing,' he told Spencer Leigh. 'I was born in London but I was christened in Birkenhead. My mother's from Liverpool and my father's from Birkenhead, so I don't know what that makes me. I went to school in London for most of my life, but my last two years in school were here in Liverpool. All my holidays were on Merseyside, so I can understand the confusion. Whenever I'm doing anything good, I'm appropriated as one of the Liverpool artists and when I'm bad, I get the opposite treatment – "Blooming southerner coming up here, trying to sell a load of old rubbish to us." '

He rarely talks about his teenage years in Liverpool, but this was the period that set him on his life's course. One afternoon in 1989, on a blustery day in Hyde Park, we sat on a damp bench outside Princess Diana's palace and talked of those times. 'It was quite funny,' he decided. 'Like anybody's first steps at doing anything, you wouldn't want to put them under the microscope ten years later. I started playing when I wasn't quite sixteen. I'd be up there with my little sensitive teenage songs, which I don't know now, 'cos I don't remember any of them. But I wrote from the start, from fifteen onwards.'

His recollections underline just how dull the Liverpool music scene had become by the early 70s, especially in sixth-form common rooms. It was now a city out of touch with the soul music it had once introduced to the rest of Britain. 'I do remember,' he said, 'how when I was at school in Liverpool it was very much two years behind London. Progressive music didn't happen until it was history in London. Before we moved up there I'd gone to school in Hounslow, and you had to like Tamla and reggae otherwise you were dead. But then I went up there and you didn't dare say you liked Tamla, it was poof's music, you had to like Deep Purple or something. I got into The Grateful Dead 'cos nobody else liked them and you had to have a group that you liked – somebody would like Caravan or something else. I used to sit at home going, "Please make me like the Grateful Dead!" It ended up I really did like them. But when I came back to London it was a relief: "Oh, you can like Lee Dorsey, terrific!"'

On Merseyside he played in a four-piece, as a solo singer and in a duo. Venues included the Yankee Clipper, the Temple Bar and the Wallasey Remploy. His strikingly loud voice was useful in overcoming the noise of the drinkers. 'I used to play those clubs, or the British Legion in Birkenhead, or in libraries, anywhere where they'd put something on for the night. One place we always used to get asked to do Slade songs, on acoustic guitars . . . The ironic thing about ending up producing the Pogues is that for a long time I hated traditional music because I had to suffer the narrow-minded attitudes in the folk clubs, the woolly-jumper folk. I used to hate the fucking "Wild Rover". I got my own back on it, I got a version on the Pogues' B-side; talk about a demolition job! And Ewan MacColl fell asleep in the first row the first time I ever played in public.'

Aptly, Costello's appointment with destiny occurred in Mathew Street, in the Grapes pub – it was on the night that Brinsley Schwarz came to town. The band's Nick Lowe told me: 'I'd known Elvis for a long time. He used to come to the Brinsleys' gigs whenever we played up Liverpool way. We'd always see him there and he was generally on his own, and he looked odd even then . . . One night we were playing at the Cavern, and we were in the Grapes across the road, sitting there having a cocktail before getting ourselves set. And he came in, and somebody said, "Look, there's that weird-looking geezer who's been at a few of the shows." And I thought, "Well, it's about time I bought him a pint and introduced myself," because he never used to come backstage or anything. So I went over and said, "Hello, I'm Nick. I've seen you at a few shows, what are you having?" ' They agreed to keep in touch, and so commenced a key relationship in Costello's professional life. Nick Lowe would one day introduce him to Stiff Records and become his producer.

As a recording artist he became celebrated for his verbal knuckle-dusters. With a touch of caricature, I think, I summed up his early work as 'a maelstrom of jealousy and vengeance, of withering scorn and sleepless guilt, of doubt, depression and fevered paranoia. A place where love lies down with treachery, and hope is a delusion in perpetual conspiracy with its old accomplice, disappointment. A world where bewildered individuals contrive their confused strategies for psychic survival, in the teeth of malign social circumstances that daily threaten to devour them, chew them up and spit their remnants into the cuspidor of oblivion.'

But his songs are broader in their emotional range than that. The River Mersey runs through them, too. In one of his best, 'New Amsterdam', he's 'down at the dockside' gazing across to the other side. He wrote '(The Angels Wanna Wear My) Red Shoes' on the train between Runcorn Bridge and Lime Street, en route to his mother's house. Two songs off Spike – 'Veronica' and 'Last Boat Leaving' – are set in Birkenhead, specifically in his grandmother's home with its view of the ships. 'Veronica', in fact, was written with Paul McCartney, though Costello will also stick up for less acclaimed stars of Merseybeat, from Cilla Black to the Swinging Blue Jeans.

Two of his most abiding passions have been the Beatles and Liverpool Football Club. I have never had a conversation with him that did not begin with a preamble on the team's form. Given his deeper family roots across the Irish Sea – he was christened Declan Patrick MacManus – and his father's career as a popular band-leader, Costello was probably a Scouser waiting to happen.

13. SCALLYWAGS AND LA'S

MEANWHILE, IN THE COUNCIL ESTATES . . .

The younger scals tend to have flicks, wear their jeans too tight and too long. Short-collared shirts, Slazenger jumpers and trainers 'zapped' from Europe. Also if it's cold they either wear sheepskin coats or anoraks (nearly always green) and maybe sheepskin mittens, borrowed off their sister. The older scals are different. They dress very 'sensible'. Short, sensible haircuts, tweed or corduroy jackets, short-collared checked shirts. Either jeans, or just normal sensible kecks. And shoes, so they can quite easily get into the poshest of clubs in Liverpool. Scals are very cocky and arrogant. They all seem to smell of some very strange-smelling oriental substances. They are nearly all unemployed. But they don't seem to give a shit about that! They totally disregard anything to do with authority. They HATE paying for things! They are also quite violent. They are very funny. And clean. They represent the REAL youth of Liverpool in these terrible, Thatcherised times . . .

That was a 1982 description, offered to me by an unemployed bricklayer called Phil Jones, of the big noise in Liverpool that year: scallies, or scals, derived from scallywag. Under a nom-de-pool of E.I. Adenoids, I wrote a report for the *NME* on this little-known trend. Eric's Club was only a memory now, but even at its peak it didn't represent the average Scouse teenager. Away from the hipper cliques of art student types and London-oriented trendies, the city's young were evolving a style of their own. For a while, there was nothing else like it in Britain.

Scallywag was never a fierce word. When grown-ups wanted to curse their wayward children there were stronger terms available. But scallywag used to capture the ambivalent tone of Liverpudlian attitudes to wrongdoing: you couldn't approve, but you might admire the cheek. The scally, however, was a different proposition. The word could extend from jack-the-lad to Jack The Ripper. Scallies could be ordinary boys, inclined to naughtiness but hardly vicious, or they could be the least lovable rogues you would never wish to meet. The scally might be carrying conkers in his pocket, or a Stanley knife.

Scally style began to define itself in the late 70s. The floppy fringe looked like a homage to Bryan Ferry, via the soul-boy wedge and some latent memory of the mop top, but the clothes owed nothing to music, and everything to football. The training shoes, the straight-legged jeans, the pullovers and kagouls, were terrace-wear, pure and simple, and lacked any resemblance to goth, punk, headbanger or hippy. There was often a strong element of upmarket European clobber, acquired somehow on the continental trips that Liverpool supporters were constantly required to take in those days. The day of the rattle, scarf and rosette was clearly over.

Phil Jones and his friend Peter Hooton, a youth-group leader, chronicled scally culture in a witty fanzine called *The End*. It was produced in the classically scally environment of Cantril Farm, one of those high-rise, overspill developments built around Liverpool's hinterland for the displaced inner city population. The magazine would sell around 4,000 copies, mainly on match days, and featured the much-imitated 'In' and 'Out' columns. (I had the honour of appearing in both.) There were interviews with Liverpool bands and club reviews, but the essence of *The End* was unrelenting satire, directed at 'teds', 'beauts', students, 'woolybacks', club doormen, badly-dressed fans of Yorkshire football teams and, most of all, scallies themselves.

The scally-word began to creep into non-Liverpudlian vocabularies, but it remained too fluid a concept to become one of those 'youth tribes' written about in the Sunday supplements. The look itself was never pinned down for long, and might take in anything from Harris tweed jackets to Adidas Sambas. Peter Hooton said: 'As soon as media people and the like define what a scally is, it will be time to change, because in Liverpool not even scallies know what a true scally is and no-one will admit to being a scal anyway. Everyone uses it as a term to discuss others.' The nearest equivalents down South would come to be known as casuals. But it was Hooton himself who made scally famous, thanks to a band he went on to form. In honour of concrete Cantril, they were called the Farm.

It was impossible to look like a scally and a rock'n'roll star at the same time. And the Farm were never mistaken for rock'n'roll stars. Hooton remarked, as he looked across at his bass player Carl Hunter, 'He knows if he turned up with a razor blade earring in, he'd be kicked out, no question.' To which Carl responded: 'People who wear razor blade earrings should be kicked out of society.' They were managed by Suggs of Madness and the journalist Kevin Sampson, who explains that lack of glam: 'I became friends with Peter Hooton; we saw how the city's music scene didn't communicate with the people who had once been so passionate about the Clash and the Jam. We liked UB40 and Madness, and you could see the common denominator: it was things that were unpretentious, that didn't involve hairspray and eye-liner. The questions asked by the proletariat weren't being answered and that was where the Farm came into it.

'Hooton had a good feel for what people wanted, for what the majority of council estate teenagers in the city would have liked. Clearly there were people who gravitated towards the Smiths and the Bunnymen, but the majority were cut adrift at that point. There was nothing for them, and that was what the Farm were trying to address. They belonged to that culture of people who went straight out on the town after matches.'

After years of effort, and various setbacks, the Farm caught on with a summer 1990 hit, 'Groovy Train', followed at Christmas by 'All Together Now' which featured Pete Wylie on backing vocals. Like the Frankies before them, they clicked by finding the right rhythmic groove. The fact they acquired some shuffling beats, the hallmark of a Soul II Soul-inspired makeover, was evidence of the links they'd built with Liverpool's rising dance culture. They'd braved the perilous rope-bridge from indie guitars to sample and DJ remixes. And, without re-vamping their scally look dramatically, they suddenly seemed to fit the pop world. The acid house and rock crossover that the media called 'Madchester' (its leading lights were Mancunian acts the Stone Roses and Happy Mondays) served to popularise a style the Farm had pioneered.

It's a contentious area, but the 'Madchester' style was undoubtedly influenced by Liverpool scallies, as well as by the neo-hippy fashions of acid house clubwear. Sampson and Hooton maintain that the Happy Mondays crowd came into the Farm's dressing room and asked, 'Lads, how do we become scals?' Bez of the Mondays had a slightly different recollection: 'Manchester was the dog's bollocks. We were well-dressed. Us and the Scousers used to try and outdo each other with our style at the football. Flares: we were all into that in 1982, although by the time we were in the Mondays we were bored of it all.'

Drugs were involved, also. It wasn't just the so-called 'Hillsborough effect' that brought a new serenity to the football terraces around this time: it was Ecstasy, too. Sweet aromas had been wafting over Liverpool for some years already, thanks to the scallies' belated discovery of cannabis. The widespread inclination to 'build up' and have a blow was a new phenomenon in local working-class life, for drugs had formerly been unknown outside of Liverpool 8. In time, the council estates would take delivery of heroin, acid and cocaine.

The take-up of dope went hand-in-hand with other adoptions of the hippy culture which had scarcely touched Scouse Liverpool in the 60s and 70s. Aside from flared jeans, there was a sudden craze for vintage 'progressive' rock. One saw 'Zappa' and 'Free' graffiti. The movement was sometimes dubbed retro-scally. As Kevin Sampson says: 'Certainly dope would have been seen as a middle-class hippy sort of thing. Your majority of urchins in Liverpool were quite anti-hippy. But this was a very interesting time. It was the forerunner of the tribute bands that are so common today.

'There was a group called Drama who played Genesis covers. Groundpig were originally called Groundhog but had to change their name for obvious reasons. They'd play to a teenage audience, boys and girls, who would go bananas to their versions of 'Solsbury Hill' by Peter Gabriel. They did 'Celia' by Simon and Garfunkel. You were seeing people now in semi-flares and training shoes, and hats. That's what was going on in the mid-80s, while you had this parallel thing of Frankie Goes To Hollywood and Dead Or Alive going through their Hi-NRG phase. People who were interested in music, but also interested in football, were getting into this strange, retro Pink Floyd scene, which is really the dawning of Acid House.'

'Skin up, yer bastards.' This, if memory serves, was the motto on the bass drum of a band who excited me greatly in the late 80s. The La's spent their career on the doorstep of greatness, with a golden key in their hand. Instead of going in, however, they shrugged and went home. Their best known track, 'There She Goes', is probably many people's definition of the perfect pop song. Its appeal endures down the years, fuelled by radio play, cover versions and soundtrack inclusions. It's doubtful, though, whether all the folks who'll sing along to it on a pub jukebox remember who it's by, or know anything of the maverick talent who created it.

After the dance-pop years of the Frankies and the Farm, Lee Mavers' La's were a return towards the traditional Liverpool sound: they were a sort of punk Merseybeat. They were formed in Huyton in 1984 by Mavers (pronounced Mavvers) and Mike Badger, after the latter saw Lee playing bass in a group, Neukoln, that Roger Eagle apparently believed would be the future of rock'n'roll. In a scally fashion that persists to this day, the La's ignored the contemporary pop universe and preferred to hole up with a bunch of old records – maybe Captain Beefheart, maybe Lightning Slim. This was deep, rootsy music that seemed to offer spiritual nourishment in a way that Bananarama didn't. Benevolent family elders enriched the band's musical resources by introducing them to the greats of yesteryear, from Louis Armstrong to Eddie Cochran, Chuck Berry and the Rolling Stones.

The bass-player, John Power, recalls: 'It's all your mates, you get into a bit of pot, and Floyd and Zep, and Hendrix and all that. That used to be what everyone I knew listened to.' And Mike Badger was well aware of Liverpool's recent past: 'The Eric's scene,' he said, 'the Bunnymen, Wah!, Teardrop Explodes, was very real. You'd be in town and see Ian McCulloch and Julian Cope sitting in cafes. It made being in a group seem possible.'

The band's name was so Liverpudlian that it cannot be pronounced by outsiders, who will say 'larze' instead of 'laa's'. Lee displayed a mystical Scouse patriotism, telling a visitor from the *NME*: 'All the souls that have come through these docks, la', from slaves to fucking merchant men – what I mean is, it's *got* something, la'. Hey! Imagine the fucking soul on a boat, a slave ship, la' – imagine that collected *feeling*. That's been through there many a time – worn them stone steps down.'

John Power told me: 'Coming from Liverpool you've got a different attitude. You do think you're better than the rest. And that's a start. I mean, fuckin' hell, you've got a good history there. It's better than coming from fuckin' Bolton. It's a melting pot. You can tell Scousers walking down the street. I can't imagine us coming from a different city. And if we had we'd be different people. Because of the way we've been brought up, and the attitudes we've got, just in school, even from a little kid of four, you can see it in them, a little cocky twat, la', starin' at you on the bus.'

They played a residency at the Pen and Wig pub, near Mathew Street, and were from the start a scally attraction. 'They could get it on with us because we were more like them,' said Lee. 'I'd rather go and see someone who looks like us that someone dressed in fucking silk clobber and stackies.' Mike Badger left eventually, as did dozens of others, but Mavers and Power persisted. They were signed by Andy Macdonald to Go! Discs and trooped off to a London studio. Their early singles included 'There She Goes' and 'Timeless Melody': neither was a big hit but their chiming catchiness echoed the best 60s guitar pop, and predictions of stardom started heaping up around the band's tousled heads.

The long-awaited LP eventually appeared in late 1990, to universally warm reviews. By now at Q magazine, I rushed across town to meet the band in their hotel, the Columbia, and offer my congratulations. But the band's response was somewhere between bitter and grim. 'We hate it,' Lee told me. His hangdog manner was not unusual, but I'd expected something more upbeat than this. Even John Power looked depressed. As with Frankie Goes To Hollywood, I'd encountered a group on what should have been the verge of their greatest triumph, only to find the end-game was already beginning.

Lee's disinclination to 'endorse the product' might seem a shade unusual, I suggested. 'Don't ask us about it, then,' he replied. 'We weren't getting our sound across, so we turned our back on it. We walked out on it, la'. We're not behind it whatsoever.' It turned out that, despite Go! Discs' best efforts, producers kept getting hired, then walking out or getting fired. There were tales of Mavers telling engineers he wanted a guitar to capture 'the sound of the tree it was made from'. On another occasion, he rejected a 60s mixing desk because it hadn't got the original 60s dust on it. (One producer, John Leckie, recalled: 'Lee was inclined to talk in a kind of Scouse psychobabble.')

What Lee was after, he explained, was 'a more organic, mono kind of sound: something like "Street Fighting Man" by the Rolling Stones or "Substitute" by the Who, even early Elvis. It was more basic in the old days. It was like people were given blocks to carve statues out of, and these days they give them buttons to press. They don't know how or why it works, they're just pissing around with toys.' Of one producer he sneered: 'He goes off and gives us a bell, on the phone: "I'm not coming in any more, I don't think it's going to work." Rather than say, "Right lads, let's sit down, let's talk, I wanna tell you what's goin' on." People are like that. They just shit out on you and run. Fickle temperament. They expect us to bend over backward but they won't bend any way. Too brittle. They'd snap.'

Most of the La's' lyrics wore a vaguely troubled air. Lee said: 'I'm just troubled by all the pretentiousness around, know what I mean? 'Cos that's the dangerous thing there is in the world. All this power shit, and greed. You can't be greedy without stepping on people . . . I'd rather be skint and doing what I wanted. Music should be left to the artists. It's not about money, is it? It's about music at the end of the day. It's a big let-down for people who've waited for that album. And even more of a let-down to me, mate.'

Over at the office of Go! Discs, Andy Macdonald reflected: 'Lee is very talented, but he can't recognise how good the record really is . . . I hate to quote another Scouse band, but John Lennon hated "Strawberry Fields Forever" until the day he died. He hated George Martin for putting it out.'

A few months later I met them again at the first Q Awards, which I presented at Ronnie Scott's club; the lads were clambering excitedly around Paul McCartney. But there was to be no happy ending for the La's. John Power left the group a few months later, Lee made some shambolic stage appearances and went to ground. Posthumously, their reputation began to grow into legendary status. They were rightly seen

'This golden light
~~ning down on you…'
~~l Sergeant and Ian
~~Culloch of Echo and
~~Bunnymen. (ANDREW
~~LIN/S.I.N.)

he music industry
r ceases to find new
s to depress me.' Andy
Cluskey of OMD,
dy hatching his sinister
erplan for Atomic
n. (ANDREW
IN/S.I.N.)

▼ Ian Broudie of Big In
Japan and the Lightning
Seeds: 'Pop is an art form.
Someone is listening to you
in sodding Siberia!' (PIERS
ALLARDYCE/S.I.N.)

un, filth and Krisco
es: Holly and Paul of
kie Goes To
ywood. (PICTORIAL
S)

Liverpool supreme soul
e, Garry of the
stians. (JAYNE
GHTON/S.I.N.)

▲ Lee Mavers of the La's: 'All
the souls that have come
through those dock, la'…'
(RONNIE RANDALL/S.I.N.)

alfway to Paradise,
Man Half Biscuit on
horeline of Liverpool's
Jersey. (RONNIE
)ALL/S.I.N.)

▼ The post-Millennium
line-up of Atomic Kitten.
(INNOCENT RECORDS)

)ap aristocracy:
kside's Sheila and
)y Grant, alias Sue
son and Ricky
inson. (Pictorial Press)

▲ The eternal Saturday night: Cream club takes the Liverpudlian spirit into a new century. (ANTONY MEDLEY/S.I.N.)

as forerunners of the mid-90s Britpop period. Noel Gallagher famously remarked that Oasis were 'finishing what the La's had started.'

'The melody always finds me,' sang Mavers, like it was a mystic force that stalked him through the Liverpool streets. But the La's' legacy is slender (although it's been boosted by some CDs of their unreleased material) and Lee has lived a reclusive existence for years. According to Badger, his greatest passion these days is for Everton FC.

There is a record shop in Liverpool that has occupied different locations down the years but has always functioned as the semi-official control room of Liverpool music. An old Cavern regular and former Liverpool rep for a national carpet company, Geoff Davies opened Probe Records in January 1971, in Clarence Street, half way up the hill from town to the university. All he wanted was a decent place that sold the records he couldn't buy in proper shops. 'I would have settled for the equivalent of dole money,' he says. 'But on the first day we took £47, which was smashing to me.'

In the early 70s, Probe was a Scouse outpost of the hippy counter-culture. I used to venture in there, embarrassed by my school uniform, to scour the underground newspapers that Geoff sold off from a cardboard box on the floor. By 1976, however, he took Roger Eagle's advice and checked out new premises, in an eye-catching corner site on Button Street, around the corner from Roger's new club, Eric's. The two establishments were inseparable in many people's minds: Probe was in a sense the retail arm of the Eric's world.

Among the waifs and strays who worked in Probe were Pete Burns and Paul Rutherford. The proprietor laughs at the memory: 'So, what with those two, this other gay fella who worked in there, and then all their gay friends comin' in, I remember shouting from the back, "Stop fuckin' mincing around, will yer! This place is full of fucking queers!" '

The legend has arisen that Davies forbade customers to buy records that he disapproved of. That's not quite correct: 'Well, it's correct in spirit, but the fact is I would always take the money. I'd sell 'em the record, and maybe just insult them. Or at least give them some advice. Make a remark, at least.'

In 1981 Probe became a wholesaler and distributor as well, part of the independent Cartel network, and then spawned the city's most enduring local label, Probe Plus. As the man who signed one of Liverpool's very few hard-core punk acts, Public Disgrace, Geoff Davies's tastes run counter to the local conventions. He's never bought into the entertainment ethos that dominates the Mersey mentality. 'I've gone against the grain of thinking Liverpool music is just great all the time,' he says. 'Some of the stuff that's done well has been piss poor. It's not personal enough. It's been like football and boxing in this town – a way for working-class lads without education to get out, make money, get sex, drugs, rock'n'roll. And this explains the blandness of much of the music.'

From Wah! to the La's, he always liked the early stuff and loses interest after that, especially when, as with the Bunnymen and Teardrops, more sophisticated production values kick in (though he disliked the Frankies' rough demo of 'Relax' as well: 'Paul Rutherford brought it in and said, "You're gonna hate this". I told him, "You're right." ').

The trouble with Liverpool music, he reckons, is that 'everything is very bland: "Me girlfriend's left me, blah blah" and hardly anything to do with the lives around them. It's always frustrated me. And everything sounds like something from the past. Where's your Nirvana? Where's your Clash? So I've always gone for something with more of an edge, and I've done more than a hundred records. I mean, take Cook Da Books: they were wild bloody boys from Kirkby; you'd probably get arrested if you had a night out with them. But you'd get them in a studio and they were trying to sing like Paul McCartney, oh so sweet.'

Davies will make one honourable exception to all this. He refers to the band who have worked with him for seventeen years, the jewel of the Probe Plus catalogue and the pride of Birkenhead: Half Man Half Biscuit.

The Biscuit's home, the Wirral peninsula, sits across the River Mersey, the River Dee on its far side, and Wales beyond that. Historically it's part of Cheshire, but the dockland district of Birkenhead is, culturally speaking, a Scouse outpost. From Birkenhead the Mersey Tunnel emerges, the trains run underground to James Street, and the view of Liverpool's waterfront is at its most spectacular, especially on a clear night when the city lights are in full glare and double up on the black Mersey surface. From here, as well, ferry boats have plied their trade for centuries.

Down river are the pleasure resorts of Seacombe and New Brighton; inland, behind the shipyards and the remnants of industry, stand suburban villas and rustic townships where the clerical classes traditionally took their refuge from the metropolis. The Wirral in general has an image in Liverpool of immense wealth and snobbishness. Ambitious Scousers dream of retiring there with their fortunes, legitimate or otherwise. But you also hear it being called the Debtor's Retreat.

Over water, at least along the Mersey strip of it, you have a place that might romantically be described as Liverpool's New Jersey. It's true that it's yet to produce its Springsteen or Sinatra, or even a Jon Bon Jovi. But the Wirral has kept the far bank well supplied with participants on the Liverpool scene: Adrian Henri, OMD, Jayne Casey, Derek Taylor and Lily Savage to name a few. Just as London's music scene has thrived on the input of immigrants from its far-flung suburbs – from David Bowie to Paul Weller – so there is something about the Wirral's position that obliges its children to decide which side they want to stay on. Do they remain here, in respectable anonymity, or go over there, to the din, the filth, the hazard and the excitement?

The genius of Half Man Half Biscuit is that they took just enough of Scouse culture to give themselves an edge, but kept their distance too. From their Wirral bastion they issue occasional dispatches of wry hilarity and downbeat, satirical bite. The songs of their leader, Nigel Blackwell, suggest a very real world of people too educated to be on the dole but too luckless or lazy to be anywhere else. They take a witty revenge on the drivel of popular culture, without denying their fascination with it. They seem flintily incorruptible, and scan the London music media with a mocking eye for cant. They were morbidly obsessed by football before it was fashionable to be so. The most famous fact about Half Man Half Biscuit is that they turned down a TV appearance so they could watch the Birkenhead team Tranmere Rovers.

They joined the Probe Plus family in 1985, as Geoff Davies recollects: 'Nigel came in to see me, in his usual style, no fuss, passes me the tape [mumbles]: "B'lieve you do records." I looked at the titles and I said, "Bloody hell, if the music is half as great as these titles, I'll be up for this!" That was it, after that.' Classics among those early titles were 'Dickie Davies Eyes', 'The Bastard Son of Dean Friedman', 'The Trumpton Riots' and 'All I Want for Christmas Is a Dukla Prague Away Kit'. If you're of the world where these Surreal collisions of reference points make sense, then Half Man Half Biscuit song titles are indeed addictive. There are websites that specialise in explaining them. Here are some more: 'Deep House Victims Minibus Appeal', 'Eno Collaboration' ('I've been from the Andes to the Indies in my undies'), 'See That My Bike's Kept Clean', 'Styx Gig (Seen by My Mates Coming out of a)' and 'Dead Men Don't Need Season Tickets'.

Their music is usually a basic punk jangle. It's not especially pretty; but as with the Fall, if it connects with you then you'll consume it by the yard. A 1993 album, *This Leaden Pall*, is the best, though it struck a slightly melancholy note. Blackwell agrees. 'But at the same time,' he says, 'there's nothing there at all. And anything clever's been stolen.'

*   *   *

Half Man Half Biscuit's greatest champion is another Wirral native, John Peel: they are almost his home town group. His passionate adoption of bands like Blackwell's was another stage in a long career as DJ and counter-cultural arbiter that has seen several transformations along the way. I once had to go with Judas Priest to a rock festival being MC'd by Peel, and the dressing room talk was not complimentary. He used to be on our side, was the view, and now he's betrayed us for all this punk rock rubbish. When Rob Halford took the stage, he said, 'I'd like to dedicate the next song to our old friend John,' which I thought was nice. 'It's called "Victim of Changes" . . .'

Like Paul McCartney, John Peel was the son of a man from the Liverpool cotton trade. Being on a higher rung of that ladder, however, the DJ's dad inhabited the Wirral's leafier depths, much grander than anything the McCartneys could afford. It was, and remains, a piece of Middle England, perched just near enough to the Mersey to have made its money from the port, but still sufficiently distant to disown any Scouse connections.

The young Peel did not share the prevalent distaste for Liverpool, however. At public school he would ape the wacker accent to sound tougher. And when he grew up and worked in America during Beatlemania, the act paid dividends: 'I was a complete phoney,' he said. 'Coming as I did from what is now Merseyside, any American who had heard of Liverpool – and in 1965 in Texas, there weren't many of those – assumed that if I wasn't related by blood to one of the Beatles, then I must be a good pal of theirs at least. I never told them I was, but then I never told them I wasn't either.'

His job, as he told *The End*, was in computer programming. 'And obviously there aren't that many computer programmers who get mobbed by gangs of screaming teenage girls, but I used to, just because I'd go on the radio and talk about Liverpool even though I hadn't been there for years. The first time it got really exciting was when a DJ and myself went down to a record shop in Dallas to give away some records. There was about 2,000 screaming girls who came and tore the place to pieces. It was wonderful. I got up on to the stage and over the PA this DJ asked me how long I'd been in Texas, and as soon as I started to speak without any hint of an American accent in what they thought quite wrongly was a Liverpool accent, they just went mad, girls shouting "Touch me, touch me" and being sick and everything.'

Back in Britain he joined the pirate radio scene of the mid-1960s and then became a founder presenter of Radio One. His Liverpool connection was more muted now, and rather eclipsed by another DJ, Kenny

Everett. (The latter man, formerly Maurice Cole of Crosby, was manic where Peel was cool: he thrived on a friendship with the Beatles, and eventually became one of television's wackiest uncles. His love for Margaret Thatcher, however, served to make him seem even more remote from Liverpool – where, by some accounts, he'd led a somewhat lonely childhood.)

Through the 70s, John Peel became the supreme voice of progressive rock, and then punk rock. In the 1980s another great Liverpool DJ, Janice Long, arrived at Radio One to boost the fortunes of many local bands, but Peel too has continued to be supportive. In later years he has become something of a scally godfather, especially by virtue of his mania for Liverpool FC (his children's middle names include Anfield, Shankly and Dalglish). There is almost no committed music fan of the past 30 years whose tastes have not been shaped by radio encounters with him. It's appalling to think how much of merit might never have got a hearing, had Peel not been in Broadcasting House to fight its corner. 'I'd like to be bit taller,' he said recently. 'And thinner, and have more hair and a bigger willy. But by and large, I'm content.'

14. DOLLYMOPS AND CREAM

THE ETERNAL SATURDAY NIGHT

Liverpool nightlife has always had an edgy quality. Traditional Liverpool clubland was a gorgeously seedy place, full of corruption, sporadically violent, always loud. By day the district was dull like factory overalls, but after dark it turned itself inside out, to become a suit of lights. The shabbiest of back streets would host a night-time wonder world of neon slums. By 2 a.m., chucking-out time, there might be savage fist fights over taxis. By 3 a.m., chucking-up time, sick and blood mingled, running down the gutters. Nowadays the up-town zone is a small triumph of urban regeneration, full of very smart bars and driven by dance culture. But certain rituals seem unchanging: the girls still wear nearly nothing.

The nastier end of clubland is a place where life is cheap, though lager might be six quid a bottle. There are joints you could enter on a whim and leave on a stretcher. The Crucial Three of our music venues – the Cavern, Eric's and Cream – were never part of this world, but then, as Pete Fulwell observed, there is the music business and there is the club business. Outside of our legendary triumvirate have been literally hundreds of establishments, more of them in these few square miles than in any other British city. Their pleasure rooms will never see daylight, and not much artificial light either. Like underwater lairs they are colourless because, where there is no light, colour has no meaning. Dirt is unchecked. Décor is uncertain: mock-Tudor walls were inexplicably popular for a time; ripped leatherette banquettes, as well. There might be a few exotic posters, possibly stolen from a travel agent's dustbin. By day these premises are silent as crypts: deserted, stale and airless. Their carpets are still sticky with beer. But by night they reek of sweat and scents, and bouncers patrol the toilets.

The bouncer – always called a doorman – is a special citizen of the Liverpool night. He'll wear his nose at a jaunty angle, and some of his colleagues have as many as two ears. Doormen are frequently foot-soldiers in the turf wars that flare between rival owners. These, in turn, boss their operations like feudal barons. The owner may have a dozen different properties, acting as licensee and protector. Licences might be revoked, but a disqualified club-owner will consider using others to front for him; so can known villains. Years ago, when the Liverpool clubs were approached by London gangsters bearing threats, they faced them down. They are big and ugly enough to be their own protectors, and doormen are their private armies. And, just occasionally, policemen are their special friends.

It's a grubby, vicious environment in some ways, fascinating, almost glamorous in others, and it's supplying the novelist Kevin Sampson with the setting for his next book, *Clubland*: 'It's about the collision of two worlds. The things that Liverpool has been great at in the past, night life and entertainment, colliding with the new deal of city regeneration, and never the twain shall meet. Those two visions don't coincide: the old style club owners don't see things in European terms, they see them in Liverpool terms.

'The great ports of the world are always the places with vibrant night life, a brilliant cultural scene, great sportsmen and big criminals. New Orleans, Chicago, Liverpool. These things all feed off each other. What you were seeing in the mid-90s when Cream came to the fore, was the people at the top of the guest list were the footballers, the most high-profile people in the city. Everyone wants to be associated with what they're not involved in: the clothes shops put their labels on the backs of the footballers who go to the clubs, who follow the bands.'

Weekend nights in town are like carnival time in Rio de Janeiro, only with much worse weather. One punk veteran of Eric's calls it 'bedlam'. Another says, 'It's like the Wild West.' In the pubs, banknotes pass like lemmings across the bar tops. Violence lurks, an abstract possibility, with sudden eruptions of typhoon fury. Away from the madding crowd you might seek out an obscure speakeasy. Knock at an unmarked door, a shutter pops open, and a jaundiced eye gives you a visual frisk.

It was always like this. In 1856, a century before the Cavern, one author displayed Victorian intrepidity by chronicling Liverpool on a Saturday night. There were respectable pleasures to be had in town, he found, wholesome shows of an improving nature. But they vied with low dives where 'dollymops', or bargain-basement whores, plied their trade among the drunken clientele. In dingy concert rooms were nearly naked girls who entertained by adopting 'poses plastiques'. At a fairground in Lime Street was a shooting gallery where you could fire at effigies of the Queen and Prince Albert. The teeming gin palaces would stay open until the first light touched the Welsh mountaintops.

Nik Cohn, at the end of the 1960s, brought back this impression of Liverpool: 'It has a certain black style of its own, a private strength and humour and awareness, real violence, and it is also grim, very much so. After the pubs close down, everyone stands out on corners and watches what happens and has nowhere much to go. Clubs are small, sweaty and dumb. Kids don't move by themselves or they get nutted by the guerillas. This is America in England: a night out ends almost inevitably with a punch on the nose.'

That's Liverpool on Saturday night, as generations of Liverpudlians have known it. But what the wider world thinks of today is something else entirely. In a word, what the world thinks of is Cream.

And Cream means James Barton: the red-headed kid from Netherfield Road in Everton who rose from ticket tout to clubland king. 'Liverpool has always been a party town,' he says. 'Before my time, my parents were big clubbers. Liverpool has always had a big appetite for a night out. One of the things we battled against for many years was the misconception of Liverpool: that it was a heavy place to come, that you'd get your car nicked or get beaten up. When Cream started booming, the big plus from everyone's point of view, was to see bus-loads of kids coming into the city.'

Given its Wolstenholme Square location, smack dab in the middle of Liverpool's night club district, it's a wonder that Cream has kept its hands clean. 'It was difficult,' concedes Barton, 'but a couple of things helped us. Cream as a company has never been about trying to run with those sorts of people. We always kept ourselves to ourselves. We avoided those people, and I think they came to realise that if they created problems at Cream we'd phone the police. We had a direct relationship with the police. We attempted to avoid using doormen that were involved in that world, although we couldn't always. But generally we acted like businessmen. Our motivation for being in that business was different to other people's. We took it out of the back alleys. We took it away from being something that the gangsters and old footballers would usually be involved in. I remember the days when people would go, "Oh, you own a night club?" And they'd look down their noses at me. Funny how it's changed.'

A self-made man who commands a business empire, Barton is nowadays a Liverpool entrepreneur in the tradition of its top-hatted Victorian merchants. 'We're big ambassadors for Liverpool,' he says. 'I have a London office now but we're a Liverpool organisation and we always will be. We love the story and we've refined it over the years: how two kids with no money started this thing, and everyone came to support it. It's a Liverpool story.'

Just as Eric's succeeded the Cavern, so Cream inherited the mantle of Eric's. As before, though, there were wilderness years in between.

Various small venues supplied live music in the early 80s. Apart from the short-lived Club Zoo, there was the Warehouse, Brady's, Adam's, Planet X, Pickwick's, the colleges as well. But there was no HQ, and the picture was fragmenting. Nor were there many groups so fascinating that they could build a scene around themselves. My own impression at the time was that the audience was discovering itself. The kids were more absorbed in one another than in wan youths on a stage, parading their pretensions to charisma. All they really required was a building, a bar, and music that hit the spot.

The orthodox clubs were, of course, terrible, as the local writer Kevin McManus recalls: 'Me and my mates had always hated the Rotters-type clubs. We hated the music and we'd rather wear jeans and trainers than the stuff you had to wear to get in there. And in town there was always that undercurrent of violence. The mainstream ones were fairly horrible, so we used to end up going to black clubs which were more fun.'

The challenge was always to get a drink after closing time: Somali-owned late drinking dens were one option, and very appealing as I recall. But drinking aside, the untapped appetites among the youthful population were the same as in their parents' day: to dance and 'cop off'. By the early 1980s an old Dale Street ballroom, the State, became the city's best big night. The former site of Littlewoods' tea dances, it was a glamorous and heady place, the location for Frankie Goes To Hollywood's 'Relax' and super-charged scenes in *Letter to Brezhnev*. It was a broad church, too: on another night you might see New Order playing live there.

There was a reservoir of energy in the city's young that had no satisfactory outlet. Even at its height, Eric's had not represented the masses. As Kevin Sampson remembers, this was about to change: 'Liverpool's dance music scene, which is now world-famous, grew out of a strange time: people in their teens going to see those retro hippy bands, and having lots of cannabis. The sort of entrepreneurs who had been behind the music scene until the mid-80s were quite ideological, quite politicised, articulate characters. What had changed by the late 80s was that people who went to football matches, read *The End* magazine and watched these weird cover version bands, became prominent in the music culture of the city. Some of them opened record shops, some started record labels, some started promoting their own dance nights.

'To a degree they were replicating what was happening elsewhere, but I'm not being Scouse-ist about this, it was different to London and Manchester. Specifically I'm talking about James Barton, Andy Carroll, John Kelly and Darren Hughes. They certainly used to read *The End*, used to attend football matches and dress in that way that was totally anti the Liverpool music scene. To be blunt, and to give a flavour of two worlds colliding, just the idea of wearing black would have been outrageous to the people going to football matches. They were dressed in flares in 1984, and a few years later they were the heart of Liverpool dance music.'

James Barton: 'Unfortunately, I was too young for Eric's, I missed that. But obviously I knew all about the heritage that came out of it. If I think back to being fourteen or fifteen in Liverpool, my brothers were into punk. They took me to see the Clash at the Royal Court, which is something I'll always thank them for. The Royal Court was a big hang-out for me. I walked in there at thirteen or fourteen and saw the Jam as my first live band. Of all the great bands! If it had been 5-Star that would have been a disaster, but I started with the Clash and the Jam.

'Then I became a ticket tout, to be frank. One reason was to make money and two, what a great way to see bands. So I spent 1985–88 travelling around Europe: got to see Prince's first European gig in Stockholm, saw U2 in the South of France, saw Michael Jackson at Wembley. Thinking about it now, it was being at those big stadium rock events that motivated me to do stuff like Creamfields. I was always a kid that was inquisitive in terms of wanting to know what was going on backstage, as well.

'In the summer of 1988 I came back after touring round Europe and checked out a couple of clubs in London. Acid House had just kicked in then and I was totally blown away. This was a sound which my brothers hadn't introduced me to, this was a sound I hadn't heard before. So I jumped on the train and whizzed back to Liverpool, expecting it to be happening there. And when I found it wasn't, I decided to start the first dance night in Liverpool.'

That night was called Daisy, and it was held at the State. 'I remember walking into the State for the first time when I was fifteen,' says James, 'and I was completely blown away. It was unbelievable. Frankie were out, "Relax" was Number 1, and I fell in love with clubs. I'd go to see Steve Proctor and Andy Carroll DJ at the Pyramid every Thursday night; at midnight they'd pack their bags and walk around to the State. I launched my first night, dance music hit Liverpool and it was all flying.'

With the exception of the La's, this was more than you could say for live music in the late 80s: 'One of my favourite bands,' he says, 'was Echo and the Bunnymen and I went to all their shows including Crystal

Day. But after that I don't think anything came along that really put Liverpool on the map . . . From my point of view, here I was in my late teens, getting really pissed off with Tony Wilson on our TV screens every Friday night, telling everyone how great Manchester was and how the Smiths were coming out of there. People always ask me where the determination for Cream came from. A lot of it was downright jealousy. I used to go to the Hacienda in Manchester for a good night out; it was only us and 8 Production doing any club nights in Liverpool. I've always had a lot of affection for Factory Records, the Hacienda and Tony Wilson; we ripped them off to death, to be honest. We were in there every Friday and Saturday and drew a lot of inspiration. So I spent my weekends travelling there or to raves and parties in London.'

Barton and Co's next venture was the Underground, in Victoria Street. Kevin Sampson: 'In a prior life it was a copping-off joint called Cindy's. The only reason they went there was a combination of friendly connections and not being screwed into the ground over the deal and the sort of music they wanted to promote. It was called indie dance or acid house or various things, but it was all centred around the Underground. They very quickly built a following there and in the World Downstairs at the Royal Court. They were doing acid house with a Liverpool spin: into the middle of it they would throw "Under Cover of the Night" by the Rolling Stones and people wouldn't walk off the dance floor, and old classics like James Brown and Sly and the Family Stone. It was unlike anywhere else at that time.'

Barton recalls the Underground as 'a great little dingy club. Instead of a dance night we wanted a dance club, where every night was DJ-based. I remember Hooton [of the Farm] and those guys coming to the Underground and they really embraced dance music, starting their own club nights and getting Terry Farley to work on the records. I was in and out of their office on a regular basis. I think I even offered to manage the Farm, when I was 20. We kept that open for about eighteen months. We did good business.'

As Sampson, who did manage the Farm, was quick to notice, his band could reach a whole new crowd outside the traditional guitar band audience: 'James is entwined with the Farm's early history. The first tour they did in their dance reincarnation was working with DJs at unusual venues – in London we did it with Andy Weatherall and Terry Farley – and in Liverpool we hooked up with the Underground and James Barton, and held it at the Royal Court. Up until then you'd been talking about hundreds of people, but here it was over 2,000. They just kept coming in.'

Apart from the Underground there was G-Love at the Mardi. 'It transformed the scene,' believes Kevin McManus. 'It became so successful it moved to the Academy where Cream is now. Loads of people still talk about it with affection: they did the whole thing of dressing up the club, having different things going on, loads of good DJs. House music had become quite snobby by then but John Kelly was just a real good-time DJ. It wasn't so much about making money as making a night out. It was totally non-threatening, and people from the London industry would be coming up for Thursday nights. If you could say what made it dead good you could make a fortune, but it was just that the organisers took a lot of care over it. And like all the best things it had a limited life, it didn't get stale.'

The Cream and Eric's stories are united in the person of Jayne Casey, the Big In Japan singer who'd one day become the dance club's Head of Communications ('that means I've got the Big Gob,' she explains). After her spell in the post-Eric's Pink Military, she found herself more drawn to electronic music and new dance sounds.

'Way back in Eric's,' she says, 'all the boys were really into the Clash, which I was never that mad on. I used to go in for reggae sound systems, and Devo, and I remember Dalek I Love You playing their first gig with a synthesiser. I believe they were the first street electronic band, because at that time the only people who played electronic music were rich boys in studios like Genesis. I used to love the Fall, for their repetition, and Joy Division for the bass and the drums. And we'd also grown up in the gay clubs. So my aesthetic and Holly [Johnson]'s was always very different to Pete Wylie and bands like that, who were all Clash boys.

'And when I started to make my own music those influences led me towards dance. A friend started sending me tapes from New York, so I was getting tuned in to early house DJs from America.'

When she looked around Liverpool for kindred spirits, it was the scally DJs she found: 'We were the only people playing with electronics in the city. All the lads hated it, because we weren't rock. There was much more of it in Manchester. I was always more into Manchester music, other than the Bunnymen. So I became a friend of James and saw this new generation coming up, and saw what they were into. I thought, "Oh, this is so close to us. This has come out of all that gay disco we heard, all that New York scene, all that electronic music." I could see that scene building.

'James was a kid that was too young to get into Eric's. His big brothers used to chase us down the streets. A few years ago I had a row with one of his brothers, and all this shit poured out of his mouth, about how we were arty fuckers. And I'd listen to all this and think, "Wow, this is the scally mentality that always hated us." Over the years they've given us leeway because they knew that we broke the deadlock in the city, it was us that did it. But still they half hate us. I remember ringing Holly afterwards and saying, "God, we had this row!" And he goes, "But they were the scallies that used to batter us!" '

In the dereliction of the north Liverpool docklands, something stirred. Quadrant Park, in Bootle, became the next magnet venue, pulling in up to 4,000 punters for its Saturday all-nighters.

'Quadrant Park was the first time I'd seen kids travel to Liverpool for a club,' says Jayne Casey. 'This was an amazing new thing, this travelling audience. It opened up after that. A scally became something that you loved, it lost some of its homophobia. I remember being at Quadrant Park in about '89 and ringing up Paul Rutherford and saying, "Oh my God, you've just got to come and see it, the scallies are taking Ecstasy!" Frankie Goes To Hollywood had been big by then, so Paul came down the following week in a T-shirt saying *Queer as Fuck*. He went on the dance floor and he couldn't believe how all the guys were hugging him. Along the way, Ecstasy had taken some of the edge off.'

Bootle boy Kevin McManus: 'It was very odd. I knew people who came up from London for it. I could walk home in ten minutes. But afterwards you'd see all these people, really wrecked, going, "How do we get home from Bootle?" It was really nice for a while but then it went horrible. A friend of mine came down from Manchester where he was used to the gangster scene, and he said it was far too heavy for him. Really nasty.'

Back in the city centre, the Underground was running into trouble with the authorities; Barton moved out to Quadrant Park. 'I got there towards the end, really, when it was going downhill,' he says. 'I remember a couple of amazing nights DJ'ing at Quadrant Park, and I was instrumental in getting them the late licence. And the Farm were great. I remember playing 'All Together Now' on New Year's Eve there, all those years ago. But it became a bad thing, because when you've got a night club that's staying open longer than any other club in the city, it attracts a lot of dregs. It went from being kids with big massive smiley faces, having the night of their lives, to being guys walking through the club with crates of beer on their shoulders, selling drugs. Beating people up. The mood of it went quickly. And none of us understood what needed to happen to keep those sort of people out.'

Clubs aside, the beginning of the 1990s saw new shops and labels arise to service Liverpool's demand for dance music. Jon Barlow's 3 Beat operation was based in the fast-reviving district around Wood Street, in a converted warehouse that became the Liverpool Palace complex. Here, Oceanic recorded their hit 'Insanity'. Symbolically, Probe Records itself moved up from the Mathew Street area to new premises nearby. Close at hand, from another age, were the Jacaranda and Blue Angel, as well as scores of far less legendary establishments. Out of the local dance scene came the 8 Productions team (including the former Lotus Eater Peter Coyle) and records by Bassheads, Apollo 440, Marina and New Atlantic. James Barton started a label called Olympic, which would license in tracks from America and Italy. He also managed DJs and acts including K-Klass, who hit big in 1991 with 'Rhythm Is a Mystery': 'Next thing you know we're on *Top of the Pops* going, Wow, this is going to be easy. Obviously it wasn't.'

James hooked up with a family friend, John Smith, who'd formerly managed Cook Da Books. They hatched a plan for Liverpool's answer to the Hacienda, to be called 051: 'And we got close,' he believes. 'John was great at experimenting with talent. On the opening night we had Adrian Sherwood, and M-People the next. He wasn't scared to book talent. Where it started going wobbly was when it became successful. I remember New Order getting turned away one night, which is not good; those guys had come all the way down from Manchester. And the door price started creeping up, to capitalise on the queues.

'What you have to understand, whether you're running a restaurant, a night club, or a bar, is that when you've got something of quality, which people like, unfortunately it attracts really bad people as well. It attracts people with loads of money, it attracts heavy faces. Gangsters. We had a few issues that went pear-shaped. So, with the combination of the original punters feeling short-changed over ticket prices, and a few gangsters giving people a few slaps, 051 went in a year from being the best thing that ever happened to me to being a real disappointment. I had situations with friends and family saying to me, You cannot stay here, it's not great, you have to get out.'

James now had a colleague called Darren Hughes. After the traumas of 051, Barton was wary of a new club launch, but Hughes was persuasive. 'Dance music had gone through its first phase,' says James. 'It had become fragmented. You had your techno clubs, your house clubs, your Balearic clubs, whereas I always loved DJs surprising me with different types of records. And I think a lot of the old faces from '88 had started staying in, they didn't like what was going on. In October 1992, about five weeks after I left the 051, we launched Cream, at the Academy.

'Cream was just an outlet for us to stay in dance music, for me to continue to DJ. We never went into it with a major plan: "Right, in ten years time this is gonna be in Argentina, millions of records sold." We took it back to where it began: a dingy room, great sound, great DJs, and the first night we opened we had all the old faces out, including Jayne Casey.'

Casey had not forgotten the potential she'd spotted at Quadrant Park. 'I had the advantage of being the older person on the scene,' she says, 'in the same way that Pete Fulwell and Roger Eagle had been the older people for me. They were my role models. I knew from the beginning how big this could become, because we had a travelling market. So all we had to do was facilitate that, build in the structure to support that market.' It was like Northern Soul and Wigan all over again. After all, if fans were willing to cross the country to visit Bootle, the chances were they would go anywhere.

Mostly, though, Cream came into being because of the local appetite for entertainment. A lull in Liverpool night life is like the vacuum that nature cannot tolerate. Something had to happen. And in 1992, that something was Cream.

On the opening night, Hughes and Barton counted 450 customers. 'We spent four grand on doing it,' says James. 'That 450 dwindled to 250 the week after. I DJ'd that week and I remember playing a brilliant set, but at the same time thinking, "This is not gonna happen." But then it steadily grew: we put another 50 in the next week, another 100 the next week, and within nine months to a year we were selling out, 900 people a week. It was a great vibe. And you'd find me on the dance floor most of the time, which was one of the reasons we were able to create a good night. We spent a lot of time jumping up and down, as opposed to trying to run a business.

'Then we did a Boxing Night party and it went through the roof. We must have locked a thousand people out. Completely ballistic, ticket touts outside, which is always a good sign. We steamed through the rest of the year, it was flying. We got to the point where we were turning away more than we were letting in. It became the worst-kept big secret.'

Kevin McManus: 'It was another one of those special times that you can't replicate or say why it happened. Right time, right place. And it was predominantly local people early on, whereas it became students and tourists. It was a lot of people like me, who'd been to the Underground and were looking for a good night again. They did it well, though it didn't seem to become massive for six or nine months.

Musically it was a lot more adventurous than it became. James and Andy Carroll were the residents, and it wasn't just the handbaggy house end. And they found the money to bring in the big DJs.

'People were desperate for a good night again. And the word spreads very quickly in Liverpool.'

Kevin Sampson: 'You could see how something that was underground, quite pure and tribal, could translate to something that was still run along the right aesthetic lines, that put the audience ahead of other considerations, but actually made money and was run as a business.'

The story soon broke in the media. Over the following few years the club expanded into Nation's vast adjacent rooms, plus the venue's courtyard, to become the super-club of Northern England, vying with its great London rival the Ministry of Sound. Customers began arriving by the coach-load. Cream became a company. 'And in 1994,' says Barton, 'dance music exploded. And we were already there with a great club. Maybe the reason dance went the way it did was because of Cream and the Ministry of Sound.'

Resident DJs, who are the soul of a club and the guarantors of its all-important personality, would include Paul Oakenfold, Judge Jules and Seb Fontaine; guest DJs would range from Boy George to Pete Tong. Barton's mission, he said, was to break down the barriers of taste and snobbery. To a 1996 visitor from the *Independent On Sunday*, Cream's great virtue was its simplicity: 'No drag queen freak show greets you at the door, no sponsored onslaught of distractions tempts you to play video games, try this perfume or otherwise deflect from the business of dancing.' Or, as *Ministry* magazine declared in 2000: 'The amazing thing about it is that nobody really gives a shit about anything but having a good time. Why shouldn't we celebrate a club where you don't have to be a stuck-up, trendy idiot to get in? This is a club that defines what a Saturday night's clubbing in the UK should be all about.'

In a curious echo of the city's rock'n'roll traditions, the locally favoured dance tunes were often at the tunier end of the spectrum. It was perhaps inevitable that somebody would come up with the label 'Scouse house'. 'It was 3 Beat who came up with that,' remembers Kevin McManus. 'The stuff that they put out tended to be on the melodic side rather than bangin' techno or trancy stuff. People who deride Cream would say Scouse house was the handbaggy, chart end of the market. Typically, the sort of stuff that went well here was the anthemic, Italian stuff, piano-driven with big vocals.' Around 1994, when Cream was at the height of its handbag phase, the biggest tune of all was probably the David Morales mix of Mariah Carey's 'Dreamlover'.

For many years Cream has had a hipper local rival in Voodoo, at Le Bateau, positioned at the harder, more techno end of things. But Barton's empire is nowadays about much more than Liverpool clubs. A falling-out between the partners led to Darren Hughes' departure for Home, in Leicester Square, while Barton turned his attentions to a pre-club bar, Mello Mello in Slater Street (run by his father), to clothes, merchandising and Cream-branded albums.

'We do about 250 Cream events around the world,' he says today. 'We're in Japan once a month, we're in Argentina once a month, Australia too. We're absolutely everywhere.' They're in Ibiza every year, obviously. In 1996 there was an April Fool's gag to the effect that Cream was going into space: they'd struck a deal with NASA's Space Station, and applications were invited for the 2012 inaugural flight. Cream claimed they were inundated with enquiries.

When Liverpool saw in the twenty-first century, its official party was Cream 2000, at the Pier Head. But the biggest event of all nowadays is Creamfields, the summer festival that brings up to 50,000 punters to Liverpool's old airfield at Speke. 'For me,' says James, 'to get 50,000 kids in Liverpool is one of the things I'm in this for.

'We have a music division which does about a million compilation albums a year. We have record deals around the world. And we have a fledgling little media business, a small TV production company, some radio licence applications. It will grow dramatically. My long-term plan is to create a music and media business, which not only operates Cream but is involved in other things as well.

'I look around me now and the entertainment business is run by people who were on dance floors ten years ago, when I was DJ'ing. The chemical generation has grown up now. At the bottom of my e-mail it says CEO. My mates laugh when I send them an e-mail: "Who the fuck's the CEO? What does that mean?" But I've got close friends who are MDs of major record companies now. So the same ambition that we had to dislodge people ten tears ago, is here again. Sweep out the old guys at radio and TV, in music. Get new guys in, make it more dynamic for the 21-year-old kids.'

And Cream in Wolstenholme Square? You're as likely now to meet someone who's arrived by the Irish ferry, or the M1 from London, as an ordinary Scouse kid of the sort who made the club happen all those years ago. Barton maintains, however, that the soul of his business will always be in Liverpool. 'I don't believe Cream could have existed in London or Manchester or anywhere else, I've said that many times. Back in 1992, the people in Liverpool felt the need for something to get behind. And the fact that I was born and bred in Liverpool, that Cream was started as a love affair, with very little investment, and grew and grew . . . Stories like that can only come from places like Liverpool.

'I don't think Cream would have got the benefit of the doubt in London, which has seen it all before. We wouldn't have got that extra bit of time to make it work. If you speak to any DJs in London, they spend a lot of their time going up the M6 to the North of England, where they'll always say the atmosphere is dramatically better than in the South.

'I've always been critical of the Liverpool music scene in as much as it's living back in its day. Once when I was being interviewed, I was asked what I hated most about Liverpool and I said the Beatles. Everyone freaked out, but where I was coming from was that, for many years, Liverpool as a city lived on its past glories. And the music scene was no different. I felt new music was being stifled. I'm not surprised that Liverpool has never really delivered a great dance band.

'Liverpool's always been very insular, and the old-arse music scene in Liverpool is very similar. We were born and bred on bands that came from the traditional two guitarists and a drummer mode, and if you can't play an instrument you're not that important. So it doesn't surprise me that we've never produced a great techno band out of this city. I think an instrumental record can be a million times better than a vocal record if the vocal's not that good. And dance music was all about creating a noise and an energy.'

What's more important than Barton's relationship with the Liverpool music scene, though, is the City Council's attitude to him. 'We learned from the Hacienda,' he says, 'and from the lack of support that they received in Manchester. For the people who were running that city not to realise how culturally important it was . . .' The penny dropped, as he recalls, on the night that Jayne Casey placed him in the front row of a TV discussion programme. Now that Liverpool had 'Objective One Status', meaning it was one of Europe's neediest areas, how should the city spend the money coming its way? 'I said we need to forget about Liverpool re-creating its industrial heritage. We need to put money into creative people, keep students in the city.' He spoke off the top of his head. But he realised, for the first time, that Cream really meant something to the local economy.

Afterwards, one of the expert panel pointed Barton out to the leader of Liverpool Council. 'He said to him, "Do you realise you could have the next Richard Branson here in your city? You need to take care of this guy." And I think that was the beginning of our relationship with the Council. Jayne was the glue that stuck it together. It set off the chain of events between being just a night club and playing an important role in local regeneration. One of the things I'll take from Cream, if and when I leave, is that we made a contribution to the re-emergence of Liverpool as a new, modern city. For somebody who started out doing this out of jealousy towards Manchester and Leeds and London, to see Liverpool talked about in the same breath as those happening places was great.

'There was definitely a shift away from the old-arse Labour way of doing things, to a new way of thinking. The City Council have been a great partner for us. We've had our ups and downs but they've supported us when we've had issues with licences and the police. Cream has had problems, dealing with drugs and gangsters. And to be fair, unlike what happened in Manchester with the Hacienda, Cream was protected by its City Council and by Merseyside Police. What people fail to grasp with Cream is that like most things, whether it's the creation of a new Ferrari, or opening a new bank, with all the great things around it, there's always a small element of shit.'

It's worth remembering that Eric's lasted for just three years. The Cavern ran from 1957 until 1973, but was either closed or broke for much of that time. Cream is now having its tenth anniversary, and has become a global brand.

Jayne Casey credits club culture with a lot that's right in Liverpool life. She reinvented herself through Eric's – arguably she saved herself through Eric's – and she believes that Cream has offered others the same opportunity. It's widely reported that students applying to John Moores University cite Cream as their main reason for choosing Liverpool. In fact there is no such statistic; Jayne Casey simply made it up. But it was readily accepted as fact, entered the cuttings files and now has a life of its own. Plus, of course, there is the distinct possibility that it's actually true.

Still, there is pain attached to building your empire in Liverpool clubland, as Barton acknowledges. Drugs and drug money are inescapable facts of life now. By 2000 Liverpool was reckoned to be Britain's leading centre in illegal pill production. The town's night life has not been hammered by the authorities in the way that Manchester's was, but it's obvious that some of the leisure-driven regeneration is drug-financed. Between the dealers and the inflow of European grant cash, you sometimes wonder how much legitimate wealth the local economy is generating from its own resources. The smartest dockside apartments might be bought by juvenile scally pushers in flash cars, sporadically pursued by demoralised police. (Yet we are still surprised by corruption. It might be more surprising that there isn't more of it.)

The Cream people are realistic that drugs are inherent in clubbing, and deal with it pragmatically. Barton has to keep a constant vigil against the dealers who pose such a threat to his business, not to mention his customers. He funds research and promotes awareness of the risks. Jayne Casey knows about dealing with the council, the police, and the grown-ups you have to keep on your side if you're to stay in business. She gives much thought to the ways you accept drug culture as a given, but find ways of dealing with its effects and looking after its victims. 'You don't just throw them out on a fire escape, for one thing.'

Finally, Jayne reflects, 'Cream is all about the audience, end of story. The stories that live on will be from the dance floor. The audience is the thing now. It was a lot about the audience at the Cavern and Eric's and it's even more so at Cream. That's the journey, from the stage to the acknowledgement of the audience.'

Cream, in a way, brings us back full circle to the dancehall days of the Grafton and Locarno. It's a social destination, where music may be an attraction but is not necessarily the point. Cream confirmed the long-term trend away from live music – at least the Grafton hired orchestras – but it stands in that timeless tradition of Saturday nights in Liverpool. The people are always the real stars in this performance. And there is your continuity, carried in the shrieks of laughing girls that pierce the night air.

15. WHOLE AGAIN

FLYING PICKETS AND ATOMIC KITTENS

Up wide, windy Hardman Street is a handsome Georgian building that was built as a school for the blind. Later it belonged to the police. Now it bears the unwieldy title of the Merseyside Trade Union Community and Unemployed Resource Centre. Through the courtyard is their pub: its name, the Flying Picket, reflects its origins in the time of Margaret Thatcher and the miners' strike. As well as a pub, though, the Picket has a live venue and a recording studio which is called the Pinball in honour of Pete Townshend, one of its benefactors and guest of honour at its opening in 1986. Other celebrity donors have included Paul and Ringo, Yoko Ono and Elvis Costello. Even Phil Collins has lent a hand. The Picket's jukebox specialises in Liverpool records, and is never short of something new to add.

The Pinball building used to house the police Black Marias. Like the venue upstairs, it was crucial to the early careers of the La's, the Farm and Space, so the Centre has earned itself a place in Liverpool music history. The man behind it all is the former High Five vocalist Philip Hayes. 'Bands don't just spring up anywhere,' he says. 'They spring up in Liverpool because we have a history of bands being here and believe we can do it, can sing and have stories to tell.'

Hayes' own life is a microcosm of that history. His older sister went out with the least remembered of Brian Epstein's acts, the singer Tommy Quickly. 'Me brother always says, Our sister would have to go out with the one who fails!' The young Philip was almost traumatised by one of Tommy's B-sides, a Merseybeat version of 'Humpty Dumpty'. But, that aside, he remembers a blissful 1960s childhood, with the Beatles playing all the time: 'Their lyrics are engraved on my mind, which must condition you. Later on when I formed my own band, the DNA of the Beatles' music was there.' He was enticed to Mathew Street and Aunt Twacky's by rumours of Deaf School rehearsing there. 'That area became the embryonic cultural location. Being an ordinary working-class lad from Croxteth, you'd walk in there and see these odd people, but something said to me, This is interesting, I want to see more. Then my older brother went to Eric's to see the Sex Pistols and the Runaways and I started to listen to that.

'Punk was where music really started to say something to me about my life. My brother, our Billy, who's now General Secretary of the Communication Workers' Union, always had lefty stuff around the house so I was influenced by that, looking for some explanation of the world, so what appealed to me most about the punk scene was the Clash. The biggest influence was going to see them at Eric's. A few years later there was Wah! and the Bunnymen, the Teardrops: people were forming bands with Eric's as their focus. I took those elements into what I do here at the Picket. You provide a place for people and it will grow. Nurture the soil and the flowers will grow.'

By 1979 he was in a band himself, the High Five: 'The idea was that you help mates in the area. Wylie was getting a profile and he'd offer us supports, we played at Julian's Club Zoo. We made a record for Probe, got a review in the NME. We were always known as the house benefit band. If there was a cause you'd ask the High Five to play: South Africa, Rock Against Racism, whatever, fighting the good fight. We kept going until about '87. It was a desperate time in some ways, the time of Thatcher and unemployment and economic decline. The opportunity to play in a band was a way to keep away the "dole-drums". I suppose I was propelled by that to do things for other bands.

'I thought about what I could do. There was this Trade Union organisation trying to create something that would direct people away from heroin and misery. They set up a network of unemployed centres, this being the central one, and one of the services they would provide was music facilities. So they brought me in and we set about making a rehearsal space. And me being naïve and straightforward thought, There's all these superstars out there, who talk about caring, so I thought I'd approach them. Pete Townshend, Peter Gabriel, Suggs from Madness, Paul Weller. They said, Set up a demo studio, that's what bands need to get recording deals.

'Through this period the La's were surfacing, Rain, the Real People, lots of bands, and we did what we set out to do, a demo studio and a live venue and we're still here. We've been the forerunner of "cultural regeneration strategies" which are now the vogue. It helps economically and it helps people's self-esteem.'

Do young Liverpool bands feel overshadowed by the Beatles' legacy, I wonder? As an old punk, Philip Hayes understands iconoclasm, the urge to smash the graven images of establishment gods: 'I remember the Clash song: "No Elvis, Beatles or Rolling Stones, in 1977". I'd also reflect on the Mott The Hoople song ['All the Young Dudes']: "My brother's back at home with his Beatles and his Stones, we never got it off on that revolution stuff." That's how it was with punk, if you had any old albums you took them to the second-hand shop and tried to buy some punk records – which were probably worse than the records you were trying to get rid of!

'So I've experienced both those feelings: Fuckin' hell, it's the Beatles again. Bands can imitate them so much it stops them being creative. We can provide all this practical support by way of a studio and venue, but how do you get bands to listen to new music or different ideas? I was thinking maybe we should get together some people to act as cultural advisors. The Eric's groups didn't sound like the Beatles. Eric's was wonderful for me, it was a great seminar in terms of being introduced to reggae. I'm indebted to Roger Eagle for that.'

The small, self-effacing figure of Ian Broudie has hovered on the fringes of our story since 1976. He was the schoolboy guitarist from Penny Lane who was drawn, as if by ancestral voices, to Mathew Street. Here he became the musical foil to Bill Drummond's fevered conceptualising, and joined him in the quintessential Eric's band Big In Japan. His earliest musical memory, he told me, was of seeing the Beatles at the Empire, where he had to cover his ears against the din. Those ears turned out to be worth protecting.

He'd first met Bill while waiting in a Mathew Street café with his brother's guitar. 'Suddenly,' he told Q, 'this massive bloke comes over, gets it out and starts singing a Kinks song at the top of his voice, smashing the strings like a nutcase. He broke three strings and I was going, Who the hell are you?'

Jayne Casey: 'Ian was sixteen and a proper musician, not as accomplished as he became, but really doggedly determined. He knew what he was into as a songwriter, classic British pop songs, and that's what he eventually became.'

'I'd always believed,' he says, 'that if you do a positive thing then it creates ripples. If it's right then things will come to it. I used to think that with Big In Japan, that at least we're doing it and something could come out of it.' After Big In Japan, he and Budgie travelled to London where the drummer joined the Slits, and Broudie stayed with Deaf School's former singer Steve Allen. These two would now form a group, Original Mirrors, who signed to a major company but, as it turned out, had neither the wit of Deaf School nor the shambolic daring of Big In Japan. It was slightly stiff electro-pop for the most part. Its lustier numbers, such as 'Sharp Words' and 'Dancing with the Rebels', featured glum, Spandau Ballet choruses, like a gang of galley-slaves having a sing-song. Broudie would later admit he hated it.

He moved back to Liverpool and formed the short-lived Care with Paul Simpson, ex of the Teardrops and Wild Swans. Though Broudie's progress was disappointingly patchy, he did begin to establish himself as a producer; from Bill Drummond's boys the Bunnymen he went on to the Fall, Icicle Works, Wah!, Shack, Dodgy and others.

Broudie's emergence from the sidelines began in 1989 with the first Lightning Seeds hit, 'Pure', and the album *Cloudcuckooland*. These and the subsequent releases like 'The Life of Riley' and 'Lucky You' confirmed him as an expert in sweet-toothed pop. Light as a first fall of snow, Broudie's confections enchanted everyone. For anyone who remembered Big In Japan it was peculiar that a product of that school should become the new exemplar of catchy songcraft. He slowly overcame a dislike of his own voice, accepting its relative wispiness would always lighten up any track it was applied to. In his own head he'd imagined the Lightning Seeds as a scruffy guitar band, but discovered that he could achieve more in the studio with loops and samples than by conventional methods.

He was frequently irritated by the 'perfect pop' tag: it misrepresented the spontaneity of his methods. All the same, he told me: 'I always call the Lightning Seeds pop music, because for me pop music is an art form and you can do what you want. All the other types of music have their parameters, but pop music can be anything . . . In a situation where there's less and less community in people's lives, and everyone's becoming more isolated, music is the thing that you can't help hearing and being affected by. You make records and they're transmitted all over the world. Someone is listening to you in sodding Siberia, and they can't even understand the words.'

Newly signed to a big label, the back room boy began to put himself about a bit more. He assembled a band around him, touring and enduring the promotional circus. Matters began to escalate when 'The Life of Riley' was adopted by *Match of the Day* to soundtrack its Goal of the Month feature. Broudie, in fact, became court musician to the national game when the Football Association commissioned him to write their Euro '96 record. In collaboration with its lyricists, the comedians Baddiel and Skinner, he came up with 'Three Lions'; its unstoppable chorus of 'Football's coming home' would make it a soccer anthem to rival 'You'll Never Walk Alone'.

Thus, with no particular contrivance on his part, Broudie became a figurehead of the laddish mood that swept across the media in those years. But his own quietly sardonic outlook was unaffected. The Surreal cover of his 1997 compilation *Like You Do* portrayed him surfing across the Mersey like the Liverpool Beach Boy his music can suggest. He wrote a tremendous song for the Liverpool dockers locked out by the port employers in a long, festering dispute: *Tales of the Riverbank* took a subject that is easy to sentimentalise, or reduce to partisan stereotyping, and made of it something simple, unaffected and stirringly human.

The La's' career faltered to a premature end, and we'll never know what they might have achieved. One of their possible futures, however, was enacted by Lee Mavers' bass-player John Power. Disentangling himself from the La's, he formed his own band, Cast – so named because it was the last word on the La's album. Cast would enjoy a few fat years in the mid 1990s, thanks to the Britpop trend the La's had pioneered. For a while there was no faster route to the top than for a young British band to steep itself in the music of the 1960s. The Who, the Beatles, the Kinks and the Small Faces were now the approved influences. Oasis, Blur, Supergrass and more would catch the moment. And so did Cast. For all their popularity, though, Cast would never have the same damaged charisma that the La's had retrospectively acquired. I often sensed that John was irritated by people's reverence toward his 'legendary' former band.

On the early hits 'Alright' and 'Walkaway' – chirpy and elegiac, respectively – Power sounded like a spliff-enhanced reincarnation of Gerry Marsden. Personally I found that wonderful, but it was not to every commentator's taste. The second Cast album, *Mother Nature Calls*, was dense with John's child-of-the-universe musings; every other song seemed to find him staring up at the stars in wide-eyed primal wonder. Full of a burning urge to share what he called 'a glimpse of the forgotten dream', John Power was one of the least ironic writers on the planet. But the melody was still king. Cast had a way of pointing themselves at a tune and kicking it 50 feet in the air.

I went with the band to Vancouver, Canada, in 1996 to watch them begin a North American tour. It was not, alas, destined to break Cast in the States, but John's optimism at the time was like a force of nature. The words raced out of his mouth in a gobby torrent: 'I have a good feeling about America, the whole theory of it, the history of rock'n'roll.' The T-shirt on his chest proclaimed John Lennon's message: We All Shine On. 'The roots are in American music and it keeps getting re-sold to them, even though the roots are already here . . . But we're gonna bug the Americans! We're the real thing, it's not a pantomime. We haven't got the yellow leotards and the long hair but we have got the rock'n'roll. I've been writing these songs on me jack, on the dole in Liverpool since I left the La's, and the feeling is so strong.'

Afterwards, in the minuscule dressing room, the mood was mellow. The band would have to climb back on their tour bus soon and drive to Seattle by morning, where they'd play two sets for radio before flying on to San Francisco for tomorrow night's gig. But there were no moans in the air, just a sweet fug of smoke. 'Forty thousand years ago,' murmured the guitarist Liam Tyson, 'there were hippopotamuses in the Mersey. I took my little dog out for a walk the other week and this fella says, Eh mate, I like yer yo-yo.' Across the room, Keith O'Neill the drummer was begging bassist Peter Wilkinson to stop calling him Bowlhead, the result of a disastrous recent haircut. 'I would, mate,' the other replied, mournfully. 'But the first thing I'll see when I wake up on the bus tomorrow is you. And I'll think, Bowlhead. What can I do?'

Back on that bus, John was already thinking about life after America: 'My head is full of new songs. I'm gagging to get on to the new stuff . . . It's a natural thing, not a planned, mathematical thing. I ain't calculating and doing the Pythagoras Theory of music. What I am doing is getting in there with spontaneity. Capture it and keep moving. We ain't got time to spare.' It was, indeed, time to leave. 'Driver, St John's Precinct, please,' said the manager Rob Swerdlow, and off they went. Cast disbanded in 2001.

The biggest of the Britpop bands was, of course, Oasis, which led to a view that our national pop capital was Manchester. It was striking how Southern journalists had taken to applying the name scally to anything from the North-west. Beneath the rivalry, though, the cities of Liverpool and Manchester have had strong musical connections. 'Between Manchester and Liverpool,' Noel Gallagher said, 'you've probably got it all in British guitar music: The La's, the Beatles, Oasis, the Stone Roses, the Smiths. I like Scousers. They're all right.' Or, as Pete Fulwell puts it: 'Oasis were the best Beatle tribute band ever.'

Back in the time of Eric's, in fact, Fulwell almost went into partnership with Granada TV's Tony Wilson: 'I went to Tony and said, Let's set up a combined Liverpool/Manchester label. Let's have Manchester's hip, grey-mac brigade and Liverpool's pop sensibility – probably best expressed at that time by Orchestral Manoeuvres. Let's do a twin city label and call it Eric's Factory. We thought of doing a double EP, one of Liverpool and one of Manchester, to start the ball rolling. And then it kind of disappeared, and the next thing Factory appeared. And that concept was gone. But there were huge supportive ties between

Liverpool and Manchester. There weren't those boundaries that came later in the '80s, with laddism and football. Manchester was a great place for Liverpool bands to go in the early stages. They got lots of support from audiences there, and the other way round. In fact you'd get more support in Manchester than you would in Liverpool.'

The affinities we'd seen between the Eric's bands and the Fall, for example, were being replicated a decade later. John Power used to stress how much the La's were followed by 'normal lads' rather than students and hipsters. Now the La's' influence was evident across the whole south Lancashire region, visible in a raft of working class guitar bands from Oasis to the Real People. On Merseyside the dole and drug culture of Liverpool's council estates had bred a new generation, receptive to an older local tradition. 'The La's don't own that particular sound,' said Bootle's Real People. 'It was given to them by people who went before, and it belongs to us all.'

This band, formed around its songwriting core of brothers Tony and Chris Griffiths, was signed to Columbia in 1989. A couple of years later they supported Inspiral Carpets on tour and struck up a friendship with that band's roadie, one Noel Gallagher. When Oasis took shape, they would rehearse and perform in Liverpool, where the Griffiths brothers produced the group's first demos. (Their early track 'Rockin' Chair' was co-written by Chris.) The Real People had a windfall thanks to Cher, of all people, who covered their song 'One by One'. But they were unlucky in that their second album, *Marshmellow Lane*, was denied a release by the record company, despite the presence of veteran American producer Jimmy Miller.

Signed to the same company around the same time were a Huyton band, Rain. Like the Real People they fell victim to record business whim – both bands having failed to achieve the overnight success that eluded the La's – and were likewise dropped. Years later, in the wake of Oasis and Britpop, Columbia would re-package old tracks by Rain and the Real People in a compilation album *The Calm Before the Storm*, lavishing the bands with all the praise of hindsight.

In a broadly similar vein were Peter 'Digsy' Deary's band Smaller. Deary was another Oasis comrade, famously commemorated in the title 'Digsy's Dinner' and in a line from 'Be Here Now': 'Your shit jokes remind me of Digsy's'. Like his earlier group Cook Da Books, Smaller never broke through the ranks, but Deary perseveres.

Though it was more or less dormant in the 70s, the legacy of Merseybeat became inescapable in the decades after. One of many ex-La's was Edgar Summertyme: he would later appear in the Big Kids and as a Paul Weller sideman, but around the early 90s could be found on the La's' label Go! Discs with the Stairs, who hovered on the cusp of 60s British R&B and psychedelia. The Hoovers, from Cantril Farm, epitomised the retro-scally tendency, but close behind were Top, who said, 'Songs are the heritage of the city, and we wanted ours to be the catchiest songs in the world.' And the Tambourines: 'There's a tradition stretching back beyond the Beatles and it's all about writing good songs and singing them well.'

Space, says the Picket's Philip Hayes, 'could have turned out as another guitar band, the same old story, but they went quirky: it wasn't the classic Liverpool sound but it brought them success.' Fronted by Tommy Scott, Space attracted notice with their comical but faintly sinister single 'Neighbourhood' in 1996. Their biggest hits were 'Female of the Species' and the Liverpool-Welsh collaboration with Cerys of Catatonia which brought us 'The Ballad of Tom Jones'. They may have looked like any other Britpop band, but their sound owed more to anything from Sparks to music hall Egyptian sand-dancers.

Scott was a born story teller whose vocals wavered in style between Noel Coward and Robbie Fowler, Marlene Dietrich and Lily Savage. There was a wiliness in their wackiness, though, and they made two fine albums in *Spiders* and *Tin Planet*. A third, provisionally titled *Love You More Than Football*, led to a falling-out with the record company, and Space were temporarily grounded.

A personal favourite of mine has been Ian McNabb. His spell as the singer of 80s group the Icicle Works put him on nodding terms with pop stardom, but he's filled the years since then with solo work of real substance. What he's mainly about is big-hearted anthems that know no restraint: a song like 'Fire Inside My Soul' is allowed to sprawl over eight minutes. He makes a warmly emotional noise, full of oily, clanging guitar chords. But he is always melodic and the effect is like receiving a drunken hug.

His second album, 1994's *Head Like a Rock*, was a Mercury Prize nominee that featured McNabb with members of Neil Young's band Crazy Horse. He named its follow-up *Merseybeast* and posed for its cover on Wallasey dock. But his greatest home town tribute is a song called 'Liverpool Girl' on the 2001 *Ian McNabb* album: its heroine is the irrepressible Everywoman, 'full of wit and intuition', going to Cream, without a coat – 'the laughter from her golden throat, can be heard from the Irish boat.' I'd say it was a masterpiece.

McNabb is an admirably uncool character who once dedicated an album to the Halifax Building Society, and ended another with a track called 'I'm a Genius'. He's willing to play the class clown if it gets him nearer to an emotional truth. But you catch his fierce idealism in a title like 'You Must be Prepared to Dream', and, above all, his boundless romantic optimism in 'You Stone My Soul'. When the appeal of irony has palled, simple sincerity can be a potent commodity.

There is an old John Lee Hooker line that Roger Eagle used to quote whenever he believed someone to be a musician to the core: 'It's in him, and it's got to come out.' For all the stuff a seasoned campaigner must contend with – the age-ism, the lack of airplay – McNabb is one of those born troubadours who does this stuff because he must. As he told Debbie Johnson in the *Liverpool Echo*: 'I spent a long time asking what my reward was for all the heartache, the lack of security, worrying about money, but this is what I do. I write songs . . . I coast for a week after writing a song I'm happy with.'

The come-back king of this post-La's wave, however, was a man who had actually preceded them. Michael Head of 80s band the Pale Fountains would reappear in the 90s as Shack. I confess I was slow to recognise his quality, but came to rate him a classic songwriter of the Liverpool school: tuneful, bruised but optimistic. Head's story is a rock'n'roll saga of bad luck, grit, self-destruction and lustrous talent. Shack came agonisingly close to a breakthrough of epic dimensions, but have had to settle for cult devotion.

Head grew up in the tough urban prairies of Everton and Kensington. (The latter district, like its neighbour Islington, had been christened by nineteenth-century bourgeois, keen to emulate London's fashionable suburbs. The contrast between their aspirations and late twentieth-century reality could not have been more stark.) He resolved to form a group after watching the Teardrop Explodes on *Top of the Pops* and, the next day, meeting one of them in a record shop in town. This had, of course, become one of Liverpool's acquired advantages: the gulf that separates pop stars and pop wannabes can occasionally vanish. He went on to discover Arthur Lee's psychedelic renegades Love, and the meticulous maestro Burt Bacharach. Ultimately, Head's own talent would possess the battered yearning of the former and the romantic poise of the latter.

In fact the Pale Fountains were at first called the Love Fountains in honour of Lee. Re-styled, they appeared on Virgin after a record company bidding war that drove their fee up to £150,000. It was a difficult time, fashion-wise, and the Fountains looked like a Hebridean version of London's New Romantics: heavy knitted jumpers, possibly with belts worn outside, fey fisherman's caps, mountaineering socks outside their rugged but ballooning trousers. Once inside the music industry process, they shared the fate of most young groups of the day, losing control of their music. It was sonically embellished, overlaid and generally transformed by studio technology, to the point where it was hard to recall the emotional impulse they'd tried to capture in the first place.

They faded from view. Worse, Michael Head's collaborator Chris 'Biffa' McCaffrey died of a brain tumour, aged 28. Head would now spend some years in a wilderness of his own making. Heroin had moved into Liverpool in a big way, and it found him ready – he was all the more susceptible, perhaps, given his attachment to a streak of nineteenth-century romanticism typified by the opium-eating Thomas De Quincey. Nevertheless, he and his brother John formed Shack; their debut, *Zilch*, was produced by Ian Broudie and carried a caustic song about one of Liverpool's worst acts of self-mutilation in 'Who Killed Clayton Square?'

The follow-up, *Waterpistol*, was stalled for years by the closure of the record label. Meanwhile, though, in 1992 there came a priceless opportunity to back Arthur Lee on some European dates. In Liverpool they played at the Academy, soon to become the home of Cream, and Lee generously declared the show 'the most memorable of my life'. He'd been touched, apparently, by the group's guided tour (they took him down to the Beatle sites in Mathew Street) and by the surprise tribute paid by fans who followed him to a restaurant afterwards, singing Love songs in his honour. The gig itself was happily captured on tape and released on an album eight years later. The unpredictable Lee, however, would spend the second half of the decade in jail on a firearms charge.

The next album, *The Magical World of . . .*, was a beauty, though Shack's lack of career momentum was scarcely helped by a temporary change of name to the Strands. Its perfect song (and every Michael Head album has one) is 'Something Like You', which Johnny Marr described as a record that could only come out of Liverpool. But that was even truer of the next album, *H.M.S. Fable*: achingly lovely, the perfect union of melody and soul. Apart from its archaic seafaring images, the record has a brutally explicit portrait of junkie routine in Liverpool, 'Streets of Kenny'.

The *NME* carried a cover shot of Michael Head, acclaiming him as the 'Greatest Songwriter'. Sadly, the waves anticipated around *H.M.S. Fable* failed to materialise, despite its great reviews. 'This could be our last chance,' he admitted at the time. 'We've had a couple of problems in the past few years. We did a photo session the other week, and I'd just had half me teeth smashed out. In January I broke me wrist, just when we found out we'd got the support slot on the Catatonia tour. But, y'know, I'm always gonna write. So you might have to put up with me until I'm 65.'

Considering that Liverpool produced, in the person of Cilla Black, Britain's biggest female pop star of the 60s, girls have rarely been central to the scene. Not even Jayne Casey became terribly well-known nationally. And all those jangling scally bands were laddish as can be.

Suddenly that's changed. If Liverpool's chart form is perking up again then it's thanks to the first great pop act of the twenty-first century, three young women from Merseyside called Atomic Kitten. They are, of course, connected to the Eric's story, even though it took place before they were even born, by virtue of their creator being Andy McCluskey from Orchestral Manoeuvres In The Dark.

There were, to be fair, a few other girls to represent the city before the Kittens came along. We must mention Sonia, who topped the chart in 1989 with 'You'll Never Stop Me Loving You' and scored a few more successes in the early 90s. She is one of those born entertainers, like Gerry Marsden – you may or may not like their output but there is no denying they have the showbiz spirit. Among the most likeable of one-hit wonders, also from 1989, were the Reynolds Girls, more protegees of Stock, Aitken and Waterman. Their 'I'd Rather Jack' has the classically brazen cheekiness of Liverpool girls. If such a substance could be bottled, it would be so dangerous they'd have to ban it by international treaty.

I think we might also include Mel C. If the Spice Girls were a true sampling of English pop life then there absolutely had to be a Scouse girl in there. She is in fact from Widnes, not from Liverpool, and therefore at the outer fringes of our catchment area. From the moment Sporty first appeared on *Top of the Pops* in a Liverpool football shirt, however, her allegiance to the city was forever sealed in the public mind. She doesn't have any particular roots in the local music scene and even her solo music is a composite of modern elements from everywhere (though one track off *Northern Soul*, 'Suddenly Monday', has a distinct 'Penny Lane' influence) but she's so far shown the keenest musical mind of the Famous Five. Perhaps her Scouse background will instil in her some of the musical ambition that you seldom see in the others. She at least has a tradition to live up to.

The Atomic Kitten story, by contrast, goes way back into Liverpool's pop past. When we last encountered Andy McCluskey he was a disappointed man: his band of eighteen years, OMD, were dissolving in the face of frenzied indifference all around. He knew the world was through with Orchestral Manoeuvres, but was the world through with him? 'I was still conceited enough to believe that I could write songs, and that it was just the OMD vehicle that was dated,' he says. 'So I thought, Screw it. I'm gonna get someone who *will* be well-received, because they're young and good-looking. And I'm gonna write songs and prove, if only to myself, that I can still do it, and fuck Radio 1 and all the rest. So I set about the idea of inventing a band and writing songs for them.'

With Stuart Kershaw, who'd written songs on the final OMD albums, he was put in touch with a group assembled from adverts placed in *The Stage*. 'But the chemistry was wrong and it self-destructed. I thought I knew the music industry, but I hadn't a clue. I didn't know how manufactured pop in the late '90s was done. And what a dirty, sordid and ruthless industry it is. But I learned a lot. A phrase involving old dogs and new tricks comes to mind.

'We'd decided that getting a band together from adverts, from different parts of the country and saying "Right, you're all in a band, now be best friends," was just a recipe for disaster. So I thought we'd try it more organically. Out of the blue, a friend in Liverpool who had a band called the Porn Kings came in and said "Are you're still writing songs for a girl band?" Well, yeah. Why? "Oh, it's just that I've got this girl in my band who's wasting her time waving her tits around behind me." And he showed us a video of Kerry Katona on stage with the Porn Kings, miming keyboards and clapping her hands, in this pink hot-pants trouser suit. And we go, Yes! We *have* to meet this girl!

'First time we met her she blew us away, She had "it". You knew she was going to be a star. She wasn't the greatest singer but she was the engine: if we put a band together around this girl, it's got something special.'

From a performing arts school they found Liz McClarnon and Heidi Range. But the new trio immediately fragmented when Heidi had to leave to do her GCSEs (she would eventually join the Sugababes). 'So we put a little piece in the *Liverpool Echo* about the "new girl band desperately seeking a third member", and Natasha Hamilton's mother read it: "Eh up, girl, this is what you want to do, isn't it?" So Natasha came in, and boy could she sing. That was the last piece of the jig-saw. When I saw all three – Kerry, Liz and Natasha – dancing together to "Right Now", that was the Eureka moment. That was Atomic Kitten.

'They were all so young, it was incredible. And without even trying we'd got a redhead, a brunette and a blonde. Everyone thought we'd done it on purpose. And their personalities fitted my original idea for the Kittens, which was Bananarama goes Manga cartoon. They were loud, obnoxious and wonderful. It was very exciting.

'Interestingly, however, the London record companies didn't want to know: "Oh, they're from Liverpool? Too provincial. And you were in OMD but you don't have a track record of writing current hit singles. And a manager from Liverpool we've never heard of?" Then all of a sudden somebody realised we had a real geographical identity, which was marketable. There was a feeding frenzy. And we signed to Innocent.

'The girls' personalities made us think in a certain way: songs like "See Ya" and "I Want Your Love" were written for the loud side of their personalities. We'd go "Would you say this? Would you use these words?" So it was a symbiotic relationship. But what set them apart, without being too big-headed, was that we were prepared to do things that were just beautiful songs. The first few singles were kitsch as hell, and I loved them. But after the Spice Girls phenomenon the media was very anti manufactured girl bands. Throughout 2000 we were swimming against the tide: the radio wouldn't play them; they were perceived as being just a Saturday morning kids' TV band. And then they were dropped. But then the record company gave it one more chance, and realised they had "Whole Again".

'I always remember being told, when I was in OMD, "Your trouble is you don't know whether to be Abba or Joy Division." And with Atomic Kitten we'd written songs that were kitsch, but also some very beautiful ones, like "Whole Again". Kerry Katona had of course left, because she was pregnant. So we baled in Jenny, who was born in Wallasey. And everyone thinks it was terribly well organised, but believe me we were winging it. Every day was another fucking trauma: "You mean Kerry's pregnant! What? We've been dropped? Oh no!"

'Then "Whole Again" comes out, with a cheap video, and storms up to Number 1. Wallop. Now everybody gets it. Another Number 1, the album sells a million. How did that happen?

'If I wasn't so naive I wouldn't have started OMD. I wouldn't have started Atomic Kitten. With more sense I wouldn't have done either. What next? I could do a boy band. After Atomic Kitten that would be a piece of cake. That's the most logical thought I've had in 25 years, so it would probably be a disaster.

'To be honest, I've been so depressed by the politics of the music industry in the last twelve months, that part of me is starting to say, You know what, Andy? Perhaps you should go back to doing your own thing again. Even if you don't sell so many records, at least it's all yours, and you don't have to answer to someone saying you've got to make the chorus sound more like a Westlife song.

'Atomic Kitten had been my knee-jerk response. I'd felt jilted by the music industry when OMD came to an end, so I went off and found another lover. It's been amazing, but there's an awful lot about it that I find disenchanting. The music industry never ceases to find new ways to depress me. But I stay in it. There's no escape. What else would I do?

'In some respects I'm like some sad old vampire, an ex-musician re-living his youth vicariously by cultivating the careers of younger people, hanging around in the wings going "I remember this!"

'I'm sure a lot of the bands in town don't think of Atomic Kitten as a Liverpool band: "That's manufactured pop crap". But apart from Mel C it's been a long time since Liverpool had Number 1s. I found that sad, because from the 60s through to the 80s Liverpool was consistently banging records up the international charts. Space and Cast did well, but they weren't on the same scale.

'And the Kittens are real Liverpool girls. Cilla Black has become a professional Scouser now, a pastiche of her former self. But when the Kittens talk and they're on stage, you can tell that Natasha's still a scally from Kensington. Liz is the slightly posh bird from Aigburth, who's upwardly mobile. But it's what they are, and that's what I like about them. Even though I'm a Wirral boy I'm delighted that Liverpool was finally able to get one over on Detroit as the musical capital of the world. And it's Atomic Kitten who've done it. With their last two Number 1s they've put Liverpool's total past Detroit. Imagine it. More Number 1s than Motown!'

16. BROTHER, CAN YOU TAKE ME BACK?
THE BEATLES AND BEYOND

'Condensed milk. I used to think, If I ever get rich . . . I'll buy a tin of condensed milk and have it all the time.'

Paul McCartney

By 1970 the whole show was over. From Fab Four to four Fabs, the individual Beatles began their awkward personal journeys. Painfully, and with a force that none of them foresaw, they learned that Beatledom was forever. No matter how long they lived, whatever they might achieve, there'd be no escaping the bloody group and its collective shadow. Ringo adjusted, eventually, with his habitual stoicism. Paul came around as well, when his populist instincts told him it was folly to fight the Beatles' popularity. George, I think, was never entirely reconciled to his role as an ex-Beatle, since he was seldom comfortable being a Beatle in the first place. Typically, John was the most militantly anti-Fab in his solo work, yet doggedly protective of their memory when they were attacked. Given the ceaseless evolution of Lennon's attitudes, he might have become the most pro-Fab of them all, had he not died in 1980.

Beatlehood wasn't the only legacy the four men would carry through life. There was Liverpool, as well. In their imaginations they never completely left it behind. In Lennon's final days, he was drawing ever closer. In the book of the Beatles' *Anthology*, taken from interviews done in middle age, the remaining members reference their home town repeatedly. Most often it's done to emphasise their humble origins in contrast to their later success. Just imagine li'l ol' me, doing all this! But its sheer repetition takes on a therapeutic quality, as if the memory of Liverpool was their touchstone, their last contact with normality. The videos they made for the *Anthology*'s two singles, 'Free As a Bird' and 'Real Love', both used images that locate the group's essence in Liverpool.

Though the teenage Beatles dreamed of equalling Elvis, their impact on the global *Zeitgeist* was quite unplanned. Their only plan had been to get a hit record. Paul was out to become a successful musician, not a legend. George and Ringo's hopes were more modest still: just to earn a living from music would keep them out of the factories.

John alone had something like a grand ambition, even if he didn't quite know what it was. He could never have settled easily for an ordinary existence. In childhood he had a recurring dream of flying over Liverpool, which he interpreted as an urge to escape. In adolescence he made a half-hearted attempt to run away to sea, like his father before him and countless Liverpudlians as well. His biographer Ray Coleman wrote of John's student days: 'The dominating characteristic at college inside everyone with ambition was a burning desire to get out of Liverpool.'

That may have been true, but if Lennon was destined to leave Liverpool, he was also fated to carry its stamp throughout his life. His upbringing was staid, in the care of respectable Aunt Mimi and decent Uncle George. He learned his first words on George's knee, being taught to pick out the headlines of the *Liverpool Echo*. But in the background, informing his sense of self, there were his real parents: his mother Julia, irreverent and spirited, and his father Fred, the shiftless and disreputable seadog. There was already a conflict in his head, then, between English propriety and Scouse subversion.

John's childhood locale, Woolton Village, is gratifyingly intact. It retains the character of a Lancashire hamlet, swallowed whole by Liverpool's sprawl and not chewed up by it. Still dominated by St Peter's Church, the place has an air of timeless stability. Lanes, like that on which Strawberry Field stands, are winding, quiet and hilly. Behind the high walls and secretive trees are the former lairs of reclusive Victorian grandees – bewhiskered bourgeois who'd forsaken the city and valued privacy over ostentation. At Woolton's hollowed-out heart was a quarry, source of the pink-brown sandstone that dominates the city. From that quarry came the name of his band, the Quarrymen. The original Beatles were made of the same rock that is the stuff of Liverpool.

And there was the legacy of language. John's capacity for cannily pointed gobbledygook – 'ladies and genital-men' – came before the more random imagery of his psychedelic period, and would outlast it too. A rush of unstoppable wordplay was one of Lennon's inherently Liverpudlian facets, for the city can scarcely express itself in any other way. In the background noise of his childhood, it might be football terrace jeering:

Holy, holy, holy,
Ten full backs and a goalie.

Or maybe playground taunts:

Oompah, oompah, stick it up yer jumper.

Nautical coarseness:

The Mersey banks
Was made for Yanks
And little girls like Ivy,
I'd twiddle with Ivy's flue, wouldn't you?

Or else the 'sky blue pink' Surrealism of ordinary conversation. There is a very old Liverpool rhyme (from at least the 1900s), entitled 'I Went to a Chinese Laundry'. This is how it goes:

I went to a Chinese laundry,
I asked for a piece of bread,
They wrapped me up in a table cloth
And sent me off to bed.

I saw an Indian maiden,
She stood about ten feet high,
Her hair was painted sky blue pink
And she only had one eye.

I saw a pillow box floating,
I jumped in rather cool,
It only took me fourteen days
To get to Liverpool.

Singing: Ah, Black Sam the Negro,
Abajou, abajou, jay,
Carder Bungalow Sam.

That was collected by the folklorist Frank Shaw off a man in Woolton. I don't know if John Lennon ever heard all of those rhymes. But in them, whether by coincidence or influence, are premonitions of so many better-known songs: 'Lucy in the Sky with Diamonds', 'I Am the Walrus', 'Happiness Is a Warm Gun', 'The Continuing Story of Bungalow Bill', 'Across the Universe' . . .

And, as to music, the rolling, hymn-like piano chords of 'Imagine' recall Lennon's earliest roots, for long before Elvis Presley and rock'n'roll, there was Church of England Sunday school. Aunt Mimi remembered him as 'a nicely-spoken boy attending church three times on Sunday of his own free will, in the church choir.'

The echoes of Anfield and Goodison, church parades and strike rallies, back alley chants and market traders: Lennon's songs resound with all the din of urban Liverpool. But he also grew up surrounded by the serenity of park lands. In his district there was an extraordinary abundance of green. Calderstones, Sefton, Princes, Reynolds, Woolton Wood, Strawberry Field, even Allerton Golf Course – these supplied him with silence and beauty to nourish his imagination. Around them all, beyond the docks, there was the graceful sweep of the Mersey river's rustic stretch: a river with nothing to do but mirror the heart-stopping vastness of the sky.

This was not the side of his childhood that he often acknowledged. He preferred to say things like, 'We were the first working-class entertainers that stayed working-class and pronounced it and didn't try and change our accents.' Back in Menlove Avenue, though, John's Aunt Mimi took a more sceptical view: 'Until John met Paul and the others,' she told the *Sunday People*, 'John spoke what I call the King's English without a trace of a Liverpool accent. One day I complained when he lapsed into broad Liverpudlian. He turned on me, saying he felt embarrassed by his accent and suddenly ran upstairs in a fit of temper. Leaning over the banisters he yelled "Dat, Dese, Dem and Dose".'

Lennon was among the first Englishmen to join the long flight from middle-class manners that would epitomise the age. As one of the Beatles, he would hasten that process. Nobody stopped loving money, but suddenly everyone wanted to be common.

In Liverpool, though, it wasn't enough to purge yourself of poshness. You had to look hard as well. Lennon became a pretend Ted, though in later life he admitted it was an act. 'Liverpool's quite a tough city,' he said in 1975. 'A lot of the real Teddy Boys were actually in their early twenties. They were dockers. We were only fifteen, we were only kids – they had hatchets, belts, bicycle chains and real weapons.' And again: 'On the street in Liverpool, unless you were in the suburbs, you had to walk close to the wall. And to get to the Cavern it was no easy matter, even at lunchtime sometimes. It's a tense place.'

In his art school girlfriend Cynthia, whom he would marry, John found a genteel young Wirral woman, a graduate of the Hoylake Parish Girls Choir. 'He was never really a macho working class man,' she told me. 'I think his talents were above and beyond that. He was like a chrysalis. He had to be macho to cope with the types he came across in Liverpool. He tried to look like the tough guys so that they wouldn't pick on him. What John became was what John really was, underneath it all.'

The cloak of Liverpudlian heaviness, though, served him well in the Beatles' early years. And below it there beat the heart of a Scouse loyalist. It may have looked, on grim winter evenings in 1957, like a city 'full of deformed people, three-foot-high men selling newspapers'. But it was also inspiring. One night, with his art school comrades Bill Harry, Rod Murray and Stuart Sutcliffe, he adjourned to Ye Cracke to discuss a beat poet they'd just seen. The trouble was, they decided, this man was imitating San Francisco style. Harry remembers: 'I'd seen John's stuff, which was very wacky and English; you could see the influence of the Goons. We knew all about Ginsberg and the angry young men, but you don't copy someone else's experiences, you should do your own stuff. We thought Liverpool had so much history and character that it was just as romantic as anywhere else. So we made a vow to make Liverpool famous: John with the group, Stuart and Rod Murray with their painting and I'd do it with my writing. I said we should call ourselves the Dissenters.'

In those days it took some nerve – or several pints of Higson's – to conceive a romantic vision of Liverpool. But John would prove himself a dissenter of international standing.

Perhaps it was always on the cards that he would gravitate to New York. Poor Herman Melville felt a pang of disappointment to find Liverpool so like New York, but John Lennon loved the Big Apple for precisely that reason.

'My love of New York,' he said on arrival in 1971, 'is something to do with Liverpool. There's the same quality of energy, of vitality, in both cities.' It was a parallel he would draw many times in his final years. In the city where he spent the last eight years of his life he found a home from home: a bigger, richer, flashier version of the city where he had spent his first 23 years.

But he made other comparisons as well. To Jan Wenner of *Rolling Stone*, he likened Liverpool to San Francisco: 'We were a great amount of Irish descent and blacks and Chinamen, all sorts there.' It that diversity, he suggested, was the creative energy that had made San Francisco, not Los Angeles, the cradle of hippy culture. His home town, he went on, was 'a very poor city, and tough. But people have a sense of humour because they are in so much pain, so they are always cracking jokes.'

In John's brief Marxist phase – when he donned dungarees, gave clenched-fist salutes and recorded 'Power to the People' – it suited him to play up his roots in downtrodden Liverpool: 'We were the ones that were looked down upon as animals by the Southerners, the Londoners.' Following his exposure to 'primal scream' therapy, he also liked to describe his past as being full of pain, generally blaming teachers or parental abandonment.

The combined cravings for victimhood and radical credibility – tricky attributes for any globally-adored multi-millionaire – were eventually satisfied by his embrace of Irish roots. John's family links to the Emerald Isle were extremely remote; his middle name was taken from Winston Churchill. Even as a Liverpudlian his childhood environment was quietly Protestant and typically English. But he was now 'Liverpool-Irish' and, in New York City where such postures played well, he'd rail against the British oppression of his people. Like most of his enthusiasms, however, it was eventually replaced by the next thing.

Right to the end, however, it was the Mersey element that lingered. The Cavern would echo in the last minutes that Lennon spent on a public stage. At Madison Square Garden on 28 November 1974, he closed his guest appearance in Elton John's show with McCartney's song 'I Saw Her Standing There', dedicating it to 'an old estranged fiancé of mine called Paul'. It had been such a staple of the Beatles' early repertoire that it became the first track on their first LP.

Unlike the other Beatles, Lennon spent the majority of his lifespan in Liverpool. They were not the most eventful years, but they were the most formative. Like most exiles he grew more homesick as he aged, and in the final years was becoming intensely nostalgic. At the foot of his bed in the Dakota Building was a trunk labelled 'Liverpool', filled with mementoes of home. He'd lately taken to wearing his old Quarry Bank school tie. (Not only for its sentimental value, perhaps: the New Wave skinny tie was a favoured device of trad-rockers looking to update their image in post-punk times.)

On 5 December 1980, he rang Aunt Mimi in England. He told her 'he was looking out of a window in New York, looking at the docks and ships and wondering whether any of them were going to Liverpool. It made him homesick. He was coming home.'

Three days later he was dead.

In the decades since Lennon's murder, Yoko Ono has been the keeper of his flame. And sometimes it flickers in Liverpool's direction. Apart from her financial support for Strawberry Fields and the Picket, Yoko organised a 1990 concert at the Pier Head. But its eccentric cast of Christopher Reeve, Joe Cocker, Cyndi Lauper and others looked more attuned to US TV than to local tastes, and attendance was poor. There was a more successful state visit in July 2001, when she unveiled the re-named Liverpool John Lennon Airport. 'Liverpool obviously meant an awful lot to him,' she said at the ceremony. 'He was always talking about it right until he passed away.' The airport's new slogan was announced as 'Above us only sky' – an echo of Lennon's atheistic hymn 'Imagine'. (Pointless, then, for nervous flyers to hope for Heavenly protection here.)

Locals wondered if the railway authorities might follow the airport's lead by re-branding their own, marginally less glamorous, terminal as Lime Street Ringo Starr Station.

It's not impossible that Yoko was pleased to be told that John Lennon Airport is situated in Paul McCartney's old neighbourhood of Speke. Dynastic rivalry between the houses of Lennon and McCartney was raging well into the new century. On the other hand, she was aware that Paul's childhood home in Allerton had become a National Trust historic site, while John's beloved Mendips, on Menlove Avenue, was just another property in the estate agent's window: 'When I came here with John and we drove past Mendips,' she said, 'he would always point at it and say "That's it, that's it." I am aware that it is up for sale and I think it should be properly honoured like Paul McCartney's place.'

So there we are. It's not what John Lennon 'believed' that makes him so interesting. It's his curiosity, his candour, his volatility. Who knows where another 20 years of life and thought would have taken him? People misunderstand him when they talk of 'what he stood for'; it was always changing. If he was a rebel, there was a streak of latent conservatism also. Perhaps it was about to emerge. He'd by no means be the first famous radical to travel that path, examples abounding from Wordsworth to Ronald Reagan. For all we know, in middle age, he might have returned to the values of Mendips, of Uncle George and Aunt Mimi.

Tomorrow never knew. Just look at any photograph of John Lennon: his eyes never looked less than 1,000 years old.

The secret strength of the Beatles was that John and Paul's talents were equal and their differences were complementary. They were on the surface two sides of the Liverpool coin – a loud-mouthed rebel wit and an all-embracing entertainer.

Obviously, the distinction is really not so clear-cut. John was always a talented balladeer, and by the final years of his life the softer side of his writing had become dominant. McCartney, for his part, is a great, raw-throated rock singer; he's always admired the avant garde and has an independent mind. Perhaps the two men's strengths will eventually be recognised and celebrated for what they are, namely an awesome force for mobilising human enjoyment. In the meanwhile, Paul has not been un-rewarded for his lack of cool esteem: the most successful pop musician in history is also rich beyond the powers of most pocket calculators.

McCartney was born in Walton Hospital in June 1942, and therefore missed the Blitz – unlike the infant Lennon, whose first eight months were spent amid the worst carnage in Liverpool's history. His parents were not well-off but would have been thought respectable: his Catholic mother a midwife and his Protestant father a cotton salesman. Mary McCartney's family were from Northern Ireland, which inspired Paul to write his own Bloody Sunday protest 'Give Ireland Back to the Irish'; the lyric acknowledges his ancestry by referring to a man who 'looks like me', there in the thick of the Troubles. She made him attend Sunday School, which he cites as one strand of influence in his writing.

But Jim McCartney had the greater impact. A trumpet and piano player, he was a product of Liverpool's unique pre-war jazz scene, itself a manifestation of American maritime connections. 'The first thing,' says Paul, 'was BBC radio, we didn't have a record player. There was a nice big family radio that the kids would sit around on the floor and listen to. Me Dad made these headphones for me and me brother out of war surplus stuff, brown electric wire which led up to the bedroom. There was the *Billy Cotton Band Show* on Sunday afternoons. You got a very broad education, you'd hear light music, a bit of classical. But classical often got switched off in our house because me Dad was a bit of a jazzer, having had the jazz band. So it was mainly British light music.'

He remembers a warmer upbringing than John, characterised by family get-togethers. McCartney Senior encouraged his son to follow his example and learn the piano (bought, of course, from the Epsteins' shop), to get more party invitations.

When the household moved to Speke, it was a brand new place, full of unfinished roads. But it was planned along enlightened lines, and promised health, air and space in contrast to the Liverpool slums. In the immediate post-war years, at least, Speke was an optimistic place to be.

'Everyone got television sets for the Coronation in 1953,' Paul recalls. 'Literally the whole street got them and you'd see the aerials going up. And then one night on telly it was talking about Bill Haley, and the scenes of devastation in cinemas, and "*This* is what's causing all the fuss" and it goes into *One two three o'clock, four o'clock rock!* And I got this electric tingle up the spine, That's for me! So I saved up, I couldn't get any schoolmates who could afford tickets to go with me, and went to the Odeon to see him.' (A decade later, the same venue would host the premiere of *A Hard Day's Night*.) 'The only disappointment was the whole first half was Vic Lewis and His Orchestra who were really not what I'd come to spend all this money on. I think I had short trousers and me school cap. Then the lights went down and you heard it again: *One two three o'clock, four o'clock rock!*'

The McCartneys now moved to Allerton, a largely white-collar suburb, separated by a golf course from John Lennon's home. Paul went to the Liverpool Institute in town, next door to the art school that John attended. In his quiet hours he liked to drift down to the waterfront, which he found romantic. 'I'd go down to the Pier Head to get the bus, because my bus was always full at the Institute, so I'd go about ten stops back to the terminus. I'd walk through town, clocking everything, and there'd be all these preachers there at the Pier Head: "The Catholic faith is the only faith!" "The Protestant faith is the only true faith, don't listen to him, brothers." I'd wonder, Do any of them know?'

By now he had discovered Elvis, and rock'n'roll became the new meaning of life. But the step from fan to practitioner was difficult. The way ahead became clear on 11 November 1956, the night Lonnie Donegan came to town. 'The skiffle craze. He became a giant. It was all guitar-oriented and that sprung up millions of skiffle groups, and everybody got a guitar that year. Somebody had to get a washboard to do the rhythm, thimbles on your fingers, metal washboard preferred. So it would always be off to Aunty Ethel to get her old washboard out of the shed. And the tea-chest bass. All over England, but particularly in Liverpool, that's what we were into.

'The people in London knew how to get into show business, they knew people at the famous 2i's coffee bar. But we didn't. So a couple of talent contests came to town, and we went along to Jim Dale's National Skiffle Competition. I went with another guy to cheer our mates Cass and the Cassanovas. So that was the start. Once you had a guitar you were in show business.'

He knew of John Lennon as a local Ted: 'There was a lot of aggression around Liverpool, there were lots of Teddy Boys and you had to try and avoid them if you saw them down alleyways.' But their famous encounter at the Woolton church fair led to friendship, musical partnership and unimaginable success. From the Allerton house came numbers that include 'I Saw Her Standing There', 'Love Me Do' and 'When I'm Sixty-Four'.

Talent contests were still the only available means of career progression: 'We lost every bloody talent contest we ever went in. Never came anywhere. We always got beaten by some terrible loser, you know, nearly always the woman on the spoons. In Liverpool they'd all get tanked up and by 11.30 when the judging went on they're all going, "Go on, Edna!" Bloody good she was, too. She always creamed us. I think she used to follow us round – bastard! "Where are the Beatles trying this weekend? I'll beat 'em!"

'For our repertoire we started doing B-sides, because everybody could do the chart stuff, and if it was a mimickry job they could do it better than us, so it was better to get round the back door and learn a B-side. We'd have a big number like 'I Remember You' and it was such a piss-off if you'd go somewhere and some other act was going on before you doing the same song. So you started looking for B-sides: that's how I got 'Til There Was You', which was a Peggy Lee record. 'Crackin' Up' by Bo Diddley, 'Havana Moon' by Chuck Berry. James Ray, 'If You Gotta Make a Fool of Somebody': nobody knew that and you should have seen the look on the faces when we came up as a rock band doing a waltz . . .'

I never got to see the Beatles and grew up lamenting it. So, when Paul McCartney brought Wings to the Empire in the early 70s, I seized the opportunity to watch his return. By 1979 I was even luckier: now that I wrote for the *NME* I could see him play the Royal Court and get to meet him at a small press conference in the downstairs bar. Just to see a Beatle in the flesh was wondrous; to speak to one was almost beyond belief. The encounter was peculiar, in that Paul and Linda faced about six of us across a table, while fans pressed their faces against the glass doors a few feet away. The irrepressible Allan Williams had turned up, and bustled about the room with great authority, though his actual role was obscure.

The Q&A session was hogged by a boring but supremely self-confident Australian journalist, demanding news of a Beatle reunion. The PR, Tony Brainsby, looked set to call a halt. Nervous of losing my chance, I lunged in with a couple of hopeless questions of my own. McCartney smiled and answered politely. The sum of human knowledge was not greatly increased by our exchange, but I left in a state of elation anyway. Outside, the Liverpool taxi drivers had called a lightning strike and were forming their cabs into a blockade of Lime Street. I couldn't care less.

I've interviewed him on dozens of occasions since then, and what's always interesting to observe is Paul's unresolved attitude towards John. Love, resentment, jealousy and sorrow seem to perform a delicate emotional dance. Attacking John's memory in public remains unthinkable, but relations with Yoko are not generally good. He could not resist a smirk in 1990, when his show at the Liverpool King's Dock drew 50,000 fans, as against the 15,000 at Yoko's all-star Pier Head event a few months earlier.

But the show was mostly famous for Paul's inclusion of a Lennon medley: 'I didn't want to get too precious with it all,' he told me. 'With the emotion of singing some John songs for the first time in my life, it should be Liverpool if I'm gonna do it. I've never sung anything of John's. I remember he did "Lucy in the Sky with Diamonds" with Elton, and his quote was he'd finally got to do Paul's part, 'cos Elton did his. So I finally got to do John's bit on "Help!", and "Strawberry Fields", which I'd always loved as a song. But the greatest thing was at Liverpool they wouldn't stop at the end, which was "Give Peace a Chance". It was a great moment.

'It was lovely anyway, being on the banks of the Mersey, because you could see the weather coming in off the top of Wales. I'm looking across to Flint, the Dee and the Wirral and all of that. In the morning it was a bit cloudy but suddenly it was, "It's gonna be great!" We did our sound-check and it got more and more beautiful as the sun started to go down. It's the power of the Mersey. There is a power in those rivers, the artery of life.'

Often, as people age, their parents' influence begins to grow instead of diminish. In McCartney's case the memory of his father emerged in songs such as 'Put it There': 'My Dad had millions of mad expressions, like a lot of these Liverpool guys. He'd say, "Put it there, if it weighs a ton." Years later when you're grown up you think, What did he mean? We lived on a little estate in Speke. He'd be talking about a kid on the estate and he'd say, "You know the one, his Dad's got a little black pen-knife." Mad. They're all full of that. Or you'd say, Why Dad? Why do we have to do this? He'd go, "Because there's no hairs on a seagull's chest." I love all that, it's why I like Surrealism so much.'

The mention of Speke sends him off: 'God, does that seem like a million miles away, from Speke to mega-ness. I've done great for some scruff from Speke. Because that's all I am. I've never met anyone better than those people, including the prime ministers of a few fair countries. Not one of them has ever came near some of those people.

'I'm not really into luxury. Where I'm from they were always dead suspicious of that: "Too far, too soon, son. Keep your head on your shoulders, moderation in all things." My Dad was always like that. If a girl was revealing a bit too much he'd say "That'll be a nice dress when it's finished." I've tried to meet people who were better and groovier and had better opinions, but I never really found any. I met people who were more far out, but in the end those basic things – "Oh, you won't find your happiness there, love" – turned out to be true.

'Which is why we sent our kids to state schools. It seemed important to keep their feet on the ground. I know it's difficult to claim I'm ordinary, because of the evidence to the contrary: no ordinary guy is as famous as I am or has the money I have. But inside I feel ordinary and inside is where I come from, that's what's speaking. I go back up to Liverpool and I really like the earthiness: "A'right Paul, don't like yer jacket, fuckin 'ell." I'm comfortable there. That's the obsession with ordinariness. I've never found anything better.'

McCartney's most fulsome tribute to the old place was the *Liverpool Oratorio*, premiered in 1991 at the same Anglican Cathedral where he had once been rejected for the choir. 'It's very loosely based on my upbringing in Liverpool, so it starts with two parents and they're going to have a baby, which is very dramatic anyway, but having a baby in wartime is even more so. It really preys on my mind, the bombs coming over, and Liverpool definitely got done in. My Dad was a fireman trying to put out all these incendiary bombs. So the first movement is very chaotic, then in the middle there is a ray of hope, the moving idea that even with all this shit going on there is hope for the future.

'I didn't want to do the Beatle thing, because that section of my life has been overdone. The other parts are just as interesting, especially to me, particularly Liverpool. It's so rich. The Liverpool Institute: a thousand boys, some nuthouse that was. Throwing piss-bombs. We used to go sagging off. Into the Cathedral graveyard, take our shirts off and sunbathe on the gravestones.'

Like its successor *Standing Stone*, the *Oratorio* has been sold as classical music by a pop composer, while McCartney himself entitled another album *Working Classical*. Though it's true the music has taken the traditional forms of symphonic, orchestral and chamber works, I wonder if its roots are really in the British light music of his wireless childhood. Before the days of rock'n'roll, when radio still emanated from mahogany cabinets with fruit bowls on top, the BBC's Light Programme was full of orchestral melodies, from which the young McCartney must have absorbed his earliest notions of composition. There was his mother's favourite, Rota's 'Legend of the Glass Mountain', and dozens more: Ketelbey's 'In a Monastery Garden', Eric Coates' 'Sleepy Lagoon' and 'Dam Busters' March'. Even Yoko recalls John Lennon's earliest impressions being formed by these BBC broadcasts.

And yet, when the Light Programme was abolished in 1967, to be replaced with the Beatle-inspired Radio 1 and the easy-listening Radio

2, an entire tradition of British music disappeared from memory. 'Light music' was a much more serious craft than its name implies nowadays; it was often dark, dramatic and intensely felt. If it has a respected modern counterpart, it's in the soundtrack work of John Barry, Morricone and the like. Put McCartney up against Mozart and he suffers in comparison; revive the notion of British light music and you have, in the *Oratorio*'s composer, a latterday master.

At the opposite end of his sonic palette sits the 'Liverpool Sound Collage' EP, recorded with the Super Furry Animals in 2000. In its uncompromising stretches of studio experiment and cut-ups of Beatle conversation, spliced with fragments from the Liverpool streets, it's McCartney's own 'Revolution 9'. But then, he's been tireless in reminding his interviewers of his avant garde dabblings in the mid-1960s, well in advance of John's work with Yoko.

Now, as Paul attains what his father used to call 'my great venereal age', he and Liverpool are on closer terms than ever. He's been a Freeman of the City since 1984, entitled 'to unsheath his sword within the city boundaries', which is nice. In 1996 he received his knighthood: at the gates of Buckingham Palace he dedicated the honour to the people of Liverpool.

And largely through his own efforts, McCartney's *alma mater* the Liverpool Institute has become LIPA: the Liverpool Institute for Performing Arts. A dignified building of 1825, it was closed in 1985 and faced an uncertain future. Paul resolved to save it. Mark Featherstone-Witty, meanwhile, had dreams of founding a British equivalent to America's 'Fame' school. When the two ambitions connected, fund-raising could begin in earnest. With the help of George Martin, McCartney secured contributions from the Queen, Paul Simon, David Hockney and others. He opened LIPA in 1996 and now it trains young people in all aspects of work in the entertainment industry.

His old Allerton house, as Yoko noticed, has become an official historic site, after an initiative by the BBC's then Director General, the Liverpudlian John Birt. Restoration work on 20 Forthlin Road removed the Artex paintwork and wood panelling, the PVC windows and the woodchip paper, to make room for carefully researched domestic styles of the 1950s. It's been open to the public since 1998.

In December 1999 he gave the new Cavern its seal of regal approval, returning there to play his last show of the twentieth century. The tiny space was naturally jammed: no ticket in town was hotter. There were, therefore, strategically leaked stories of sexual favours being offered to the organisers for admittance. (If true, the scenario would have been in a tradition dating all the way back to the Beatles' first trip to America. Alas, the Cavern tales were not true.) An alternative means of entrance was offered by the Internet. A medium un-dreamt of when Paul last played the Cavern, the Net now staged the largest web-cast the world had seen to that point. McCartney played a storming set, backed by the band from his rock'n'roll covers album *Run Devil Run*. He also raised a cheer for special guest Bob Wooler.

In the early years of the twenty-first century, Paul McCartney found a partner, Heather Mills, to succeed his beloved Linda. He also saw his daughter, Stella, becoming almost as famous as he was, and more frequently photographed. He remained busy and surprisingly accessible: I'd usually arrange to meet him at his London office, and see him sauntering up the street, hands in pockets. In his own head, he never became the superstar he'd become in everyone else's.

Where George or John saw humans as a mass, to be spiritually or politically uplifted, Paul sees only individuals, with sorrows to serenade or spasms of hope to be nurtured in song. He never stops marvelling at the mis-match between his ordinary origins and his destiny. He once described to me how astronomers had named a star after him. He seemed almost frightened by the idea: 'Imagine being at school,' he said, 'and being told that was going to happen.' As ever, he was reaching out to the Liverpool past to steady himself.

If you like your celebrities to be strange, enigmatic or angst-ridden, McCartney will always disappoint. The magical things about him are in his music. He himself remains in awe of Liverpool, more than anything else, and what he calls 'the strange brilliance' of its people. They have kept him human. In a TV interview he remembered driving through the city, cruising Memory Lane. A passer-by recognised him, and raised a hand in salutation. Only slowly did Paul McCartney realise that the stranger was sliding two fingers up either side of his nose.

Like Paul, George Harrison's early years were spent in some very modest suburbs of Liverpool: Wavertree, then Speke. Also like Paul he had an Irish Catholic mother; his father worked as a steward on the White Star transatlantic liners, and then became a bus driver. He attended the same primary school as John, though their age difference kept them apart, and the same secondary school as Paul, who in turn introduced him into John's skiffle group.

In his own book, *I, Me, Mine* and in the group's autobiography *The Beatles Anthology* (both memoirs prepared with the help of Derek Taylor) he recalled a busy port with trams and cobbled streets and bomb sites.

At Speke he watched his father tend the tiny garden – lupins and golden rod out front for show, cabbages round the back – as well as the council allotment down the road in Hale. Gardening would become a passion of Harrison's. The seeds sown on Liverpool Corporation property came to full bloom in the magnificent grounds of his last home, Friar Park in Oxfordshire.

He didn't see the fabled Buddy Holly show in Liverpool, and could not afford the fifteen shillings Paul paid for the Bill Haley concert, but he did see Lonnie Donegan and Eddie Cochran, two of the biggest influences on Liverpool musicians of the Merseybeat era. His first job after leaving school was apprentice electrician at Blackler's department store in the city centre, where his maintenance jobs included the children's Christmas grotto. I remember it well. The whole ground floor is now a giant pub.

His loyalty to Liverpool, and to the North, could sometimes express itself as chippiness. In the *Anthology* his memory is of London companies telling the Beatles, 'You'll never do anything, you Northern bastards.' He adds, 'But that's the thing, as anybody knows who's had the experience of being down and being downtrodden (which we have, as working-class Liverpool lads).' Elsewhere he contrasts his early life – 'Lime Street, Liverpool, just being a Scouse kid' – to what happened later, but tries to make the point that no external changes affect the essentially spiritual journey, which is the core of our existence. He also explains his old track 'Only a Northern Song' as being on two levels: the reference to 'Liverpool, the Holy City' and a sardonic comment on the music being owned by its publisher, Northern Songs.

He never lost an affection for one particular trapping of Northern culture, namely the ukulele-playing of George Formby. An American call-girl, though seemingly unfamiliar with Formby's *oeuvre*, did recall pleasuring Harrison on her knees at a party: he played his ukulele throughout the encounter. True professionals, both.

In the experimental solo albums he released before the Beatles' split, there is a track on *Wonderwall Music* named after the Mersey resort Seacombe, and, on 1969's *Electronic Sound*, a long piece entitled 'Under the Mersey Wall'. The latter was a wry nod towards a famous old *Liverpool Echo* column, written by a stout old boy in a trilby hat who covered some early Beatle stories. The reporter's name was George Harrison.

It's well-known that he felt resentment, in the Beatle years, at the dominance of Lennon and McCartney. But even in solo life he could often seem frustrated. The initial triumphs, like 'My Sweet Lord' and *All*

Things Must Pass, were followed by some disappointing records that suggested it was not just John and Paul who had held him back. The best music of his later years was made with the Traveling Wilburys (including Bob Dylan, Tom Petty and Jeff Lynne), where George was once again allowed to be one of the boys instead of the leader. He had always been a subtle guitar-player, whose genius was not to draw attention to himself but to flatter the song he was embellishing.

Many found Harrison to be kind and gregarious, though most agree that he was prone to sullen moods. His personal life was a puzzling contrast of spiritual piety and physical indulgence. Though he is often admired for his generosity towards Eric Clapton, who took away his wife Pattie, it's less widely remembered that he had an affair with Ringo's wife Maureen. And yet, like Ringo and Paul, he eventually made a long-lasting and apparently loving marriage. He married Olivia Arias in 1978, the same year that his son Dhani was born.

His impact on the British film industry was significant. Through his company, Handmade, he financed an impressive list including Monty Python's *Life of Brian*, *Mona Lisa*, *The Long Good Friday* and *Withnail and I*. Though it was not a great film, he deserved credit for his damage-limitation work on *Shanghai Surprise*, where he worked to soothe both crew and press objections to its stars Madonna and Sean Penn. 'While she's in a warm trailer,' he explained to *Q*, 'the crew are trying to drink a cup of tea to keep warm and a little "Hello, good morning, how are you doing?" goes a long way in those circumstances. Why are they like that? You're asking me! I don't know. They should have done their apprenticeship in Liverpool.'

At a press conference for the same film he said, '*Letter to Brezhnev* resurrected my original belief in the character of the Liverpool people. It's a fantastic example of how someone with no money and no hope can get through that. I think it's fabulous. I've not spent a great deal of time in Liverpool over the years, but I'm happy to say the film has revitalised my image of the Liverpool people.'

In 1992 at the Royal Albert Hall, I watched him play an election benefit for the Natural Law Party. The crowd were neat, not shaggy; the party candidates were extremely ordinary-looking people, perhaps at pains to counter the impression they were mad. The Hall was full, but the touts outside could do no business – as if, in some strange way, precisely the right number of people had turned up. George entered to huge applause, reflecting our sense of the occasion's historic value. But he shrugged, nervously. 'It's not all it's cracked up to be, really,' he said, in that funny side-of-mouth way of his. He was equally diffident at the end: 'Thank you for coming. It would have been terrible for us up here on our own.' And in between, acknowledging our applause: 'I'm always paranoid about whether people will like me. You never know.' The show was a mixture of his Beatle and solo songs, which sounded terrific. Yet, as a frontman, George made a great sideman. The visual focus was often his percussionist Ray Cooper, who looked like a man trying to restrain a frisky bat. The most exuberant outburst came from Ringo, onstage for the encore: 'Hasn't it been a great show? Let's hear it for Georgie!'

In 2001, the re-packaged CD version of his greatest work, *All Things Must Pass*, did much to restore his reputation. It should have been the beginning of a revitalised period in Harrison's career: there was a reservoir of press affection waiting for him. But in fact he was already too ill to take advantage. On 30 December 1999, while the rest of us were preparing our exit from the twentieth century, he'd been brutally attacked in his home by a mentally disturbed man from – of all places – 200 miles away in Liverpool. It was, in a macabre way, virtually George's last contact with home.

The injuries and upset cannot have been helpful to a man already weakened by throat and lung cancer. He succumbed to a brain tumour soon afterwards. In the last month of his life he was visited in hospital by Paul and Ringo; the three men talked quietly of the old days. He died on 29 November 2001.

Twice a day, when I had an office on London's Oxford Street, all life came to a halt as we heard the chanting of Krishna devotees, filing loudly beneath the window. I always felt a pang of displeasure at George in those moments, reflecting that his patronage had done so much to promote this noisy cult. Yet, when he was dead, I was happy that 'My Sweet Lord' was chosen to be his memorial single and that it became a Number 1 hit all over again. Spirituality was his deepest interest, even if sex and money were never entirely forgotten. The opening of Western minds to Eastern ideas should in theory be helpful to us all, and Harrison used his position as a Beatle to bring that about on a grand scale. I confess that I haven't noticed any benefits, generally, but these affairs no doubt take time. Only John Lennon thought that karma could be instant.

Ringo Starr is the Beatles' link to an older Liverpool, of dockside terraces and corner pubs and close-knit proletarian communities. His beginnings were much tougher than the others', and his outlook correspondingly slushier. Contempt for sentimentality is a privilege of the affluent, not the poor. On the *White Album*, just as John's savagely fractured 'Revolution 9' is prefaced with Paul's plaintive call, 'Brother, can you take me back?', so the wound is healed, at the end, by Ringo's whispered lullaby 'Good Night'.

In his childhood there was bitter and sweet: bomb-site playgrounds, violence and poverty, but also the family get-togethers where everybody did a turn. He was an only child, and frequently ill. His father, Richard Starkey, left Ringo's mother when the boy was three. About ten years later she married Ringo's stepfather, Harry Graves. His district, the Dingle, is at the foot of Toxteth, at what used to be the southern end of the Liverpool dock system. In former times it was a place of sailors, whores, emigrants in transit and those who'd simply run out of steam. By Ringo's time the Dingle was more settled, though still rough at closing time; in most respects it mirrored Cilla's Scotland Road district to the north. These are the Scouse heartlands.

The slums were unhealthy but fate was leading him in the right direction: 'No drummer really turned me on at the beginning,' he told me. 'I was in hospital with TB, and they sent me out of Liverpool to a place called Heswall, where they used to have this big greenhouse for children, so we could breathe and get well, 'cos there's not a lot of oxygen in Liverpool. A woman came once a week with instruments for us to play, tambourines, maracas, little snare drums with one stick. She'd put this huge music sheet up, she'd point to the yellow and you'd hit the drum, she'd point to the red and you shook the maraca. It was all pretty primitive but it kept us entertained. I was in there for a year, so they used to make you do things just to keep your spirits up, I suppose. And that's where I started, in the hospital with this one drum.

'And I decided that next time she came, if I didn't get a drum I wouldn't play. That's where the dream started. Then I would walk around Liverpool, to the music stores, and I would just look at the drums, I was never interested in the other instruments at all. My grandparents, who played mandolin and banjo, gave me them, and I'd no interest; my Grandad bought me a harmonica, I'd no interest. We had a piano at home that I used to walk on. But a lot of people sang around that piano, and people would bring instruments to the parties when I was growing up. There'd always be a harmonica player, banjo player, guitar. It was a party town.'

But his Plan B was to go 'deep sea' as they used to say, and work on the ocean liners. To get himself qualified he worked on a Mersey pleasure steamer that plied the North Wales run. When he got back in the evening he'd try to impress girls in the pub by pretending he'd been away to sea: 'Yeah, just got back from Menai.' 'Oh yeah, when did you leave?' 'Ten o'clock this morning.' Then they would tell him to piss off.

He was of the first post-war wave to escape National Service, the nightmare that had haunted John Lennon's childhood. Still, this was Liverpool, and a young man of fighting age still faced conscription of sorts: 'I was a Teddy Boy, you had to be,' he says in the *Anthology*. 'Where I lived, you had to associate with some gangs otherwise you were "open city" for anybody. The choices were: you could either be beaten up by anybody in your neighbourhood or by people in other neighbourhoods, which I was, several times . . . It was like New York or Hamburg.'

Just as nostalgic Cockneys will reminisce about the Krays' East End, he believes the gangs had moral standards: children and old people were safe. You hear this a lot in Liverpool: the 'old violence' was better, because it was not as random as today's. On the other hand, 'There was a terrible thing in Liverpool where you'd walk past somebody and they'd say, "Are you looking at me?" If you said "No" they'd say "Why not?" and if you said "Yes" they'd get you anyway . . . There were a lot of really angry people around.'

He had a Teddy Boy suit: 'My cousin who went to sea – it all revolves around sailors – would give me his old clothes.' The wanderlust took him so badly that, at one point, he thought of moving to Texas, and got a list of Houston factory jobs. But the call of the drums was stronger: 'I just always wanted to drum. I used to make little kits, mainly a snare drum and a tom-tom out of biscuit tins, and then I bought a huge bass drum for 30 bob, I used to whack that. Then I was eighteen and my stepfather, he was from Romford, Essex, he went down there for a funeral or something and found this drumkit for me for twelve quid, and brought it back. That's how it started. A month later I was in a band, 'cos I had the instrument.

'I started with the Eddie Clayton Skiffle Group. I started on brushes and one snare. Then I went to the Dark Town Skiffle Group, which was like this big skiffle group in Liverpool. I auditioned for Rory, the only time I ever auditioned. Got the gig, played with him for a year. Then we got a gig in Butlin's, went professional and then we went to Germany. We were at one club, the Beatles were at another, we used to go and watch them. I loved the front line. We got to know each other, got back to Liverpool. Their drummer couldn't make it one day, Brian Epstein said, "Could you play?" Couple of months later they asked me to join.'

It was not the first attempt to poach Ringo. He'd already turned down an offer from Kingsize Taylor, which is something few had the courage to do. Weirdly, he was also asked by Gerry Marsden to join the Pacemakers on bass guitar: 'We were young,' he laughs. 'You know Paul only played bass because the other two wouldn't play it, after Stu went. John went "Oh no, not me" and George was definitely not going to play it. So Paul just said, "Shit, I'll play it." Wasn't like his instrument of choice. Things happen in strange ways.'

The film of A Hard Day's Night was clever in the way it picked up and amplified aspects of the Beatles' four personalities. And yet, when it came to Ringo, the impression was misleading. Like the movies and the books that followed, not to mention a few of the Beatle tracks as well, it suggested 'little Ringo', the group mascot. 'But Ringo was older than us,' Paul points out. 'He'd worked Butlin's, he had a suit, he'd grown a beard, he was a grown-up.

'He was the sophisticate among us,' says Paul. 'He always was. If there was anything American, like Lark cigarettes, Ringo knew it all. He had a big car. He might have been a GI, Ringo, the way he lived. He had a GI kind of lifestyle. He had a Zephyr Zodiac. And he used to drink bourbon. I'd never heard of bourbon. I think I heard Ringo order it once, so I said I'll have one of those too. He's always been like a grown-up. I suspect when he was about three he was a grown-up.'

And, in a city so conscious of neighbourhoods, it would not be lost on the grammar school fruits that Ringo was from the Dingle. That made him harder, whatever he lacked in height.

Brian Epstein became convinced the Beatles had obeyed some uncanny impulse when they insisted on bringing Ringo into the group. Epstein had been dubious: he was no judge of drumming, but he knew a pretty boy when he saw one, and Ringo wasn't. And yet, said the manager, when Ringo's face completed the quartet a magical transformation occurred. They were suddenly more than the sum of their parts. The chemistry was not only visual. Ringo was the Beatles' allocation of pure Scouse. The others were educated, they'd tasted bohemia, up the hill in Liverpool 8. But Ringo was another sort: down-to-earth, sceptical, humorous, patient. Whatever the alchemy that made the Beatles work, he was one quarter of the formula.

There was a natural assumption, after the Beatles' split, that Ringo would have the toughest struggle. He'd shown some promise in films, including Candy, The Magic Christian and That'll be the Day. But there could not be an infinite supply of roles within his range, as even David Bowie had to learn. Against all expectations, however, he had a brilliant run of hit singles: 'It Don't Come Easy', 'Back Off Boogaloo', 'Photograph' and 'You're Sixteen'. The albums, too, were an interesting mixture. Of the first, a collection of old-fashioned standards called *Sentimental Journey*, he says, 'That was after the break-up, and I was lost for a while. Suddenly the gig's finished that I'd been really involved in for eight years. "Uh-oh, what'll I do now?"

'And I just thought of all those songs that I was brought up with, all the parties we'd had in Liverpool at our house and all the neighbours' houses. Songs my uncles and aunties sang, songs my stepfather sang. So I called George Martin and said, Why don't we take a sentimental journey?'

The LP sleeve was a picture of a Dingle pub, the Empress, in his old neighbourhood. The tracks, such as 'Stardust' and 'Love is a Many Splendoured Thing', were chosen to please his Mum.

The next album, *Beaucoups of Blues*, was just as rooted in his Dingle days, being a record of country songs: 'George was making an album [*All Things Must Pass*] and I sent my car for this steel guitarist and producer Pete Drake, from Nashville. So Pete came and he noticed in my car I had all these country tapes. I don't know why he was shocked at this but he goes, "Wow, you've got all these country tapes!" "Yeah. I love country music." He said, "Well, why don't you come to Nashville and we'll make a record?" And we actually did it in two days. Far out. We picked and learned five songs in the morning and we recorded five songs at night, and had a lot of fun in between.'

The best, however, was 1973's *Ringo* album: a full-on rock-and-pop affair with contributions from the other three Beatles, including John's opening track 'I'm the Greatest', which has Ringo recalling his mother's encouragement back in Liverpool. (John was really using Ringo as a surrogate voice here, deciding a track called 'I'm the Greatest' might seem too brazen if it came from him.) A minor hit single, 'Only You', was culled from Ringo's 1974 set, *Goodnight Vienna*. But, from this point, as Ringo candidly admits, 'it started going downhill.' It's a sorry coincidence that 'Goodnight Vienna' should be boozer's slang for 'hello oblivion'. On the album cover, Ringo's arm is lifted in salutation. But in reality, he could just as easily have been waving farewell.

He speaks with a deep, deliberate voice; behind the dark glasses are a pair of sad, smiley eyes. 'On the downhill slide there,' he recalls of his wilder years, 'I forgot what I really liked to do, which is play, and I still do.' The drummer's taste for transglobal high life was starting to wreck his career. He'd flit between the jet-set destinations of London, Monte Carlo and Los Angeles, his watch set permanently to the cocktail hour.

With his thirsty pals Keith Moon and Harry Nilsson, he was a regular playmate of John Lennon's during the notorious fifteen-month 'lost weekend'. Though he'd bought John and Yoko's white mansion at Tittenhurst, where the *Imagine* film was made, he took up residence in Monaco for tax purposes. His marriage to Maureen Starkey, the Liverpool girl he'd met in the Cavern, ended in divorce in 1975. And as for the records . . . For some reason, people stopped talking about Ringo's records. In some instances, record companies stopped releasing them altogether.

His health was never good, even at the best of times, and in 1979 he nearly died of intestinal problems in a Monte Carlo hospital. Soon after that, his LA house burned down, destroying much Beatle memorabilia. In 1980 John Lennon was killed, but Ringo has said he was almost too stoned to notice. On a happier note, in 1981 he married the actress Barbara Bach, who'd been a Bond girl in *The Spy Who Loved Me*; she'd met Ringo when they appeared together in the movie *Caveman*, and the couple have been together ever since. In 1984 he took a new role, as the lugubrious narrator of *Thomas the Tank Engine*. Today there is a generation of children who know him for this alone. In 1989 he entered a rehab clinic, and re-emerged as the leader of his All-Starr Band.

Ringo Starr has spent the past few years confronting a couple of key realities: one is that he's an alcoholic who must stay away from booze; the other is that he's a Beatle and this is all anyone really wants to know. Gamely, when he tours, he serves up versions of 'Octopus's Garden' and the inevitable 'With a Little Help from My Friends', interspersed with oft-told yarns about their origins. Similar fates befall his solo hits, while pride is salvaged by a few cuts off a recent album. The newer songs are often much better than, say, 'Don't Pass Me By' – but the realist in him will say to the crowd: 'Let's hear it for the *White Album*. I loved it!' And the crowd appears to swoon at the magic of witnessing a near-Beatle experience. His lot in life, it seems, is not to be an artist, but a much-loved celebrity turn.

I asked him if he were content, nowadays, with the Beatle legacy he cannot walk away from. 'Well, it's something we'll never get away from,' he says. 'When I was 30 I thought "Well, what about *me*? Just *me*, you know? It's always related to the Beatles." Now you realise it doesn't matter what you do, it's gonna be related, so you just live with it.'

Like Paul and George, he's kept a sense of Beatledom being the outer layer of himself, the one that the world sees. If he could simply step away from it, he said, there would be 'Richard Starkey, 10 Admiral Grove, Liverpool 8', waiting for him.

'I haven't been back to Liverpool since my stepfather died a couple of years ago,' he adds. 'I used to go more often when my Mum was alive, less after that. I still have a lot of family there, but it's just that life changes. I took my son Zak there when we toured in '92, and mainly all I could say was "Well, what *used* to be there was . . . " The Cavern's moved next door, which we went down to and saw it all. But when we went to Madryn Street, the house I was born in, some woman just got hold of me arm saying, "Ooh, it hasn't changed has it?" Well, what happened to all the shops? "Oh they've gone." And what happened to that? "Oh that's gone." I suppose if you live there you don't notice the change so much, 'cos you're there while it's happened. But, y'know, it's not like I've moved to London – I've moved to the world.'

17. HEAVEN UP HERE?

LAST TRAIN FOR SUBLIME STREET STATION

Who steals my purse steals trash . . .
But he that filches from me my good name
Robs me of that which not enriches him
And makes me poor indeed.

Shakespeare, Othello

Around the corner from Lime Street I remember a night club called the Shakespeare. It was actually an historic theatre, whose nineteenth-century edifice wore the stone inscription 'Comedy – Tragedy – Music'. The words could almost have served as Liverpool's civic motto.

Isn't it the grit in the oyster that makes the pearl? Liverpool is big on grit, but has also given us a string of pearls. It can be a terrible place, but an extraordinarily creative one, too. Actually, I don't entirely understand why this should be: there is something literally wondrous about the process. But I walk around this city and I am amazed by it, just as I am occasionally appalled.

Comedy, tragedy, music . . . The city has survived so much in its time, up to and including the new-slums-for-old approach of its own planners. But the last twenty years have seen another misfortune, in the city's spectacular fall from national grace. Within my time I have seen it descend from hip esteem to an object of derision. By tradition it was Liverpool's role to be the source of jokes and not the butt of them. Enter the comedy Scouser, with his grubby shell suit, his curly perm and nasty 'tache. Cue the *Sun* gags: 'What do you call a Scouser in a semi-detached? A burglar.' 'What do you call a Scouser with a tie? The accused.' And so forth.

What fresh Hell was this? Liverpool can live with notoriety. It has had centuries of practice. But ridicule?

To be at the bottom of the heap is bad enough, but to be mocked as lacking in style is intolerable. Living outside of Liverpool I was probably more aware of its poor reputation. I was always surprised to find how little the locals knew of outsiders' opinions, and I certainly admired their magnificent lack of interest. You can revile Liverpudlians for anything you like: dishonesty, fecklessness, brutality, vulgarity. At least one of them will reply, in all sincerity, 'You're just jealous.'

More thoughtful Liverpudlians, however, are conscious of a problem that needs to be tackled. In 1999, one correspondent to the *Liverpool*

Echo offered the Shakespearean lines quoted above. The occasion had been an unguarded remark by the then Home Secretary, Jack Straw, that 'Scousers are always up to something'. It goes without saying that a similar quip directed against any other minority would have spelled the end of his ministerial career. Three months later, in a *Guardian* article called 'Why has everyone got it in for Scousers?', the writer Linda Grant made an eloquent defence of her home town: 'What had happened? How did what I thought of as the best place in Britain turn into what everyone thought was the worst?'

Her conclusions were optimistic. But two years later, from another *Guardian* columnist came a suavely argued piece ('Why the Bulger mourning marathon sickens me') of a less sympathetic sort. The infant Jamie Bulger was murdered by two boys in Liverpool in 1993. The decision, in 2001, to release the killers on licence provoked protests, not least from Bulger's mother Denise Fergus. Like the *Sunday Times* man who thought the week after Hillsborough an appropriate time to air his contempt for Liverpool, so the *Guardian* woman took this opportunity to parade her own distaste. In a twist on the more conventional imbecility that the murderers were typical Scouse psychopaths, she found the mother far less appealing: 'Scousers' propensity to linger over every misfortune until another comes to replace it makes them uniquely suited to the demands of the Bulger mourning marathon.'

In fact, there was a widespread degree of scepticism about Denise Fergus in Liverpool, something which escaped the liberal pundit's rigorous research, no doubt. But in her opinion, Liverpudlians were merely a red-necked lynch-mob given to emotional self-indulgence.

Well, I blame the impression of perpetual whinging on *Brookside*, myself.

Around the same time as Jack Straw's jibe, the Comic Relief charity granted £46,000 to a local arts organisation, for research into negative stereotyping, epitomised by Harry Enfield's famous 'Scouser' sketches (though I always found them funny and know of nobody in the real world who was offended by them). 'Young people in Liverpool have a poor self-image,' said the recipient of this hand-out. 'We don't want them to be locked into living a self-fulfilling prophecy. It is as though the city has become a huge *Brookside* set and we are all bit players and everyone else is amused by our behaviour.'

My own impression was that Liverpool had come into the last of its Irish inheritance. By the turn of the millennium the real Ireland was more widely liked than before; Paddy jokes were very poor form, and any overt expression of prejudice was socially unacceptable. If you wished to stigmatise any group as lazy, thick and violent, the Scousers would do instead. There was a sort of displaced racialism at work. At those 'gentlemen's evenings' organised by London football clubs, the type of after-dinner wag who'd formerly favoured the Pakistani gags nowadays conformed to more enlightened standards: 'I go to Liverpool sometimes, you know.' Whoops and jeers break out in anticipation of the punch-line. 'I go to visit my hub-caps.'

For a while the image problem looked insurmountable. And Liverpool, for all its bearded playwrights and curly-headed poets, had no one to hymn its praises. Step forward Bet Lynch of *Coronation Street*. The actress Julie Goodyear – she was, unfortunately, from Manchester – was in 1989 appointed by the Council as Liverpool's 'cultural ambassador'. It was a vague and ill-conceived role that she struggled honourably to fill, with few apparent qualifications for the job apart from liking the place and having played Widow Twanky in pantomime there.

Adrian Henri suggested England's disdain for Liverpool was a reaction against its popularity in the Beatles' era. But he was too intelligent to suppose that everything was the fault of the outside world. He thought that some of Scousedom's most famous entertainers were lamentable parodies. He wondered how it had come to be so utterly forgotten that this was the city of William Roscoe, the immensely civilised nineteenth-century scholar and campaigner against slavery; or that it was once the alternative capital of English painting. For all the modernity and populism of his work, Henri spent his final years deploring the eradication from memory of Liverpool's contributions to a certain British tradition of excellence.

Matters had come to a sad pass by the end of the twentieth century. How much of Liverpool's miserable reputation was self-inflicted? The city did not invent the notion of dumbing-down, but has shown a horrible aptitude for it, just the same.

'If you grew up in Liverpool in the 1960s,' wrote Michael Elliott in *Newsweek* in 1995, 'the rest of life has been about as exciting as toothpaste.' But now he deplored the 'wilful act of self-dumbing' by which the city had disowned its white-collar traditions of clerks, commercial lawyers and nonconformist chapels. 'If you spoke to any of Liverpool's politicians, bishops or academics in the 1970s and 1980s, you went away thinking that the first three syllables of "culture" were "working-class".' The problems of reviving a dying seaport were big enough already, he argued; it doesn't help if citizens are saddled with the image of aggressive layabouts.

Though not so bad as its economic collapse, the cultural dumbing of Liverpool was a sorry thing to watch. I now believe the position to be improving, and not before time. However it was often impossible to imagine that this had ranked among the most sophisticated places in the world. By the time I was old and pretentious enough to expect a decent wine with dinner, I found that Liverpool restaurants no longer served any. Strange to think that Admiral Nelson made a point of stocking up whenever he was in port, so renowned were its vintners. In the Adelphi, where Dickens once dined in splendour, the young staff of the 1990s took a request for the wine list with expressions of bewilderment. (In the same historic establishment, I found my telephone disabled. The receptionist wanted a credit card imprint: ' 'Cos, like, yer might be robbin' us, mightn't yer?')

'Liverpool gentleman, Manchester man' was once the phrase, popular among the nabobs of Mersey commerce, who fancied themselves a cut above their factory-owning Northern neighbours. What's more, they had the neo-Classical libraries, the galleries and the concert halls to prove it. Naturally they could sometimes be a tiresome crew. 'When I was young,' wrote the London essayist William Hazlitt, of the period around 1800, 'I spent a good deal of my time at Manchester and Liverpool; and I confess I give the preference to the former. There you were oppressed only by the aristocracy of wealth; in the latter by the aristocracy of wealth and letters by turns. You could not help feeling that some of their great men were authors among merchants and merchants among authors. Their bread was buttered on both sides and they had you at a disadvantage either way. The Manchester cotton-spinners, on the contrary, set up no pretensions beyond their looms . . .'

Nobody wants that snobbery back. But where is the true Liverpool gentleman today? He still lives, but he is elusive. (Adrian Henri and Derek Taylor are two examples I mourn.) You are more likely to notice his counterpart, the Scouse slob. He will be there, in the strip-lit ghastliness of the shopping malls that Georgian Liverpool was trashed to accommodate, wearing his baseball cap and pseudo-sportswear, surveying his domain with a lustreless eye and a belch of burger gas.

Traditional snobbery might have given way to slobbery, but there is still a problem with inverted snobbery, the most insidious of Liverpool's self-destructive tendencies. The democratic instincts and the stout refusal to tolerate pomposity are attractive traits, but there is a less likeable characteristic, in the aggressive dislike of anyone breaking rank. It's this malign flipside to social solidarity that promotes a culture of under-achievement and leads to poverty of aspiration. Much as I loved Liverpool, I took the first opportunity to leave. I had to escape the Bucket of Crabs syndrome: the fisherman may leave his captured crabs in a bucket overnight, knowing that any which try to climb out will merely be clawed back by the rest. For all the rhetoric I heard of capitalist oppression, nothing seemed so limiting as the Scousers' own mistrust of ambition.

Inverted snobbery is the true religion of Liverpool. For years there was a peculiar streak of civic one-downmanship: You've never seen slums like *our* slums; there's no crime like *our* crime . . . In long years of industrial struggle the workers perfected the art of opposition to the bosses. But it ill-prepared them for the day when the bosses simply walked away, and handed them the keys to the city. The Militant administration of Derek Hatton was dramatic proof. Efforts to save the city's past from demolition were denounced as middle class. But the new developments were an insult to the working class.

There was an impulse to sneer at 'gentrification'. Yet the de-gentrification of Liverpool had been on a scale unseen in Britain since the evacuation of the Roman nobility. The bourgeoisie abandoned Liverpool in haste, leaving those Hanoverian terraces and Edwardian villas to an uncertain fate. The subsequent gentrification that saw some properties saved was not the importing of something alien, but the restoration of something lost. Quite correctly, it is now thought wrong to deny the diversity of Liverpool's racial make-up, but the richness of Liverpool's history is also a composite of social strata. It's telling the way that 'Scouser' has come to apply to all Liverpudlians, whereas Cockneys are still a working-class sub-set of Londoners. The implication is that, on Merseyside, we're all proletarians now. Lenin himself could never have hoped for such success.

The least attractive product of Liverpool's period in the spotlight was the Professional Scouser. Pride in identity can easily be reduced to something twee and rather mercenary. The universal indulgence that Liverpool enjoyed in the 60s helped to create – in a few individuals – a certain Uncle Tom mentality that plays up its cuteness and surrenders its claim to be taken seriously. Praise of a place corrupts its unself-consciousness; it also encourages the complacency that breeds ultimate failure. If the Scousers come to accept a view of themselves that they are good at entertaining – singing, boxing, acting the happy fool – they need to be sure they don't settle for it.

They don't have to settle for anything.

*   *   *

When hard times arrived they made themselves at home. No sooner had Liverpool recovered from the Great Depression than the second world war broke out. When that was over, the port began to die as a source of employment. Manufacturing likewise crept away. By the 1980s it seemed the city itself had lost its job.

Everyone likes to dress-down now and talk common, but actual poverty is never in fashion. Liverpool was left high and dry. In 1998, in Paul McCartney's old neighbourhood of Speke, unemployment reached 30 per cent. For all their expensively advertised, customer-facing mission statements, the High Street banks decided to pull out of the area. Now loan sharks prowled the pubs and the shoppers' cafes. They used intimidation on bad debts, and charged up to 1,000 per cent. The locals formed a credit union for self-help. In the same year, a *Times* survey declared the Knowsley area of Merseyside to have the lowest quality of life. By 2000, a *Sunday Times* report ('Where You Live May Be the Death of You') found Liverpool dependably high in every table of medical deprivation, usually vying with Manchester and East London. It excelled in particular at cancer, premature death and heart disease.

Poorer parts of Liverpool, it seemed to me, increasingly resembled the old, crumbling Dublin I knew from family reunions. But Dublin was reviving, and Liverpool was not. There was the familiar sight of middle-aged men, shuffling to the shops with their mothers; the sense of lives that had never quite achieved lift-off; the impression that energy and talent had found somewhere else to go. And there were the devastated communities, ruined by drugs and the crime that drugs encourage. There was the silent blight that modern poverty brings: the invisible erosion of hopes, health and happiness. Babies are born into the results and grow up knowing only those results; their spiritual vision is stunted, their ideas degraded. Yet a rapacious culture commands them to consume and they must find a way. I admire anyone who stays and tries to fight against it all.

Such are the scenes that accompanied Liverpool's transition from cloth cap to baseball cap. Earlier generations of working men might take a pride in mighty enterprises they had helped to fruition: prodigious feats of engineering, tunnels, towers and ships built, trade and commerce advanced, wars won. What had their grandsons to compare? They owned more stuff and could go to more places, but there was no equivalent to that sense of shared achievement. The older Scouse solidarity was underpinned by family, workplace, union, religious and political affiliation. Now, only football remained intact: the rest were being dismantled piece by piece.

Assuming that money does not grow on EU trees – not forever, at any rate – then Liverpool must find its own way forward. It cannot depend on subsidies: the hand-out system is flawed because the hand in question has no nerve-endings in its fingertips. Clumsiness and corruption are the results. Nor should Liverpool play the victim card and complain, as some do, about the brutality of free markets. Even the hated Thatcher regime did not abandon Merseyside to remorseless economics. The city owes more than it likes to admit to the intervention of her 'Minister for Merseyside' Michael Heseltine.

The last time Liverpool was in such a state was in the reign of Elizabeth I. Weakened by plague and unfavourable trading conditions, the city appealed for help and was advised to try crime: specifically theft. Piracy on the High Seas, directed against Her Majesty's enemies, was officially encouraged and Liverpool got stuck in there. Crime is always an option, of course, and many Liverpudlians have exercised it on a freelance basis. But it can hardly become a civic policy again.

Or can it? The monumental St George's Hall, which stands in magnificent isolation across Lime Street, was designed by its Victorian founders to be a hybrid of concert hall and courts of justice. A civic building dedicated to Music and Crime might seem appropriate to Liverpool, as if in tribute to its patron deities. The British people believe Liverpudlians to be uncannily gifted in both pursuits.

A recent magazine joke told of three Scousers at the Pearly Gates, asking for admission. St Peter replies that he isn't sure: 'We've never had Scousers here before. I'll have to ask the Boss.' He goes to God who recommends they be welcomed into Heaven. St Peter leaves but soon comes running back. 'They've gone,' he cries. 'Who? The Scousers?' says God. 'Not just them,' says Peter. 'The friggin' Pearly Gates as well!'

This gag had an awful echo in reality when the gates of Strawberry Field went missing, in 2000. Happily they were recovered in a local scrap metal yard. But the episode naturally reinforced a national stereotype; worse still, it pointed up the decline of Liverpool's image, from mystic source of a great piece of art, to thieves' paradise. Around the same time came a tale much relished in London newspapers, concerning the theft of an entire Liverpool street. Its cobblestones were apparently taken up and removed overnight.

And yet, Liverpool is slipping down the crime league tables. By 2000, it was placed a mere 22nd among Britian's urban areas. It is now less violent than Bedfordshire. More cars are stolen in Cambridgeshire. Burglary is worse in all sorts of places. Nobody believes it, but Scousers are losing their pre-eminence in crime. Or perhaps the rest of the country has finally caught up.

Perhaps music would be the better bet after all.

But nobody with sense makes long-term predictions about pop music. Brian Epstein used the say the next big thing would be 'a good tune, because it always is'. If the Liverpool tradition consists of anything specific, then good tunes are probably it. Guitar bands have been common, from Merseybeat to scally days, but there have been plenty of solo singers, and some electronic acts as well. Melody is the thread through all of them.

Though Cream continues to be the favourite place to hear music, its audience are not especially given to making music themselves. Dance music is loved but seldom emulated. Today's inheritors of the Cavern and Eric's tradition – of watching an act on stage and being inspired to compete with them – would, I suppose, be the crowd at the Lomax club. As I write this a band called the Coral are tipped to be the next Liverpool noise and have certainly had the customary rock press build-up. ('It's like these little pixies have been bottling the magic fog that floats over the Mersey to cast their spells on their music,' wrote the *NME*.) Less in the scally guitar band mode and more eclectic are Clinic, while another act, Ladytron, have an icy electro cool that picks up on the Kraftwerk and glam influence. From Birkenhead, Dean Johnson is evidence of the enduring scope for simply picking up a guitar and singing with it.

According to Andy McCluskey, 'A true Liverpool trait is to sign, get a big advance and then self-destruct.' And Ian Broudie, who is producing the Coral, once told me the defining characteristic of Liverpool groups was 'to shoot themselves in the foot as soon as they learn to walk,' so we must hope his latest clients are different. At worst they'll wander into that misty oblivion shared by so many nearly bands, from Rory Storm and the Hurricanes to Ellery Bop and Rain. At best they'll join the pantheon of greats defined by you-know-who, the Bunnymen and the La's. There is no shame in either fate.

Nothing in life is so bad that we cannot – with hard work and determination – manage to make it even worse. The problems are immense, but Liverpool is equal to the challenge and music will be at the heart of its recovery.

Liverpool is a busker, deep down. When you've no job, nor any income to speak of, you look to what talent you do possess, and put the hat on the pavement. When all else fails – and sometimes it does – this town will sing for its supper. After decades of rejection, Liverpool's musical industries – from the mega dance events to Beatle tourism – are getting official support. Music is at last considered part of Liverpool's social capital. It's an employer, an ambassador and a potential money-spinner that's big enough to offset some of the economic carnage of recent times.

The regeneration of its waterfront, the upgrading of its greatest buildings, the opening of new hotels and the upsurge of night-life, especially in the twin pleasure zones around Cream and the new Cavern – all of these improvements are making Liverpool a more welcoming place than ever. Sympathetic outsiders are still beguiled, like the NME's Sylvia Patterson, visiting Shack in 2000: 'Liverpool shares the spirit of Jamaica; everyone's a cartoon character, even more ridiculous than reality, which round here is as ridiculous as it gets, a population insulated from the world through the survival mechanism of the psychedelic mindset, some of which is drug-related and some of which just is.'

I hope that many more visitors will come and be beguiled, too. Liverpool's recovery from the nadir of the 1980s has been encouraging. For all the damage and neglect that were permitted, the town still has a wealth of great architecture and cultural attractions in abundance. Renovation proceeds apace. New city festivals – including that in Mathew Street – are invented daily. That's not to say it's Disneyland. Liverpool can never be entirely sanitised. There is too much of the old sailor town in its soul for complete respectability, but there is something heroic in that soul as well.

This book celebrates roughly four decades of Liverpool music, from the early 1960s into the first years of the twenty-first century. It was a time of spectacular activity, and extraordinary success. I don't know if it will prove an isolated period or not. The great comic author P.G. Wodehouse looked back on his world, of silly toffs in stately homes and Mayfair *pieds-à-terre*, wistfully concluding: 'It has gone with the wind and is one with Nineveh and Tyre. In a word, it has had it.' For all I know, the world I write about has had it too. I hope at least that it leaves something of itself for the future to enjoy.

In Florence I was astonished to be told that Michelangelo made an ice sculpture. Why would he do that? Why would he submit his genius to inevitable ruin? But then I came across an article by Elvis Costello. Reflecting on the impermanence of art, he quotes Michelangelo himself: 'We too were men joyful and weary like you, and now we are lifeless, we are only earth, as you see. All that is created must end. All, all around us must perish.' *Sic Transit Gloria* Liverpool?

An even more dramatic notion is the disappearance of Liverpool itself. An alarming report in 1999 predicted global warming would melt the polar ice-caps and eradicate the coastal plains of Britain. This would be ironic, not to mention all the other drawbacks, since the River Mersey was where the global measurement of 'Sea Level' was originally fixed, back in the nineteenth century.

Perhaps we'd spy the Liver Birds, finally like cormorants off the coast, their rocky perches being all that was still visible of the waterfront's tallest building. They'd scan the swollen estuary that now lapped up against Hope Street and Everton Heights. Schools of fish would inhabit the Cavern. Future explorers would search this silent new Atlantis for some signs of that once world-famous noise. There are in fact occasional octopuses in the Mersey, slithering over shipwrecks: they might create an octopus's garden in Ringo's old district of the Dingle. It could be reached, perhaps, in yellow submarines.

As on the final page of Herman Melville's *Moby Dick*, 'the great shroud of the sea' would cover the source of all the old commotion. And all you would hear is the seagulls.

And yet, I am sure that something would happen. The sound of this city would rise in bubbles to the surface. I do not think Liverpool will be one with Nineveh and Tyre for a while. I rather suspect there are more wonders to come from this wondrous place.

FINALE: THE TOP 100 LIVERPOOL SONGS

The list which follows is no more than the sum of my own irrational prejudices. It has no statistical basis, nor any relation to sales charts. It's simply a personal selection of music that is either by artists from Liverpool, or is directly connected to Liverpool.

You will find a few inclusions to be tenuous. On the other hand I have denied myself several hundred perfectly decent songs by imposing a limit of one entry per artist: the Beatles, therefore, get exactly the same allocation as Sonia. (But their solo records are allowed, of course. This rule is technically known as the Pete Wylie Exemption.)

Some tracks are included because they're so well-known, others because they are obscure but deserve not to be. When faced with a choice of great songs by one act, I've tended to favour tracks that have a specifically Liverpool theme, like the Christians' 'Greenbank Drive'.

Readers of a more statistical disposition might like to see the 2001 figures produced by Guinness World Records, suggesting that Liverpool is Britain's capital city of pop. Their method was to count the Number 1 singles by artists linked to each particular town, measured against the relative populations. In a result much celebrated by the local music tourism industry, Liverpool came out top with 54 Number 1 hits, or one for every 8,485 Liverpudlians. Surprisingly, perhaps, Cardiff came next (eight Number 1s, or one for every 43,750 residents) and London third (104 hits, one for every 75,240 Londoners). Had it been eligible, Dublin would apparently have come second. The Guinness system might have its drawbacks, but the Celtic showing is certainly striking, especially if we take account of Liverpool's Welsh and Irish element. (Latest additions include George Harrison's second release of 'My Sweet Lord' in 2002; it may now be the case that Liverpool outstrips any city in the world on this reckoning.)

With one eccentric exception at Number 81, I have not tackled classical music. Apart from the city's very fine Philharmonic Orchestra, I might have gone for any of Liverpool's three renowned conductors: Sir Adrian Boult, Sir Thomas Beecham or Sir Simon Rattle. It was the robust Beecham, I think, who was asked if he had ever played any Stockhausen and replied, 'No, but I have trodden in some'. Simon Rattle, from

Menlove Avenue, made his name with the City of Birmingham Symphony Orchestra and in 2001 took the top job in classical music, succeeding Claudio Abbado and Herbert von Karajan as Director of the Berlin Philharmonic.

One last category that I was tempted to include was any vinyl bearing the inscription 'A Porky Prime Cut'. It's a tribute to Liverpool's burning urge to get itself on record that one of its sons actually colonised the run-off groove itself. George Peckham, alias the man behind Porky's Prime Cuts, was a former member of Merseybeat groups including the Olympics and the Fourmost. His nickname, he told Adrian Deevoy, derived from 'all the old slagbags I used to chase and the ale I put away.' Peckham possessed hidden depths of professionalism, however, as he showed when he started 'cutting' records for the Beatles at Apple: there was an art to capturing the studio sound to its fullest effect on the master disc given to the factory. This led Porky into a distinguished career of record-cutting, during the course of which he carved his name on countless vinyl artefacts, and won himself a niche in the hearts of collectors all over the world.

And now, that chart in full . . .

1. The Beatles: 'Penny Lane' 1967
Paul's soaring celebration of random lives you might just glimpse from a Corporation bus. Everyone had realised that pop could do astonishing things in 1967, but no one had suspected it could run to an immortal portrait of an ordinary English high street. Chosen in preference to its companion piece, 'Strawberry Fields Forever', but only because John's song is more about the contents of his own head than the specific site that inspired the song.

2. The La's: 'Timeless Melody' 1990
If you could distil the entire history of Liverpool music into one song, this would be that song.

3. Echo and the Bunnymen: 'Killing Moon' 1980
McCulloch knew immediately that the Bunnymen had recorded their finest song to date. But have they ever bettered it? Maybe not, although I believe it's rivalled by the 1997 comeback song 'Nothing Lasts Forever': played consecutively, they make beautiful companion pieces.

4. Pete Wylie: 'A Heart As Big As Liverpool' 2000
The spirit of Bill Shankly is hovering over this record like the Holy Ghost. 'Writing it was a challenge,' says Wylie. 'It wasn't really about Liverpool. Bill Drummond told me my thing was all about heart, and said to me "Why don't you write something about a heart as big as a city?" But I went to the circus in Sefton Park with my daughter Mersey, and wrote a song about falling in love with the girl on the tightrope in her fish-nets, looking mad and fabulous, and about my daughter looking at the girl. And that turns into "Heart As Big As Liverpool". Of course when

Sony heard it they say, No one outside of Liverpool will like it. Now they play it at Anfield and it's becoming a Liverpool folk song. But the key word is not Liverpool, it's about being big-hearted. Passion and generosity are the things.'

5. The Searchers: 'When You Walk in the Room' 1964
Picked at random from an embarrassment of riches.

6. The Real Thing: 'You to Me Are Everything' 1976
Few are the British-made soul hits that sit well on compilations in the company of Barry White, Curtis Mayfield and Harold Melvin, but this one certainly does. The Real Thing's Number 1 will radiate forever beneath the dancefloor glitterball.

7. Cilla Black: 'I've Been Wrong Before' 1965
She was the first to cover a Lennon and McCartney song ('Love of the Loved') and Paul, in particular, saw a cool jazz possibility in her style ('It's for You' and 'Step Inside Love'). Randy Newman, meanwhile, considers that this extremely chic track is the best cover anyone has ever done of one of his songs.

8. John Lennon: 'Instant Karma!' 1970
Lots of echo and thump, courtesy of Phil Spector, in Lennon's greatest solo moment: a distillation of the spiritual light within. 'We all shine on.'

9. Gerry and the Pacemakers: 'I Like It' 1963
'The world was made for you and me.'

10. Billy Fury: 'Wondrous Place' 1960
So spookily beautiful that someone ought to name a book after it.

11. The Swinging Blue Jeans: 'You're No Good' 1964
A stinging guitar part, crisp rhythm and vocal moans make this a fascinatingly dramatic version, so much darker than most recorded Merseybeat.

12. Big Three: 'Some Other Guy' 1963
Epstein found the Big Three were just too troublesome to persevere with. But, in 'Some Other Guy' they may have made the greatest rock'n'roll single of the Merseybeat era.

13. Ian McNabb: 'Liverpool Girl' 2001
An absolute gem of observation, descriptive precision and warm Scouse patriotism.

14. Frankie Goes To Hollywood: 'The Power of Love' 1984
Third of the Frankies' all-conquering singles (after 'Relax' and 'Two Tribes') and easily the best tune. Still a much-requested radio favourite, apparently. When all the hype has decayed into history, a simple and utterly straightforward song survives, preserved by its own purity.

15. Orchestral Manoeuvres In The Dark: 'Stanlow' 1980
A wonderfully atmospheric picture of a Mersey oil refinery. Andy McCluskey: 'With so many of our concerts being out Manchester and Sheffield way, we'd always drive home to the Wirral afterwards along the M53, and Stanlow became like a beacon for us. At four in the morning, we'd see its gantries lit up and flames burning in the sky, and know we were almost home. Because my father worked there, he got me inside one day and I tape recorded all the machines, which you can hear on the

track. We liked to write songs about aeroplanes and telephone boxes. We had a good line in inanimate objects.'

16. The Chants: '1000 Stars' 1964
A hit for Billy Fury, but covered here with immense grace by the city's outstanding harmony group of the era.

17. Atomic Kitten: 'Right Now' 2001
Though surpassed by 'Whole Again' this was a classic of crackling pop energy, and a song that bristles with the urgent hedonism of Liverpool after dark. I must admit I love it to death.

18. Half Man Half Biscuit: 'Floreat Inertia' 1993
The Tranmere laugh-in takes a bleaker turn in this song, perhaps: less of the lofty mockeries of junk-culture and something of a piece with its parent album's title, *This Leaden Pall*.

19. Shack: 'Comedy' 1999
From their cult triumph *H.M.S. Fable*, and in the best Michael Head tradition of songs that carry a whole freight of hope and heartbreak.

20. Wah! Heat: 'Story of the Blues' 1982
A song for Liverpool, written in one of its darkest hours, inspired by a combination of Alan Bleasdale and the spoken bits of Philadelphia soul numbers: 'In my head, it's the Chi-Lites doing *Boys from the Black Stuff*,' says Wylie. 'But it's a very Liverpool song, all heart-on-your-sleeve emotion. I should have called it "Just Give Me a Big Fucking Hug".'

21. The Mojos: 'Everything's Alright' 1964
A rollicking R&B thing from one of the younger Merseybeat groups. Like the other post-Beatle groups they were more open to blues influences than the skiffle boys who'd preceded them, which is possibly one reason it appeared on Bowie's collection of Marquee mod favourites, *Pin-Ups*. (Though another might be the presence in Bowie's band of the Mojos' old drummer Aynsley Dunbar.)

22. The Christians: 'Greenbank Drive' 1990
A dreamy celebration in the lineage of its neighbour 'Penny Lane': as the grimy town can be uplifted by the rays of the sun, so an entire city can be transformed by one girl's interest. She says she loves him and everything turns magical. There's even a sitar at the end.

23. Deaf School: 'Hi Joe Hi' 1976
A breezy affair, the much-loved combo's most delicious pop confection.

24. A Flock Of Seagulls: 'Wishing (If I Had a Photograph of You)' 1982
One of Liverpool's few contributions to early 80s synth pop. There are middle-aged men who still flinch at the mention of Mike Score's hairstyle.

25. The Justified Ancients Of Mu Mu: 'It's Grim Up North' 1991
Absurdly exciting techno-tribute to Bill Drummond's favourite end of England, climaxing in Blake's 'Jerusalem'.

26. Lightning Seeds: 'Tales of the Riverbank' 1999
Not for the first time, Liverpool dockers of the late 1990s were at loggerheads with the port employers, the national media and their own trade union. Not for the first time, they lost. But this had been a particularly brave fight, and it receives a fittingly dignified anthem from Ian Broudie.

27. 23rd Turn-off: 'Michelangelo' 1967
Jimmy Campbell's post-Merseybeat masterpiece, eternally veiled in a soft psyche-delic mist.

28. Michael Head and the Strands: 'Something Like You' 1997
Basically Shack under another name, but a cunning way to sneak in a second and quite delicious Michael Head song.

29. The Spinners: 'The Ellen Vannin Tragedy' 1965
It's horrifying to look across Liverpool Bay and be conscious of its innumerable shipwrecks. The spirits of the drowned are summoned from the deep in this powerful telling of an 1899 disaster that befell the Isle of Man mailboat.

30. George Harrison: 'All Things Must Pass' 1970
The Beatles missed a trick in ignoring this incredible song despite George's requests. It would eventually be the centrepiece of his first post-Beatle album. You can also hear a wonderfully tender demo version on the *Anthology 3* album.

31. Jimmy Campbell: 'Don't Leave Me Now' 1970
The greatest lost legend of Liverpool music is not the La's' Lee Mavers (whose records are all available and send him a pleasing stream of royalties), but Jimmy Campbell, who is remembered by only a few. If you ever chance upon this record (on the long-deleted LP *Half-Baked*), buy without hesitation.

32. Speed: 'Good Luck Charm' 1998
Guest vocal by Monica Queen. Extraordinarily beautiful song.

33. Cast: 'Live the Dream' 1997
John Power is the archetypal cosmic scally, and none the worse for it. Of the several fine tracks on their second album *Mother Nature Calls*, I've chosen this for Power's immaculate Scouse pronunciation of 'girl' in the chorus: not 'gurl' but 'geerl'.

34. Melanie C: 'Goin' Down' 1999
The Spice Girls' solo careers have served to confirm early suspicions that Sporty was, if not exactly the group's Brian Wilson-style genius in residence, then at least the most musical of the bunch. This was the first single off her first album *Northern Star*. And it rocks.

35. Lotus Eaters: 'The First Picture of You' 1983
Their career seemed no longer than the shimmering summer that their song celebrates, but it's a sweet contribution.

36. The Fourmost: 'Respectable' 1963
They were recipients of some lesser Lennon and McCartney songs, and had some tiresome comedy tendencies, but the Fourmost are pleasingly frantic on this breathless Isley Brothers cover that appeared on the B-side of 'I'm in Love'.

37. Dead Or Alive: 'You Spin Me Round (Like a Record)' 1985
The production was by Stock, Aitken and Waterman, the sleeve photos by Mario Testino, and the song by Dead Or Alive. At last, the boy who'd starred in Eric's was just as famous everywhere.

38. Paul McCartney and Wings: 'Warm and Beautiful' 1976
Even around the fringes of McCartney's repertoire, where the compilation albums never go, there are superlative songs like this.

39. Lori and the Chameleons: 'Touch' 1979
Essentially a front for Drummond and Balfe of Zoo, looking for a novelty dance hit with a breathlessly sexy story of Lori's romantic adventure in Japan. For this and other lost treasures from Chicago Buildings, try the compilation *The Zoo Uncaged 1978–1982* on Document.

40. Last Chant: 'Run of the Dove' 1981
Nicely likened in *Record Collector* to 'the Velvet Underground in a monastery garden', and produced by the future Waterboy Mike Scott. Available on Viper's CD *Unearthed: Liverpool Cult Classics Volume 2*.

41. Elvis Costello: 'New Amsterdam' 1980
A small, waltzing masterclass in lyrical word-play that finds Costello bewildered by his first time in New York, down by the docks and thinking back to Liverpool and London.

42. Beryl Marsden: 'Breakaway' 1965
A big hit in 1983 for Tracey Ullman, but Beryl Marsden's cover of this Jackie de Shannon/Sharon Sheeley song was better.

43. Johnny Keating and His Orchestra: 'Theme from Z-Cars' 1962
Liverpool boy goes off to sea, leaves Liverpool girl crying buckets. Boy come home, finds girl quite recovered and fully equipped with new sailor. The sad story of Johnny Todd, a song of ancient origins, got jazzed up for the TV cop show by the Liverpool-Viennese musicologist Fritz Spiegl.

44. The Teardrop Explodes: 'Great Dominions' 1981
Julian Cope was delighted by his own preposterous conceit in this lyric (which veers from a lecture on the 'blunders of history' to stuff about being stuck in a pickle-jar). It's fairly apparent that the singer had already slipped his moorings from the rest of the group, and perhaps from more besides.

45. Cherry Boys: 'Kardomah Café' 1983
A Whitechapel shopper's refuge, opposite NEMS, where Sam Leach had an 'office' and Adrian Henri saw Marcel Proust 'eating Madeleine butties dipped in tea'. The Cherry Boys' lost classic can now be found on the Viper label's CD *Unearthed: Liverpool Cult Classics Volume 2*. It's claimed this song beat Michael Jackson's 'Thriller' in the Spanish charts.

46. Wild Swans: 'Revolutionary Spirit' 1982
The last and, in Bill Drummond's view, the greatest single on the Zoo label was this stirring affair from Paul Simpson's post-Teardrop Explodes band. It was produced and financed by Pete DeFreitas of the Bunnymen, but Paul describes it as 'virtually

bass-less and in mono due to Pete being off his head on cocaine and the band too stoned to notice'.

47. Michael Holliday: 'The Runaway Train' 1956
A regular request on BBC Radio's *Children's Favourites*, from a time when tastes were simpler and railways more loved.

48. Black: 'Wonderful Life' 1987
Colin Vearncombe's bittersweet hit, forever doomed to make people feel good despite its author's intentions.

49. Freddie Lennon: 'That's My Life (My Love and My Home)' 1965
I know of no curio more curious than this. John's renegade father made this uninvited sequel to the Beatles' 'In My Life' after he'd emerged from nowhere to declare himself to the newspapers. It's like a Scouse 'My Way' crossed with a pub-singer's sea shanty: old Fred croons nostalgically about his supposed past as seafarer, ladies' man and bar-stool philosopher. Crashing waves and MOR strings frame his thick, old-fashioned accent rather attractively. Not that John was impressed. It's believed he asked Brian Epstein to use his influence and get the record stopped.

50. Big In Japan: 'Nothing Special' 1978
Holly took the idea from a TV show planned by his hero Andy Warhol, built around a psychopathically egotistical host: 'Me me me!' shouts Jayne Casey. 'I I I!' In other words, a deeply Eric's 1978 sort of song.

51. Pete McGovern: 'In My Liverpool Home' 1961
Though he began it in 1961, McGovern's immortal folk song has picked up a new verse at every turn. It will possibly go on growing for centuries. Somebody once told him it had been written by an Irish emigrant in 1846.

52. The Merseys: 'Sorrow' 1966
Crane and Kinsley's attempt to escape the albatross of being called the Merseybeats in 1966. It was also the subject of a Bowie tribute on his *Pin-ups* LP.

53. Marina: 'Sly One' 1990
A sweet dancefloor hit from the 8 Productions team who, with singer Marina Van Rooy, were at the heart of the Wood Street scene that eventually gave us Cream.

54. The Real People: 'She' 1991
Big, droning, hypnotic bash-about from the Griffiths brothers' debut album, rather overlooked in the interlude between baggy and Britpop.

55. China Crisis: 'King in a Catholic Style (Wake Up)' 1985
One of several Liverpool bands to get their start from Pete Fulwell's Inevitable label, China Crisis had a low-key style of delivery that seemed almost too self-effacing to make the charts, and yet they did, repeatedly. This was from *Flaunt the Imperfection*, made with Steely Dan's Walter Becker.

56. The Coral: 'Shadows Fall' 2000
The first EP by a Hoylake group who'd soon become the subject of a record company bidding war. The singer James Skelly kept up the best La's traditions by declaring himself unaware of anything on contemporary radio: he'd rather just lock

himself away with some Harry Nilsson. The Coral obeyed another Liverpool tradition by using Ian Broudie to produce them.

57. High Five: 'Working for the Man' 1984
The former group of Picket boss Philip Hayes, on stirringly indignant form, the subject being a mate who has joined the police. To be found on the Viper CD *Unearthed: Liverpool Cult Classics Volume 1*.

58. Space: 'Me and You vs the World' 1996
Not so well remembered as their glorious Scouse-Welsh collaboration with Cerys Matthews, 'The Ballad of Tom Jones', this was still a deserved hit and a song which Tommy Scott describes as summing up the Liverpool mentality.

59. Rain: 'Taste of Rain' 1991
The pulsing bassline points to a Nick Lowe production job on this, the title track of Rain's album. Utterly exciting.

60. The Reynolds Girls: 'I'd Rather Jack' 1989
The story goes that Linda and Aisling Reynolds met the DJ and producer Pete Waterman at his Radio City show, where they agreed upon their common dislike of oldies records on the airwaves, and a song was born. Alas for the girls, Fleetwood Mac (than whom they would rather jack, if you recall) proved immune to this attack. But the Reynolds Girls made their point wonderfully well, and didn't stick around any longer than they needed to.

61. Bette Bright and the Illuminations: 'My Boyfriend's Back' 1978
From her short but hugely enjoyable run of post-Deaf School records, produced by her band-mate Clive Langer. A cover of the Angels' 1963 hit, it's the sort of thing the Merseybeat boys would have covered if the lyric had fitted their gender. Conscious or not, there's an hilarious Scouse spin to the chorus warning: 'Hey la', my boyfriend's back.'

62. It's Immaterial: 'Driving Away from Home' 1986
John Campbell puts his foot down on the pedal – ever so gently – to cruise out along the M62. A mini-Midwestern road movie transposed to Merseyside.

63. The Dubliners: 'The Leaving of Liverpool' 1964
Applies a lump to the throat with surgical precision.

64. Thomas Lang: 'Fingers and Thumbs' 1987
Though a handsome and convincing crooner, Lang never quite located the male Sade niche his record label seemed to be aiming for with his over-stylised *Scallywag Jaz* album. Still, this track was superb.

65. Mott The Hoople: 'All the Way from Memphis' 1973
Song of praise to the rock'n'roll adventure, 'from the Liverpool docks to the Hollywood Bowl'; Ian Hunter pays a passing tribute to the city whose audiences he loved more than any other.

66. Badfinger: 'Come and Get It' 1970
Their greatest hit, recorded to a blueprint already laid down by Paul McCartney for the soundtrack of *The Magic Christian*. It would take Badfinger another year to prove they were more than mere recipients of Beatle charity.

67. The Monkees: 'Alternate Title (Randy Scouse Git)' 1967
Wacky titles were becoming par for the course in 1967. Even so, this one must have looked incomprehensible in Kansas.

68. Rockin' Horse: 'Baby Walk Out with Your Darling Man' 1971
From the Dark Ages of Liverpool music, in between Merseybeat and Eric's, comes this Jimmy Campbell classic off the *Yes It Is* LP.

69. Scaffold: 'Liverpool Lou' 1974
Its release coincided with Alan Price's Geordie-oriented single 'Jarrow Song'. And, as Liverpool were playing Newcastle in the FA Cup Final, Derek Taylor at Warner's arranged to flood London with song-sheets carrying the two lyrics side by side. The match proved a glorious finale to Bill Shankly's career, and the fans gave their greatest rendition of 'You'll Never Walk Alone'. That night, Piccadilly Circus was ankle-deep in these song-sheets, while supporters of both teams, united in Northern solidarity and drunken bonhomie, danced and chanted 'Scousers and the Geordies'. Two tribes that did not go to war.

70. Cook Da Books: 'Piggy in the Middle Eight' 1982
First in a trilogy of Liverpool-oriented singles by Peter 'Digsy' Deary's first band. Riot-inspired, the working title was 'Tocky on TASS' after Soviet news coverage.

71. The Room: 'Things Have Learned to Walk That Ought to Crawl' 1982
One of those songs whose name alone deserves respect. It's a tense, driven thing, more in the dark Mancunian vein of Joy Division than of their contemporaries on the post-Eric's scene.

72. The Bangles: 'Going Down to Liverpool' 1984
Written by Kimberley Rew for Katrina and the Waves, though better known in this version. It's impossible to miss the sheer peculiarity of hearing the Bangles sing of UB40s and English dole misery – but on the other hand their sound was very neo-Merseybeat, like a feminised update of the Searchers.

73. Glide: 'Excerpts from a Space Age Freak-out Part II: Wise Baby Dreams' 1995
Alias the 'psychedelic tripscape project' of Bunnyman guitarist Will Sergeant. Not recommended for jukeboxes, but deeply absorbing.

74. The Farm: 'All Together Now' 1991
The Farm's finest hour, when their lyrical idealism found a tune that gave it wings to fly

75. Skyray: 'Mind Lagoons' 1999
The title track of a gently gorgeous, largely instrumental album by Paul Simpson, assisted by Henry Priestman. A softly-spoken Bill Drummond intones a tale of romantic mystery over the band's quasi-oriental reverie.

76. The Boo Radleys: 'Wake Up Boo!' 1995
One of those insanely happy songs that will never entirely die.

77. The Dennisons: 'Nobody Like My Babe' 1964
Unwisely billed by Decca's publicity department as 'five seventeen-year-old stormtroopers from Aintree', the Dennisons were denied a hit with 'Walkin' the

Dog' when the Stones recorded a version too. This, their third and last single, has a milder R&B feel. By late 1964, they'd missed the last train from Lime Street.

78. Faron's Flamingoes: 'Do You Love Me' 1963
Acceptably wild cover of Berry Gordy's composition for the Contours; said to be the first British cover of a Motown number.

79. Bassheads: 'Is There Anybody Out There' 1991
Hammered at Cream in its opening year, and one of remarkably few dance hits created by a Liverpool act.

80. Ringo Starr: 'Photograph' 1973
The best of his solo LPs, *Ringo* arrived with songs contributed by the other three Beatles, but this one – written by George and Ringo – was easily the stand-out, and gave the drummer another of those surprise hit singles.

81. Donizetti: 'Confusa e l'alma mia' from *Emilia di Liverpool* 1824
Nobody knows for sure whether this Neapolitan opera was really set in Liverpool: Donizetti might just have fancied the sound of it. But I like the heroine's final aria: 'My spirit is confused/And whatever it hears and sees/Believes it is a dream/Which will fade away.' If that's not a Liverpool girl on Sunday morning I don't know what is.

82. The Liverpool Scene: 'I've Got Those Fleetwood Mac Chicken Shack John Mayall Can't Fail Blues' 1969
The band were at their best supplying backdrops for Adrian Henri's poetry, but there was something endearingly clumsy about his rock posturing, as in this parody of the white boy blues boom of the day.

83. Chuck Berry: 'Liverpool Drive' 1964
A shame it's only an instrumental. Chuck's analysis of the Beatle phenomenon would have made for an interesting lyric, though not necessarily a warm-hearted hymn of approval. As it is, one suspects, a rather grudging sop to current teen tastes, knocked off in a few minutes of Chess Studio downtime.

84. Billy J Kramer with The Dakotas: 'Sugar Baby' 1965
From his EP *Billy J. Plays the States*, a live rocker with an object lesson in very polite crowd control.

85. Ellery Bop: 'Fire in Reflection' 1983
Another Ian Broudie production and probably the closest Ellery Bop ever came to capturing Jamie's idealistic intensity.

86. Two People: 'Rescue Me' 1985
The two in question were Mark Stevenson and Mark Ram, to be filed forever under Ones That Got Away. Having rejected the standard Liverpool names of the period (stuff like Richard Is Himself Again, or Niagara Falls Under Moonlight), they went for something they hoped would get people asking 'Why the hell did they pick such a bad name?' A run of supremely melodic singles failed to catch on, but as Mark said to me at the time: 'If all this turns to dust tomorrow, it's good to have something to play hour after hour to yer kids. Until they hate you.'

87. The Stairs: 'Weed Bus' 1991
One of Edgar Summertyme's periodic trips in time, on this occasion to an imaginary lay-by of the mind where the Pretty Things, the Who and the La's confer behind a thick, smoky veil.

88. Suzanne Vega: 'In Liverpool' 1992
One of the American songwriter's best, inspired by a Merseyside hotel stop-over on Sunday, 29 April 1990, listening to church bells, looking at the river and meditating on the pale, thin light.

89. Cecil: 'The Most Tiring Day' 1998
Very interesting single, by a little-known group, performed with a certain heavy complexity that is rare in Liverpool music. Even among the scallies who adopted prog rock ten years after, there was never much inclination to try playing it.

90. Alexei Sayle: 'Ullo John! Gotta New Motor?' 1982
For decades the South has mocked the North, so here's a nice reversal. When Sayle wasn't skitting London trendies he was taking on Cockney wideboys, and it's the latter who catch it here. 'I'm dead popular in Essex – loads and loads of Lonsdale swea'ers. It's just through living round here, being subject to it, in my local or down the market, all selling dodgy motors to each other. It's partly affectionate, and partly, Oh fucking hell, they're annoying, noisy bastards!' Strangely, this was the first record Robbie Williams ever bought.

91. Hambi and the Dance: 'L'Image Craque' 1981
As a band-leader, manager and studio owner, Hambi has been a persistent presence on the Liverpool music scene since his early band Tontrix. He went the usual route of looking for a London label. On one early trip he was so poor he offered the bus conductor a postage stamp in payment. At length he was signed by Richard Branson to Virgin, for the price of many, many stamps. But the group's majestic edge got lost along the way, in those synth-obsessed times. I always preferred their demo tapes. This, however, was the best of the eventual singles.

92. Hank Walters and the Arcadian Ladies: 'Progress' 1992
The grand-daddy of Liverpool country music performs for a Radio Merseyside show with his three daughters, on a song that puzzles over the Liverpool authorities' vision of the future.

93. Liverpool Express: 'Every Man Must Have a Dream' 1976
Billy Kinsley's band between his spells in the original and revived Merseybeats. I spent 1976 watching the Sex Pistols at the 100 Club and this was not the Liverpool sound I really wanted to hear, but it's grown on me since.

94. Sonia: 'You'll Never Stop Me Loving You' 1989
She made it! With just six places to go!

95. Palais De Sand: 'The Harbour Song' 1996
A Liverpool chart needs seagull sound effects. There is no finer way to obtain them than in this haunting Henry Priestman piece, with a lyrical overdub by his It's Immaterial colleague John Campbell. To be found on the Viper CD *Unearthed: Liverpool Cult Classics Volume 2*.

96. The Merseysippi Jazz Band: 'All the Girls Go Crazy 'bout the Way I Walk' 1957
The early Cavern jazzers, still blowin'. The sleevenote to their . . . *All The Girls* LP suggests this song has three titles, 'the other two being indelicate'.

97. David Garrick: 'Dear Mrs Applebee' 1966
Unusual instance of a Liverpool singer ditching Merseybeat for a bit of Swinging London mod-pop, alias Carnaby Street psychedelic. Garrick had been to school in Egypt, claimed his sleeve-notes, and could write the lyric out in hieroglyphics.

98. Rory Storm and the Hurricanes: 'I Can Tell' 1963
The B-side to one of the only two singles he ever released; this track taken from the Rialto Ballroom session.

99. Oceanic: 'Insanity' 1991
The Wirralites' dancefloor triumph on the Dead Good label.

100. Frankie Vaughan: 'Green Door' 1956
Subject of a 1981 homage by Shakin' Stevens, but, as his grandmother nearly said, Frankie will always be our Number Vorn Hundred.

BIBLIOGRAPHY & SOURCES

1 BOOKS

Armstrong, Thomas, *King Cotton*, Collins, 1947
Badman, Keith, *The Beatles: The Dream is Over*, Omnibus, 2001
Beatles, The, *The Beatles Anthology*, Cassell, 2000
Beynon, Huw, *Working for Ford*, Penguin, 1973
BFI Dossier 20, *Boys from the Black Stuff*, British Film Institute, 1984
Burke, John & Alun Owen, *A Hard Day's Night*, Pan, 1964
Channon, Howard, *Portrait of Liverpool*, Robert Hale, 1970
Cohen, Sarah & Kevin McManus, *Harmonious Relations: Popular Music in Family Life
    on Merseyside*, National Museums & Galleries on Merseyside, 1991
Cohn, Nik, *Awopbopaloobop Alopbamboom*, Paladin, 1970
Coleman, Ray, *Lennon*, Pan, 1995
Cooper, Mark, *Liverpool Explodes!*, Sidgwick & Jackson, 1982
Cope, Julian, *Head-On/Repossessed*, Thorsons, 1999
Cornelius, John, *Liverpool 8*, John Murray, 1982
Crick, Michael, *The March of Militant*, Faber & Faber, 1986
Davies, Hunter, *The Beatles*, Mayflower, 1968
Drummond, Bill, *45*, Little, Brown, 2000
Du Noyer, Paul, *We All Shine On*, Carlton, 1997
Epstein, Brian, *A Cellarful of Noise*, Souvenir, 1964
Evans, Mike, *The Art of the Beatles*, Anthony Blond, 1984
Forsyth, Ian, *The Beatles' Merseyside*, SB Publications, 1991
Frame, Pete, *The Beatles and Some Other Guys*, Omnibus, 1997
Geller, Deborah, *The Brian Epstein Story*, Faber and Faber, 2000
Giuliano, Geoffrey & Brenda, *The Lost Beatle Interviews*, Virgin, 1995
Harrison, George, *I, Me, Mine*, Simon & Schuster, 1982
Haslam, Dave, *Manchester England*, Fourth Estate, 1999
Hazlitt, William, *On Coffee-House Politicians*, from *Table-Talk*, Cassell, 1903
Henri, Adrian, Roger McGough & Brian Patten, *The Mersey Sound*, Penguin, 1967
Hibbert, Christopher, *The English: A Social History 1066–1945*, Paladin, 1998
Hocking, Silas K, *Her Benny*, Frederick Warne, 1879
Jenkins, Tricia, *'Let's Go Dancing': Dance Band Memories of 1930s Liverpool*, Institute
    of Popular Music, 1994
Jewell, Derek, *The Popular Voice*, Sphere, 1981
Johnson, Holly, *A Bone in My Flute*, Century, 1994
Jones, Ron, *The American Connection*, Ron Jones, 1986
Jones, Ron, *The Beatles' Liverpool*, Ron Jones, 1991
Lane, Tony, *Liverpool, Gateway of Empire*, Lawrence & Wishart, 1987
Leach, Sam, *The Rocking City*, Pharaoh, 1999
Leigh, Spencer, *Brother, Can You Spare a Rhyme?*, Spencer Leigh, 2000
Leigh, Spencer, *Drummed Out! The Sacking of Pete Best*, Northdown, 1988
Leigh, Spencer & John Firminger, *Halfway to Paradise: Britpop 1955–1962*, Finbarr,
    1996

Leigh, Spencer & Pete Frame, *Let's Go Down the Cavern*, Vermilion, 1984

Lewisohn, Mark, *The Complete Beatles Chronicle*, Pyramid, 1992

Long, Cathy, *The Sound and the Crowd: Football and Music in Liverpool*, Unpublished manuscript, 2002

MacDonald, Ian, *Revolution in the Head*, Fourth Estate, 1994

Macnaughton, Donald A, *Roscoe of Liverpool*, Countryvise, 1996

Matovina, Dan, *Without You: the Tragic Story of Badfinger*, Frances Glover, 1997

McCann, Graham, *Morecambe & Wise*, Fourth Estate, 1998

McCauley, Peter, *Music Hall in Merseyside*, Overseal Press, 1982

McClure, James, *Spike Island*, Macmillan, 1980

McIntyre-Brown, Arabella & Guy Woodland, *Liverpool, The First 1,000 Years*, Garlic Press, 2001

McManus, Kevin, *Ceilis, Jigs & Ballads: Irish Music in Liverpool*, Institute of Popular Music, 1994

McManus, Kevin, *Nashville of the North: Country Music in Liverpool*, Institute of Popular Music, 1994

Melly, George, *Revolt Into Style*, Penguin, 1972

Melville, Herman, *Redburn*, Richard Bentley, 1849

Merseyside Socialist Research Group, *Merseyside in Crisis*, MSRG, 1980

Miles, Barry, *Paul McCartney: Many Years from Now*, Secker & Warburg, 1997

Milner, Frank, *Adrian Henri: Paintings 1953–1998*, National Museums & Galleries on Merseyside, 2000

Nowell, David, *Too Darn Soulful: The Story of Northern Soul*, Robson, 1999

O'Connor, Freddy, *Liverpool: It All Came Tumbling Down*, Brunswick, 1990

O'Donnell, Jim, *The Day John Met Paul*, Penguin, 1994

O'Mara, Pat, *The Autobiography of a Liverpool Irish Slummy*, Vanguard Press, 1933

Redhead, Steve, *Sing When You're Winning*, Pluto, 1987

Roberts, David (ed.), *British Hit Singles*, Guinness, 2001

Rylatt, Keith & Phil Scott, *Central 1179: The Story of Manchester's Twisted Wheel Club*, Bee Cool, 2001

Sampson, Kevin, *Powder*, Jonathan Cape, 1999

Sampson, Kevin, *Outlaws*, Jonathan Cape, 2001

Sayle, Alexei, *Barcelona Plates*, Sceptre, 2000

Schreuders, Piet, Mark Lewisohn & Adam Smith, *The Beatles' London*, Hamlyn, 1994

Schwartzer, Klaus, *The Scouse Phenomenon Part 1*, Druckerei und Verlag Bitsch, 1987

Scott, Walter Dixon, *Liverpool 1907*, re-pub. Gallery Press, 1979

Shallice, A, *Liverpool Labourism & Irish Nationalism in the 1920s and 1930s*, North West Labour History Society Bulletin 8, 1983

Shaw, Frank, *My Liverpool*, Gallery Press, 1971

Shaw, Frank, *You Know Me Anty Nelly?*, Wolfe, 1970

Sinclair, Iain, *The Kodak Mantra Diaries*, Albion Village Press, 1971

Smith, Tommy, *I Did It the Hard Way*, Arthur Barker, 1980

Smout, Michael, *Mersey Stars*, Sigma Leisure, 2000

Thomson, Douglas, *Cilla Black: Bobby's Girl*, Simon & Schuster, 1998

Wenner, Jan, *Lennon Remembers*, Penguin, 1971

Willis-Pitts, P, *Liverpool, The Fifth Beatle*, Amozen Press, 2000
Woodham-Smith, Cecil, *The Great Hunger: Ireland 1845–1849*, Penguin, 1962

2 PERIODICALS
Q
Mojo
NME
Melody Maker
The Sunday Times
The Liverpool Echo
The End
HotLine
The Guardian
The Daily Telegraph
Record Collector
Vanity Fair

3 WEBSITES
www.cavern-liverpool.co.uk
www.liverpoolmusic.com
www.liverpool-music-city.com
www.geocities.com/soulpooluk

4 TV
Heroes of Comedy: Ken Dodd, Channel 4, 1999
Rock Family Trees, BBC, 1998
Tales from the Riverbank, Granada, 1999
Who Put the Beat in Merseybeat?, 1996

5 RADIO
Dancing in the Rubble, BBC Radio 4, 1982
Liverpool: The New Wave, BBC Radio 2, 2001

6 DVD
The First US Visit; You Can't Do That! The Making of A Hard Day's Night, Apple/MPI
Home Video, 1998

7 VIDEO
Liverpool, The Swinging 60s, Pleasures Past, 1995

INDEX

Fulwell, Pete 107–8, 110, 111–14, 115, 133, 193, 214–15, 263
Fury, Billy (Ron Wycherley) 10–12, 54, 59, 65, 80, 98, 259
Fuseli, Henry 49

Gabriel, Peter 210
Gaelic 7
'Gal with the Yaller Shoes, The' 59
Gallagher, Noel 52, 187, 214, 215
'Garden of Eden' 59
Garland, Judy 63
Garrick, David 98, 99, 268
Gaye, Marvin 62
Gerry and the Pacemakers 34, 39, 57, 66–8, 73, 74, 171, 242, 259
'Get Back' 100
Gill, Alan 125
Ginsberg, Allen 93, 95, 160, 227
Girl Can't Help It, The (film) 57
'Give Me the Moonlight' 59
'Give Peace a Chance' 53, 233
'Glass Onion' 29
Gleason, Ralph J. 90
Glide 265
Go! Discs 185, 186, 216
'Goin' Down' 261
'Going Down to Liverpool' 160, 265
'Good Golly Miss Molly' 75
'Good Luck Charm' 262
'Goodbat Nightman' 96
'Goodbye Dolly Gray' 84
'Goodbye My Love' 73
Goodyear, Julie 249
Gordy, Berry 79, 266
Gorman, John 93, 95–6
'Got My Mojo Working' 83
Grant, Linda 248
Grapes, The (pub) 15, 16, 19, 35, 133, 170, 178
Graves, Harry 58, 240
'Great Dominions' 262
Green, Paul 131
'Green Door' 59, 268
'Green Eyed American Actress' 98
'Greenbank Drive' 176, 256, 260
Griffiths, Brian 72
Griffiths, Ron 99–100
Griffiths, Tony and Chris 215, 263
Grimms 97
Grimshaw, Atkinson: paintings 48
Groundpig 184
Guardian (newspaper) 248
Guinness World Records 256–7
Gustafson, Johnny 72
Guthrie, Woody 61, 81
Guyler, Deryck 140, 146

Haggard, Merle 55
Haley, Bill 12, 230–1, 237

Half-Baked (LP) 98, 261
Half Man Half Biscuit 188, 189–90, 260
Halford, Rob 190
'Halfway to Paradise' 11
Ham, Pete 99, 100, 101–2
Hambi and the Dance 171, 267
Hamburg 31–2, 66, 74, 75, 76, 83, 84; Beatles in 31–3, 34, 38, 91
Hamilton, Natasha 220–2
Hamilton, Russ 59
Handley, Tommy 28, 64, 140, 147
Handmade (film company) 238
'Happiness' 141
Happy Mondays 183
'Harbour Song, The' 267
'Hard Day's Night, A' 73
Hard Day's Night, A (film) 22–3, 44, 87–8, 151, 242
Harpo, Slim 91
Harrison, George 7, 15, 40, 56, 75; early life 41, 55–6, 65, 236–7; with Beatles 45, 99, 223, 237, 242; after Beatles 223, 237–9; music 73, 76, 91, 101, 237, 257, 261, 266
Harrison, Pattie 238
Harry, Bill 32, 63–4, 76, 115, 167, 227
Hart, Mike 94
Hatch, Tony 72
Hatton, Derek 45, 161–2, 251
Hawthorne, Nathaniel 5–6
Hayes, Philip 109–10, 209–10, 216, 264
Hazlitt, William 250
Head, Michael 154, 174, 217–19, 261
'Heart as Big as Liverpool, A' 132, 135, 258
Hebrides 120–1
'Hello Dolly' 59
'Hello Little Girl' 71
'Help!' 233
Help! (album) 56
Help! (film) 8
Hendrix, Jimi 91
Henri, Adrian 93, 93–5, 97, 115, 150, 162, 166, 249, 250, 262, 266
Herman's Hermits 80, 81
Heseltine, Michael 253
Heswall (hospital) 240
'Hey Jude' 28
Heysel Stadium, Belgium 159, 164–5
'Hi Joe Hi' 260
Hideaways, the 89
High Five 209, 210, 264
Hillsborough Stadium, Sheffield 147, 159, 165–6, 176, 248
Hippodrome, Liverpool viii
hippy culture 183–4
'Hippy Hippy Shake' 75, 83
Hitler, Adolf 10, 38
Hitler, Bridget 10
H.M.S. Fable (album) 53, 218, 260
'Hold Tight' 75
Holliday, Michael 59, 263